DISSONANT VOICES

DISSONANT VOICES

*Religious Pluralism and the
Question of Truth*

Harold A. Netland

William B. Eerdmans Publishing Company
Grand Rapids, Michigan

 APOLLOS
LEICESTER, ENGLAND

First published 1991 in the USA by Wm. B. Eerdmans Publishing Co.,
255 Jefferson Ave. S.E., Grand Rapids, Michigan 49503
and in the UK by APOLLOS (an imprint of Inter-Varsity Press)
38 De Montfort Street, Leicester LE1 7GP, UK

Printed in the United States of America

Library of Congress Cataloging-in-Publication Data

Netland, Harold A., 1955-
    Dissonant voices: religious pluralism and the question of truth /
Harold A. Netland.
        p.   cm.
    ISBN 0-8028-0602-3
    1. Religious pluralism.   2. Religion — Philosophy.   3. Evangelism.
    I. Title.
    BL85.N37   1991
    261.2 — dc20   91-13553
                                                             CIP

British Library Cataloguing in Publication Data

A catalogue record for this book is available from the British Library.

ISBN 0-85111-426-1

The author and publisher gratefully acknowledge the publishers and individuals
listed on p. vi, who have granted permission to reprint from copyrighted works.

For my parents,
Anton and Bernice Netland,

and my wife's parents,
Einar and Blanche Ford,

whose many years of missionary service in Japan provide
a model of gracious, culturally sensitive, yet bold witness
for Jesus Christ in a highly resistant culture.

Acknowledgments

The author and publisher gratefully acknowledge the publishers and individuals who have granted permission to quote from the following sources:

Kenneth Cragg, *The Call of the Minaret*, 2nd ed. (1985). Reprinted by permission of Orbis Books and Kenneth Cragg.

Don Cupitt, "Anti-Realist Faith" (unpublished paper, 1988). Reprinted by permission of Don Cupitt.

J. D. Douglas, ed., *Let the Earth Hear His Voice: International Congress on World Evangelization, Lausanne, Switzerland.* Copyright 1975 by World Wide Publications. Reprinted by permission of World Wide Publications.

Mircea Eliade, ed., *The Encyclopedia of Religion* (1987). Reprinted by permission of Macmillan Publishing Company.

John H. Hick, *An Interpretation of Religion* (1988). Reprinted by permission of Yale University Press.

John H. Hick, "Jesus and the World's Religions" in John H. Hick, ed., *The Myth of God Incarnate.* © SCM Press Ltd., 1977. Used by permission of SCM and Westminster/John Knox Press.

John H. Hick and Paul F. Knitter, eds., *The Myth of Christian Uniqueness* (1987). Reprinted by permission of Orbis Books and SCM Press.

Paul F. Knitter, *No Other Name? A Critical Survey of Christian Attitudes toward the World Religions* (1985). Reprinted by permission of Orbis Books, SCM Press, and Claretian Publications.

Sarvepalli Radhakrishnan and Charles A. Moore, eds., *A Source Book in Indian Philosophy* (1957). Reprinted by permission of Princeton University Press.

Contents

Introduction   viii

I. The Challenge of Religious Pluralism   1

II. The Scandal of Pluralism:
Conflicting Truth Claims (I)   36

III. Conflicting Truth Claims (II)   73

IV. Religion and Truth   112

V. Evaluating Religious Traditions   151

VI. All Roads Lead to . . .   196

VII. No Other Name: The Question of Jesus   234

VIII. Evangelism, Dialogue, and Tolerance   278

Bibliography   315

Index   319

Introduction

We live in a religiously pluralistic world. Of course, I did not become acquainted with the term "religious pluralism" until much later in life, but even as a child I knew that not everyone shares the same religious beliefs and practices.

My parents were devout, conservative evangelical missionaries in a farming town in rural northern Japan. Among my earliest memories is that of my father going out to a small neighboring fishing village to hold a Bible study with a family interested in Jesus Christ. We believed in God and Jesus. We went to church on Sunday. But most Japanese did not. They went to the temples or shrines — if they went anywhere at all. The tolling of bells in nearby temples, the haunting chants of Buddhist priests, the burning of small fires during the annual *bon* festival to welcome back the spirits of the dead — these are vivid memories from my early years in Japan. Even a young child can to some extent grasp the importance of such differences in religious practices. And although my understanding was obviously limited, even as a child I knew that most Japanese did not worship the God of the Bible, and that my parents were in Japan to tell them the Good News about Jesus. I grew up, then, in an environment in which most people were not Christian, but rather were immersed in Japanese folk religion, that fascinating mixture of Buddhism, Shinto, Taoism, and shamanism.

Although I had been interested for some time in the problems posed by religious pluralism, it was not until graduate studies in philosophy that I began to grapple with them seriously. I had the privilege of studying under Professor John Hick at Claremont, and it was largely due to his influence that religious epistemology, and especially the problem of conflicting truth claims among religions, became the focus of my attention. It will be obvious in what follows that Professor Hick and I disagree sharply on some fundamental issues, but this in no way detracts from my genuine respect for and appreciation of him, both as a person and a scholar. In a sense, this book can be regarded as a response to the pluralism that John Hick has so vigorously championed in recent years.

More recently I have returned to Japan as a missionary educator, and I now struggle, along with my Japanese brothers and sisters, with the difficult question of how we are to live as disciples of the one Lord and Savior Jesus Christ in the midst of a highly relativistic and pluralistic society. The issues addressed in this book, then, are for me not merely of academic interest. They emerge out of real-life situations, from daily contact with men and women whose religious worldviews and commitments are very different from my own.

છ   છ   છ

Until fairly recently Christians have generally held that the basic claims of Christianity are true, and that where the claims of other religions conflict with those of Christianity the former are to be rejected as false. It has also been generally accepted that salvation is available only through the person and work of Jesus Christ. Thus, followers of other religions must accept Jesus Christ as Lord and Savior in order to be saved. This traditional position is frequently referred to in contemporary theological and missiological literature as exclusivism.

But exclusivism has fallen on hard times in recent decades. Many Roman Catholic and Protestant theologians, missiologists, and even missionaries are abandoning it in favor of alternative perspectives that are much more accepting of other religious traditions. While fully aware of the difficulties — both real and imagined — associated with exclusivi :n, I am convinced that its widespread rejection today is unwarranted and is based largely upon faulty reasoning as well as a misunderstanding of its implications. After carefully reflecting upon the various alternatives advanced in the current debate, I am persuaded that the proposed alternatives suffer from even greater difficulties than those associated with exclusivism.

Although the central issues in the current discussion on the relation of Christian faith to other faiths are inextricably linked to epistemology, it is difficult to find rigorous and responsible treatment of basic epistemological issues in recent literature on religious pluralism.[1] The unfortunate result has been some extravagant and far-reaching claims that demand close scrutiny. Clear thinking on this important topic requires careful and rigorous work in epistemology, as well as a thorough understanding of the teaching of Scripture and the phenomena from the various religions themselves. In the following chapters certain central epistemological issues will be examined and clarified. The discussion, however, is not overly technical and does not presuppose any previous background in philosophy. I will argue that if we are to have a view of the relation among religions which (a) is epistemologically sound, (b) accurately reflects the phenomena of the various religious traditions, and (c) is faithful to the clear teaching of Scripture, then something very much like the traditional exclusivist position is inescapable.

Briefly, the argument of the book is this: Since there are many today who deny that the central claims of the various religions are in fact mutually incompatible, in chapters 2 and 3 I show, in a very summary fashion, that some of the fundamental claims advanced by Hinduism, Buddhism, Islam, and Shinto are prima facie mutually incompatible.

1. The outstanding exception to the general pattern is John Hick's *An Interpretation of Religion* (New Haven: Yale University Press, 1988), which is considered in chapter 6.

At the heart of the epistemological confusion in much of the current debate lie some erroneous assumptions about the nature of religious truth. Thus, some of the more prominent misconceptions of religious truth are dealt with in chapter 4.

Exclusivism presupposes that one can make accurate judgments about the truth or falsity of the major religions. But many today deny that it is possible to apply objective, nonarbitrary criteria in the assessment of various religious traditions. That it is possible to do so is argued in chapter 5.

Without question John Hick is the most influential and articulate spokesman today for the view that all religions constitute, in their own culturally and historically conditioned manner, responses to the same ultimate reality. In chapter 6 I argue that, despite its undeniable appeal, Professor Hick's theory of religious pluralism is seriously flawed.

The watershed issue in the current debate is, of course, the question of Jesus Christ. Is he merely *a* savior, one among many, or is he *the* unique Savior of humankind? Chapter 7 is concerned with the traditional understanding of the person and work of Jesus Christ, particularly with respect to the implications of this position for those who, through no fault of their own, have never heard the gospel of Jesus Christ. The pluralistic Christologies of John Hick and Paul Knitter are also critically examined.

And finally, any defense of exclusivism today must grapple with the serious charge of intolerance routinely levelled against it because of its emphasis upon evangelism and conversion. In chapter 8 the questions of evangelism and interreligious dialogue, as well as the charge of intolerance, are considered.

A comprehensive defense of Christian exclusivism would need to include at least two elements: first, demonstration, based upon careful and rigorous exegesis of all relevant biblical texts, that it is indeed demanded by the biblical data; and, second, a careful response to the various criticisms currently levelled against exclusivism. There is today a great need for a rigorous, systematic study of the biblical data as they relate to the question of the relation of Christian faith to other faiths. But this book is not that study. This is not primarily a theological or biblical study. Rather, it is hoped that

this book will serve as a kind of defense of Christian exclusivism —
as a prolegomenon to an evangelical theology of religions — by
clarifying some basic epistemological issues in the current debate
over religious pluralism, responding to some criticisms of exclusivism, and pointing out weaknesses in alternative views.

Obviously this is not intended as the last word on the
subject. Much more can, should, and undoubtedly will be said. But
if this study can clarify some issues and stimulate further discussion, then its intention will have been achieved.

ᔕ   ᔕ   ᔕ

I am grateful to all who contributed in one way or another toward
the writing of this book. Not everyone can be mentioned by name,
of course, but special gratitude should be expressed to several
individuals. My appreciation for Professor John Hick has already
been noted. Although I cannot embrace his theory of religious
pluralism, I am grateful for the opportunity of studying with him,
discussing together problems of pluralism, and being challenged
in fresh ways by his probing questions. Special thanks are due Dr.
Philip B. Payne for his encouragement, generous assistance, and
advice. Professor Arthur Glasser provided invaluable advice and
assistance during the early stages of research and writing. I am also
grateful to Dr. Mark M. Hanna, not only for his reading and commenting extensively upon an earlier draft of the manuscript, but
for the example he has provided by his life. For his life demonstrates that not only is philosophical rigor compatible with commitment to world evangelization, but the two can have a mutually
enriching relationship. And most of all, I am grateful to my wife
Ruth for her consistent support and encouragement throughout
all phases of the preparation of this book.

CHAPTER ONE

The Challenge of Religious Pluralism

"How can you possibly believe that one can be saved only by accepting Jesus Christ as Lord and Savior?" Initially, Joe had not meant to enter into the discussion at all. He had agreed to come to the campus Bible study only to please Jan, the girl he had been dating recently. And so, there he was, sitting on the floor with twenty other university students, deeply engaged in a study of Jesus' troubling statements in the Gospel of John, chapter 14. The obvious sincerity of those in the Bible study impressed him. And the students certainly seemed normal enough — no weird religious freaks or fanatics that he could see. In fact, they were every bit as decent and intelligent as the crowd with which he usually associated. But he was increasingly bothered by what he was hearing — for example, Jesus' statement about no one coming to the Father except through him. Now that may have been alright for the Jews in the first century; after all, they obviously knew nothing about the many different religions and cultures in our world. But surely no one who has been exposed to the tremendous variety in cultures and religious beliefs in our world today can seriously maintain that there is only *one* way to God and that those who do not happen to accept it are eternally damned! Yet these students actually believe that Jesus is somehow uniquely divine and the only one able to save people. How can apparently intelligent and normal people have such narrow and naive beliefs? If there really is a God and he is a God of love as these Christians claim, would it not make much more sense for this God to reveal himself in his own way in each culture and to provide saviors within each of them? Why should we believe that there is only *one* way to reach God and that Christians happen to be the lucky ones who know about it?

℘   ℘   ℘

Sue took another sip of coffee and listened carefully as her friend continued talking quietly. She had taken a special interest in Yoriko who, along with her husband and family, had arrived in the United States from Japan a year ago. Yoriko had initially seemed totally bewildered by the changes, so Sue had gone out of her way to help her adjust to life in a large American city. They quickly became close friends. Sue had helped her with her English and, in general, with her adjustment to life in the States, all the while praying that she would have an opportunity to share her faith in Christ with Yoriko. And now, this evening, for the first time, Yoriko had joined her in attending a special evangelistic talk at church, after which they had gone out for coffee. As they were eating pie and ice cream, Sue asked Yoriko what she thought of the special speaker. Yoriko quickly responded that since she is Japanese of course she is Buddhist. All of her family are Buddhist. They have always been Buddhist and would never consider changing religions. Why should they change? Besides, she said, surely there are many ways to get to God. You in the West are Christian, we in the East are Buddhist. Each culture has its own religion. The most important thing is not so much what religion one belongs to, or what one happens to believe. The crucial thing is that one is sincere and lives a morally respectable life. Yoriko then asked Sue a troubling question: Why do Christians have to be so exclusive and insist that theirs is the only right way? As Sue continued to listen silently, Yoriko became visibly excited, saying that she felt that it was time for different religions to stop fighting and competing with each other and to start working together to solve the world's many problems. After Yoriko finished, Sue remained quiet, unsure just how to respond to her new friend.

 භ භ භ

George toyed with his pen as he listened to his professor lecture. He was beginning to have second thoughts about signing up for this course on world religions. He had heard such positive things about the course — the professor was one of the most popular teachers on campus, and since it fulfilled a general education requirement he had enrolled. But nothing in his many years of involvement at church had prepared him for this. The professor had just completed talking about Mahayana Buddhism, and he was now drawing some disturbing parallels between Buddhism and Christianity. Sure, there are some significant differences between them, he said. But when one gets beneath the external cultural and historical trappings it is clear that both Jesus and the Buddha were teaching basically the same thing. Each expressed the Truth in terms appropriate to his own time and culture, and thus we have the many external, and really quite insignificant, differences between the religions today. But the essential Truth underlying both religions is the same. George had been particularly troubled by the professor's earlier lecture on Shinran and Jodo Shinshu Buddhism. He had always been told that only in Christianity do we have a religion of pure grace and mercy. He recalled the statement made by a visiting missionary at church: "Christianity is God reaching down to man; all other religions are man reaching up to God." But in Jodo Shinshu Buddhism George encountered for the first time a powerful and attractive non-Christian religion of grace. The professor had emphasized that Shinran was to Buddhism what the apostle Paul was to Christianity. Some troubling questions were beginning to haunt George: Is Christianity really unique after all? What sets Jesus apart from Shinran or other religious leaders? If Buddhism has someone like Shinran, how can we maintain that Christianity is uniquely true and that Buddhism is wrong? Perhaps, he thought, he had better drop the class after all.

The Fact of Pluralism

The three fictional cases above illustrate some of the tensions Christians face when confronted by the growing religious pluralism of the West. Not only do increasing numbers of non-Christians respond to the Christian message of salvation only in Jesus Christ with incredulity, but many Christians too are becoming perplexed about the implications of the exclusiveness of the gospel for their friends and neighbors who follow other religious traditions.

In a sense, of course, our world has always been characterized by religious pluralism. For as far back as recorded history takes us, there have been divergent religious beliefs and practices. When the ancient Assyrians were worshiping the war god Ashur, for example, far away in the Indian subcontinent the *Brahmin* priests were offering sacrifices to Agni, the fire god. While the Old Testament prophet Jeremiah was proclaiming judgment against Judah, in distant China Confucius was extolling the virtues of the *chün-tzu* (gentleman). And we must not forget that throughout history, in addition to the followers of the so-called major religions, there have been millions who have been part of lesser-known ethnic and tribal religious traditions. So in itself, religious pluralism — diversity in religious practice and belief — is nothing new in our world.

What is new today in the West, however, is the widespread awareness of religious pluralism resulting from an unprecedented exposure to many different religious traditions. For centuries people in the West lived their lives with little, if any, direct exposure to other religions. Until the nineteenth century, with the exception of periodic unhappy encounters with Muslims and the exotic tales of China by Marco Polo and Jesuit missionaries, the West plodded along largely in isolated ignorance of other religious traditions. All of this has, of course, changed. It is virtually impossible today to live in a major Western city and not come into contact with some aspect of a major non-Christian religion.

Part of the reason for this change is the enormous number of immigrants to the West from Asia, the Middle East, and Latin America. For along with the large influx of non-Western immigrants come the various religious and cultural traditions of the homeland. Religions long regarded as exotic and distinctly ir-relevant to the West are now thriving in North America and Europe.

Most Americans have little grasp of the astonishing degree to which religious pluralism is already characteristic of American society today. There are, for example, an estimated three million Muslims and over six hundred mosques in the United States alone.[1] Most of the mosques are located in large urban centers, many of them near universities. In 1982 the Islamic Society of North America, an umbrella organization for five smaller Islamic societies, was formed, thereby providing greater unity and cohesion to the movement of Islam in North America. Muslims are generally zealous in spreading their faith in the West and have targeted in particular the university as the focus for *da'wah,* or the propagation of Islam. Robert C. Douglas, director of the Zwemer Institute of Muslim Studies, reports that at a recent conference in Los Angeles Muslims announced a goal of winning fifty to seventy million Americans to Islam.[2] Their target is the various strata of society "suffering from the bankruptcy of the social order." They declared that they are in North America for the long haul, willing to invest centuries if necessary to achieve their objectives. Dr. Yvonne Haddad, an Islamicist at the University of Massachusetts, says, "Those who have studied Muslims in the United States estimate that if the Muslim community continues to grow at the present rate, Islam will be the second largest religion in the United States by 2015, overtaking Judaism."[3]

Muslims are not alone in seeing the West as a mission field. There are an estimated three to five million Buddhists living in the United States. The Nichiren Shoshu sect of Japanese Buddhism alone claims 500,000 members.[4] In 1987 forty-five American

1. Terry Muck, "The Mosque Next Door," in *Christianity Today,* February 19, 1988, p. 15.
2. Robert C. Douglas, "The Challenge of the Muslim World," *World Evangelization,* November-December 1988, p. 15.
3. As quoted in "Da'wah and the Koran: Islam Grows in America," by Kent Hart, in *Eternity,* March 1988, p. 6.
4. See Terry Muck, "The Mosque Next Door," p. 15.

Buddhist organizations joined together to form the American Buddhist Congress, a national body that will assume an increasingly high public profile and will speak out on national issues from a Buddhist perspective. The Buddhist Churches of America, a denomination affiliated with Japanese Jodo Shinshu (Pure Land True Sect) Buddhism, has established The Institute for Buddhist Studies, the first professional institution of higher education created by a Buddhist organization in the United States. Significantly, the Institute in 1985 established an affiliate relationship with the prestigious Graduate Theological Union in Berkeley, California.[5]

Although not as aggressive as Muslims or Buddhists in propagating their faith, Hindus also are becoming increasingly prominent in North America. There are over forty Hindu temples scattered throughout the United States, from major urban centers such as Los Angeles, Chicago, and New York, to smaller communities such as Aurora, Illinois and Springfield, Virginia.[6]

North America is not alone in experiencing rapid growth in non-Christian religions. In France Islam is second only to Roman Catholicism, with Protestantism in third place. In Britain there are large numbers of Muslims as well as sizeable Hindu and Sikh minorities. London is today one of the world's most pluralistic cities; more than 170 languages are spoken by pupils of London's schools.[7] The strategic importance of London has not been lost on Muslims. Robert Douglas tells of a Muslim leader at an Islamic conference who stated: "Unless we win London over to Islam we will fail to win the whole of the Western world."[8]

In addition to the major non-Western religions which are finding greater acceptance in the West, we must also mention the

5. Cf. E. Allen Richardson, *East Comes West* (New York: The Pilgrim Press, 1985), p. xiv.
6. Terry Muck, "The Mosque Next Door," p. 15.
7. Cf. Ralph C. Wood, "British Churches Encounter the Challenge of Pluralism," in *The Christian Century*, October 19, 1988, pp. 923f. Wood states, "British Christianity, once the bastion of European culture-Protestantism, now approaches something akin to the New Testament situation. It is making a valiant minority witness in a pluralistic culture." Ibid., p. 924.
8. Robert C. Douglas, "The Challenge of the Muslim World," p. 15.

many newer, nontraditional religions, often referred to as "cults" by Christians. No picture of the religious scene in the West is complete without including the significant impact of the Jehovah's Witnesses, the Church of Jesus Christ of the Latter-Day Saints (Mormons), The Theosophical Society, Spiritism, The Unification Church, The Worldwide Church of God (Herbert W. Armstrong), Scientology (L. Ron Hubbard), Rajneeshism (Bhagwan Shree Rajneesh), and the International Society for Krishna Consciousness.

And along with these relatively well-defined religious traditions must be included the amazing recent phenomenon of the New Age Movement, a loose network of self-proclaimed religious leaders whose teachings combine themes from ancient spiritism, Eastern religion, and more recent positive thinking. Whereas in the turbulent sixties interest in Zen and other forms of Eastern religion was largely confined to the counterculture, one of the distinctives of the New Age Movement is its widespread appeal to those very much a part of the establishment — "yuppies," entertainers, professionals, educators. The impact of New Age beliefs and values is pervasive. *Los Angeles Times* religion writer Russell Chandler reports that "roughly 30 million Americans — about one in four — now believe in reincarnation, a key tenet of the New Age, and 14 per cent endorse the work of spirit mediums, what New Agers often call 'trance channelers'."[9] A 1978 Gallup poll indicated that ten million Americans were engaged in some aspect of Eastern mysticism and nine million in spiritual healing.[10]

Clearly, North American society is already religiously highly pluralistic. The days when Western religious society could be thought of in terms of the "Big Three," Protestantism, Catholicism, and Judaism, are long gone. And yet most Westerners — certainly most Western Christians — are only now beginning to realize the extent of this pluralism and to grapple with some of the issues that follow from it.

The extent of religious pluralism today is magnified when

9. Russell Chandler, *Understanding the New Age* (Dallas: Word, 1988), p. 20.

10. Ibid., p. 21.

considered in the global context. In 1990 David Barrett estimated that worldwide there were 1.7 billion Christians, 934 million Muslims, 705 million Hindus, 323 million Buddhists, seventeen million Jews, eighteen million Sikhs, as well as millions who followed various tribal religions and new nontraditional religions.[11] In Japan alone, in addition to the major religions, there are literally hundreds of so-called "new religions" — syncretistic offshoots of Shinto, Buddhism, Taoism, or Christianity — which have emerged during the twentieth century. But it would be difficult to find a more pluralistic society today than that of Singapore. Paul Hiebert reports that forty-one percent of the population of Singapore is Buddhist, eighteen percent Christian, seventeen percent Muslim, five percent Hindu, and seventeen percent Secularist.[12]

From Exclusivism to Inclusivism to Pluralism

With increased awareness of religious pluralism has come a host of disconcerting questions: Why are there so many diverse religions? If Christianity is the true religion, why is it that so much of the world rejects it in favor of diametrically opposing religious traditions? Is it theologically and morally acceptable to maintain that one religion is uniquely true and that the others are at best incomplete or even false? Is Jesus Christ really unique after all? The challenge to Christian theology posed by pluralism should not be minimized. Canon Max Warren seems to have had prophetic insight when he observed in 1958 that the impact of agnostic science upon theology will turn out to have been as mere child's play when compared to the challenge to Christian theology posed by the faith of other men.[13] In a similar vein, sociologist Peter Berger claims

11. David Barrett, "Annual Statistical Table on Global Mission: 1990," in *International Bulletin of Missionary Research*, January 1990, p. 27.

12. Paul Hiebert, "Christianity in a World of Religious Turmoil," *World Evangelization* 16 (May-June 1989): 19.

13. As quoted in Wilfred Cantwell Smith, "The Christian in a Religiously Plural World," in *Religious Diversity: Essays by Wilfred Cantwell Smith*, ed. Willard G. Oxtoby (New York: Harper & Row, 1976), p. 7.

that "modernity has plunged religion into a very specific crisis, characterized by secularity, to be sure, but characterized more importantly by pluralism."[14] Berger contends that the contestation between the major religions, especially those emanating from the Far East and the Indian subcontinent, will be an important theme for theology in the foreseeable future.[15] And missiologist Gerald H. Anderson asserts that the most critical aspect of the task of forging a viable theology of mission today "deals with the Christian attitude toward religious pluralism and the approach to people of other faiths."[16] Even a cursory survey of recent theological literature indicates the soundness of this analysis. For over the past quarter century questions concerning the relation of Christianity to other faiths have been addressed in the writings of such prominent theologians as P. Tillich, K. Barth, H. Kraemer, S. C. Neill, K. Rahner, H. Küng, R. Panikkar, W. Pannenberg, J. A. T. Robinson, J. B. Cobb, Jr., J. Macquarrie, J. Moltmann, J. Hick, W. Cantwell Smith, H. Cox, G. Kaufman, and L. Gilkey, as well as a host of lesser-known figures.

It has been customary in recent literature on religious pluralism to distinguish between three broad perspectives on the relation of Christianity to other religions: exclusivism, inclusivism, and pluralism. *Exclusivism* maintains that the central claims of Christianity are true, and that where the claims of Christianity conflict with those of other religions the latter are to be rejected as false. Christian exclusivists also characteristically hold that God has revealed himself definitively in the Bible and that Jesus Christ is the unique incarnation of God, the only Lord and Savior. Salvation is not to be found in the structures of other religious traditions.

Inclusivism, like exclusivism, maintains that the central claims of Christian faith are true, but it adopts a much more positive view of other religions than does exclusivism. Although

14. Peter Berger, *The Heretical Imperative* (New York: Anchor Press, 1979), p. xi.

15. Ibid.

16. Gerald H. Anderson, "American Protestants in Pursuit of Mission: 1886-1986," in *International Bulletin of Missionary Research* 12 (July 1988): 114.

inclusivists hold that God has revealed himself definitively in Jesus Christ and that Jesus is somehow central to God's provision of salvation for humankind, they are willing to allow that God's salvation is available through non-Christian religions. Jesus is still held to be, in some sense, unique, normative, and definitive; but God is said to be revealing himself and providing salvation through other religious traditions as well. It is the attempt to strike the delicate balance between the affirmation of God's unique revelation and salvation in Jesus Christ and openness to God's saving activity in other religions that distinguishes inclusivism.

Pluralism parts company with both exclusivism and inclusivism by rejecting the premise that God has revealed himself in any unique or definitive sense in Jesus Christ. To the contrary, God is said to be actively revealing himself in all religious traditions. Nor is there anything unique or normative about the person of Jesus. He is simply one of many great religious leaders who have been used by God to provide salvation for humankind. Pluralism, then, goes beyond inclusivism in rejecting the idea that there is anything superior, normative, or definitive about Christianity. Christian faith is merely one of many equally legitimate human responses to the same divine reality.

Exclusivism

Historically, exclusivism has been the dominant position of the Christian Church regarding other religions. The roots of Christian exclusivism can be traced back not only to the New Testament but also to the many unambiguous denunciations of pagan idolatrous practices and beliefs found throughout the Old Testament.[17] The first Christians were strict monotheists who believed that the one eternal God had decisively revealed himself to humankind through the long-awaited Messiah, Jesus of Nazareth. Salvation was available to all — Jews and Gentiles alike — because of the unique

---

17. See Ex. 20:1-5; Deut. 5:6-7; 7:1-6, 16, 25; 13:1–14:2; Josh. 24:14-25; Ps. 115; Isa. 40:18-20; 41:5-7; 44:9-20; 46:5-7; Jer. 10:1-16; 44:2-4; John 14:6; Acts 4:12; 1 Tim. 2:5.

person and work of Jesus Christ. Moreover, early apostolic preaching asserted that such salvation was possible only through Jesus Christ (Acts 4:12). The inevitable result of such an exclusive view of God's revelation and salvation was to reject alternative religious practices and beliefs as idolatrous. Thus the early church held a consistently critical posture toward the religious practices and beliefs of Hellenistic paganism.

It is tempting to assume that the perplexing problems of religious pluralism we face today are unique to the modern world, and that the New Testament is not really that relevant to the contemporary discussion, since the early church did not have to struggle with its relation to other religious traditions. In fact, however, nothing could be further from the truth. The world of the New Testament was characterized by tremendous social, intellectual, and religious ferment.[18] Traditional Jewish religious and social values and beliefs were being challenged by powerful competing forces within the Hellenistic-Roman world. Even within Palestine itself, Jews were confronted with alien values, beliefs, and practices. The many Jews in the Diaspora, scattered throughout the Mediterranean world, were forced to come to grips with the relation between their traditional Jewish religious and cultural heritage and the new, invigorating, intellectual and religious currents from Greece and Rome. Not only did they face the formidable challenge presented by Greek philosophy and literature, but they also had to contend with the many popular religious movements of the day — the cults of Asclepius or Artemis-Diana, the "mystery religions" of Osiris and Isis, Mithras, Adonis, or Eleusis, the ubiquitous cult of the Roman emperor, and the many popularized versions of Stoicism, Cynicism, and Epicureanism.[19] Although this should not be pressed too far, with respect to pluralism there are striking parallels between the first-century Mediterranean world and that of the West today.

18. See Eduard Lohse, *The New Testament Environment*, trans. John E. Seely (Nashville: Abingdon, 1976), for a helpful discussion of the religious, social, and intellectual background to the New Testament.

19. A helpful introduction to the religious milieu of the Roman Empire in the first century is John Ferguson's *The Religions of the Roman Empire* (Ithaca: Cornell University Press, 1970).

Historian John Ferguson observes that the attitudes of many in the Roman Empire in the first century concerning alien religious beliefs and practices were marked by tolerance, accommodation, and openness to syncretism.[20] The outstanding exceptions to this general pattern were the Jews and the early Christians. For the strict mono-theism of the Jews and Christians allowed no room for accommo-dation with the polytheistic traditions of Hellenism and Roman religion. The early Christians were highly critical of the surrounding religious values and practices. Initially little more than a small minority movement within the empire, the early Christians faced hostility on all sides. They were attacked by Jews as heretics, per-secuted by Rome as a seditious movement, resisted by the masses for their rejection of the popular cults and mystery religions, and rid-iculed by the philosophers for their seemingly crude views.[21]

Perhaps the outstanding exception to this general pattern was Justin Martyr (ca. 100-165), who had a high view of Hellenistic culture and developed a doctrine of the divine Logos, according to which every human being possesses a seed *(sperma)* of the Logos. Thus, even pagan philosophers such as Plato and Socrates had a seminal element of the Logos *(Logos spermatikos)*, and it was due to the Logos that they were able to discern the truth they so persuasively taught.

> Christ is the Word [Logos] of whom all man partakes. Those who lived by reason [Logos] are Christians, even though they have been considered atheists: such as, among the Greeks, Socrates, Heraclitus, and others like them; and among foreigners, Abraham, Elias, Ananias.[22]

Although the pagan's knowledge of the Logos is distorted and incomplete — and thus there are various contradictions and errors in their teachings — the Logos is operative in all persons. Thus he

20. Ferguson, *Religions of the Roman Empire,* chap. 12.

21. See E. C. Dewick, *The Christian Attitude Toward Other Religions* (Cam-bridge: Cambridge University Press, 1953), pp. 101f.

22. Justin Martyr, "The First Apology," par. 46 in *Writings of Saint Justin Martyr,* trans. Thomas B. Falls (New York: Christian Heritage, Inc., 1948), p. 83.

could say, "The truths which men in all lands have rightly spoken belong to us Christians."[23] We have in Justin Martyr an early anticipation of what was later to become a major theme in twentieth-century theology.

However, in spite of the openness of Justin Martyr (and also Irenaeus and Origen), during the early Middle Ages the Christian Church became increasingly negative and exclusive regarding God's presence in and work through other religious traditions. Part of the reason for this is no doubt the fact that from the time of Constantine until the end of the Middle Ages the Christian Church was largely isolated from other religious traditions. What contact the Church did have with other religions — for example, encounters with Muslim invaders in the eighth and ninth centuries — was generally unpleasant and did little to encourage mutual respect and understanding. Thus, by the thirteenth century the stance of the Church had become rigidly exclusive; salvation was identified with the Church and there naturally developed the view that outside the Church there is no salvation. Centuries before, Cyprian (ca. 200-258) had introduced the formula, and at the Fourth Lateran Council in 1215 it was restated formally: *salus extra ecclesiam non est* — there is no salvation outside the Church. A century later, in his bull *Unam Sanctam,* issued in 1302, Pope Boniface VIII reaffirmed the earlier formula. And in the following century the Council of Florence (1438-45) made the position even more explicit:

> [The Council] firmly believes, professes and proclaims that those not living within the Catholic Church, not only pagans but also Jews and heretics and schismatics, cannot participate in eternal life, but will depart "into everlasting fire which was prepared for the devil and his angels," unless before the end of life the same have been added to the flock. . . . [N]o one, whatever almsgiving he has practiced, even if he has shed blood for the name of Christ, can be saved, unless he has remained in the bosom and unity of the Catholic Church.[24]

23. "The Second Apology," par. 13, *Writings*, pp. 133-34.
24. Henry Denzinger, *Enchiridion Symbolorum*, trans. by Roy J. Deferrari in *The Sources of Catholic Dogma* (St. Louis: B. Herder, 1957), p. 230.

The prevalent attitude toward other religions throughout the Middle Ages was, "outside the Church there is no salvation."

Although there were always those who accepted more accommodating views, it can hardly be denied that Christian exclusivism remained dominant within both the Roman Catholic and Protestant churches until the nineteenth century. Certainly exclusivism played a major role in the emerging missionary movements of the Catholic and Protestant communities. For it was the firm conviction of Catholics that those outside the Church were eternally damned, and the Protestants held equally firmly that those who had never responded in faith to Jesus Christ were forever lost. And it was this conviction about the lostness of humankind that drove early missionaries to bring the gospel of Jesus Christ to the remote peoples of China, Africa, Latin America, and the islands of the Pacific. One cannot understand the Catholic missionary movements of the sixteenth and seventeenth centuries or the remarkable Protestant missionary effort of the nineteenth century, including the work of missionary pioneers such as William Carey, Adoniram Judson, David Livingstone, and Hudson Taylor, without appreciating the fundamental assumption of the missionary movement: salvation is to be found only in the person and work of Jesus Christ, and those who die without having made a commitment to Christ face an eternity apart from God.

Inclusivism

And yet, even while the modern missionary movement was enjoying unprecedented success and the gospel of Jesus Christ was spreading to all parts of the globe, dramatic changes were occurring in Europe which were to alter forever the Christian community's understanding of itself and its mission in the world. The very foundation of Christian exclusivism — the assumption that God had revealed himself and his will in a unique manner in the Bible, and thus that the Bible was absolutely trustworthy in all it says — was being eroded by the emerging higher-critical views of Scripture and the conclusions of Darwinian science. The uniqueness of Jesus Christ and Christian teaching was being challenged by the developing discipline of the history of religions. The common perception of non-Europeans as heathens and uncivilized pagans, in need not only of the saving gospel of Jesus Christ but also of the civilizing influence of the West, was being refuted by extensive contact with the impressive cultures of China, Japan, India, and Latin America. To be sure, most of those who came to reject exclusivism still held on to the view that Christianity is somehow superior to other religions, and that other cultures need to be exposed to the positive values and teachings of Christianity. While the possibility of other ways and other saviors might be admitted, it was still emphatically maintained that Jesus is the superior Savior and that Christianity is the superior faith.

Thus, Christian exclusivism, for centuries virtually unchallenged from within Christendom, has during the past century not only been vigorously disputed but has been rejected by many theologians and mission leaders in favor of more positive views of other faiths. Roman Catholic and Protestant relations with other religions in the twentieth century have been characterized increasingly by an emphasis upon interreligious dialogue and the desire for mutual understanding and enrichment through extensive contact with those of other faiths. Significantly, although religious pluralism has been a fact for as long as recorded history, the concerted effort to bring together representatives from various religions for the express purpose of enhancing mutual understanding through dialogue is a phenomenon of roughly the last hundred years. Indeed, a major assumption underlying the current emphasis upon interreligious dialogue — that religious variety is a positive rather than a negative fact, and that pluralism should have an enriching rather than a divisive effect upon religions — is a relatively modern one.

The first, and in many ways the most remarkable, attempt to bring together on a large scale representatives from many different religious traditions occurred in 1893 in Chicago at the World's Parliament of Religions.[25] For many in the West, this was

25. See John Henry Barrows, ed., *The World's Parliament of Religions*, 2 vols. (Chicago: The Parliament Publishing Company, 1893). A helpful overview of the Parliament can be found in Marcus Braybrooke, *Inter-Faith Organizations, 1893-1979: An Historical Directory* (New York: The Edwin Mellen Press, 1980), chap. 1.

the first exposure firsthand to articulate and devout spokesmen
for Hinduism, Buddhism, Shintoism, and Islam. Particularly impressive to many Westerners was the Hindu Swami Vivekananda
(d. 1902), founder of the Ramakrishna Mission, who was hailed
in glowing terms by *The New York Times* as "undoubtedly the
greatest figure in the Parliament of Religions."[26] A staunch op-
ponent of proselytizing and conversion, he stated,

> I am proud to belong to a religion that has taught the world both
> tolerance and universal acceptance. We believe not only in uni-
> versal toleration, but we accept all religions to be true. . . . The
> Christian is not to become a Hindu or a Buddhist, nor a Hindu
> or a Buddhist to become a Christian. But each must assimilate
> the others and yet preserve its individuality, and grow according
> to its own Law of growth.[27]

Although conducted during the heyday of Protestant liberalism
and dominated largely by liberal concerns, a surprisingly wide
variety of positions concerning the relation among religions was
evident at the Parliament. Most of the positions on religious pluralism that have emerged in recent decades were foreshadowed at
the 1893 Parliament.

And yet, as David Bosch notes, the World's Parliament of
Religions remained something of an isolated and anomalous
event.[28] For the dominant tone within Protestantism during the
early twentieth century remained one of confidence in the superiority of Christianity and the need for all peoples of the world to
come to saving faith in Jesus Christ. But there were other, increasingly strident, voices vying for attention as well. Serious disagreement over the mission of the Church and its relation to other
religious traditions became evident in the second missionary conference of the International Missionary Council, held in 1928 in
Jerusalem, where the focus of discussion was "The Christian Life

26. Braybrooke, *Inter-Faith Organizations*, pp. 6-7.
27. Ibid.
28. David Bosch, "The Church in Dialogue: From Self-Delusion to Vulnerability," in *Missiology: An International Review* 16 (April 1988): 132.

and Message in Relation to Non-Christian Systems of Thought and Life." As Gerald Anderson points out, the two major challenges to mission were then perceived to be secularism and syncretism.[29] The official statement of the Jerusalem Meeting indicates a much more open and affirming view of other religions than that of the first missionary conference at Edinburgh in 1910. The following is a brief part of the International Missionary Council's official statement:

> We rejoice to think that just because in Jesus Christ the light that lighteth every man shone forth in full splendor, we find rays of that same light where he is unknown or even rejected. We welcome every noble quality in non-Christian persons or systems as further proof that the Father, who sent His Son into the world, has nowhere left himself without witness. Thus, merely to give illustration, and making no attempt to estimate the spiritual value of other religions to their adherents, we recognize as part of the one Truth that sense of the Majesty of God and the consequent reverence in worship which are conspicuous in Islam; the deep sympathy for the world's sorrow and unselfish search for the way of escape, which are at the heart of Buddhism; the desire for contact with Ultimate Reality conceived as spiritual, which is prominent in Hinduism; the belief in a moral order of the universe and consequent insistence on moral conduct, which are inculcated by Confucianism; the disinterested pursuit of truth and human welfare which are often found in those who stand for secular civilization but do not accept Christ as their Lord and Savior.[30]

The third missionary conference of the International Missionary Council, held at Tambaram, India, in 1938, witnessed an important debate concerning the question of whether God's revelation, as expressed in Christian faith, is continuous or discon-

29. Gerald H. Anderson, "American Protestants," p. 106.
30. The International Missionary Council's official statement, "The Christian Life and Message in Relation to Non-Christian Systems of Thought and Life," in *The Jerusalem Meeting of the International Missionary Council: March 24–April 8, 1928*, 8 vols. (New York: International Missionary Council, 1928), vol. 1, pp. 410-11.

tinuous with the beliefs and values found in other religious traditions. The outstanding figure here was clearly the Dutch missiologist and theologian Hendrik Kraemer, who had been profoundly
influenced by Karl Barth and Emil Brunner.[31] Influenced by the
dialectical theology in vogue at the time, Kraemer insisted upon a
radical discontinuity between God's revelation in Christ and all
human religiosity, or, in other words, between authentic Christian
faith and other religions. Kraemer affirmed in no uncertain terms
the uniqueness and sufficiency of the Incarnation — the ministry,
death, and resurrection of Jesus Christ. Although Kraemer was the
towering figure at Tambaram, and although his treatment of the
subject was to dominate Protestant reflection on theology of religions for the next two decades, the fundamental issues raised at
Tambaram were not resolved.[32]

In the years after World War II there was increasing accep-

31. See Hendrik Kraemer's *The Christian Message in a Non-Christian
World* (London: Edinburgh House Press, 1938), which was prepared at the request
of the IMC for the Tambaram conference. This is often regarded as the classic
expression and defense of Christian exclusivism.

32. The disagreements at Tambaram focused largely upon the question
of the appropriateness of the "promise and fulfillment" approach to other religions.
Critics of Kraemer held that other religions should be regarded as analogous to
the religion of Israel of the Old Testament. Thus they represented preparation for
the supreme revelation of God in Jesus Christ. Fifty years after Tambaram, in
January 1988, the World Council of Churches sponsored an international seminar
on mission and dialogue. As Mark Heim reports, the focus of the discussion has
shifted dramatically since 1938.

> The questions of Tambaram 1938 have taken on new form. The fullness of
> the revelation of God in Christ and the unique decisiveness of that event are
> themselves matters of debate among Christians. The "promise and fulfillment"
> scheme by which many opposed Kraemer has come to be viewed by some as
> itself an unacceptably triumphalist approach. Conversely, the stress Kraemer
> put on the unique character of each religious tradition has been adopted by
> many who disagree with him and who argue that these faiths offer alternate
> and parallel avenues of God's saving action. The very notions and practice of
> Christian "mission" that were the occasion for discussion in 1938 have become
> suspect or have been significantly reformulated among some branches of the
> church.

Mark Heim, "Mission and Dialogue: 50 Years After Tambaram," *The Christian
Century,* April 6, 1988, p. 340.

tance among Protestants of the idea that God is present in, and at work through, both the secular realm and the non-Christian religious traditions. The more open posture toward those of other faiths was increasingly being reflected in the policies and activities of the World Council of Churches.[33] Questions about the relation of Christian faith to other faiths, and in particular concerning the place of dialogue with other religions, were becoming increasingly urgent.[34] The problem of interreligious dialogue emerged at the Fourth General Assembly of the World Council of Churches at Uppsala, Sweden, in 1968, and a brief section on dialogue was included in the Assembly's final statement. The statement affirms the place of dialogue in the Christian's encounter with those of other faiths and concludes by saying that "as Christians we believe that Christ speaks in this dialogue, revealing himself to those who do not know him and correcting the limited and distorted knowledge of those who do."[35] Consistent with this new emphasis, in 1971 a new subunit, Dialogue With Men of Living Faiths and Ideologies, under the Programme Unit on Faith and Witness of the World Council of Churches, was formed. Dr. Stanley Samartha of India was named its director. In March 1970 the first multilateral consultation on religious pluralism under the auspices of the World Council of Churches was held at Ajaltoun, Beirut. Participating were forty persons from seventeen countries, representing four religions — Christianity, Hinduism, Buddhism, and Islam. Four years later, in Colombo, Sri Lanka, a second multilateral consultation was held. Five religions were represented this time, with Judaism joining the four represented in the earlier consultation. Although always controversial, and in spite of the fact that

33. For a helpful review of major developments within the World Council of Churches and changes in its understanding of the relation between Christian faith and other faiths, see the fine discussion in Robert B. Sheard, *Interreligious Dialogue in the Catholic Church Since Vatican II* (New York: The Edwin Mellen Press, 1987), pp. 135-272.

34. Cf. *Living Faiths and the Ecumenical Movement,* ed. Stanley J. Samartha (Geneva: World Council of Churches, 1971). See especially Samartha's article, "Dialogue as a Continuing Christian Concern," pp. 143-57.

35. As quoted in Sheard, *Interreligious Dialogue,* pp. 154-55.

there is not a consensus on basic theological issues as well as the purpose of dialogue itself, since 1970 dialogue with persons of other faiths has been an important part of the World Council of Churches' understanding of the mission of the Church. The ongoing debate over the place of dialogue in Christian witness is indicative of a more fundamental dispute over the relation between Christian faith and other religions and whether God can be said to be genuinely "at work" in other religions. Missiologist David Bosch notes how the terminology used in ecumenical circles has undergone a subtle shift in recent years, this in itself revealing a more fundamental change in the Church's perception of its mission in the world.

> The Mexico City meeting of 1963 still employed the "old" concept of "witness": "the *witness* of Christians *to* men of other faiths." A year later, at an East Asian Christian conference in Bangkok, the word *witness* was dropped; the theme was "The Christian *encounter with* men of other beliefs." Three years later, in Sri Lanka, the word *encounter* was also dropped. The theme now ran: "Christians in *dialogue with* men of other faiths." Throughout, however, the major participants are still identified as *Christians* who dialogue *with* others. In 1970, in Ajaltoun (Lebanon) this was also dropped; the theme was "Dialogue *between* men of living faiths." (The women were apparently still outside of the dialoguers' field of vision!) In 1977, in Chiang Mai, Thailand, the theme was "Dialogue in Community."[36]

An even more dramatic change in the perception of other religious traditions is to be found in the recent history of the Roman Catholic Church. So remarkable has been the transformation in perspective that the inclusivist view of the relation of Christianity to other faiths is today most frequently identified with recent Roman Catholic theology, particularly that of Karl Rahner. The Council of Florence in 1442 had declared unambiguously that "no one, whatever almsgiving he has practiced, even if he has shed blood for the name of Christ, can be saved, unless he has remained

---

36. David Bosch, "The Church in Dialogue," p. 134. Emphasis in original.

in the bosom and unity of the Catholic Church."[37] With only minor variations, the formula "outside the Church there is no salvation" was to be characteristic of Catholic views of other religions until well into the twentieth century. As exposure to other traditions increased, however, there were increasing efforts to soften this stance by relating God's desire for the salvation of all humankind to the accepted necessity of the Church for salvation. Catholic theologian Paul Knitter observes that theologians came up with various "ingenious concepts" so as to include within the Catholic Church devout and morally exemplary adherents of other faiths, even when they were not explicitly tied to the Church in any way: "saved" non-Christians belonged to the "soul" of the Church; they were "attached," "linked," "related" to the Church; they were members "imperfectly," "tendentially," or "potentially."[38] In part, this was simply a reaffirmation of what had been acknowledged much earlier at the Council of Trent (1545-63) — that baptism, and thereby salvation, could be received not only, as by Christians, with water *(in re)* but also by desire *(in voto)*. Such "baptism by desire," it was said, could admit into the Church anyone who lived a morally good life but could not, for whatever reason, receive the sacrament of water baptism. The more moderate modern views, however, should not be taken as necessarily indicative of a more positive estimation of other religions themselves. For there was no suggestion that God's grace might be operative through the structures of other religions. Rather, what was in view here was simply a private, individual, implicit desire for baptism and thus inclusion within the Church.

It would be difficult indeed to exaggerate the impact of the changes ushered in by Vatican II (1962-65). Nowhere is the shift in perspective more evident than in the position of the Catholic Church concerning other faiths.[39] There is a certain tension, even

37. Henry Denzinger, *Enchiridion Symbolorum,* p. 230.

38. Paul Knitter, "Roman Catholic Approaches to Other Religions: Developments and Tension," in *International Bulletin of Missionary Research* 8 (April 1984): 50.

39. For an excellent overview of the impact of Vatican II upon Roman Catholic theology of mission see the special issue of the *International Bulletin of*

inconsistency, among the statements of the documents of Vatican II regarding the relation of the Church to other religions, due, no doubt, to the internal struggles between the theologically conservative and more liberal participants in the Council.

Several prominent themes emerge from the documents of Vatican II. First, there is an important sense in which Jesus Christ is held to be normative for all persons, for, in the words of *Nostra Aetate*, the Declaration on the Relation of the Church to Non-Christian Religions, it is "in [Christ], in whom God reconciled all things to himself (2 Cor. 5:18-19), [that] men find the fulness of their religious life."[40] Furthermore, there is still a sense in which the Church is held to be necessary for salvation. This is evident from the following statement from *Lumen Gentium*, the Dogmatic Constitution on the Church:

> Basing itself upon scripture and tradition, [this holy Council] teaches that the Church, a pilgrim now on earth, is necessary for salvation: the one Christ is mediator and the way of salvation; he is present to us in his body which is the Church. He himself explicitly asserted the necessity of faith and baptism (cf. Mk. 16:16; Jn. 3:5), and thereby affirmed at the same time the necessity of the Church which men enter through baptism as through a door. Hence, they could not be saved who, knowing that the Catholic Church was founded as necessary by God through Christ, would refuse either to enter it, or to remain in it.[41]

Given the supremacy and normativity of Christ and the necessity (in some sense) of the Church for salvation, it follows that the Church cannot escape its solemn responsibility to proclaim to all

---

Missionary Research 9 (October 1985) on "Mission Since Vatican Council II." Especially helpful are W. Richey Hogg's "Vatican II's *Ad Gentes:* A Twenty-Year Retrospective" and Thomas F. Stransky's "The Church and Other Religions"; see also "Catholic Teaching on Non-Christian Religions at the Second Vatican Council" by Mikka Ruokanen, "Interpreting Silence: A Response to Mikka Ruokanen" by Paul Knitter, and "Comments on the Articles by Ruokanen and Knitter" by William R. Burrows, all in *International Bulletin of Missionary Research* (April 1990): 56-64.

40. A. P. Flannery, ed., *Documents of Vatican II* (Grand Rapids: Eerdmans, 1975), p. 739.

41. Ibid., pp. 365-66.

peoples the gracious gospel of Jesus Christ. The evangelistic imperative is reflected in the Decree on the Church's Missionary Activity, *Ad Gentes*:

> [T]he Church, in obedience to the command of her founder (Mt. 16:15) and because it is demanded by her own essential universality, strives to preach the Gospel to all men. . . . Hence the Church has an obligation to proclaim the faith and salvation which comes from Christ. . . . The reason for the missionary activity lies in the will of God, "who wishes all men to be saved and to come to the knowledge of the truth. For there is one God and one Mediator between God and men, himself a man, Jesus Christ, who gave himself a ransom for all" (1 Tim. 2:4-5), "neither is there salvation in any other" (Acts 4:12). Everyone, therefore, ought to be converted to Christ, who is known through the preaching of the Church, and ought, by baptism, to become incorporated into him, and into the Church which is his body.[42]

And yet, despite such perspicuous statements reaffirming a more traditional understanding of the place of Jesus Christ and the Church in salvation, Vatican II clearly opened the door to a very different way of looking at other religions. For example, *Lumen Gentium* 8 makes it clear that no longer can the Roman Catholic Church be identified as the sole Church of Jesus Christ. Instead of saying that the Church of Jesus Christ *is* the Catholic Church it was now stated that Christ's Church *subsists in* the Catholic Church — a subtle but significant departure. Further, *Lumen Gentium* 16 affirms "that those who have not yet received the Gospel are related to the Church in various ways."[43] And, in an oft-quoted passage from the same document, the possibility of salvation apart from actually hearing and responding to the gospel of Jesus Christ is explicitly acknowledged.

> Those who, through no fault of their own, do not know the Gospel of Christ or his Church, but who nevertheless seek God with a

42. Ibid., pp. 813, 817, 821.
43. Ibid., p. 367.

sincere heart, and, moved by grace, try in their actions to do his
will as they know it through the dictates of their conscience —
those too may achieve eternal salvation. Nor shall divine providence deny the assistance necessary for salvation to those who,
without any fault of theirs, have not yet arrived at an explicit
knowledge of God, and who, not without grace, strive to lead a
good life. Whatever good or truth is found amongst them is
considered by the Church to be a preparation for the Gospel and
given by him who enlightens all men that they may at length have
life.[44]

Moreover, the remarkable text of *Nostra Aetate* makes it plain that
non-Christian religions are not to be condemned but should be
viewed positively. "The Catholic Church rejects nothing of what is
true and holy in these religions."[45] Dialogue with adherents of
other faiths is encouraged: "The Church urges her sons to enter
with prudence and charity into discussions and collaboration with
members of other religions."[46]

Obviously, there is a fundamental tension between the emphasis upon the necessity of Jesus Christ and the Church for salvation and the affirmation of the possibility of salvation for those
with no explicit relation to the Church. This tension is reflected
also in the following statements by Pietro Rossano, Secretary of
the Vatican Secretariat for Non-Christians, made in 1979:

> As for the salvific function of these religions, namely, whether
> they are or are not paths to salvation, there is no doubt that "grace
> and truth" are given through Jesus Christ and by His Spirit (cf.
> John 1:17). Everything would lead one to conclude, however, that
> gifts of "grace and truth" do reach or may reach the hearts of men
> and women through the visible, experiential signs of the various
> religions. The Second Vatican Council is explicit on this point. . . .
> In this perspective we can conclude by saying that Christ is seen
> as the origin, center, and destiny of the various religions, as He
> who brought them to birth, takes them up, purifies them, and

44. Ibid., pp. 367-68.
45. Ibid., p. 739.
46. Ibid.

fulfills them in order to take them to their eschatological goal, so that "God may be all in all" (1 Cor. 15:28).[47]

Paul Knitter states that the majority of Catholic theologians interpret the documents of Vatican II as affirming that the non-Christian religions provide ways of salvation.[48] Post-Vatican II Catholic theology of religions has thus struggled to reconcile the fresh recognition of salvation through non-Christian religions with the traditional emphasis upon the normativity of Jesus Christ and the necessity of the Church for salvation. Undoubtedly, the most influential Catholic theologian of religions has been the great Karl Rahner, whose thought helped to shape the declarations of Vatican II. Rahner, of course, is best known in missiology for his theory of the "anonymous Christian," according to which one could be regarded as an anonymous or implicit Christian and thus saved, even without having any contact with the preaching of the gospel or the visible Church.[49] Rahner's views have come to be widely accepted, not only within Roman Catholicism but by Protestant theologians as well.

Pluralism

Although it was Rahner who was largely responsible for opening the door for Roman Catholicism to a complete reassessment of the relation of Christianity to other faiths, a number of prominent

47. Pietro Rossano, "Christ's Lordship and Religious Pluralism," in *Mission Trends No. 5: Faith Meets Faith*, ed. Gerald H. Anderson and Thomas F. Stransky (Grand Rapids: Eerdmans, 1981), pp. 27-28, 34.

48. Paul Knitter, "Roman Catholic Approaches to Other Religions," p. 50. For a contrasting perspective see Mikka Ruokanen's "Catholic Teaching on Non-Christian Religions at the Second Vatican Council."

49. See especially Rahner's "Christianity and Non-Christian Religions," in *Theological Investigations*, vol. 5 (Baltimore: Helicon Press, 1966), pp. 115-34; "Anonymous Christians," in *Theological Investigations*, vol. 6 (Baltimore: Helicon Press, 1969), pp. 390-98; "Atheism and Implicit Christianity," in *Theological Investigations*, vol. 9 (New York: Seabury Press, 1972), pp. 145-64; and "Anonymous Christianity and the Missionary Task of the Church," in *Theological Investigations*, vol. 12 (New York: Seabury Press, 1974), pp. 161-78.

Roman Catholic theologians — including Raimundo Panikkar, Paul
Knitter, and Aloysius Pieris — have gone far beyond Rahner, rejecting outright the suggestion that Christian faith is in any sense
superior to other religious traditions. In this they join a growing list
of Protestant thinkers who dismiss both exclusivism and inclusivism
as untenable. Often referred to as pluralists, these thinkers repudiate
the suggestion that there is anything unique, normative, or superior
about Jesus Christ or the Christian faith. Salvation/enlighten-
ment/liberation is said to be a reality in all major religious traditions,
and no single religion can be considered somehow normative or
superior to all others. All religions are in their own way complex
historically and culturally conditioned human responses to the one
divine reality. Pluralists include some of the most influential theologians and philosophers of religion today.

      An indication of the direction the contemporary theology
of religions is taking can be found in the significant meeting of
theologians and philosophers held at the Claremont Graduate
School on March 7-8, 1986. The major papers of the conference
were later published in *The Myth of Christian Uniqueness*,[50] a book
that was intended by the contributors to serve as a kind of "crossing
of a theological Rubicon," or a public rejection of both exclusivism
and inclusivism and acceptance of a genuinely pluralistic view of
religions. Editor Paul Knitter, in the preface, states, " Through this
collection of essays we hope to show that such a pluralist turn is
taking shape, that it is being proposed by a variety of reputable
Christian thinkers, and that therefore it represents a viable, though
still inchoate and controversial, option for Christian believers."[51]
Participants in the conference were theologians who "were exploring the possibilities of a pluralist position — a move away from
insistence on the superiority or finality of Christ and Christianity
toward a recognition of the independent validity of other ways."[52]
Contributors to the volume include some of the most influential

------

      50. *The Myth of Christian Uniqueness*, ed. John H. Hick and Paul F. Knitter
(Maryknoll, N.Y.: Orbis, 1987).
      51. Ibid., p. viii.
      52. Ibid.

figures in contemporary theology, such as Gordon Kaufman, John Hick, Langdon Gilkey, Wilfred Cantwell Smith, Raimundo Panikkar, Rosemary Radford Ruether, Paul Knitter, and Tom Driver.

Clearly, Christian exclusivism has fallen upon hard times. Not only is it being rejected by non-Christians as naive and arrogant, but it is increasingly being criticized from within the Christian community as well for alleged intolerance and for being a vestige of an immoral religious imperialism. Thus Waldron Scott, former general secretary of the World Evangelical Fellowship, speaks of the "sheer incredibility to the modern person of an exclusivist approach" to the relation among religions.[53] The evangelical Christian who maintains the unique truth of Scripture and rejects as false any rival claim is very much on the defensive in the accommodating climate of contemporary theology. Current discussions of religious pluralism take it as virtually axiomatic that the traditional exclusivistic position is no longer tenable. Inclusivists and pluralists debate the relative merits of their respective positions, but few bother to engage seriously with exclusivism. For many it is no longer even a live option.

Reasons for the Rejection of Exclusivism

How is it that exclusivism — so long the dominant position within Christendom — is today being rejected not only by the secular public but also by those claiming to be Christians? Why has it fallen into such disrepute? Undoubtedly many factors could be mentioned, but several stand out as particularly significant. The cumulative effect has been widespread acceptance of a general approach to religious issues which dismisses out of hand any suggestion that one particular religion is uniquely true and thus universally valid, and that salvation (however this is understood) is available only through one particular religious tradition.

---

53. Waldron Scott, " 'No Other Name' — An Evangelical Conviction," in *Christ's Lordship and Religious Pluralism*, ed. Gerald H. Anderson and Thomas F. Stransky (Maryknoll, N.Y.: Orbis, 1981), p. 69.

1. A major factor contributing to the undermining of an exclusivist approach to other religions is the unprecedented exposure people in the West have today to adherents of other faiths. Muslims, Hindus, Buddhists, Sikhs, among others, are no longer exotic novelties seen only in magazines such as *National Geographic* or in quaint slide presentations during periodic missionary conferences at church. In the major urban centers of the West it is no longer unusual to have Buddhists or Muslims for neighbors, to go to school with Hindus, or to work with Sikhs. So long as one has no contact with, say, Muslims or Hindus it is easy enough to dismiss them casually as "heathen" in need of Christianity. It is an entirely different matter, however, when one's neighbor, friend, or classmate is a Hindu or a Muslim. Once there is the opportunity to develop a personal relationship with followers of other faiths, it is much more difficult to categorize them as lost "pagans." After all, one might suppose, they are not so different from us — they are decent human beings who enjoy life, love family, work hard, and try to live morally respectable lives. What right do we have to tell them that our religion is correct and theirs is false?

An exclusivistic approach becomes especially difficult for many people to maintain once they are exposed to the great religious figures in other traditions. For those led to believe that morally Christianity is vastly superior to other religions, and that only those who acknowledge the lordship of Jesus Christ can exemplify saintly virtues, it is a rude shock indeed to be confronted with outstanding religious figures from other traditions. How are we to account for the towering figure of Mohandas Gandhi? If Hinduism is false, how is it that Gandhi could live such a morally exemplary life as a Hindu? How can one say that Hinduism is false when it produces such great men? Or what are we to make of the compassion of the Buddha? Or the moral sensitivity of Confucius? Or the insights of Shinran? Surely it is the height of arrogance to maintain that Christianity is uniquely true when there are so many good and respectable persons in other religious traditions!

2. The demise of exclusivism can also be traced to the pervasive influence of skepticism about religion during the twentieth century. The roots of modern skepticism go back at least to

philosophers such as Hume and Kant, although within the twentieth century the legacy of logical positivism, as well as the fideistic themes of the later Wittgenstein, have also contributed to widespread suspicion of claims to knowledge in religious matters. Such skepticism is not limited to the philosophical community. It is pervasive throughout the academic world and cannot help but be felt by students who enter the university. Much of contemporary academia — including theology — is inundated with an epistemological skepticism which regards any claim to religious truth as problematic and which views with incredulity those who hold that God has revealed himself definitively in one religious tradition.

Closely related is a biblical skepticism, characteristic of much twentieth-century higher criticism of the New Testament, which casts suspicion on any attempt to justify theological positions merely by appealing to what the New Testament record portrays Jesus as saying and doing. No longer can one justify Christian exclusivism simply by referring to texts such as John 14:6 or Acts 4:12. For many biblical scholars claim that we cannot conclude that Jesus actually said what is attributed to him in John 14:6 and deny that Peter's statement in Acts 4:12 can be interpreted as supporting the idea that salvation is available only through Christ. Add to this the current controversy over Christology among biblical scholars — there is no clear consensus on just what the New Testament picture(s) of Jesus is — and the very foundation of Christian exclusivism is shaken.

3. Along with skepticism we must note the growing impact of relativism. Philosopher Roger Trigg has observed that historically epistemological and moral relativism have always been attractive options when people who had previously led settled and complacent lives are suddenly confronted with new and different ideas and practices.[54] It is hardly suprising, then, that an increasingly influential relativism has accompanied the growing awareness of other cultures and religious traditions. The social sciences — and anthropology in particular — have both been influenced by and

54. Roger Trigg, "Religion and the Threat of Relativism," in *Religious Studies* 19 (1983): 297.

contributed toward the seductive lure of relativism. [55] Relativism has been particularly attractive during the modern era. Peter Berger notes that the history of Western thought over the past several centuries can be regarded as "one long effort to cope with the vertigo of relativity induced by modernization."[56] In his recent provocative work *The Closing of the American Mind,* philosopher Allan Bloom provides an incisive analysis of the impact of relativism in American higher education. He states, "There is one thing a professor can be absolutely certain of: almost every student entering the university believes, or says he believes, that truth is relative."[57] Tolerance and openness — radical openness to anything and everything — are prized as the greatest of virtues, and frequently the implication is that critically evaluating or rejecting as false the beliefs of others is incompatible with this spirit of tolerance. Consequently, the rigorous quest for truth, traditionally the hallmark of a genuinely liberal education, is replaced by a bland and patronizing acceptance of any and every opinion. One is left with a vacuous relativism in which all beliefs are granted equal status and no one perspective is allowed to have priority over or rule out competing alternatives.

The growing impact of relativism can be seen in a subtle shift, over the past half century or so, in the nature of the attacks upon Christianity. Until fairly recently Christianity was rejected by many intellectuals because they thought that its central beliefs about God and humankind had been disproven by philosophy, modern science, or archeology. For many today, however, it is Christianity's claim to possess absolute, unchanging, universally valid truth about God and humankind which disqualifies it from serious consideration. Many people today find the idea of religious truth which is unchanging and valid for all cultures and at all times simply incredible.

4. A further factor is what Lesslie Newbigin and others have

---

55. See Elvin Hatch, *Culture and Morality: The Relativity of Values in Anthropology* (New York: Columbia University Press, 1983).

56. Berger, *The Heretical Imperative,* p. 10.

57. Allan Bloom, *The Closing of the American Mind* (New York: Simon & Schuster, 1987), p. 25.

referred to as the tendency today to make a sharp distinction between the public realm of facts and the private world of values, opinions, and preferences. Truth is held to belong to the public realm of facts — preeminently in the physical sciences — and not to the private world of values and preferences. Since religion is said to be limited to this private world of values and preferences, questions of truth and falsity are inappropriate in religious matters. Certainly one cannot expect that religious questions can be settled on the basis of public criteria which clearly adjudicate between truth and falsity. Newbigin points out the implications of this perspective for the problem of pluralism:

> In contrast to traditional societies, modern Western society leaves its members free, within very wide limits, to adopt and hold their own views about what is good and desirable, about what kind of life is to be admired, about what code of ethics should govern one's private life. As a natural extension of this, with the growing presence of large numbers of Muslims, Sikhs, Hindus, and Buddhists in areas formerly designated as Christendom, it is assumed by a large number of Christians that the principle of pluralism applies here also. The rival truth-claims of the different religions are not felt to call for argument and resolution; they are simply part of the mosaic — or perhaps one should say kaleidoscope — of different values that make up the whole pattern.[58]

This dichotomy between the public domain of "fact" and the private realm of "values" and the banishment of religion to the latter result in the reduction of fundamental religious questions to simply a matter of preferences. Just as some people prefer Bach to the Beatles, or Westerns to romantic love stories, so some people prefer Buddhism to Roman Catholicism. The question of truth is no more appropriate in religion than it is in music. What matters is one's taste, one's preferences.[59] The operative principle here is

58. Lesslie Newbigin, *Foolishness to the Greeks: The Gospel and Western Culture* (Grand Rapids: Eerdmans, 1986), p. 16.
59. In a fascinating discussion Peter Berger calls attention to the peculiar phrase "religious preference." " 'Preference', of course, is a term that is associated with the marketplace, with the possibility of options and choices. To speak in terms

openness and tolerance. Each person should be encouraged to choose a religious option most suited to his or her particular needs and tastes. It is just as nonsensical to claim that there is one true religion which is universally valid for all persons in all cultures as it is to say that there is one kind of music or literary genre which is "true" and thus valid for all people at all times.

5. Christian exclusivism is also undermined by what we might call the pragmatic view of religion, which minimizes questions of truth and falsity and emphasizes instead what religion does for its adherents. For many people the purpose of religion is simply to help people cope in our complex and bewildering world. One looks to religion in times of major crisis (such as serious illness or death) to provide peace, solace, and encouragement. It is simply something to help us to attain inner peace and tranquility in a complex and uncertain world. Thus, to look to religion to answer ultimate metaphysical questions about the nature of humankind and its relation to God — if there even is a God! — is to misunderstand the nature and role of religion. It follows, then, that different religions should be evaluated on the basis of how effective they are in providing the desired solace and tranquility. If an Indian finds that Advaita Vedanta Hinduism works for him, then it is the right religion for him. If a Japanese finds Jodo Shinshu Buddhism to be effective for her, then it is the right religion for her. Clearly, on such an understanding it makes little sense to speak of one religion being exclusively right and true for all people in all cultures. Since people and cultures differ widely and people's needs are so varied, it is only to be expected that a variety of religious traditions will be necessary.

6. It is frequently assumed that there is something necessarily arrogant and intolerant about holding that one religion is

---

of religious preferences, as many do today, is to suggest that choosing a religion is somehow similar to choosing a brand of toothpaste or model of car. The implication is that one could have made another choice if desired. The notion of there being — in some objective sense — a *right* choice (a right model of car for everyone?) is out of place here." Cf. Peter Berger, "The Pluralistic Situation and the Coming Dialogue Between the World Religions," *Buddhist-Christian Studies* 1 (1981): 33.

true, and that those incompatible with it are false. Similarly, it is often claimed that exclusivism must be rejected because it has such reprehensible effects upon the relations between various cultures and religious traditions. Since we are today all members of an increasingly interdependent global community, and all face common threats of nuclear annihilation, famine, and overpopulation, we must at all costs strive for harmony and peaceful cooperation among various cultures and traditions. Maintaining that one particular religion is uniquely true and that followers of other faiths embrace false beliefs is, it is said, somehow incompatible with this.

7. Finally, we should note the growing acceptance — even within Christian circles — of the doctrine of soteriological universalism, according to which all persons, regardless of religious affiliation, will in the end enjoy God's salvation. Christian exclusivism, which rejects soteriological universalism, is regarded as morally questionable and out of touch with the realities of our pluralistic world. It is often taken for granted that if God is indeed a God of love, he is morally obligated to provide all persons with equal opportunity of responding to him. Maintaining that salvation is necessarily linked to personal response to the person and work of Jesus Christ is said to be incompatible with God's goodness and love, since it allegedly cuts off from the possibility of salvation those who through no fault of their own have never heard of the gospel of Jesus Christ. Accordingly, Christologies which see Jesus Christ as uniquely and exclusively divine and thus normative for all persons are increasingly being criticized for being obscurantist and untenable in our pluralistic world.

A Definition of Christian Exclusivism

Christians have traditionally held that incompatible truth claims are being made by the various religions and thus that not all of the claims of the many religions can be true. At least some must be false. It has traditionally been maintained, for example, that the Muslim and the orthodox Christian cannot both be correct in their respective beliefs concerning the identity of Jesus of Nazareth. At least one must be incorrect. Convinced that the central affirmations of the Bible are true, Christians have regarded the person and work of Jesus Christ as unique, definitive, and normative, and the beliefs of other faiths conflicting with Scripture as, at best, distorted or incomplete, if not simply false. This traditional position is reflected in the widely accepted Lausanne Covenant of 1974:

> We also regard as derogatory to Christ and the Gospel every kind of syncretism and dialogue which implies that Christ speaks equally through all religions and ideologies. Jesus Christ, being himself the only God-man, who gave himself as the only ransom for sinners, is the only mediator between God and man. There is no other name by which we must be saved.[60]

Exclusivism is not simply an isolated belief about the relation of Christian faith to other religions, a dogma which somehow stands on its own. It should be understood as part of a comprehensive perspective rooted in certain fundamental beliefs about the person and work of Jesus Christ, the nature of God, and God's self-revelation in Scripture. Accordingly, Christian exclusivism — as I use the term in this study — can be defined as the position which accepts as the basis for its view of other religions the following four propositions: (a) Jesus Christ is the unique Incarnation of God, fully God and fully man; (b) only through the person and work of Jesus Christ is there the possibility of salvation; (c) the Bible is God's unique revelation written, and thus is true and authoritative; and (d) where the claims of Scripture are incompatible with those of other faiths, the latter are to be rejected as false.

The use of the term "exclusivism" is somewhat unfortunate since it has for many people undesirable connotations of narrow-mindedness, arrogance, insensitivity to others, self-righteousness, bigotry, and so on. In the context of the current debate, however, the term is perhaps unavoidable, because of its widespread use today to refer to the position represented by the Lausanne

60. J. D. Douglas, ed., *Let the Earth Hear His Voice* (Minneapolis: World Wide Publications, 1975), p. 4.

Covenant. Use of "exclusivism" is adopted in this book, then, not because of any fondness for the word itself, but rather because of its current extensive use to refer to the traditional position of the Christian Church concerning other religions. To introduce fresh terminology at this point would merely confuse the discussion. I will argue that, properly construed, Christian exclusivism need not have the negative connotations often associated with it.

In concluding this chapter, three things should be noted briefly about Christian exclusivism as defined above. First, Christian exclusivism does not entail that all of the claims of the other religions must be false. It is perfectly consistent with exclusivism, as defined above, to maintain that some of the claims of other traditions are true. Similarly, Christian exclusivism does not entail that other religions are completely without value, or that Christians cannot learn anything from adherents of other faiths. And finally, it should be recognized that Christian exclusivism is but one example of exclusivism in religion. For Christian exclusivism is not the only kind of exclusivism. An exclusivist religion can be thought of in broad terms as a religion which maintains that its own central affirmations are true, and that if the claims of another religion appear to be incompatible with its own claims, the former are to be rejected as false.

What is often overlooked is that most, if not all, religious traditions are exclusivist in this sense. Most followers of any given religion regard their own religion as true and others which conflict with it as incomplete or false. Theravada Buddhists, for example, characteristically reject as false those claims made by Christians which are incompatible with Theravada Buddhism. Muslims reject as false those views about the prophet Muhammad which conflict with the teachings of Islam. Even Hinduism — widely hailed as the apotheosis of tolerance — is no exception. One finds in Shankara and Radhakrishnan vigorous argument against those who do not accept their particular perspectives on reality. So Christian exclusivism is by no means an oddity when considered in the broader context of the global religious traditions.

CHAPTER TWO

The Scandal of Pluralism:
Conflicting Truth Claims (I)

Most religions presuppose that human beings, and in some cases the cosmos at large, are presently in some kind of undesirable predicament, and that, in contrast to this predicament, an ultimately good and desirable state can be achieved — either through one's own individual efforts or through the benevolent assistance of one or more higher beings or powers. Given this common structure, three questions naturally emerge which can profitably be put to the various religious traditions: What is the nature of the religious ultimate? What is the nature of the human predicament? What is the nature of salvation/enlightenment/liberation? The three questions are clearly interrelated, for one's views on the human predicament and the religious ultimate will have profound implications for beliefs about salvation and how it is to be achieved. Just as in medicine the physician's prescription and advice to the patient will largely be determined by the diagnosis of the problem and the available resources for treating that condition, so too in religion any prescription for the human predicament will presuppose a particular understanding of the nature of the predicament and the resources available for its treatment.

How do the major religions answer the three questions posed above? Is it plausible to maintain, as many do today, that the different religions all make essentially the same claims and teach basically the same truth? Careful examination of the basic tenets of the various religious traditions demonstrates that, far from teaching the same thing, the major religions have radically different perspectives on the religious ultimate, the human predicament, and the nature of salvation. Any attempt to produce an essential unity in outlook among the many religions will result in distorting at least some of the actual religious beliefs of followers of the various traditions.

We will look briefly at four religious traditions — Hinduism, Buddhism, Islam, and Shinto — to see what answers they provide to our three questions.[1] Hinduism and Buddhism will be considered in this chapter, Islam and Shinto in the next. Some explanation for including Shinto is in order, since discussions of religious pluralism generally focus upon relations among major religions such as Christianity, Islam, Buddhism, Hinduism, and possibly Judaism. Although this is understandable, it tends to elevate in importance the numerically largest religions and obscures the fact that there are hundreds of other religious traditions in our world today competing for people's allegiance. An adequate understanding of religious pluralism must take into account not only the "major" religions but also the many "minor" religious movements and traditions. For example, in addition to followers of the many new, nontraditional religions[2] there are millions of people

1. What follows is a highly selective introduction to the major tenets of these religions; obviously a comprehensive discussion of each tradition is impossible here. Good general introductions to the major religions, which treat the subject in much more depth, include Ninian Smart, *The Religious Experience of Mankind*, 3rd ed. (New York: Charles Scribner's Sons, 1984); David S. Noss and John B. Noss, *A History of the World's Religions*, 8th ed. (New York: Macmillan, 1990); and *Religion and Man: An Introduction*, ed. W. Richard Comstock (New York: Harper & Row, 1971).

2. In 1980 as many as 22 percent of the Japanese population claimed to be followers of so-called "new religions." Cf. Robert S. Ellwood, "New Religions in Japan," in *The Encyclopedia of Religions*, vol. 10, ed. Mircea Eliade (New York: Macmillan, 1987), p. 411.

today who participate in religious traditions that are broadly animistic. That is, their worldview is one in which the cosmos is
understood to be permeated with unseen spirits, powers, or deities
that directly affect one's well-being and the events in the visible
world. Shinto can be understood as a kind of animism. Although
an ancient tradition with roots in Japan's prehistoric past, Shinto
today remains a vigorous and thriving religion. One of the many
paradoxes of contemporary Japan is that the assumptions, values,
and traditions of Shinto are still very much accepted by many
modern, sophisticated, "Westernized" Japanese. Thus, in order
both to emphasize the great variety among religious traditions
today and to include in our discussion a representative of the
animistic family of religions, Shinto will be considered along with
the other three major religions.

Dimensions of Religious Phenomena

Religion is a multifarious phenomenon that can be approached
from various perspectives. Philosopher and phenomenologist of
religion Ninian Smart, for example, suggests that there are at least
six dimensions of religion.[3] His analysis is most instructive. What
he calls the *ritual* dimension includes the visible rites, ceremonies,
institutions, and buildings that are used in a carefully prescribed
manner by the religious believers. Religious services, prayers, offer-
ings, baptisms, sacrifice, and so on are thus part of the ritual
dimension. The collection of myths, images, and stories through
which the invisible, transcendent world is symbolically expressed
is called the *mythological* dimension. (We should note that Smart
is not using the term "myth" to imply that the content is necessarily
false. What he means by "myth" is similar to a story, whether true
or false.) A third dimension is the *doctrinal* dimension. Doctrines
can be thought of as the systematic attempt to clarify and integrate

3. Ninian Smart, *Religious Experience*, pp. 6-12; cf. also N. Smart, *Worldviews: Crosscultural Explorations of Human Beliefs* (New York: Charles Scribner's
Sons, 1983), chaps. 3-8.

the central beliefs of a religious tradition. Yet another aspect is the *ethical* dimension, which includes the moral teachings of a tradition bearing directly upon the manner in which the believer is to live his or her life. And closely related to the ethical is the *social* dimension, which reflects the patterns and mores that dictate desirable relationships among the believers in the religious community, as well as the institutions which provide necessary structure and organization to the tradition. And finally, the *experiential* dimension is that part in which the religious believer participates actively in the various rites and patterns of the religious tradition (e.g., through worship, prayer, meditation, etc.). A genuinely comprehensive understanding of religion will include appreciation of all six dimensions.

Of particular importance for our purposes, however, is the doctrinal dimension. Now, to be sure, religion cannot be reduced simply to a tidy set of beliefs or doctrines. For, as Smart reminds us, religion includes much more than mere beliefs. But neither can one ignore the central place of beliefs in religion. The major religious communities characteristically teach their members to live in certain ways, to have certain values, and to regard all of life from certain perspectives.[4] The particular religious perspective of a tradition can be articulated in terms of basic beliefs about the cosmos and humankind's place in the cosmos. It is helpful in this connection to think of a religious tradition as embracing a particular religious worldview. A worldview, in turn, can be thought of as a comprehensive set of basic beliefs and values regarding reality which regulate characteristic patterns of behavior.[5] Following Smart, we might use "worldview" in a very general sense to include

4. Cf. William A. Christian, Sr., *Doctrines of Religious Communities: A Philosophical Study* (New Haven: Yale University Press, 1987), p. 5.

5. Anthropologist Michael Kearney defines a worldview as "a way of looking at reality. It consists of basic assumptions and images that provide a more or less coherent, though not necessarily accurate, way of thinking about the world." M. Kearney, *World View* (Novato, Cal.: Chandler & Sharp Publishers, 1984), p. 41. Similarly, Charles H. Kraft speaks of a worldview as "the central systematization of conceptions of reality to which members of [a] culture assent (largely unconsciously) and from which stems their value system." C. Kraft, *Christianity in Culture* (Maryknoll, N.Y.: Orbis, 1979), p. 53.

both religious traditions, such as Islam or Buddhism, and secular ideologies, such as Marxism or secular humanism.[6] Religions such as Christianity, Judaism, Shinto, or Buddhism would then provide examples of different religious worldviews. It seems clear that each religious tradition demands from its adherents a particular religious "way of life" which accords with its particular religious worldview. And undergirding this religious way of life are fundamental assumptions or beliefs about the nature of the cosmos, the religious ultimate, the place of the human person in the cosmos, the relation of the person to the religious ultimate, the human predicament, and the possibility of deliverance from this predicament. The importance of such basic beliefs must not be minimized, for, as Smart observes, "the world religions owe some of their living power to their success in presenting a total picture of reality, through a coherent system of doctrines."[7] These fundamental beliefs about reality, particularly those concerning the religious ultimate and its relation to human beings, are what William Christian calls the *primary doctrines* of a religious community.[8] We might also think of them as *defining beliefs* of a given religious tradition, in that they define the acceptable parameters of that tradition and help to determine the nature of the other dimensions (ritual, ethical, experiential, etc.) of the tradition.

Now, in passing on its primary doctrines to new members, a religious community does not merely mention them or indifferently suggest them as possible options for acceptance. Primary, or defining, beliefs are not "up for grabs," so to speak. The religious community proposes them for acceptance and it fully expects new members of the community to accept them. And accepting the doctrines involves, among other things, taking what is asserted by them as true. The fundamental assumptions about reality that define the worldview of a given religious community are accepted by that community as true.[9] Thus, while we can readily admit that there is much more

6. N. Smart, *Worldviews*, p. 2.
7. Idem, *The Religious Experience*, p. 8.
8. W. Christian, *Religious Communities*, pp. 1-2, 5-11.
9. Ibid., p. 42.

to a religious tradition than simply its beliefs or doctrines, it should be clear that basic beliefs defining the worldview of a religious community are of great significance in understanding that particular religious tradition. One cannot understand evangelical Christianity or Tendai Buddhism, for example, without having a good grasp of the defining beliefs of these religions. And I will argue that careful examination of the defining beliefs of the major religions shows that the various traditions are making very different, and at times what appear to be actually incompatible, claims about humankind and its place in the cosmos.

A caveat is in order here. What follows is not intended to be a comprehensive survey of the four religions, but merely a concise overview of some of the distinctive teachings of each as they pertain to the three questions raised earlier. And yet, any attempt to summarize the central teachings of the great religions will be somewhat controversial. For religions such as Hinduism and Buddhism in particular are best thought of as vast families of religious traditions, including within their family trees an enormous variety of sometimes competing and conflicting sects. Thus, virtually any statement about, say, Hinduism can be challenged by some Hindu who maintains that it does not accurately reflect his or her own particular religious tradition. I trust, however, that the discussions which follows accurately represents the main currents within each tradition and thus would be acceptable to many Hindus, Buddhists, Muslims, and Shintoists.

HINDUISM

Hinduism does not fit many common expectations of what a religion should be. There is no single founder of Hinduism; it has no prescribed ecclesiastical structure nor does it put forward a carefully defined creed. What is known today as Hinduism is really a family of religious traditions that are the product of some 4,000 years of development. Hindu scholar Kshiti Mohan Sen says, "Hinduism is more like a tree that has *grown* gradually than like a

building that has been *erected* by some great architect at some
definite point in time."[10] The term "Hindu" itself seems to have
been originally a generic term used by the early Persians to refer
to the people of India (those who lived beyond the River Indus),
and only later came to be used to refer specifically to the religious
ways of life of the Indian people.[11]

A bewildering variety of religious beliefs and practices fall
under the rubric "Hinduism." For example, although most Hindus
believe in a Supreme Being, variously conceived in the different
traditions, some Hindus do not believe in any kind of higher
Being.[12] Although many, if not most, Hindus are vegetarians, some
are not. Some Hindus worship Shiva; others worship Vishnu, or
one or more of his manifestations *(avataras)*, such as Krishna. A
Hindu may believe in one God, a few gods, or in many gods. Many
Hindus believe in a supreme Being or God while simultaneously
worshiping other "lesser gods" who are taken to be manifestations
or appearances of the one supreme Being. Some Hindus conceive
of the religious ultimate in personal, somewhat theistic categories;
others conceive of the religious ultimate in nonpersonal, monistic
categories.

Is there, then, any unity to the rich diversity, anything that
unifies the disparate traditions and marks them as belonging to
one identifiable family of traditions? The unity in the great diversity of beliefs and practices within Hinduism is generally said to
lie in the prominent role played by the concepts of transmigration

10. K. M. Sen, *Hinduism* (Baltimore: Penguin Books, 1961), p. 14. Emphasis in the original.
11. Cf. Nirad C. Chaudhuri, *Hinduism* (New York: Oxford University
Press, 1979), p. 24.
12. There are traditions within Hinduism which are often referred to as
atheistic, although, as Ninian Smart reminds us, atheism in the Indian context is
somewhat different from atheism in the West, since it does not carry with it any
irreligiousness. Atheism rejects belief in a Creator or Supreme Being, but in the
Indian context is compatible with belief in salvation, or liberation from the round
of rebirth, as well as with prayer and worship of the gods. The gods are simply
regarded as part of, rather than transcendent to, the cosmos. Cf. Ninian Smart,
Doctrine and Argument in Indian Philosophy (London: George Allen & Unwin,
1964), p. 23.

and *karma* (the cosmic law of cause and effect, determining the conditions of existence) in the understanding of the human predicament, and in the common recognition of the Vedas as sacred scripture. For the notions of transmigration and *karma* are central to all major schools of Hinduism, and all Hindus regard the Vedas as authoritative, although they may disagree sharply over their proper interpretation.

In spite of the obscurity of the origin of the earliest Indian religious practices and beliefs, it is generally agreed that sometime during the middle of the second millennium B.C. a group of tribes, referring to themselves as Aryans, invaded and gradually established their dominance over what is now northern and central India. Although religious traditions were already established among the pre-Aryan Indus Valley civilizations, relatively little is known about them. However, an identifiable and distinctive religious life on the Indian subcontinent can be traced back to the time of the Aryan migrations into India. The Aryans brought with them a religious culture which was on the whole polytheistic, and which had some similarities to the religions of the ancient Greeks and Romans, as well as that of ancient Iran. Most of the gods of the Aryan pantheon were identified with forces of nature. These influences, combined with indigenous practices and beliefs of the pre-Aryan Indus Valley civilizations, helped to produce some of the central themes and motifs that were to dominate Indian religious and philosophical thought for centuries.

Sometime between roughly 1500 and 800 B.C. the Vedas appeared, a collection of sacred hymns and treatises concerned largely with details of sacrificial ritual. The term "Vedas" is often used in a strict sense to refer to the four Samhita Vedas — the Rigveda Samhita, the Atharvaveda Samhita, the Samaveda Samhita, and the Yajurveda Samhita. But it can also be used in a more general sense to refer not only to the Samhita Vedas but also to the Brahmanas, prose texts dealing with sacrificial ritual, as well as to the Upanishads, sacred writings which date from roughly the eighth to the fourth centuries B.C. In this more general sense the Vedas can be said to form the essential canon of sacred scriptures for orthodox Hindus. The Vedas, including the Upanishads, are sometimes classified as *sruti* ("that which is heard"),[13] scriptures embodying eternal truths which the seers *(rishis)* discerned or "heard," and thus comprising the most authoritative sacred texts of Hinduism. In addition to the *sruti* are the *smriti* ("that which is remembered") — the many writings which developed as interpretative commentary or elaboration of the truths contained in the *sruti*. These include the law books; the two great epics, the Ramayana and the Mahabharata (which includes the most famous of Indian scriptures, the Bhagavad Gita); the Puranas, the principal scriptures for theistic Hinduism; the Agamas, theological treatises and manuals of worship; and the sutras of the six major schools of Hindu philosophy.

Vedic religion — the religious beliefs and practices of the period from roughly 1500 B.C. to 900 B.C. — was characterized by polytheism — the identification of various deities with forces of nature — and carefully prescribed rituals of sacrifice, the object of which was to please the nature gods and thereby secure for one's self or clan health, wealth, fertility, long life, and victory in battle. As sacrifice played a central role in Vedic religion, the priestly or *Brahmin* caste, which held the secrets necessary for effective sacrifice, came to occupy an increasingly prominent place in the religious life of the people. Although a variety of deities such as Indra, Varuna, Vishnu, and Rudra appear in the Vedas, there are indications of a rudimentary monotheism in some of the Vedas. In a famous passage, for example, the Rigveda declares, "He is one, (though) wise men call Him by many names."[14] The notion of one infinite Being projecting Himself in many different forms, which is introduced in the Rigveda, is later elaborated upon in the Upanishads and becomes a prominent theme in later Hindu thought.

The period from roughly the eighth through fourth centuries

13. The origin of the use of the term *sruti* to refer to this body of texts is sometimes explained on the basis of the fact that for centuries the Vedas were passed on orally from generation to generation. The Vedas, then, were literally "what is heard." Also included, perhaps, is the idea that the Vedas were *apauruseya* — "not produced by human agency." The truths of the Vedas were taken to be eternal truths which the *rishis* have merely "seen" or "discerned." Cf. R. N. Dandekar, "Vedas," in *The Encyclopedia of Religion*, vol. 15, p. 214.

14. Rigveda, 21, 164, 46. Cited in Sen, *Hinduism*, p. 48.

B.C. saw the emergence of the Upanishads, sacred writings concerned primarily with explaining the "hidden meaning" or the "real message" of the many religious practices and rituals which had developed around the earlier Vedas. The central teaching of the Upanishads revolves around the notion that behind the changing phenomenal world of our experience is a timeless, unchanging, unifying Reality which is ultimately to be identified with the eternal essence of the human person.[15] Thus, a recurring theme in the Upanishads is the question of the relation between Brahman (ultimate Reality) and *atman* (the self). While recognizing the difficulties of apprehending the truth of Brahman, the Upanishads maintain that through disciplined meditation and rigorous cultivation of mental perception ultimate Reality — Brahman — can be discerned.

Some Basic Concepts of Hinduism

One cannot understand Hinduism without an appreciation of the significance of the notions of transmigration and *karma*. Thomas Hopkins states that by the sixth century B.C. the concepts of transmigration and the law of *karma* had been generally accepted as basic facts of existence and were rarely challenged from that time on by any major Indian system of thought.[16] Physical death was not regarded as the termination of life and existence. Persons and other living beings were considered to be continually being reborn. Although the physical body may die, there is an indestructible element to the living organism — the soul — which passes on from one life to another. What regulates the endless cycle of deaths and rebirths is *karma*. The term *"karma"* literally means "deeds" or "action," but it came to be used to denote

> the impersonal and transethical system under which one's current situation in the world is regarded as the fruit of seeds planted by

15. Cf. William K. Mahony, "Upanishads," in *The Encyclopedia of Religion*, vol. 15, pp. 147f.

16. Thomas J. Hopkins, *The Hindu Religious Tradition* (Belmont, Cal.: Dickenson Publishing Company, 1971), p. 50.

one's behaviour and dispositions in the past, and the view that in all of one's present actions lie similar seeds that will have continuing and determinative effect on one's life as they bear fruit in the future.[17]

Birth leads inevitably to death. Death, in turn, inevitably results in rebirth in another body. And it is the impersonal cosmic law, *karma*, which determines the conditions of each existence. One's present existence is determined by the effects of past actions and dispositions, and one's future states are determined by present (and past) actions and dispositions. Unless checked by counteractive measures, the influences of moral actions in the present will extend into subsequent lives. The Chandogya Upanishad, from the seventh or eighth century B.C., states:

> Those who are of pleasant conduct here — the prospect is, indeed, that they will enter a pleasant womb, either the womb of a *brahmin* [priestly caste], or the womb of a *ksatriya* [warrior] or the womb of a *vaisya* [merchant]. But those who are of stinking conduct here — the prospect is, indeed, that they will enter a stinking womb, either the womb of a dog, or the womb of a swine, or the womb of an outcast.[18]

The entire repetitive process of birth, death, and rebirth, impersonally regulated by *karma*, came to be referred to as *samsara* (literally, "to wander or pass through a series of states or conditions").[19] *Samsara* increasingly took on a negative, pessimistic note,[20] and the religious objective of all three major Indian

17. William K. Mahony, "Karman: Hindu and Jain Concepts," in *The Encyclopedia of Religion*, vol. 8, p. 262.

18. Chandogya Upanishad 5.10.7, as cited in *A Source Book in Indian Philosophy*, ed. Sarvepalli Radhakrishnan and Charles A. Moore (Princeton: Princeton University Press, 1957), pp. 66-67.

19. Brian K. Smith, "Samsara," in *The Encyclopedia of Religion*, vol. 13, p. 56.

20. "The succession of finite births has traditionally been regarded by Hindus pessimistically, as an existential misfortune and not as a series of 'second chances' to improve one's lot, as it is often viewed in the West. Life is regarded not only as 'rough, brutish, and short' but as filled with misery *(dukkha)*. Thus, the

religions — Hinduism, Jainism, and Buddhism — came to be identified with release or liberation *(moksha)* from the bondage of *samsara* by rendering ineffective the principle of *karma*. As we shall see, various religious movements in India provided different answers to the question of how one was to achieve liberation from *samsara*. But the idea of release from the cycle of rebirths as the primary religious goal was common to all the major Indian religious traditions.

Although the notion of Brahman as the sustaining power of the cosmos had been introduced in the earlier Vedas, it is in the Upanishads that we first find serious concern with the nature of Brahman and its relation to the human person. Most schools of Hinduism accept the notion of an all-pervading ultimate reality, Brahman, although the specific details vary widely. Brahman is generally said to be the ultimate reality, the Supreme Being, the ground underlying all that is, that upon which all else depends. "Verily, this whole world is Brahman. Tranquil, let one worship It as that from which he came forth, as that into which he will be dissolved, as that in which he breathes."[21] The central question of the Upanishads was the relation between this ultimate reality (Brahman) and the human self *(atman)*, and in what is perhaps the most famous passage in the Upanishads the *atman* is identified with Brahman — "That thou art" *(tat tvam asi)*.[22] Thus the one eternal Reality underlying all the appearances of the phenomenal world is in actuality identical to the self. The problem is that humans ascribe independent reality to individual entities in the world, not realizing that they are but manifestations of that which is ultimately Real. The individual self is mistakenly taken to be self-existent in its own right, when in fact it is one with that ultimate Reality pervading all that is. Brahman is present in the phenomenal world as the human self. And attainment of true

---

multiplication of births within this 'vale of tears' merely augments and intensifies the suffering that is the lot of all creatures." J. Bruce Long, "Reincarnation," in *The Encyclopedia of Religion*, vol. 12, p. 266.

21. Chandogya Upanishad 3.14.1, cited in Radhakrishnan and Moore, *Source Book*, p. 65.

22. Cf. Chandogya Upanishad 6.9-13.

insight into the ultimately Real results in release from the cycle of deaths and rebirths caused by one's ignorance of the fact that one's essential self (which is identical with Brahman) does not die.[23] What breaks the cycle of rebirths and the bondage of *samsara,* then, is the knowledge of the unchanging Brahman and of one's essential identity with Brahman. Thus, the religious goal in the early Upanishads was to become one with the ultimate Reality, Brahman, or rather to recognize that one's true self is already identical with Brahman, and through this knowledge to attain *moksha* or release.

Brahman was generally held to be utterly beyond characterization, incapable of being expressed in human concepts or linguistic symbols and without qualities — nonpersonal Being (*nirguna* Brahman). But the later Upanishads reveal a growing interest in the personal aspect of Brahman and give evidence of an emerging theistic emphasis. This shift is apparent in the Svetasvatara Upanishad (fifth or sixth century B.C.), which, while still concerned with release from *samsara,* suggests that such release comes not from knowledge of the nonpersonal *nirguna* Brahman but rather from knowledge of the personal Lord identified as Rudra or Shiva, the personal manifestation of Brahman.[24]

> Him who is without beginning and without end,
>   in the midst of confusion,
> The Creator of all, of manifold form,
> The One embracer of the universe —
> By knowing God one is released from all fetters.[25]

Thomas Hopkins states, "Saving knowledge is not knowledge of the impersonal Brahman but of the personal Lord, and it is gained by coming to know Him as resident within one's self."[26] Such

---

23. Thus the Adhyatma Upanishad states, "he is a free person who through insight sees no distinction between his own self and Brahman, and between Brahman and the universe." Quoted in Mahoney, "Upanishads," p. 148.

24. Cf. Hopkins, *Hindu Religious Tradition,* p. 70.

25. Svetasvatara Upanishad 5.13. Cited in Radhakrishnan and Moore, *Source Book,* pp. 91-92.

26. Hopkins, *Hindu Religious Tradition,* pp. 70-71.

knowledge was said to come through rigorous self-discipline and meditation *(dhyana)*.

The theistic emphasis can also be seen in the growth of the popular cults of Shiva and Vishnu. By the fourth century B.C. Shiva and Vishnu were clearly the two most popular deities. Shiva was worshiped as the great creator of the universe and was identified with fertility (thus his association with the symbol of the phallus, or *lingam*), creation, destruction, and, curiously, also asceticism. Perhaps even more important than Shiva, however, is the figure of Vishnu, who is referred to in several Brahmanas as "the highest of the gods." Characteristic of the cult of Vishnu was belief in various manifestations or appearances *(avataras)* of the deity on earth, principally as Rama or Krishna.[27]

The theistic tendency and the accompanying emphasis upon devotion *(bhakti)* are clearly evident in the Bhagavad Gita (ca. 200 B.C.), in which Krishna, as a manifestation of Vishnu, is presented as the Supreme God who, if made the object of proper devotion, will provide salvation. Krishna is depicted as the culmination of all the previous religious forms and as bringing a higher and better way of salvation or release. Three ways of attaining spiritual perfection or release are delineated. First is *karma marga,* or the way of selfless or disinterested action — that is, action done without any attachment to its consequences. The second is *jnana marga,* or the way of higher knowledge or insight, culminating in the realization of the identity between the *atman* and Brahman. The third is *bhakti marga,* or the way of exclusive devotion to God. Although Krishna does not discount the other two ways, he makes it clear that the superior way is exclusive devotion to him. "And of all the *yogins,* he who full of faith worships Me [Krishna], with

27. Shiva and Vishnu were sometimes linked in the popular mind with Brahman as a kind of divine triumvirate. Ninian Smart cautions against drawing any analogy here with the Christian doctrine of the Trinity — three in one. The three divine figures are rather alternative ways of expressing the same truth about the Supreme Being; the Supreme Being can be represented in a threefold form — as Shiva, Vishnu, and Brahman. The one Supreme Being can be worshiped either as Shiva, Vishnu, or Brahman. Cf. N. Smart, *The Religious Experience of Mankind,* p. 136.

his inner self abiding in me — him I hold to be the most attuned to me."[28] The nonpersonal Brahman of the Vedas and the ways of release through rigorous discipline and meditation are not rejected. But a better way, easier and available to all, is now revealed.

> For those who take refuge in Me [Krishna], O Partha [Arjuna], though they are lowly born, women, *vaisyas* [merchants or traders], as well as *sudras* [workers] — they also attain to the highest goal — How much more, then, holy *brahmins* [priests/ teachers] and devoted royal saints, having entered this impermanent sorrowful world, do thou worship Me. On Me fix thy mind; to Me be devoted; worship Me; revere Me; thus having disciplined thyself, with Me as thy goal, to Me shalt thou come.[29]

Thus *bhakti* directed to Krishna becomes the highest form of religious activity as well as the key to true renunciation and release (*moksha*).

The Puranas, sacred writings from roughly A.D. 300 to 1200, reflect the great upsurge in theistic development and *bhakti* within popular Hinduism. The present age was said to be a time of such degeneracy and deterioration of standards that, whereas in the past, when persons were purer and capable of greater achievement and it was possible to attain *moksha* through rigorous mental and physical discipline resulting in the requisite spiritual knowledge, during the present evil age an easier way of salvation was necessary. Salvation now was said to be available through devotion to the Lord. One should seek refuge in Vishnu (or Shiva), worship him, and call upon his name in love and devotion for help and he would graciously save. Significantly, with the development of theistic devotionalism there comes also a shift in the understanding of salvation/liberation. According to Thomas Hopkins,

> The goal they sought was salvation, but it was salvation in very personal terms; not union with the impersonal Brahman or even

28. Bhagavad Gita 6.47. Cited in Radhakrishnan and Moore, *Source Book*, p. 126.

29. Ibid. 9.32-34, p. 134.

merger with the Lord, but an eternal relationship of blissful devotion in which the distinction between devotee and the Lord would be preserved. The spirit of their devotion was well expressed by the later Hindu saint Sri Ramakrishna when he declared that he wanted "to taste sugar, not become sugar."[30]

Such popular devotion, or *bhakti,* finds clear expression in the Bhagavata Purana, whose central focus is the worship of Vishnu through devotion to Krishna. Rama and Krishna, technically *avataras* of Vishnu, became so popular that in time they came to assume the position of supreme deity for their respective devotees. David Kinsley notes that followers of Krishna tended to regard Krishna as no longer an *avatara* himself but rather as the source of all *avataras.* Even Vishnu was regarded by some as a lesser manifestation of Krishna.[31]

Schools of Hinduism

Traditionally, six distinct schools of thought, or viewpoints, have been recognized among the strands of orthodox Hinduism. The six branches have been usually grouped together in three pairs: Sankhya and Yoga, Vaishesika and Nyaya, and Vedanta and Mimamsa.[32] The latter of each of the pairs — Yoga, Nyaya, and Mimamsa — present more of a methodology than a metaphysical system. The Sankhya and Yoga schools emphasize the distinction between eternal souls *(purushas)* and nature *(prakriti),* and the Sankhya school in particular held that release from the cycle of rebirths comes through proper knowledge of the soul's essential distinction from nature. The Vaishesika tradition argued that nature is composed of ultimate, indestructible atoms and, in its later

30. T. Hopkins, *Hindu Religious Tradition,* p. 118.

31. David Kinsley, "Avatara," in *The Encyclopedia of Religion,* vol. 2, p. 15.

32. For helpful expositions of the major tenets of each school see Ninian Smart, *Doctrine and Argument in Indian Philosophy,* chaps. 1, 4-9, and Stuart C. Hackett, *Oriental Philosophy: A Westerner's Guide to Eastern Thought* (Madison: University of Wisconsin Press, 1979), chap. 4.

theistic forms, held that it is God who imparts motion and order
to the atoms. Both the Sankhya and the Vaishesika traditions embrace what is frequently called metaphysical pluralism, or the view
that a plurality of eternal, individual souls exist in their own right
and confront an equally independent order of nature.[33] This perspective was vigorously denied by major exponents of Vedanta,
perhaps the most influential of the schools. Underlying all six
viewpoints, however, were two fundamental assumptions: first,
that the religious goal was release from the cycle of rebirths and,
second, that the most effective means of achieving such release was
through cultivation of a proper insight into reality that would
dispel the clouds of ignorance and render impotent the chains of
karma and *samsara.*

Given the tremendous influence of Vedanta, brief attention should be given the major traditions within this school of
Hinduism. The three major divisions within Vedanta — often
called the schools of Non-Dualism, Dualism, and Qualified Non-
Dualism — accept the ultimate authority of the Vedas and the
Upanishads, although they differ significantly in their interpretations of these scriptures.

Non-Dualism, or Advaita Vedanta, has its chief architect in
the person of Shankara (A.D. 788-820), arguably the most influential Hindu thinker of all time.[34] The central insight of Shankara
was the essential identity between the self and the one ultimate
Reality sustaining and permeating the phenomenal world. The sole
Reality was said to be the nonpersonal *nirguna* Brahman, or Brahman devoid of all qualities or characteristics. Advaita Vedanta thus
accepts an ontological monism in which the sole reality is Brahman. It follows, then, that the entire phenomenal world, the cosmos, is in an important sense illusory *(maya)* and has no ultimately
real existence. Now, Shankara does not deny that we normally
experience the world around us as having an independent reality

33. Cf. Stuart Hackett, *Oriental Philosophy,* p. 126.
34. For good introductions to Shankara and Advaita Vedanta see Eliot
Deutsch, *Advaita Vedanta* (Honolulu: University of Hawaii Press, 1969), and
N. Smart, *Doctrine and Argument in Indian Philosophy,* chap. 7.

of its own. He would not deny, for example, that if one walks randomly into a busy intersection one will be struck by oncoming traffic. He accords the phenomenal world a functional reality but maintains that from the perspective of Brahman — that which alone is ultimately real — this world is illusory.[35] Central to Shankara's thought is a fundamental distinction between levels of reality and truth. The phenomenal world of our experience is not wholly unreal; it has a provisional reality which must be respected, but it must be distinguished from the realm of absolute reality, of nondifferentiated Being, or Brahman. Similarly, "truths" that are applicable on the lower level of phenomenal reality must be regarded as provisional at best, superseded by the ultimate Truth pertaining to Brahman.

If all distinctions and attribution of qualities are ultimately illusory, then conceptions of the ultimate reality in terms of a personal God are inadequate at best. The notion of a personal God is the result of mistakenly attributing qualities to the nonpersonal Brahman. Similarly, it follows that there can be no permanent souls or individual selves. And if individual selves are ultimately illusory, then the perceived bondage of rebirth — *samsara* — is itself also ultimately illusory. The widely accepted perception of *samsara* as bondage is due to ignorance *(avidya)* and the mistaken assumption of the independent reality of individual selves.[36] Although Shankara accepts the notion of *moksha* as release from *samsara*, there is a sense in which even *moksha* must be regarded as illusory. For what is called release from the cycle of rebirths is really merely the "release" that comes from the knowledge that ultimately there is no reality apart from Brahman and thus nothing from which to be released. Genuine spiritual liberation, and thus release from the illusion of rebirth, is possible solely through attaining right knowl-

35. Deutsch points out that for Shankara the term "real" means that which is permanent, eternal, infinite, that which is never substrated at any time by another experience. This, according to Shankara, can only be Brahman. The phenomenal world, then, is not wholly unreal, but neither is it granted reality in any ultimate sense. Deutsch, *Advaita Vedanta*, pp. 29-34.

36. There are clear parallels here with earlier Buddhist thought, causing Shankara's enemies to accuse him of being a crypto-Buddhist.

edge *(jnana)* concerning the self *(atman)* and what is ultimately real (Brahman). From the perspective of supreme Truth the inner self is identical with Brahman. As the Upanishads put it, "That art thou" *(tat tvam asi)*.

Although Shankara does not entirely dismiss *karma marga* (the way of right action) and *bhakti marga* (the way of devotion) as possible paths to salvation, they are clearly considered to be subordinate to *jnana marga* (the way of knowledge). Whereas the former two ways could lead to a better rebirth either in this world or the world of the gods, they are at best preparatory and cannot in and of themselves lead to complete spiritual liberation. For it is only through the discipline of *jnana marga* that one can find absolute liberation. Knowledge is thus the key to liberation, while, conversely, the source of the present predicament is ignorance concerning the true nature of reality.

A contrasting perspective is found in the thought of Ramanuja (A.D. 1017-1137) and the Qualified Non-Dualistic school of Vedanta. With Shankara, Ramanuja held that ultimately the sole reality was Brahman. However, he differed from Shankara in also maintaining that this does not entail that the cosmos, the phenomenal world, must be illusory. For Brahman, the sole reality, was said to be an all-inclusive unity which includes within itself real ontological differences and distinctions, such as real distinctions between individual selves and the selfhood of Brahman, as well as real distinctions between both selves and the material world. The distinctions are objectively real, although they ultimately fall within the one inclusive reality, the all-encompassing Brahman. Thus the material world and individual selves are regarded as the "body" of Brahman, created by Brahman out of his own creative being. Just as human selves animate human bodies, so Brahman is the Higher Self underlying the individual human selves. Shankara's view that ultimately each individual self is identical to the one Self, Brahman, is thus clearly rejected by Ramanuja, who maintained instead that individual selves are objectively real and eternal.

Ramanuja's primary concern was to argue for the legitimacy of the way of theistic devotion, *bhakti,* as an effective means of salvation. He held that *samsara* and *karma* are objectively real and that, contrary to Shankara, knowledge alone was inadequate for liberation. True liberation is possible only through the grace of the ultimate Self, Brahman, which accompanies the devout meditation of the worshiper. Further, in such release the individual self is not completely absorbed into the Higher Self but maintains its own consciousness of blissful devotion to the Lord. Thus, while accepting much of the broader structure of Shankara's thought, Ramanuja turns his soteriology upside down; it is devout worship — *bhakti*—and not knowledge alone which produces release.

Madhva (1197-1276), whose views defined the Dvaita or Dualist school of Vedanta, reacted even more strongly against the monism of Shankara than did Ramanuja. For Madhva Brahman, individual souls, and the material world are all objectively real and are to be clearly distinguished from one another. Although ultimately Brahman is the only independent reality, the world and individual selves are also eternal and are not created by him, although there is a sense in which they are dependent upon Brahman. Madhva advocated devotion to Vishnu and held that there are three classes of souls: those who are devoted to God alone and are destined to attain liberation, those who will never attain liberation but are destined to perpetual rebirth, and those who reject Vishnu and are thus subject to damnation.[37]

We see, then, that even within one school of thought, Vedanta, quite different views were advanced regarding the nature of the cosmos and its relation to Brahman and the way to attain liberation from *samsara* and *karma*. Such diversity of views on basic issues within a major school of Hinduism — to say nothing of the sharp differences between the broader Hindu traditions themselves — is frequently regarded by non-Hindus as evidence of fundamental internal inconsistency within Hinduism. However, such diversity is not necessarily considered problematic by Hindus

37. Robert D. Baird notes that in the whole of Indian philosophy this doctrine of damnation is peculiar to Madhva and the Jainas. Much more common is the view that hell is a temporary abode where the bad *karma* are allowed to spend themselves, thus enabling the soul to work its way upward again. Cf. Baird, "Indian Religious Traditions," in *Religion and Man: An Introduction,* p. 195.

themselves. For, as K. M. Sen observes, essential to Hindu thought is the assumption of there being many ways to God. One can approach him through knowledge *(jnana)*, proper action *(karma)*, or devotion *(bhakti)*. Each is in its own way legitimate and effective.

> Since Hinduism denies the existence of any exclusive way of reaching God, this is only natural. As the age-old *Mahimna-Stotra* puts it: "All these paths, O Lord, *Veda, Samkhya, Yoga, Pasupata, Vaishnava,* lead but to Thee, like the winding river that at last merges into the sea." This, in fact, is the message of Hinduism, if it has one. He is infinite, omniscient, omnipotent, omnipresent, but He may appear different to different people. There are various ways of reaching Him, each as valid as every other. Apparently conflicting views of God may be nothing more than the infinite aspects of the same Supreme.[38]

BUDDHISM

Buddhism, like Jainism, is frequently regarded as having been initially a kind of reform movement within the broad religious tradition stemming from the Vedas and the Upanishads, although it was a reform movement that resulted in the establishment of a genuinely new and different religion. Early Buddhist belief accepted the basic concepts which defined the religious worldview of most Indians — concepts such as *karma* and *samsara*,[39] and the idea of *moksha* or release from the cycle of rebirths as the spiritual goal. But it differed radically from accepted traditions in the way

---

38. K. M. Sen, *Hinduism*, pp. 39-40.

39. Noble Ross Reat states, "The Upanishads and Buddhism have basically identical ideas on rebirth: Beings are, by ignorance, desire, and will, entangled in an ongoing process of repeated birth and death conditioned by actions *(karma)* and operating in such a way that it is possible to link a given being to a chain of past existences. Both systems encourage release from the chronic trauma of birth and death through ethical conduct, wisdom, and meditation." Noble Ross Reat, "*Karma* and Rebirth in the Upanishads and Buddhism," *Numen* 24 (December 1977): 163.

it understood the nature of the human predicament and the way of release from that predicament. In two ways in particular Buddhism stands apart from the broader Hindu tradition: (1) it denies outright the authority of the traditional scriptures, the Vedas and Upanishads; and (2) it denies the existence of individual souls which transmigrate in the cycle of rebirths. Because of this, Buddhism is recognized as constituting a genuinely different religion and not merely another alternative school of Hinduism.

The Buddha

Etymologically, the Sanskrit/Pali word "buddha" means "one who has awakened or been enlightened," and although it had wide circulation among various Indian religious traditions prior to the rise of Buddhism, it came to be used by Buddhists to refer to the historical Gautama, the founder of Buddhism.[40] Although there can be little question about the historicity of Gautama, there is considerable uncertainty concerning details of his life and thought. Indeed, there is lack of certainty about even the dates of his birth and death. Our access to the historical Gautama is complicated by the fact that the earliest Buddhist scriptures were not put into writing until roughly four hundred years after his death. Prior to this time the authoritative discourses were passed on orally by monks from one generation to the next.[41] Further, the extant ver-

40. For good discussions of the Gautama Buddha see "Buddha," in *The Encyclopedia of Religion*, vol. 1, pp. 319-31; Michael Carrithers, *The Buddha* (New York: Oxford University Press, 1983); Walpola Rahula, *What the Buddha Taught*, 2nd ed. (New York: Grove Press, 1974); Hajime Nakamura, *Gotama Buddha* (Tokyo: Buddhist Books International, 1977). See also the helpful essay "Biographies of the Buddha" by David Edward Shaner, *Philosophy East and West*, July 1987, pp. 306-22.

41. On the oral and written sources for the Buddhist scriptures see Michael Carrithers, *The Buddha*, pp. 6f., and Richard H. Robinson and Willard L. Johnson, *The Buddhist Religion*, 2nd ed. (Belmont, Cal.: Dickenson Publishing Company, 1977), pp. 19f. The distinguished Buddhist scholar Edward Conze states,

> For the first five hundred years the [Buddhist] Scriptures were orally transmitted. They were written down only at the beginning of the Christian era, because at that time the decline in faith threatened their continued survival

sions of the complete life of Gautama, which are widely recognized as containing legendary and mythological elements as well as historically reliable material, were all composed five hundred or more years after his death. Thus, one must exercise considerable caution in making claims about the life and teachings of the historical Gautama.

However, certain details about the life of Siddharta Gautama are generally accepted by scholars as historically reliable. These include the facts that Gautama lived sometime between roughly 566 B.C. and 486 B.C., that he was born in Kapilavastu in what is today Nepal, that he was born into the *ksatriya* (warrior) caste and into the Sakya clan, that his father was a noble or chieftain of the Sakya clan, that he was married and had a child, that he rejected the comfortable lifestyle of his family and against his father's wishes took up the ascetic life, that his first attempts to share the insights of his Enlightenment met with failure, that he eventually attracted a considerable following of devoted adherents, and that he died in a remote place after eating a meal.

The legends concerning his life which we find in the Buddhist scriptures contain, of course, much more fascinating material. For example, in the Buddhacarita of the first-century Indian poet Ashvaghosa, the first full-length "biography" of the Buddha, young Gautama is portrayed as being brought up in a life of luxury, isolated from the cares and sorrows of the real world. And yet one day, as he ventured outside the palace confines, the young prince saw an old man — the first of the famous "four sights." Having never before been exposed to old age, young Gautama was perplexed and asked his charioteer the meaning of this strange sight. The charioteer

---

in the memories of the monks. Different schools wrote down different things. Much of it was obviously composed centuries ago, and some of it must represent the direct and actual sayings of the Buddha himself. At present we have, however, no objective criterion which would allow us to isolate the original gospel. All attempts to find it are based upon mere surmise, and the discussion of the subject generally leads to nothing but ill will and fruitless disputes.

"Introduction," in *Buddhist Scriptures*, ed. Edward Conze (New York: Penguin Books, 1959), pp. 11-12.

replied that such was the fate of all persons. On later excursions he encountered a man with a diseased body and then a corpse. Confronted with the reality of death, Gautama was greatly dismayed and said, "This is the end which has been fixed for all, and yet the world forgets its fears and takes no heed! . . . Turn back the chariot! This is no time or place for pleasure excursions. How could an intelligent person pay no heed at a time of disaster, when he knows of his impending destruction?"[42] On yet another occasion Gautama encountered a wandering ascetic, who inspired in him the ideal of renouncing the life of comfort and pleasure he had known in order to discover the secret and cure of suffering.

Determined to discover for himself the cause and cure for suffering, young Gautama resolved to abandon his comfortable lifestyle in favor of that of a wandering ascetic. Taking one last look at his infant son and wife, he quietly slipped out of the palace one night and from then on lived the life of a wandering recluse. He initially sat at the feet of various ascetics, or *yogis,* mastering their techniques of meditation and self-mortification; but failing to find ultimate satisfaction and release from *samsara* in their practices, he moved on.

Then on a night of the full moon (traditionally April or May, 523 B.C.) Gautama passed through the four stages of *dhyana* (trance) and, fully enlightened, attained a state of complete spiritual insight into the nature of reality. From this point on he is a Buddha ("Awakened" or "Enlightened One"). Just what he was awakened to — what he was made aware of in the Enlightenment — constitutes the fundamental core of Buddhist belief. We might summarize the insight here by saying that Gautama was made aware of the fundamental causes and effects of existence and how to make them cease. Although initially tempted to remain in the state which he had entered, out of compassion for all living beings the Buddha returned to his fellow ascetics and began to proclaim the new insight he had gained through his Enlightenment. At Benares he preached his famous First Sermon to the five ascetics with whom he had formerly associated. They accepted his teaching

---

42. Buddhacarita 4, in *Buddhist Scriptures,* ed. and trans. by Edward Conze, p. 40.

and became the first of many followers who were to comprise the
sangha or community of monks who accepted, practiced, and
passed on the Buddha's teaching.

What was this insight which the Buddha realized and which
he then passed on to others? The heart of the Buddha's new teaching is contained in what is often called the Four Noble Truths.[43]

> (1) Now this, O monks, is the noble truth of pain: birth is painful,
> old age is painful, sickness is painful, death is painful, sorrow,
> lamentation, dejection, and despair are painful. Contact with un-
> pleasant things is painful, not getting what one wishes is painful.
> In short the five *khandas*[44] of grasping are painful. (2) Now this,
> O monks, is the noble truth of the cause of pain: that craving
> which leads to rebirth, combined with pleasure and lust, finding
> pleasure here and there, namely, the craving for passion, the crav-
> ing for existence, the craving for non-existence. (3) Now this, O
> monks, is the noble truth of the cessation of pain: the cessation
> without a remainder of that craving, abandonment, forsaking,
> release, non-attachment. (4) Now this, O monks, is the noble
> truth of the way that leads to the cessation of pain: this is the
> noble Eightfold Path, namely, right views, right intention, right
> speech, right action, right livelihood, right effort, right mindful-
> ness, right concentration.[45]

The First Truth is the truth concerning *dukkha*. The Pali
word *dukkha* is often translated "suffering," or, as in the above
passage, "pain," and this is adequate so long as certain qualifica-
tions are made. Suffering must be understood in a very broad sense
to include not only physical pain and discomfort but also lack of
emotional or psychological well-being. The Buddhist scholar Walpola Rahula suggests that it includes the idea of a pervasive im-

43. For good discussions of the Four Noble Truths see Walpola Rahula,
What the Buddha Taught, chaps. 2-5, and Michael Carrithers, *The Buddha,* chap.
4.

44. The five *khandhas,* or Five Aggregates, are Matter, Sensations, Perceptions, Mental Formations, and Consciousness.

45. This is taken from the traditional account of the Buddha's first sermon,
in Samyutta-nikaya v.420, in Radhakrishnan and Moore, *Source Book,* pp. 274-75.

perfection, impermanence, emptiness, or insubstantiality.[46] Michael Carrithers prefers to translate *dukkha* as "discomfort, dissatisfaction, or discontent."[47] The First Noble Truth asserts that all of existence is characterized by *dukkha* — that is, *dukkha* is found in every aspect of existence.

The Second Noble Truth concerns the origin of *dukkha* and holds that there are discernible causes of suffering and that the root cause of suffering is *tanha* (literally "thirst," but often translated "craving" or "desire"). It is the desire or craving not only for sensual pleasures but for existence itself — and even for nonexistence — which results in *dukkha*. That is, it is the very condition of desiring, craving, or thirsting for anything at all which causes human suffering.

The Third Noble Truth affirms that the disease of *dukkha* is curable and that when *tanha* ceases then *dukkha* ceases as well. The Fourth Noble Truth states that the cessation of *dukkha* is achieved through following the Noble Eightfold Path: (1) right views, (2) right intention, (3) right speech, (4) right action, (5) right livelihood, (6) right effort, (7) right mindfulness, and (8) right concentration. The eight constituents fall into three general categories: moral self-discipline, meditation, and wisdom.

We noted earlier the concepts of *samsara, karma,* and rebirth that were current in the Indian subcontinent at the time of the Buddha. Although he operated within the general framework of this religious worldview, as a result of his Enlightenment the Buddha gave a much more subtle and creative interpretation to these familiar concepts. He contended that all things constituting the world as we know it, including persons, are marked by *dukkha* (suffering), *anatta* (absence of self), and *anicca* (impermanence).

The doctrine of rebirth or transmigration current at the time of the Buddha held that there are eternal souls which transmigrate from one psychophysical organism to another in a succession of lives. There was considerable dispute over the nature of such souls and whether they were in fact distinct souls or merely reflections of the one ultimate reality; but that there were such souls which passed

46. Walpola Rahula, *What the Buddha Taught*, p. 17.
47. Carrithers, *The Buddha*, p. 56.

on from one life to the next was widely accepted. However, the
Buddha held that there is *nothing* permanent in the world — only
nirvana is permanent. Everything else is in constant flux, an unend-
ing process of coming into being and passing out of existence. But if
nothing in the world is permanent then there cannot be any permanent or enduring souls either. Thus, one of the fundamental
tenets of the Buddha's teaching was the denial of any enduring,
substantial, or permanent soul. What we think of as "a person" or "a
soul" — an enduring identity — is really no more than an ever-
changing combination of psychophysical forces which, according to
Buddhism, can be divided into the "Five Aggregates" — Matter,
Sensations, Perceptions, Mental Formations, and Consciousness. In
reality there is no substantial person or soul behind what is commonly taken to be an enduring individual. And it is the illusion of
just such a permanent, enduring soul that produces *dukkha*. As the
Buddha put it, "In short these five aggregates of attachment are
dukkha."[48] The illusion of a permanent self merely fans the flames
of *tanha* or craving, which in turn commits one to further rebirth
within *samsara*, and thus subjects one to still more suffering.

The Buddha, then, did not accept the doctrine of the transmigration of souls. And yet he apparently did accept the notion of
samsara, the successive cycle of births and rebirths. But here we
encounter an obvious problem: If there is no soul to pass on from
one life to another, what sense can we make of the notion of
repeated rebirths? The answer given this question reveals one of
the Buddha's great innovations. What is passed on, it was claimed,
is simply the cumulative effects of actions. The Buddha accepted
the notion of *karma* and the notion that the effects of one's actions
continue beyond the present life. Although there is no substantial
self or soul who engages in the actions[49] but merely the peculiar

48. Cited in Rahula, *What the Buddha Taught*, p. 20.
49. As Buddhaghosa put it in the Visuddhi-magga,

Misery only doth exist, none miserable,
No doer is there; naught save the deed is found.
Nirvana is, but not the man who seeks it.
The Path exists, but not the traveler on it.

Cited in *A Source Book in Indian Philosophy*, p. 289.

combination of forces known as the Five Aggregates, the effects of volitional action can continue to manifest themselves in a life after death. For death is merely the total non-functioning of a physical body. The forces and effects of the Five Aggregates continue even after the physical body dies.

For the Buddha, then, the human predicament is to be thought of in terms of bondage to *samsara*, the cycle of rebirths characterized by pervasive suffering or dissatisfaction. If *samsara* is the disease, what then is the cure? How can one be free of *dukkha* and the chains of *samsara*? What is needed is not simply improvement of one's lot within *samsara*, the endless cycle of birth and rebirth. Rather, what is sought is escape or complete liberation from *karma* and *samsara*. This is possible, according to the Buddha, through the elimination of *tanha* — desire, thirsting, or craving. To accomplish this, strict adherence to the Noble Eightfold Path is necessary, and we should note that an essential element of this Path, right view, involves having an accurate understanding of the nature of the cosmos. In other words, the key to eliminating desire and craving, and thus release from the chains of *samsara*, lies in accepting and appropriating the Buddha's analysis of reality, one of the most important aspects of which is the denial of any enduring, substantial self. In this way alone can one be released from *samsara* and attain *nirvana*.

Nirvana (*nibbana* in Pali) can thus be viewed as the spiritual goal of the Buddhist. But just what is *nirvana*? Generally, although not always, *nirvana* is described in Buddhist literature in negative terms — as "cessation," "absence of craving," "detachment," or "the unconditioned." Positively, however, *nirvana* is release from the cycle of rebirths, or, in other words, from the chains of *karma*.[50] And yet it cannot be likened to notions of paradise or heaven found in, for example, Christianity or Islam. For strictly speaking, one

---

50. An important issue is whether *nirvana* and *samsara* are to be interpreted as referring to psychological or ontological states. Are *samsara* and *nirvana* merely "states of mind" or are they extra-mental ontological states of existence? If the former, then the transition from *samsara* to *nirvana* is really no more than a profound change in attitude, perspective, and motivation. If the latter, then the transition is more than simply a change in attitude. It is a transition from one ontological state — a highly undesirable one — to another. Support for both interpretations can be found among Buddhist scholars.

cannot even speak of the Buddha (or anyone else for that matter) entering *nirvana*. It is not a place. And besides, as noted above, there is no enduring soul or person to "enter" *nirvana*. However, it would be equally misleading to think of *nirvana* as total annihilation of the self, since, again, there is according to Buddhism no self to annihilate.

Two aspects of *nirvana* should be distinguished. First, a monk may attain what is often called *nirvana* "with substrate."[51] This means that the monk has, in this life, attained supreme insight into the nature of reality, and that, although he will continue to go on living as before, upon death there will be no more rebirth. For at death he will have attained the second phase, *nirvana* "without substrate." Of course, we should not think here in terms of someone entering this state of pure *nirvana*, for as noted above there is no self to survive death. This is, to say the least, a dark saying, and the more one tries to sort out the subtleties in the Buddhist notion of *nirvana*, the more perplexed one becomes. This much, however, is clear: the Buddha held that there is a deathless, permanent, unconditioned realm *(nirvana)* which can be attained and that attainment of *nirvana* rules out the possibility of rebirth in another life. Although details concerning the precise nature of *nirvana* are left a mystery, its importance for Buddhism can hardly be exaggerated. For it serves as the religious ultimate, the only thing unconditioned and permanent, the attainment of which is the goal of the devout Buddhist. Walpola Rahula summarizes the Buddha's fundamental insight as follows:

> According to Buddhism, the Absolute Truth is that there is nothing absolute in the world; that everything is relative, conditioned and impermanent, and that there is no unchanging, everlasting, absolute substance like Self, Soul or *Atman* within or without. This is the Absolute Truth. . . . The realization of this Truth, i.e., to see things as they are without illusion or ignorance, is the extinction of craving, 'thirst', and the cessation of *dukkha*, which is *Nirvana*.[52]

51. Cf. Ninian Smart, *The Religious Experience of Mankind*, pp. 100f.
52. Rahula, *What the Buddha Taught*, p. 40.

We might conclude our discussion of the Buddha with two observations about his teaching. First, as near as we can tell, there was in the teaching of the Buddha no explicit reference to God or a Supreme Being. Nor, apparently, did his Enlightenment take place within the context of a prior belief in God. There is no hint in any of the accounts of his Enlightenment, or in his teaching as contained in the *sutras,* of anything like the later Christian and Muslim mystics' notion of union with God. Further, he made no claim to special inspiration from God or any divine source. One is given the distinct impression that his insights into reality were the product of his own human self-discipline, intelligence, and endeavor. If he was concerned about the question of the existence of God or other higher beings, on this matter he remained silent.[53]

Second, there is within the early teachings attributed to the Buddha a strong sense of the human individual being responsible for his or her own salvation. There is no higher Being or Power to whom one can turn for salvation. True, the Buddha himself did proclaim the *dharma,* the teaching which results in liberation, and in this way he can be said to assist all sentient beings. But it is up to the individual to grasp the Truth, to appropriate it, and thereby to attain *nirvana.* As Rahula puts it, "If the Buddha is to be called a 'saviour' at all, it is only in the sense that he discovered and showed the Path to Liberation, Nirvana. But we must tread the Path ourselves."[54]

Mahayana Buddhism

By the first or second century A.D., roughly six hundred years after the time of the Gautama Buddha, a significantly new movement

---

53. "Buddhist tradition does not exactly deny the existence of a creator, but it is not really interested to know who created the Universe. The purpose of Buddhist doctrine is to release beings from suffering, and speculations concerning the origin of the Universe are held to be immaterial to that task. They are not merely a waste of time but they may also postpone deliverance from suffering by expending ill-will in oneself and in others." Edward Conze, *Buddhism: Its Essence and Development,* 2nd ed. (New York: Harper & Row, 1959), p. 39.

54. Rahula, *What the Buddha Taught,* pp. 1-2.

within Buddhism had emerged. The result was a division of Buddhism into two major schools, Theravada Buddhism and Mahayana Buddhism. Theravada Buddhism, also referred to as the Teaching of the Elders, is today found largely in Sri Lanka, Burma, Thailand, Laos, and Kampuchea. Mahayana Buddhism, sometimes also called the Great Vehicle (in contrast to Hinayana Buddhism, the Small Vehicle), is today most prominent in China, Tibet, Mongolia, Korea, Japan, and Vietnam.

Mahayana Buddhism is itself an amalgam of many different schools and traditions that developed over the centuries as Buddhism spread throughout East Asia and in the process came into contact with, and was significantly influenced by, various indigenous religious cults and traditions. In-depth discussion of Mahayana Buddhism is impossible here, but several striking contrasts between later Mahayana teachings and the earlier teachings of Theravada Buddhism should be mentioned briefly.

Although all Buddhists accept the authenticity and authority of the Pali *Suttas* (sacred scriptures), Mahayanists also accept many other sacred writings as authoritative, writings largely rejected by the Theravadins. Thus, various schools of Mahayana Buddhism appeal to writings from Tibet, China, Korea, or Japan in support of their distinctive teachings, although they would be quick to emphasize that their teachings do not deviate from the teaching of the Buddha as contained in the Pali texts, but rather are contained in rudimentary form in the earlier texts. Mahayana texts are said to represent the final, mature doctrine of the Buddha, which was revealed only to his most astute followers.

The Buddha is portrayed in the earlier Pali texts as having discouraged metaphysical speculation as unprofitable. Even the question whether the *Tathagata* (a term used by the Buddha to refer to himself after his Enlightenment) exists or ceases to exist after death was dismissed by the Buddha as not conducive to the realization of *nirvana* and thus not to be entertained. But later Mahayana teaching exercised no such caution concerning metaphysical questions. One can see this increased interest in metaphysical issues in the growing prominence of *bodhisattvas* in the Mahayana tradition during the first four centuries A.D.

Bodhisattvas are those said to have experienced enlightenment (or more precisely, those about to experience supreme enlightenment) but who have taken a special vow to continue being reborn into *samsara* rather than entering *nirvana,* so as to deliver others from suffering by assisting in their enlightenment. The *bodhisattva* thus came to represent the ideal of compassion.[55] There developed in Mahayana a vast pantheon of *bodhisattvas* and Buddhas, who came to be regarded as a kind of savior figure for the masses. *Bodhisattvas* residing in various "heavenly realms" and, out of compassion, interacting with and helping human beings on their way to enlightenment became a prominent part of many Mahayana traditions. The *bodhisattvas,* in turn, became objects of meditation, reverence, supplication, and even worship on the part of believers.[56] This of course is in sharp contrast to Theravada Buddhism, which characteristically discourages metaphysical speculation about higher beings and

55. "The bodhisattva is endowed with wisdom of a kind whereby he looks on all beings as though victims going to the slaughter. And immense compassion grips him. His divine eye sees . . . inumerable beings, and he is filled with great distress at what he sees, for many bear the burden of past deeds which will be punished in purgatory, others will have unfortunate rebirths which will divide them from the Buddha and his teachings, others must soon be slain, others are caught in the net of false doctrine, others cannot find the path [of salvation], while others have gained a favorable rebirth only to lose it again. So he pours out his love and compassion upon all those beings, and attends to them, thinking, 'I shall become the savior of all beings, and set them free from their sufferings.'" From Astasahasrika Prajnaparamita 22.402-3; cited in *The Buddhist Tradition,* ed. William Theodore DeBary (New York: Random House, 1969), pp. 81-82.

56. Japanese Buddhism, in particular, has accommodated itself to the ubiquitous penchant for worship of deities and higher beings. Popular Buddhism in Japan recognizes various classes of higher beings who are worshiped by the faithful: *nyorai* (*tathagata* in Sanskrit) refers to "enlightened ones," and can denote separate Buddhas, the four most popular being Shaka (the enlightened Gautama Buddha), Yakushi, Amida, and Dainichi; *bosatsu,* or *bodhisattvas,* the most popular being Kannon, Miroku, Monju, Fugen, and Jizo; *myo-o* or "kings of light," fearsome and awe-inspiring lesser deities assigned the task of assisting the Buddhas, among whom the fiercest and most famous is Fudo; and *ten* (*deva* in Sanskrit), or folk deities. The importance of the Buddhist pantheon is reflected in the large number of statues and images of the various deities and Buddhas in most Japanese temples. See Stuart D. B. Picken, *Buddhism: Japan's Cultural Identity* (Tokyo: Kodansha, 1982), chap. 8.

powers, frowns upon images and statues of the Buddha, and
rejects prayer to and worship of the Buddha.

The interest in metaphysics is also exemplified in the
Mahayana doctrine of the Three Bodies *(Trikaya)*, three distin-
guishable, but closely related, levels of "Buddhahood," or the
Buddha essence. According to this doctrine, the historical Gautama
Buddha was a human manifestation of an underlying, all-inclusive
Buddha essence. This ultimate, all-inclusive Buddha essence is the
Dharmakaya, or Law Body. As the highest level of Buddha essence,
the *Dharmakaya* is free from all multiplicity, duality, and variability
which characterize our phenomenal world. This Buddha essence
was later identified by Mahayanists as the equivalent of the Void,
or Suchness, or Emptiness. On a second level the Buddha essence
is manifest as the Body of Bliss or *Sambhogakaya*, and it is on this
level that *bodhisattvas* and Buddhas (those who have attained
enlightenment) apprehend and enjoy the Buddha essence. And
finally, there is the Transformation Body of the Buddha essence,
or the *Nirmanakaya*, in accord with which the historical Gautama
can be regarded as a concrete, historical manifestation of the one
eternal Buddha essence.[57]

One feature of Mahayana Buddhism has been its remarkable flexibility and adaptability to new cultural and religious traditions.[58] As Buddhism moved from the Indian subcontinent north
into China sometime during the first century A.D. and then later
on into Korea and Japan, it encountered very different cultures
with distinctive indigenous religious traditions. When Buddhism
entered China, for example, Confucianism and Taoism were already well established. The notions of *samsara* and *karma*, so central to Indian religious and philosophical thought, were lacking in
the Chinese context. Release from *samsara* was thus not the burn-

57. The Mahayana doctrine of the Three Bodies is sometimes said to
resemble the Christian doctrine of the Holy Trinity. However, while there are some
superficial similarities, the differences between the doctrines are far more pronounced than any similarities.

58. See "The Buddhist Transformation in Japan," in Joseph Kitagawa's *On
Understanding Japanese Religion* (Princeton: Princeton University Press, 1987), pp.
203-19.

ing issue for Chinese that it had been for the Indians. Consequently, one finds in the Mahayana tradition as it developed in China, Korea, and Japan a decreasing emphasis upon the notion of *nirvana* as release from *samsara* and greater stress upon the much more positive notion of enlightenment. Thomas Kasulis notes that "Mahayanists were generally more interested in the truth to which enlightenment was an awakening than the pain from which it was a release. This emphasis on the positive aspect of enlightenment also caused to be diminished the importance of *nirvana* as the release from rebirth."[59] The concept of *nirvana* as release came to be replaced with that of enlightenment as "awakening" (*satori* in Japanese) or "realization."[60] The ideal became not so much release from *samsara* but rather harmony within the social and cosmic order, which is to be achieved through attaining a penetrating and liberating insight into the actual nature of reality. This shift in emphasis is particularly evident in the Chinese schools of T'ien-t'ai (Tendai in Japan), Hua-yen (Kegon), and Ch'an (Zen) Buddhism.

The contrast between Theravada and Mahayana is perhaps most pronounced in the Amida cult of Mahayana, which became established in Japan as Pure Land (Jodoshu) and the True Pure Land (Jodo Shinshu) sects of Buddhism. Sometime before the first century A.D., texts appeared which dealt with a Western paradise — the Pure Land — over which the Amida (Amitabha in Sanskrit) Buddha reigned. The Amida cult flourished in China and later in Japan, greatly influencing several other established Buddhist sects. The cult eventually became established as a separate Buddhist sect,

59. Thomas Kasulis, "Nirvana," in *The Encyclopedia of Religion*, vol. 10, p. 450.

60. The emphasis upon enlightenment, the experience of "seeing" intuitively things as they really are and not simply as they appear to be, is of course central to Zen Buddhism. *Satori*, or "awakening," is an intuitive, nonrational insight into the way things actually are, the "suchness" of reality. It is an enlightenment which all beings, who have already within them the Buddha nature, can in principle realize. Conspicuous by its absence is any serious concern with *samsara*, the cycle of rebirths, which so vexed the Indian mind. Cf. *Zen Buddhism: Selected Writings of D. T. Suzuki*, ed. William Barrett (New York: Doubleday Anchor Books, 1956), chap. 4.

which later developed under the Japanese monk Honen (1133-1212) and his disciple Shinran (1173-1262) into two major schools of Japanese Buddhism.

Honen maintained that in Buddhism there are two paths leading to Enlightenment: the "path of sages" *(shodomon)* and the "path of Pure Land" *(jodomon)*. The path of sages is the difficult path in that it advocates reliance upon one's own efforts and power *(jiriki)* and strict adherence to monastic precepts and rigorous meditative disciplines in attaining salvation. The path of the Pure Land, on the other hand, is the easy path in which one depends upon the power and merit of another *(tariki)* — namely, the salvific power of the Amida Buddha — for salvation. Honen claimed that the present world had entered *mappo,* a period of such widespread degeneracy and decadence that it was all but impossible for one to attain enlightenment through one's own efforts. He thus proclaimed that the only way now to attain salvation was to declare one's absolute faith in the Amida Buddha and his original vow *(hongan)* to save all sentient beings. It was said that Amida had fulfilled a series of vows taken eons ago, while still the *bodhisattva* Dharmakara, and thus he has stored up enough merit for the salvation of all sentient beings. All that is necessary for salvation is placing complete faith in Amida Buddha and reciting the *nembutsu* ("adoration be to Amida Buddha") — that is, placing sole reliance upon the invocation of Amida's name as a means to salvation. Constant repetition of the *nembutsu* — in faith — will eventually result in the purification of the mind, lead to a moment of awakening *(satori)* in this life, and ultimately produce rebirth in the Pure Land. Shinran, Honen's disciple and the founder of the True Pure Land sect, followed his master in most of the fundamental teachings but differed from him in emphasizing that nothing in the salvation process can be ascribed to one's own effort.[61] Even the faith in the Amida Buddha, the very decision to exercise faith

61. A helpful introduction to the Pure Land tradition, and Shinran in particular, is Alfred Bloom's *Shinran's Gospel of Pure Grace* (Tucson: University of Arizona Press, 1965). See also Gerhard Schepers' "Shinran's View of the Human Predicament and the Christian Concept of Sin," in *Japanese Religion* 15 (July 1988): 1-17.

in the Buddha, is not the product of one's own will but is entirely a result of Amida's boundless grace. Whereas Honen had stated that the individual must choose to exercise faith in the Amida Buddha and that this choice must be reaffirmed through repeated invocations of the *nembutsu,* Shinran stressed that in actuality it is the Amida Buddha who chooses us, along with all sentient beings, to be saved.

Three features of Pure Land (and True Pure Land) Buddhism stand in stark contrast to the teaching of Theravada Buddhism. First, whereas Theravada Buddhism and, so far as we can tell, the original teaching of Gautama Buddha emphasize that *nirvana* is to be attained through one's own efforts and not through reliance upon a higher being or power, Pure Land Buddhism teaches the very opposite. It is claimed that, given the present condition of the world, one is utterly incapable of attaining Enlightenment through one's own efforts and so must rely totally in faith upon the power and merit of the Amida Buddha. Buddhist scholar Dale Saunders states that "the essential idea of the Amida cult — that is, of transfer of merit from the Buddha to the worshiper; in other words, of salvation through the good works of others — stands in opposition to early Buddhist ideas, which instead stressed self-responsibility and a system of self-advancement toward Enlightenment."[62] Similarly, whereas in Theravada Buddhism release from *samsara* was available only to the few who, as a result of rigorous self-discipline through many lives had achieved the elimination of desire, in Mahayana Buddhism and in the Pure Land tradition in particular salvation was made available to all beings in this life.

Second, the notion of the Pure Land itself is quite different from that of *nirvana* in Theravada Buddhism. Originally regarded as a place of blissful sojourn on the way toward *nirvana* (those born into the Pure Land were assured of eventually attaining *nirvana*), the concept of the Pure Land *(Sukhavati)* tended to become an end in itself, sometimes regarded as virtuously synonymous

62. E. Dale Saunders, *Buddhism in Japan* (Tokyo: Charles E. Tuttle, 1972), p. 188.

with *nirvana* and at other times as a kind of heaven or paradise. It was said to be a place of no evil and endless bliss, and in the popular imagination rebirth in the Pure Land came to be viewed as the spiritual goal and the culmination of the salvation provided by Amida.

Third, there is in popular Amidism and Pure Land Buddhism a strong devotion to Amida suggestive of theism. Especially in True Pure Land Buddhism there is a strong devotion to Amida which finds expression in prayer to and worship of the Amida Buddha. Although other Buddhas are invoked during the funeral ceremony, for example, Amida is singled out for worship and veneration. There are in Pure Land Buddhism no relics or images of Buddhas or divinities other than Amida and, occasionally, the Gautama Buddha. This devotion to and worship of Amida is quite alien to the spirit of Theravada Buddhism.

It is evident, even from this brief survey, that although the religious traditions that developed in the Indian subcontinent were largely concerned with the same problems and shared certain common assumptions about the human predicament, they presented quite different answers to the question of how we are to find release from this predicament. The differences between Hinduism and Buddhism on the nature of liberation/release/enlightenment and how it is to be achieved are fundamental and not simply a matter of different emphases. Significantly, there are also striking differences in perspective within each religion. The views of Pure Land Buddhists concerning the nature of and conditions for salvation, for example, are remarkably different from those of Theravada Buddhists. And Shankara and Ramanuja disagree sharply over the proper means for achieving liberation. Thus, even within the cluster of religious traditions originating in the Indian subcontinent we do not find complete uniformity of perspective, but rather markedly different answers to certain common questions. And as we shall see in the next chapter, fundamental differences in outlook become even more pronounced when consideration is given a monotheistic religion, Islam, and a somewhat amorphous polytheistic tradition, Shinto.

CHAPTER THREE

Conflicting Truth Claims (II)

ISLAM

Islam must rank as one of the most remarkable religions in history. Emerging from within the polytheistic milieu of the seventh-century Arabian desert under the charismatic and dynamic leadership of the prophet Muhammad, it quickly spread, so that within a century of the prophet's death in A.D. 632 the Islamic world stretched from southern France through Spain, North Africa, central Asia, and even into what is now China. In 1453 the most impressive city of Christendom, Constantinople, was conquered by Muslim invaders. And by the eighteenth century there were millions of Muslims in China, Indonesia, India, the Philippines, and Africa, as well as in the Middle East. Today, Muslims can be found in virtually any part of the world, including Europe and North America. Islam continues to grow at an astonishing rate and is increasingly being accepted in the West as a viable alternative to established religions such as Christianity and Judaism. Although Muslims reject the suggestion that Islam was founded by Muhammad — Islam is said to be God's eternal religion and Muhammad simply the last and greatest in a long line of prophets — any consideration of Islam must begin with the prophet Muhammad.

Muhammad

Muhammad was born around A.D. 570 in Mecca, where he spent most of his first fifty years.[1] His father died about the time of his birth and his mother died when he was only six. Muhammad was brought up first by his grandfather and then by his uncle, both of whom, like his parents, were from the Arab tribe of Quraysh, the dominant tribe of Mecca.

Little is known about Muhammad's early life, although legends abound about his unusual childhood. For example, tradition maintains that as a boy of twelve Muhammad accompanied his uncle, Abu Talib, on a journey to Syria, during which he met a Christian monk named Bahira who, recognizing the boy for who he really was, hailed him as God's messenger and advised the uncle to take great care to protect him from the Jews.[2] We do know, however, that Muhammad grew up an orphan, and that at the age of twenty-five he married a wealthy widow named Khadija, who is said to have been forty years old at the time. After marriage Muhammad seems to have been occupied primarily in commercial trading ventures, although very little is known about the fifteen years which intervened between his marriage and his call as a prophet.

1. The classic English work on the life of Muhammad is the two-volume set by W. Montgomery Watt, *Muhammad at Mecca* (Oxford: Clarendon Press, 1953) and *Muhammad at Medina* (Oxford: Clarendon Press, 1956). A shorter version of Muhammad's life is found in W. Montgomery Watt's *Muhammad: Prophet and Statesman* (New York: Oxford University Press, 1961). Also helpful are Michael Cook's *Muhammad* (New York: Oxford University Press, 1983); Alfred Guillaume, *Islam,* 2nd ed. (New York: Penguin Books, 1956), chap. 2; Fazlur Rahman, *Islam,* 2nd ed. (Chicago: University of Chicago Press, 1979), chap. 1; and W. Montgomery Watt, "Muhammad," in *The Encyclopedia of Religion,* vol. 10, ed. Mircea Eliade (New York: Macmillan, 1987), pp. 137-46. Good introductions to Islam can be found in Kenneth Cragg, *The Call of the Minaret,* 2nd ed. (Maryknoll, N.Y.: Orbis, 1985); idem, *The House of Islam,* 2nd ed. (Encino, Cal.: Dickenson Publishers, 1975); Richard C. Martin, *Islam: A Cultural Perspective* (Englewood Cliffs, N.J.: Prentice-Hall, 1982); and Sir Norman Anderson, "Islam," in *The World's Religions,* ed. Sir Norman Anderson (Grand Rapids: Eerdmans, 1985).

2. On the legend see W. Montgomery Watt, *Muhammad: Prophet and Statesman,* pp. 1f.

Arabian society at the time of Muhammad was largely nomadic and tribal. Mecca was an important trading center and trade
was the major source of livelihood for its citizens. Montgomery
Watt suggests that by the sixth century the merchants of Mecca
had largely gained control of the trade between the Indian Ocean
and the Mediterranean.[3] Consequently, Mecca was a thriving, pros-
perous community in which one could readily come into contact
with peoples and ideas from various parts of the Middle Eastern
world. Perhaps partially as a result of its cosmopolitan nature and
the stiff competition of commerce, during the early seventh century Mecca was characterized by social turmoil and a kind of
malaise due to the breakdown of traditional morality.

The Arabs of Mecca were largely polytheists, although there
are indications that about the time of Muhammad there was a
general trend toward some kind of monotheism. The center of
popular religious focus was the *Ka'bah* in Mecca, a rectangular
building in which was enshrined a sacred black stone.[4] Sacrifices
to the various deities were commonplace, as were pilgrimages to
the sacred *Ka'bah*. Popular religious sentiment was broadly animistic. Alfred Guillaume observes that "the primitive worship of
the Arabs was given to the god or spirit who was believed to inhabit
blocks of stone, rocks, trees, or wells."[5] And yet even in the midst
of the polytheistic and animistic milieu there was what Watt calls
"a vague monotheism," that is, "a monotheism not expressing itself
in definite acts of worship and not fully conscious of its distinction

3. W. Montgomery Watt, "Muhammad," p. 138.

4. Although the *Ka'bah* had great significance in the pre-Islamic polytheistic religious traditions, Muhammad did not reject the *Ka'bah* but rather retained
it as a religiously significant object, in the process giving it a new interpretation.
The sacred *Ka'bah* was said to be founded by Abraham, who escorted Hagar and
Ishmael to Mecca where he helped Ishmael construct a house for the sacred black
stone. The *Ka'bah* was thus the first house of worship, and, according to Muslims,
by the time of Muhammad it had degenerated into a polytheistic shrine of idols.
One of Muhammad's last acts was to perform the pilgrimage to Mecca, where he
reestablished the original Abrahamic meaning of pilgrimage and the *Ka'bah*. Cf.
Richard C. Martin, *Islam: A Cultural Perspective*, pp. 30-32.

5. Alfred Guillaume, *Islam*, p. 8. On the religious and intellectual background of Mecca see W. Montgomery Watt, *Muhammad at Mecca*, pp. 23-29.

from paganism."[6] Above all the gods, distant and remote, was Allah, *the* God, creator of the world.[7]

The premonitions of monotheism among the Arabs were probably due largely to the Christian and Jewish influences in the Arabian peninsula. Monophysite Christianity was widespread in the Arab kingdom of Ghassan; Nestorian Christians were well established in Persia and scattered throughout the peninsula as well; and Byzantine monks were said to be present in the Hijaz, the district in which Mecca and Medina are located. Jews were well represented at Medina. Significantly, there are reports of both Christians and Jews attempting to proselytize the Meccans, and although converts to either religion — if any — were undoubtedly very few, there seems to have been some familiarity with the Judeo-Christian tradition among the Meccan community. Some Arabs seem to have embraced a general monotheism as well.[8]

Muhammad was evidently a highly sensitive person religiously. Profoundly troubled by the crass polytheism, superstition, and moral degeneracy around him, he is said to have spent a month each year meditating in a cave near Mecca. He was apparently convinced of the existence of the one true God, although it is not clear just how he came to embrace monotheism, given the pervasive polytheistic influences all around him. There can be little doubt, however, that at some point early in his life he came into contact with some form of Christianity and probably Judaism as well. This is hardly suprising, since some Christians and Jews would undoubtedly have been among the many travelers and merchants

6. W. Montgomery Watt, *Muhammad at Mecca*, p. 158.

7. Kenneth Cragg states, "It is clear from the negative form of the Muslim creed, 'There is no god except God,' that the existence and lordship of Allah were known and recognized in pre-Islamic Arabia. The Prophet's mission was not to proclaim God's existence but to deny the existence of all lesser deities." *The Call of the Minaret*, p. 31.

8. On the Christian and Jewish presence in Arabia and its possible influence on Muhammad see Alfred Guillaume, *Islam*, pp. 10-19; Fazlur Rahman, *Islam*, pp. 26-28; Frants Buhl, "Muhammad," in *First Encyclopedia of Islam: 1913-1936*, vol. 6 (Leiden: E. J. Brill, 1987), pp. 642-44; and W. Montgomery Watt, *Muhammad at Mecca*, pp. 25-29, 158-61. On Muhammad and the Jews see W. Montgomery Watt, *Muhammad at Medina*, pp. 192-220.

passing through Mecca. It is perhaps of some significance that Khadijah's cousin Waraqah is said to have been a Christian and to have had some familiarity with the Bible, although he evidently did not have extensive knowledge of the contents of the Bible. Careful examination of the Qur'an reveals that, whatever the nature of Muhammad's contact with the Judeo-Christian tradition, it did not result in a clear and accurate understanding of either the Old or New Testament. The possibility that Muhammad had access to and read the Jewish or Christian scriptures has been ruled out by scholars of Islam.[9]

About the year 610, at the age of about forty, Muhammad began to have some profound experiences that convinced him that he had been called to be the "Messenger of God" who would bear messages or revelations from the one true God to the people of Mecca. One night, while meditating alone in the hills, the angel Gabriel appeared to Muhammad and commanded him: "Recite in the name of the Lord who created, created man from clots of blood! Recite! Your Lord is the Most Bountiful One, who by the pen taught man what he did not know."[10] Greatly troubled by the vision initially, Muhammad was encouraged and supported by his wife Khadijah and her cousin Waraqah, who is said to have assured Muhammad that his experience was similar to those of the earlier Old Testament prophets who received revelations from God. Muhammad became fully convinced that he had indeed been given a unique calling as a prophet of God, and over the next twenty years, until the end of his life, Muhammad continued to receive

9. W. Montgomery Watt states, "The form of the biblical material in the Qur'an, however, makes it certain that Muhammad had never read the Bible; and it is unlikely that he had ever read any other books. Such knowledge, then, as he had of Judeo-Christian conceptions must have come to him orally. . . . The conclusion of this matter is that Muhammad received his knowledge of biblical conceptions in general (as distinct from the details of some of the stories) from the intellectual environment of Mecca and not from reading or from communication with specific individuals." *Muhammad: Prophet and Statesman*, pp. 40-41.

10. Surah 96:1-5, in *The Koran*, trans. and ed. by N. J. Dawood (New York: Penguin Books, 1974), p. 26. (Cf. also Surah 53:1-18 and 81:15-25.) This passage is generally held to be the first revelation to Muhammad, although some suggest that 74:1-7 contains an even earlier revelation.

revelations. The contents of the revelations were memorized by
Muhammad and his followers and were repeated in the worship
and prayer which became a part of the early Muslim community.
Most of the divine messages were probably written down during
Muhammad's lifetime, although the final "collection" of all the
passages of revelation and the assignment of the present order of
the Qur'an took place about twenty years after Muhammad's
death.[11] The Qur'an is thus the written collection of the revelations
received by Muhammad. It is difficult, if not impossible, to recon-
struct the chronology of events surrounding the call of Muhammad, but he probably received the first of his many revelations at
about A.D. 610, and about three years later he began preaching to
the people of Mecca and claiming to be a prophet of God.

The early preaching of the prophet "spoke of God's power
and his goodness to human beings, called on them to acknowledge
their dependence upon God and to be generous with their wealth,
and warned them that all would appear before God on the Day of
Judgment and be assigned to Paradise or Hell according to whether
their deeds were good or bad."[12] Increasingly, however, the dominant theme in Muhammad's preaching became the unity and
transcendence of the one true God, combined with a strict denun-
ciation of the idolatry of paganism. His wife Khadijah was probably
the first convert, and Muhammad soon attracted a small circle of
followers, including his cousin Ali and his adopted son Zayd. As
Muhammad's following increased and his message became known,
bitter opposition was stirred up by the wealthy merchants of
Mecca. The opposition was due to a variety of socioeconomic as
well as religious factors: Muhammad's message was a direct threat
to popular religious rites and the pilgrimage associated with the
Ka'bah — something which caused alarm not only for its religious
but also for its economic implications, as Meccan merchants had
no interest in seeing the pagan rites cease; by setting himself up as
a prophet of God, Muhammad was a threat to the established
authority structure in Mecca; and Muhammad's condemnation of

11. W. Montgomery Watt, *Muhammad: Prophet and Statesman,* p. 16.
12. Idem, "Muhammad," p. 138.

unethical practices and call for the wealthy to be generous with their wealth antagonized many among the upper classes.[13]

So intense was the opposition at Mecca that in A.D. 622, upon the invitation of some of the leaders at Medina, Muhammad and his followers (probably numbering around 200) withdrew from Mecca and migrated to Medina, about 250 miles to the north. This migration to Medina is known as the *Hijra* and proved to be so significant for Islamic history that the calendar used in the Islamic world recognizes year 1 (A.H.) as the year of the *Hijra*. (Thus A.D. 622 corresponds to year A.H. 1 of the Islamic calendar.) The move to Medina brought about a dramatic change in the fortunes of Muhammad. Whereas at Mecca he had been the persecuted prophet, at Medina, through his considerable diplomatic and leadership skills, he became the leading statesman, legislator, and judge. Under his leadership Medina was transformed into the first Muslim theocracy, and the religious and social structures of early Islam began to take definitive form. At Medina the first mosque was built. Weekly worship services on Fridays set the pattern that has been observed ever since, and idolatrous practices in the city were stopped.

From early on Muhammad seems to have been convinced that his message was essentially a continuation of that of the earlier Hebrew prophets. Apparently he initially expected Jews and Christians — whom he referred to positively as "People of the Book" — to accept his message readily and to welcome him as a prophet. There was a considerable Jewish population at Medina, but, far from accepting Muhammad, they ridiculed him and dismissed him as standing outside the tradition of their prophets. In particular, Muhammad's claim that his message, embodied in the Qur'an, was the very Word of God was emphatically rejected by the Jews. Numerous inconsistencies between the Old Testament and the

13. "The Meccans not only feared Muhammad's challenge to their traditional religion based on polytheism but they felt that the very structure of their society, commercially vested interests, was being directly threatened by the new teaching with its emphasis on social justice which, as time went on, became more and more specific in its condemnation of usury and its insistence on the *zakat* or poor rate." Fazlur Rahman, *Islam,* pp. 14-15.

Qur'an concerning the same events were taken as decisive proof that the Qur'an could not be the Word of God. In response, Muhammad became increasingly hostile to the Jews and claimed that in fact they had corrupted their own scriptures. Although earlier references to Christians and Jews had been quite favorable, from the time of Medina on Muhammad assumed a highly negative attitude toward Jews, banishing and even massacring Jewish tribes and rejecting outright Jewish practices and influences that once had been adopted.

We cannot here pursue the fascinating story of Muhammad's consolidation of power in Medina, the extension of his authority, and the spread of Islam throughout Arabia, culminating in his triumphant return to Mecca shortly before his death in 632.[14] Suffice it to say that within ten years of his departure from Mecca for Medina, through a brilliant system of alliances with nomadic tribes and military victories, Muhammad was recognized as political ruler and prophet of God by the citizens of Mecca and Medina, as well as by most of the tribes in the Arabian peninsula. "The tribes in a broad region around Mecca and Medina were all firmly united to Muhammad and had all professed Islam."[15] In March 632 Muhammad led the *Hajj*, the greater pilgrimage to Mecca, in person. The pilgrimage was now a strictly Muslim rite; all idolaters were forbidden to attend.

And then suddenly, with little warning, on Monday, June 8, 632, Muhammad died. Although revered as the last and greatest of the prophets, Muhammad is regarded by orthodox Muslims as strictly human. This is reflected in the comment attributed to Abu-Bakr, an early convert to Islam and the first caliph ("successor" of the prophet Muhammad, chosen to head the Islamic community): "Let those who worship Muhammad know that he is dead and gone! Let those who worship God know that He is ever living, never dying!"[16]

14. But see W. Montgomery Watt, *Muhammad: Prophet and Statesman*, chaps. 5-8.
15. Ibid., p. 223.
16. Richard C. Martin, *Islam: A Cultural Perspective*, p. 39.

Basic Tenets of Islam

A complete overview of Islam would, of course, include discussion of the history and expansion of Islam, the development of the caliphate, the rich cultural heritage of Islam, the major sectarian divisions within Islam, as well as the manner in which Islam is today struggling to come to grips with its place in the modern world. Important as it is, such discussion is well beyond the limited scope of this chapter. We must be content to outline in broad strokes some of the fundamental beliefs of Muslims as they pertain to the central questions of the religious ultimate, the human predicament, and the nature of salvation. In what follows our concern is primarily with beliefs and practices of the Sunni Muslims, who comprise about 90 percent of the Muslim population, although much will be applicable to the Shi'ite Muslims as well.[17]

Five times daily the *muezzin* summons the faithful to stop what they are doing and to pray. The *Adhan*, or call to prayer, contains within it the basic creed of Islam, and it was for this reason that Bishop Kenneth Cragg structured his classic study of Islam around the phrases of the familiar call to prayer.[18]

> God is the greatest, God is the greatest,
> God is the greatest. I witness that
> There is no God but Allah; I witness that
> There is no God but Allah. I witness that
> Muhammad is His Apostle; I witness that
> Muhammad is His Apostle.
> Come to the prayer! Come to the prayer!
> Come to the betterment! Come to the betterment!

17. The vast majority of orthodox Muslims are Sunni Muslims. Shi'ite Muslims differ from Sunni Muslims in tracing their spiritual heritage to the prophet Muhammad through his cousin Ali, who is said to have had special knowledge of the meaning of the Qur'an and the example of the prophet *(Sunna)*, and to have passed on this special knowledge to five, seven, or twelve *Imams* (special spiritual leaders) who descended from Ali. The Sunni Muslims acknowledge the authority of the Qur'an and the *Sunna* but do not recognize the special authority of the Shi'ah *Imams*.

18. Cf. Kenneth Cragg, *The Call of the Minaret.*

God is the greatest. God is the greatest.
There is no God but Allah.[19]

Contained within the call is the simple affirmation, "There is no
god but Allah and Muhammad is the Apostle of God." Sincere
confession of this creed, with proper intention, is sufficient to make
one a Muslim. Although there are of course many significant ramifications from this for one's broader worldview, the central thrust
of the Muslim's faith lies in declaring boldly the utterly unique and
incomparable greatness of Allah and submitting ritually to his
sovereign will in all aspects of life.

Allah

The doctrine of God is central to all Muslim faith and practice. There
is but one God, the eternal, sovereign creator. Islam thus joins
Judaism and Christianity in affirming a strict and uncompromising
monotheism. Cragg points out that the word "Allah" itself is
grammatically incapable of a plural; it is a proper name and literally
means "the God."[20] Fundamental to the concept of God is his unity.
Surah 112 of the Qur'an, the Surah of Unity, declares,

Allah is One, the Eternal God.
He begat none, nor was He begotten.
None is equal to Him.[21]

Muhammad is said to have proclaimed God in a series of descrip-
tives that have been called the ninety-nine "Beautiful Names." The
most significant of the divine names are the titles "the Compassionate, the Merciful." This double title appears in the *Basmalah*
— "In the Name of Allah, the Compassionate, the Merciful" —
which is found at the beginning of each of the 114 Surahs in the
Qur'an, with the exception of Surah 9.

19. Cited in Richard C. Martin, *Islam: A Cultural Perspective*, p. 2.
20. Kenneth Cragg, *The Call of the Minaret*, p. 33.
21. Surah 112:1-4, in *The Koran*, p. 265.

Allah alone is said to be eternal and uncreated. Islam thus affirms the Judeo-Christian doctrine of the creation of the world out of nothing. Allah is entirely self-sufficient, omnipotent, omniscient, and absolutely sovereign. The tension between divine sovereignty and human responsibility — an inescapable problem for any monotheistic faith — is evident in the Qur'an. Many passages suggest that the will of God is the immediate source of all events; God is absolutely sovereign and all things, good and bad, are the product of his inscrutable will. Sir Norman Anderson states that, according to orthodox Islam, God

> maintains the whole creation in being, moment by moment, by a continual miracle: even the impression of choice present to the mind of men is his creation. He is the source of both good and evil; his will is supreme, untrammelled by any laws or principles, whatever they may be; whom he will he forgives, and whom he will he punishes.[22]

And yet the Qur'an also assumes that humans are responsible for their conduct. God is the direct source of all existence and events; however, men and women are also responsible, and thus, in some sense, "free" beings. One way of dealing with the paradox is to ascribe all good things to God while holding humans responsible for all evil that occurs to them: "Whatever good befalls you, man, it is from Allah: and whatever ill from yourself" (Surah 4:79).[23]

Not only is Allah absolutely sovereign, but he is utterly transcendent and cannot be identified with anything in the created world. Given the transcendence of God, the problem of the meaningfulness of religious discourse is inevitable: What is the meaning of terms such as "merciful" or "wise" when used of God? Is God merciful and wise in the same sense that creatures are said to be merciful and wise? If not, in what sense can we speak of God as merciful and wise? Classic Muslim theology developed the notion of *mukhalafa* (difference), which held that Allah is so utterly different from his creatures that terms such as "merciful" and "wise,"

22. Sir Norman Anderson, "Islam," p. 115.
23. *The Koran*, p. 374.

when used of Allah do not retain their normal connotations but only that meaning appropriate to God. But we humans cannot specify just what that meaning is. And thus we use these terms "without knowing how" they apply to God and without implying any similarity between God and creatures.[24]

The notion of Allah's radical transcendence leads to the concept of *shirk,* the ultimate sin in Islam. *Shirk* is the sin of identifying anything in the created order with deity. This accounts for the strong condemnation of idolatry in the Qur'an, for idolatry blurs the distinction between the eternal Creator and the creature and associates the creature with the Creator. Thus, it is not enough merely to recognize that God exists. One must also affirm that God *alone* is deity and is to be worshiped.[25]

Qur'an

Muslims see themselves as standing in continuity with a long tradition of God's dealings with humankind. God is said to have sent his messengers to all peoples throughout history, leaving none without guidance (Surah 35:24; 13:7). A large number of prophets are recognized by Islam — some claim as many as 124,000 — but the six greatest are Adam, Noah, Abraham, Moses, Jesus ('Isa), and Muhammad. God communicated his messages through the prophets, some of which were preserved as written scriptures. "Every age has its scripture" (Surah 13:39).[26] Thus the Law was "sent down" to Moses, the Psalms to David, the Gospel to Jesus, and the Qur'an to Muhammad. All scriptures are said to have originally corresponded to a heavenly prototype and proclaimed essentially the same message: a call for humankind to reject *shirk* and to submit to the will of God by living in accordance with his law. However, it is claimed, the Jews rejected the prophets and corrupted the

24. Cf. Cragg, *The Call of the Minaret,* pp. 48-49.

25. The Qur'an does assume the existence of angels and *jinn,* creatures which fall somewhere between angels and humans, but these are never regarded as deities.

26. *The Koran,* pp. 146-47.

scriptures, as did the Christians who followed them (cf. Surah 5:9-16, 44-48, 57-61, 70-75, 109-20). Nevertheless, in his great mercy God has revealed his will definitively to Muhammad, and this final revelation is the Qur'an. The Qur'an thus consummates and transcends all earlier revelations. Muhammad is the final and greatest of the prophets, the "Seal of the Prophets" (Surah 33:40).

The Qur'an[27] is held to be, quite literally, the Word of God. The prevailing orthodox view among Muslims is that the Qur'an is the written transcript of an eternal tablet in heaven, the "Mother of the Book," which is also the source of all earlier revelations. In no way is it to be regarded as the product of Muhammad's creative activity. Muhammad was merely the passive recipient of God's revelation transmitted through the angel Gabriel. Tradition maintains that Muhammad was illiterate and thus could not have written the Qur'an. He simply passed on what had been "sent down," that is, what he received through divine revelation. Indeed, the incomparable beauty of the Arabic Qur'an is taken to be conclusive proof of its supernatural origin (cf. Surah 2:23; 10:38; 11:13). As God's revelation, however, the Qur'an is not so much a matter of the divine self-disclosure (God revealing himself) as it is a message telling us how humankind is expected to live with respect to God.

Although unrivalled in its authority, the Qur'an is not the sole source of guidance for living among orthodox Muslims. The *Shari'a*, or divinely authoritative law prescribing proper conduct for all Muslims, comprises not only the Qur'an but also the authoritative tradition of Muhammad *(Hadith, Sunna)*, the consensus of the *Ulema* or religious leaders, and proper reasoning by analogy from the teachings of the Qur'an or the tradition of Muhammad to new problems that emerge in each generation.

The Muslim views on God and his revelation are conveniently summarized in a creed from the twelfth-century Muslim theologian Al-Nasafi:

27. On the Qur'an see Fazlur Rahman, *Islam,* chap. 2; Alfred Guillaume, *Islam,* chap. 3; Kenneth Cragg, *The House of Islam,* chap. 3; and idem, *The Event of the Qur'an: Islam in its Scripture* (London: Allen & Unwin, 1972).

The Originator of the world is God Most High, the One, the
Eternal, the Decreeing, the Knowing, the Hearing, the Seeing, the
Willing. He is not an attribute, not a body, nor an essence, not a
thing formed, nor a thing bounded, nor a thing numbered, nor
a thing divided, nor a thing compounded, nor a thing limited: He
is not described by quiddity, *Mahiyah,* nor by modality, *Kaifiyyah,*
and He does not exist in place or time. There is nothing that
resembles Him and nothing that is beyond His Knowledge and
Power. He has qualities from all eternity existing in His essence.
They are not He, nor are they any other than He. They are Knowledge and Power, and Life and Strength and Hearing and Seeing
and Doing and Creating and Sustaining and Speech. And he
Whose Majesty is majestic speaks with a Word. This Word is a
quality from all eternity, not belonging to the genus of letters and
sounds, a quality that is incompatible with coming to silence and
that has a weakness. God Most High speaks with this Word, com-
manding and prohibiting and narrating. And the Quran is the
uncreated Word of God, repeated by our tongues, heard by our
ears, written in our copies, memorized in our hearts, yet not
simply a transient state in these. And creating is a quality of God
Most High from all eternity. . . . and Willing is a quality of God
Most High from all eternity, existing in His essence. . . . And God
Most High is the Creator of all actions of His creatures whether
of unbelief or belief, of obedience or rebellion: all of them are by
the Will of God and His sentence and His conclusion and His
decreeing.[28]

The Five Pillars

The religious, intellectual, and social life of the devout Muslim is
structured around the "Five Pillars": (1) the *Shahada* or "witness"
of the basic creed of Islam, (2) prayer, (3) fasting, (4) *Zakat* or
almsgiving, and (5) the pilgrimage to Mecca. The creed is simple
and concise: "There is no god but Allah and Muhammad is the

28. Translated by Duncan B. Macdonald, cited in Kenneth Cragg, *The Call
of the Minaret,* pp. 53-54.

Prophet of Allah." The oneness and unity of Allah are clearly and unequivocally affirmed. Muhammad is revered as the Prophet of Allah, but there is no suggestion that he was anything more than human; certainly there is no hint of his having a divine nature.[29]

Ritual prayer, *Salat,* is central to the life of Muslims.[30] Five prayers daily are obligatory for all Muslims, and each prayer is to be conducted in a carefully prescribed manner and in a state of ritual purity. Particularly significant is the congregational prayer at noon on Fridays at the local mosque. Obviously, the daily prayers make a considerable demand upon the faithful, and Kenneth Cragg suggests that the stringent requirement is to reinforce "the obligation of the believer to recognize God in the midst of, rather than in escape from, distractions and duties."[31]

During *Ramadan,* the ninth month of the Muslim calendar, all Muslims except the ill, travelers, pregnant women, nursing mothers, and young children are expected to fast from dawn until sunset. This should not be mistaken for a form of asceticism. Evenings, after sundown, are times of feasting and joyous gatherings together with family and friends. The point of fasting is not to emphasize the evils of sensual delights but rather to reaffirm that "human nature has larger needs than bread, that the body is to be the servant, not the master, and that ordered voluntary privation is a fine school of patience and endurance."[32]

The *Zakat,* or almsgiving, is a form of giving to those who

---

29. Dispute soon arose within Islam regarding what constitutes a Muslim and the place of recitation of the creed in defining a Muslim. "The more exacting require that it be recited aloud at least once; that it be understood with the mind and believed in the heart; that it be recited correctly and professed without hesitation; and that it be held until death. To the majority of Muslims, however, a mere recital of the creed is enough to enroll a new convert in the ranks of Islam; and any more stringent requirement is left to divine omniscience." Sir Norman Anderson, "Islam," p. 118.

30. The *Salat,* or ritual prayer, is to be distinguished from the more private, spontaneous prayer, or *Du'a,* in which one may address Allah through words and phrases of one's own choice without necessarily following any prescribed pattern. Cf. Cragg, *The Call of the Minaret,* pp. 96f.

31. Ibid., p. 97.

32. Ibid., p. 105.

are less fortunate and is obligatory upon all Muslims who have the means to do so. Although like fasting almsgiving is considered meritorious, it is also regarded as an act of worship "because it is a form of offering thanks to God for the means of material well-being one has acquired."[33]

The fifth Pillar requires all Muslims who are physically and financially capable of doing so to make the pilgrimage *(Hajj)* to Mecca at least once during their lifetime. The popular perception of the meritorious nature of the pilgrimage is indicated in such traditional sayings as "Every step in the direction of the *Ka'bah* blots out a sin," and "He who dies on the way to Mecca is enrolled in the list of martyrs."[34]

Day of Judgment

Eschatology is prominent in Muslim thought. Almost every surah in the Qur'an makes some reference to eschatology.[35] Muslims believe that our present world will one day be destroyed by Allah and that all humankind, past and present, will then be raised to face divine judgment over the degree to which they followed the faith and practice enjoined upon them by the prophets. On that day each person's deeds will be impartially weighed in the balance. Some will be consigned to Hell *(Jahannam)*, others to Paradise *(Jannah)*. Hell is graphically pictured as a place of intense physical torture and torment which never ends (cf. Surah 22:19-20). Paradise, by contrast, is depicted as a place of unimaginable sensual delights: "On that day the dwellers of Paradise shall think of nothing but their bliss. Together with their wives, they shall recline in shady groves upon soft couches. They shall have fruits and all that they desire" (Surah 36:55-57).

The Qur'an holds that the Devil, Iblis, was originally an

33. Richard C. Martin, *Islam: A Cultural Perspective*, p. 15.
34. Cited in Norman Anderson, "Islam," p. 120.
35. Cf. Marilyn Robinson Waldman, "Islamic Eschatology," in *The Encyclopedia of Religion*, vol. 5, pp. 152f.

angel who fell when he refused to pay homage to Adam, the first man (cf. Surah 2:34). Iblis was granted power to lead astray those who do not believe in Allah, and the paradigmatic example of his seductive power is the story of his tempting Adam and Eve to eat of the forbidden tree of immortality and power (Surah 20:116-22).[36] On the Day of Judgment Iblis and his evil host will be cast into the fiery pit of Hell.

Although Islam does acknowledge Adam's sin and expulsion from the Garden, it does not have anything corresponding to the Christian doctrine of original sin and the total depravity of human nature. There is, of course, a sense of sin in Islam, but it seems to signify more a weakness, defect, or flaw in human character rather than the radical corruption of human nature. There is in humankind a tendency to sin. Humans are liable to seduction and temptation from Iblis, but it is within their power to resist and to remain faithful to the will of Allah.[37] Men and women can turn and be obedient to the will of Allah, if they only will do so. The late Bishop Stephen Neill draws a sharp contrast between the Muslim sense of sin and that found in Christianity:

> And the Muslim objects strongly to Christian stress upon the sinfulness of man. This seems to him to be mere evasion. By pleading his weakness man tries to excuse his failure to obey, and so to withdraw himself from the last judgment of God on disobedience. Instead, he should gird himself to the not overwhelmingly difficult effort of obedience. At the heart of the Muslim-Christian disagreement, we shall find a deep difference in the understanding of the nature of sin. It is not true to say that the Muslim has no sense of sin or of the need for forgiveness. He has both. But an understanding of sin is directly related to an understanding of the nature of God. The New Testament doctrine of God as love involves a deepened understanding of the nature of sin, such as

36. Cf. Martin, *Islam: A Cultural Perspective*, p. 93.
37. "In its discussion of Adam as the archetypal man, the Qur'an does not see him as rebellious. That would be to enlarge his stature over against God. It sees him rather as weak and forgetful, or lacking in firmness and resolve. Though still his responsibility and sternly requited if God so wills, his sins are nevertheless more weakness than revolt." Kenneth Cragg, *The Call of the Minaret*, pp. 39-40.

seems not to be involved in the Islamic concept of the relation between the believer and the God in whom he believes. The believer may sin against the law and the majesty of God, and if he does so he deserves to be punished. The idea that man by his sin might break the heart of God makes sense only on the basis of the Christian understanding of the nature of God as love.[38]

The choice facing humankind, then, is unmistakably clear: at the Judgment one will either be consigned to the torments of Hell or be allowed to experience the delights of Paradise, and, in either case, each person is solely responsible for his or her own fate. There is no place in Islam for anything resembling the orthodox Christian doctrine of the substitutionary atonement. Not only does Islam rule out the need for a Savior, but the Qur'an emphatically states "that no soul shall bear another's burden and that each man shall be judged by his own labours" (Surah 53:38).[39] Allah is a fair and righteous Judge who will impartially determine each person's just reward. "On that day no soul shall suffer the least injustice. You shall be rewarded according only to your deeds" (Surah 36:54; cf. 82:19).[40] Salvation by faith is rejected by Islam.

> One earns one's fate by choosing to adhere or not adhere to clearly specified spiritual and behavioral norms. Judgment is as fair as a business transaction: one's deeds are weighed in the balance, neither wealth nor kin availing. If one has been faithful and grateful, accepted [Allah's] signs and messengers as true, prayed, and given charity, one is rewarded. If one has been faithless and ungrateful, given the lie to the signs and the messengers, given God partners, prayed insincerely or not at all, and been selfish with and prideful of one's material goods, one is punished.[41]

No one can presume to know with certainty his or her fate prior to the Day of Judgment. The idolaters and polytheists face certain

38. Stephen Neill, *Crises of Belief: The Christian Dialogue With Faith and No Faith* (London: Hodder & Stoughton, 1984), p. 88.
39. *The Koran*, p. 116. Cf. also Surah 39:7 and 6:164.
40. Ibid., p. 176.
41. Waldman, "Islamic Eschatology," p. 153.

condemnation — on this there is no question. But not even the sincere and devout Muslim can presume admittance to Paradise. Only Allah knows who will, and who will not, be admitted. There are some traditions suggesting that sinning Muslims will temporarily face the Fire, after which they will be permitted to enter Paradise. In any event, there is no ground for presumptive assurance; Allah is the one who decides, and only on that Day will his judgment be known.

Jesus

Undoubtedly the major source of controversy between Muslims and Christians concerns their respective beliefs about Jesus of Nazareth. Although we cannot here treat the subject in depth, some mention of the relevant issues is called for.[42]

Jesus ('Isa in the Qur'an) is mentioned in fifteen surahs and ninety-three verses, and is given a number of honorable titles: he is said to be a "sign," a "mercy," a "witness," and an "example." He is called the Messiah, Son of Mary, Messenger, Prophet, Servant, Word, and Spirit of God.[43] Jesus is always spoken of in the Qur'an with reverence, for he is the Messiah of God. Jesus is portrayed as being a great miracle worker and one of the greatest of the prophets. And although there are numerous discrepancies between the brief references in the Qur'an to Jesus' life and the accounts of his life in the Gospels, apart from the fact that the Qur'an omits Jesus' teachings contained in the Gospels (hardly a minor omission), the major differences center upon two issues — whether Jesus regarded himself as divine and whether he actually died upon the cross.

The Qur'an depicts Jesus as explicitly disclaiming deity (cf. Surah 5:115-18). Also in the Qur'an are numerous denunciations of what seem to have been current views on the Christian doctrines

42. For a full discussion of the Muslim understanding of Jesus, see Geoffrey Parrinder, *Jesus in the Qur'an* (New York: Oxford University Press, 1977).
43. Ibid., p. 16.

of the Incarnation and the Trinity. Surah 4:171 states, "The Messiah, Jesus the son of Mary, was no more than Allah's apostle and His Word which he conveyed to Mary: a spirit from Him. So believe in Allah and His apostles and do not say 'Three.' Forbear, and it shall be better for you. Allah is but one God. Allah forbid that He should have a son!" (cf. also 9:30-31).[44] Although he was a great prophet of God, Jesus was in no sense divine. Particularly offensive to Muslims is the Christian title "Son of God." There can be little doubt that Muhammad understood this to refer to physical generation. "Never has Allah begotten a son, nor is there any other god besides Him" (Surah 23:93; cf. 112:1-4).[45] Muhammad seems to have conceived of the Trinity as consisting of the Father, the Virgin Mary, and their Child. It is hardly surprising, then, that he would vehemently denounce such a view, which had certain parallels to the pagan polytheism all around him, as blasphemous. For what he took to be the Christian doctrines of the Trinity and the Incarnation were clear examples of the sin of *shirk* — associating the creature with the one Creator. However, as Parrinder points out, what is denied in the Qur'an is not so much the orthodox doctrines of the Trinity and Incarnation but rather expressions of the heresies of Adoptionism, Patripassianism, and Mariolatry.[46]

Did Jesus actually die on the cross? The cross and the resurrection are, of course, absolutely central to Christian faith, but it may come as a surprise to Christians to discover that most Muslims believe that Jesus in fact did not die on the cross. The key passage here is Surah 4:155-59:

> They [the Jews] denied the truth and uttered a monstrous falsehood against Mary. They declared "We have put to death the Messiah Jesus the son of Mary, the apostle of Allah." They did not kill him, nor did they crucify him, but they thought they did. Those that disagreed about him were in doubt concerning his

44. *The Koran*, p. 384.
45. Ibid., p. 224.
46. Parrinder, *Jesus in the Qur'an*, p. 137. See also Kenneth Cragg, "Islam and Incarnation," in *Truth and Dialogue in World Religions*, ed. John H. Hick (Philadelphia: Westminster, 1974).

death, for what they knew about it was sheer conjecture; they were not sure that they had slain him. Allah lifted him up to His presence; He is mighty and wise.[47]

There are difficult questions concerning the precise meaning of this passage but, exegetical questions aside, a widely accepted Muslim interpretation has been that the Jews tried to kill Jesus but were unable to do so, and that God rescued him and carried him away to a safe place in the heavens. One tradition tells of Jesus hiding in a niche in a wall and one of his companions being killed in his place.[48] Did Jesus actually die on the cross? Or was a substitute killed in his place? The New Testament Gospels make it clear that the answer to the first question is yes; no serious historian today would dispute that Jesus was in fact crucified on the cross. Most Muslims, however, emphatically deny this. Further, there is no hint in the Gospels of a substitute being crucified in Jesus' place. And yet many Muslims maintain that this is precisely what happened. The differences between Muslims and Christians, then, over the person and work of Jesus of Nazareth are fundamental and cannot be casually dismissed. It is unfortunate that Muhammad does not appear to have been presented with a clear picture of the orthodox understanding of Jesus, the Trinity, and the Incarnation. For what he encountered — and rightly rejected — was not so much the New Testament understanding of Jesus and God but rather a heretical distortion of the person of Jesus and his relation to God the Father.

SHINTO

It would be difficult to find an example of a contemporary religious tradition more radically different from Islam than Shinto.[49]

47. *The Koran*, p. 382. For a full discussion of the problems in interpreting this passage see Geoffrey Parrinder, *Jesus in the Qur'an*, pp. 108-21.

48. Parrinder, *Jesus in the Qur'an*, p. 109.

49. Good discussions of Shinto can be found in Naofusa Hirai, "Shinto," in *The Encyclopedia of Religion*, vol. 13, pp. 280-94; Joseph M. Kitagawa, "Shinto,"

Whereas Islam maintains an uncompromising monotheism, Shinto unashamedly embraces polytheism. Shinto has no known founder; its origins are lost in the obscurity of Japan's prehistoric past. Moreover, it does not have an accepted canon of sacred scripture, although some texts, such as the Kojiki (Records of Ancient Matters) and the Nihon-shoki (Chronicles of Japan) play a significant role in Shinto tradition. There is no carefully defined creed, no systematic theology of Shinto. Unlike religions such as Buddhism, Islam, and Christianity, which are clearly intended to be universal in scope and thus genuine world religions, Shinto makes no claim to universal applicability. It is a particularist, ethnic religion, intimately linked to the Japanese people and nation.

The insular nature of Shinto is reflected in the following definition by the Japanese scholar Naofusa Hirai: "I define the word 'Shinto' as the traditional indigenous religious practices of the Japanese people as well as their worldview, based on their concept of *kami*."[50] Similarly, Joseph M. Kitagawa defines Shinto as "the ensemble of contradictory and yet peculiarly Japanese types of religious beliefs, sentiments, and approaches, which have been shaped and conditioned by the historical experience of the Japanese people from the prehistoric period to the present."[51] As an ethnic religion Shinto is inconceivable apart from the Japanese people and culture.

It is perhaps significant that prior to the introduction of Buddhism to Japan in the sixth century A.D. there was no special term denoting the web of indigenous religious practices and beliefs already in place in Japan. In order to distinguish the indigenous tradition from Buddhism, the term "Shinto" was coined. Shinto literally means "the way of the *kami*"[52] and thus the indigenous religious tradition was differentiated from Buddhism (*Butsudo*, "the way of the Buddha"). Early Shinto was largely hostile to the

in *On Understanding Japanese Religion* (Princeton: Princeton University Press, 1987); Sokyo Ono, *Shinto: The Kami Way* (Tokyo: Charles E. Tuttle, 1962); Stuart D. B. Picken, *Shinto: Japan's Spiritual Roots* (Tokyo: Kodansha, 1980); Clark B. Offner, "Shinto," in *The World's Religions,* ed. Sir Norman Anderson (Grand Rapids: Eerdmans, 1975), pp. 191-218.

50. Naofusa Hirai, "Shinto," p. 280.
51. Joseph M. Kitagawa, "Shinto," p. 139.
52. For the meaning of *kami*, usually translated "god," see pp. 100f.

new foreign religion. However, the succeeding centuries were to witness fascinating transformations in the relationship between the two traditions, as well as between Shinto and Confucianism.[53] During the eighth and ninth centuries, for example, Buddhism and Shinto were to achieve a remarkable rapprochement, in which the original nature of the Shinto *kami* was said to be Buddha and the various *kami* were seen to be the Buddha's manifestations in Japan. Shinto shrines were established within the confines of Buddhist temples, and Buddhist chapels, in turn, were constructed on the outskirts of Shinto shrines. And in the seventeenth century, Banzan Kumazawa tried to unify Shinto and Confucianism by asserting that the Way of the *kami* (Shinto) and the Way of the True Kingship in China *(wang-tao)*, although different in name, were essentially the same. Such irenic overtures, however, did not go unchallenged by Shinto purists. In the eighteenth and ninteenth centuries, under such leaders as Norinaga Motoori and Atsutane Hirata, there was a resurgence of Shinto which stressed the unique and superior nature of the Shinto faith and the Japanese collective identity. The Meiji Restoration of 1868, which, at least in principle, placed Japan under direct rule by the emperor, carefully prescribed Shinto values and principles as part of the new national policy. The following decades saw the manipulation of Shinto and the emperor cult by militarists and ultranationalists, thrusting Japan down a precarious path culminating in the disastrous Second World War. While it cannot be denied that Shinto does contain within it elements that were conducive to the aims of the militarists and ultranationalists, it would be erroneous to conclude that Shinto values and beliefs entail Japanese militarism and expansionism.

It is helpful to distinguish several kinds of Shinto, although we should note that a clear distinction between types is not possible.[54] There is considerable overlap in beliefs, values, and practices of the various types. *Folk Shinto* is a broad category including within it the many practices and traditions associated with Japanese

53. For the historical development of Shinto, and its relation to Buddhism and Confucianism, see J. M. Kitagawa, "Shinto," pp. 155-68, as well as Kitagawa's classic study *Religion in Japanese History* (New York: Columbia University Press, 1966).

54. See C. Offner, "Shinto," pp. 192f.

96 DISSONANT VOICES

folk religion, such as divination and magical shamanic rituals. Folk Shinto thus contains an assortment of practices, some of which are part of the indigenous Japanese tradition and others of which are of Taoist or Buddhist origin. *Shrine Shinto* refers to the religious practices and beliefs, particularly the worship of *kami,* which are centered upon the numerous local shrines. It is this aspect of Shinto that is usually meant by the term "Shinto." One can actively participate in Shrine Shinto without being a member of any particular Shinto sect or organization, although each local shrine usually has a loose association of parishioners taken from the immediate community. *State Shinto* was the product of the nationalistic policy of the architects behind the Meiji Restoration. In 1868 the Department of Shinto was established and Shinto was officially distinguished from Buddhism. State Shinto was said to be a nonreligious or suprareligious cult of national morality and patriotism to which all Japanese, regardless of religious affiliation, must adhere.[55] The disestablishment of Shinto in 1945 marked the end of State Shinto, although there have been some ominous indications in recent years of a growing sympathy among many Japanese for a return to an official tie between the state and Shinto values and practices. *Sect Shinto* originally referred to the various Shinto denominations — organized groups with an identifiable tradition, some of which have historical founders, canonical scriptures, and creed — in an effort to distinguish them from the supposedly nonreligious nature of State Shinto. The term also came to refer to the many sects that developed in the nineteenth and twentieth centuries and are usually known now as "new religions." *Domestic Shinto* designates the carefully prescribed rituals performed within the home rather than in the local shrines. And *Imperial Household Shinto* includes the special rites performed by the imperial family at the special shrines set apart for this purpose.

Those who, impressed by the apparent "Westernization" of Tokyo or Osaka, conclude that Shinto probably has little, if any,

55. See J. M. Kitagawa, *On Understanding Japanese Religion,* pp. 167f. For an excellent discussion of State Shinto in modern Japanese history see Helen Hardacre's *Shinto and the State: 1868-1988* (Princeton: Princeton University Press, 1989).

role to play in modern Japan fail to understand the extent to which traditional values and practices have become embedded in the Japanese cultural identity. Shinto is very much alive and flourishing in contemporary Japan. According to the Agency for Cultural Affairs, in 1982 there were 79,700 shrines nationwide, most of which belong to the Association of Shinto Shrines. A total of 74,660,000 Japanese were reported to be believers in Shrine Shinto.[56]

But the influence of Shinto upon contemporary Japan cannot be measured by statistics alone. For, as Hirai puts it, Shinto "has permeated the life of the Japanese people, not so much through a firmly established theology or philosophy as through its basic code of values, its behavior pattern, and its way of thinking."[57] The keen observations of Edwin O. Reischauer, the leading interpreter of modern Japan to the West, are worth quoting at length:

> Shinto pervades the sophisticated, highly developed society of modern Japan, but it remains very much what it was as we know it from history. . . . The shrines of Shinto are to be found everywhere throughout the land — the great Ise Shrines of the Sun Goddess, unchanged from prehistoric times through continual faithful reproductions of their original form; the equally moving and magnificent shrine in Tokyo built in this century to the memory of the Emperor Meiji; the village shrines dedicated to the progenitors of some long-vanished tribal *uji;* the shrines that celebrate the spirit of some great waterfall or mountain; the tiny boxlike shrines in front of gnarled old trees; the shrines tucked into tiny corners of the busy downtown sections of cities or placed on roofs of many-storied buildings; and the *kamidana,* or "god shelves," for worship of the ancestors within private homes. The *kami* are still to be found everywhere throughout the islands of Japan, and Shinto ways still permeate life.[58]

Even Japanese who claim not to believe in Shinto and who look with amused skepticism upon the ancient Shinto myths have nevertheless

56. Naofusa Hirai, "Shinto," p. 292.
57. Ibid., p. 280.
58. Edwin O. Reischauer, "Introduction," in *Shinto: Japan's Spiritual Roots,* p. 8.

been influenced profoundly in their basic worldview by Shinto values. In times of serious illness in the family, for example, a highly educated computer engineer or heart surgeon will still visit the local shrine to pray for the speedy recovery of a loved one. Prior to the construction of a new building a Shinto priest is summoned and the *jichinsai* (a ceremony to purify the site of the new building) is performed. Thirty-two days after the birth of a son (thirty-three days for girls) the baby is taken to the local shrine for the *hatsu-miyamairi* (literally "the first shrine visit"), through which he becomes a parishioner. During February of each year, as students prepare to take the rigorous university entrance examinations, over 2,000 people a day visit the Yushima Tenjin Shrine in Tokyo, where the *kami* of learning is said to be enshrined, to pray for success in the upcoming examinations. The simplicity of contemporary Shinto faith and ritual is illustrated in the following report by a young Japanese student:

> The sun rises early, but cannot be seen for some time because of the walls of high buildings that surround the house. Yet an old woman rises with the sun. Climbing slowly out of her heavy bedding, she walks across the *tatami* floor to the window. Opening it, she faces the east and twice claps her hands loudly: "Please protect everyone today, too." The small cup of water and offering of rice are replaced with new ones on the white wood *kamidana* in the shape of a shrine, in the heart of which is a small mirror. Again she claps twice. Having thus satisfied her *kami*, she goes outside to sprinkle the front porch with water. By then, her daughter-in-law is up and together they begin setting breakfast. This is a typical morning for my eighty-year-old grandmother.[59]

Mythology

The central theme of the early Japanese myths concerns the divine origin of the imperial clan and, by extension, of the Japanese people as a whole. Various myths, which had undoubtedly been trans-

---

59. The report is found in Stuart D. B. Picken, *Shinto: Japan's Spiritual Roots*, p. 28.

mitted orally for centuries, were compiled and included in the two quasi-historical writings of the eighth century A.D., the Kojiki and the Nihon-shoki.[60]

The ancient Japanese mythology presupposes a three-dimensional universe: the Plain of High Heaven (where male and female *kami* dwell), the Phenomenal World (where humans and other beings reside), and the Nether World (where unclean spirits are found).[61] In the Kojiki account, prior to the "creation" of the world there emerged spontaneously in the Plain of High Heaven three *kami* — Ame-no-minakanushi, Takamimusubi, and Kamimusubi. Subsequently, numerous other *kami* also emerged or were born to already existing *kami*. Two such *kami*, Izanagi (male) and Izanami (female), stood on the Floating Bridge of Heaven and stirred up the formless, watery chaos beneath with their jewelled spear. When they lifted their spear, the brine dripping from the spear became an island. The two *kami* descended to the island and proceeded to give birth to numerous other islands and other *kami* — including *kami* of the wind, trees, mountains, and plains. Thus the islands of Japan came into being.

However, Izanami was fatally burned when she gave birth to the *kami* of fire, so she departed to the Nether World. Izanagi followed her in hopes of bringing her back, but once in the Nether World he saw her putrefied body. Horrified, Izanagi returned to the Phenomenal World, where he purified himself in a river. This act of purification resulted in the generation of many more *kami*, among them the Sun Goddess, Amaterasu O Mikami. Later, the grandson of the Sun Goddess, Ninigi, accompanied by numerous heavenly *kami*, was sent to rule the Japanese islands. Ninigi is said to have married a daughter of a local *kami* in the southern island of Kyushu, and one of their grandchildren grew up to be the Emperor Jimmu, the legendary first

---

60. Cf. *Kojiki,* trans. Donald L. Philippi (Tokyo: University of Tokyo, 1968), and "Nihongi: Chronicles of Japan From Earliest Times to A.D. 697," 2 vols., trans. W. G. Aston, *The Transactions and Proceedings of the Japan Society, London,* Supplement I (London: Kegan, Paul, Trench, and Trübner, 1896). Selections from the Kojiki and Nihon-shoki can be found in *Sources of Japanese Tradition,* ed. William Theodore de Bary (New York: Columbia University Press, 1958), pp. 14-35.

61. Cf. J. M. Kitagawa, *On Understanding Japanese Religion,* pp. 143f.

emperor of Japan. Thus, the imperial family is said to be directly
descended from the Sun Goddess Amaterasu.

Kami

It is obvious from the preceding discussion that the concept of
kami is central to the Shinto worldview. The term *kami* is
frequently translated into English as "god" or "deity," but given
the unique meaning it has in Shinto it is probably best left un-
translated. The classic definition of *kami* was provided by the
eighteenth-century Shinto scholar Norinaga Motoori:

> Speaking in general, however, it may be said that *kami* signifies,
> in the first place, the deities of heaven and earth that appear in
> the ancient records and also the spirits of the shrines where they
> are worshipped. It is hardly necessary to say that it includes
> human beings. It also includes such objects as birds, beasts, trees,
> plants, seas, mountains and so forth. In ancient usage, anything
> whatsoever which was outside the ordinary, which possessed su-
> perior power or which was awe-inspiring was called *kami*.[62]

A wide variety of entities fall into the category of *kami*. The twentieth-century Shinto scholar Sokyo Ono states that included within
the concept of *kami* are the qualities of growth and fertility; natural
phenomena, such as wind, thunder, the sun, mountains, trees;
some animals; ancestral spirits; the imperial family; spirits of noble
families; guardian spirits of certain occupations and skills; and
spirits of people who have demonstrated exemplary bravery or
courage, or who have made great contributions to society.[63] Many
scholars trace the notion of *kami* back to the concept of the *ujigami*, the guardian deity of a local clan, and even today often a
particular community will have its own *ujigami*.

The notion of *kami* is deliberately kept vague in Shinto, and

62. As quoted in H. Byron Earhart, *Religion in the Japanese Experience:
Sources and Interpretations* (Encino, Cal.: Dickenson Publishing Company, 1974),
p. 10.

63. Sokyo Ono, *Shinto: The Kami Way*, p. 7.

attempts to make its meaning precise are resisted. But there is no question that the concept of *kami* is polytheistic. Shinto tradition refers to the *yao yorozu no kami* (literally, "eighty myriads of *kami*"). This is sometimes taken to mean that there are literally 80,000,000 *kami* in the Shinto pantheon, but the phrase probably should not be taken to be an enumeration of the actual number of *kami* so much as an indication that the *kami* are innumerable, ubiquitous, and the fountainhead of all life. The *kami* are considered to be directly involved in the affairs of the living; they are the source of blessings and prosperity.

> The real faith of Shinto is necessarily a faith in individual *kami* as proximate beings who bestow many kinds of blessings; behind this lies no monistic reality. The *kami* are not abstract existences. They are beings who respond to the sincere prayers of humanity and who have separate, divine personalities. The pious *ujiko*, parishioners of shrines, believe that their *ujigami* make possible their life and prosperity in this world.[64]

Three points in particular distinguish the notion of *kami* from the concept of God in the Judeo-Christian tradition. First, there is in Shinto no clear ontological distinction between the natural realm and the supernatural realm. The line of demarcation between *kami* and humans, as well as animals and natural objects, is fluid and unclear. Persons and even animals can become *kami*. Thus *kami* does not refer to a divine reality transcending the universe but rather to a reality which, while in some sense distinct from the world, also exists within the continuum of the universe itself. Thus, in a sense the cosmos itself can be regarded as *kami* or as manifesting the *kami* presence.

Second, there is no place in Shinto for the concept of an eternal, self-sufficient, creator God. Although historically there have been at times certain theistic strains in Shinto (notably in the thought of the nineteenth-century Shinto apologist Atsutane Hirata), the mainstream of Shinto tradition unequivocally rejects monotheism. Ono states categorically, "In Shinto there is no ab-

64. Naofusa Hirai, "Shinto," p. 288.

solute deity that is the creator and ruler of all."[65] And Kenji Ueda
observes that today "the Association of Shinto Shrines rejects any
monotheistic interpretation that could detract from the independent dignity of individual *kami* in the Shinto pantheon." He goes
on to assert that "Shinto is a polytheistic religion, permitting worship of many *kami* at the same time, although Amaterasu retains
the central and highest position."[66]

Third, one does not find in Shinto the notion of deity being
the basis for the moral order. The *kami* are not presented as the
source of moral good and righteousness; they do not engage in
dramatic battle for the sake of righteousness; nor do they divide
up humankind into opposing camps of good and evil.[67] To the
contrary, one finds both good and evil exemplified in the conduct
of the *kami*, who are depicted, much like the earlier gods and
goddesses of Greek mythology, as susceptible to the same moral
failures found in humans. As Joseph Spae puts it, there are both
good *kami* and bad *kami*, but ultimately all *kami* are benevolent.[68]
Thus, one finds in Shinto neither a clearly defined ethical system
nor a strong religious foundation for moral judgment.

Humankind

The picture of humankind found in Shinto is largely optimistic.
Hirai observes that the fundamental assumption underlying
Shinto's views on humankind is the idea that "human beings are
children of the *kami*."[69] This calls for an intimate relation between
humankind and the ubiquitous *kami*. Not only is a person's life
derived from the *kami* (and thus human life is to be regarded as
sacred), but the continued well-being of each person is due to the
ongoing blessing of the *kami*. Ono states,

65. Sokyo Ono, *Shinto: The Kami Way*, p. 8.
66. Kenji Ueda, "Kami," in *The Encyclopedia of Religion*, vol. 8, p. 244.
67. Cf. Joseph J. Spae, *Shinto Man* (Tokyo: Oriens Institute for Religious
Research, 1972), pp. 46f.
68. Ibid., p. 52.
69. Naofusa Hirai, "Shinto," p. 288.

Man is a child of the *kami*, he is also inherently good. Yet there is no clear line of distinction between himself and the *kami*. In one sense men are *kami*, in another they will become *kami*. Man owes his life, which is sacred, to the *kami* and to his ancestors. He is loved and protected by them.[70]

Noticeably lacking in Shinto is the notion of human sin as willful rebellion against a holy and righteous God. Not only is there in Shinto no holy God against whom one rebels, but there is no sense of a radical fallenness, a pervasive evil in human nature itself which is the root cause of the human predicament. Hirai puts it this way:

> In Shinto there is no conspicuous conception of original sin. Instead, since man is believed to have received life from the *kami*, man has within him the sacrality that is the essence of *kami*. However, actual human beings seldom exhibit that sacred essence. In order to "polish" the light of this essence, it is necessary to purify the heart, removing from it the dust and pollution obscuring its surface.[71]

To be sure, Shinto recognizes that something in humankind at present is amiss. All is not well in our world. But the problem is not so much a radical perversion of the will as it is a failure on the part of humankind to recognize its own intimate relation to the *kami* and to live, in a spirit of sincerity and gratitude, in harmony with the will of the *kami*. "Evil" in Shinto is thought of in terms of pollution *(kegare)* and impurity and has traditionally included things regarded as abnormal, unclean, or unpleasant to the *kami* — death, sickness, parturition, menstruation, abnormal sexual activity, and so on. As Joseph Kitagawa observes, in the early records evil was not thought of so much in moral categories as in physical or mental categories. The tendency in Shinto was to regard *tsumi* (sin) or *ashi* (evil) as something caused by external factors. "In effect, evil was not viewed as a reality; rather, evil was a lack of

70. Sokyo Ono, *Shinto: The Kami Way*, p. 103.
71. Naofusa Hirai, "Shinto," p. 288.

harmony and beauty, and could be corrected by purificatory ceremonies *(haraye)* performed by the ablutionist."[72]

This essentially is the perspective of contemporary Shinto as well and accounts for the prominence — even today — of carefully prescribed rituals of ceremonial purification. Humankind is basically pure and good; it is contact with what is impure (blood, sickness, death), the action of evil spirits, or failure to cultivate the inherent goodness within which results in disharmony and requires ritual purification. Joseph Spae points out that in Shinto evil is essentially a "lack of natural harmony *(shizen aku)* to be removed by various ritual means at hand." He cautions, however, "that these ritual practices do not 'forgive sins', nor relieve man of his responsibility for them. Rather, they restore his capacity to do good by making him more aware of his obligations."[73]

A variety of purification rites are performed, some by specially trained priests and others by ordinary laypeople. For example, an ordinary believer can perform the rite of *temizu* (literally "hand water"), in which one rinses the mouth and pours clean water over the fingertips, symbolizing inner purification and pacification of spirit. Or laypeople might participate in *misogi,* a ritual of purification by bathing in a prescribed manner at the mouth of a river or under a waterfall. Priests will be called upon to perform the *oharai,* a ceremony to remove various pollutants and evil spirits by the waving of a *haraigushi,* a kind of purification wand made from a sacred tree with white linen cloth or paper streamers attached. The *oharai* ceremony can be adapted to a variety of needs; it might be performed in a shrine, at the dedication of a new building, or even upon the purchase of a new automobile. Or priests might be called upon to perform the *yakubari* ceremony, in which *kami* who have been offended by some impurity are appeased.

Integral to proper observance of ceremonial purification rites is a general attitude of reverence and worship of the *kami.* A spirit of worship can be expressed in different ways. In a sense, all

72. Joseph Kitagawa, *Religion in Japanese History,* p. 13.
73. Joseph Spae, *Shinto Man,* p. 57.

of one's daily activities are to be performed in a spirit of worship, as a service *(matsuri)* to the *kami*. More tangible expressions of worship are seen in the offering of food to the *kami (shinsen)*, offering of special sacred prayers by the priest *(norito)*, or participation in sacred feasts with the *kami (naorai)*. Central to the proper response of worship is an attitude of *magokoro* ("the true heart") — that is, an attitude of sincerity and truthfulness based upon purity of life. Authentic worship of the *kami*, then, is not simply a matter of following certain carefully prescribed external rituals; it involves the pacification of one's spirit and the purification of one's mind.

Shinto does not speculate about the end of the world. Its concerns are remarkably "this-worldly." There is no clear eschatological emphasis, no sense of history progressing toward a definite denouement in the future. Shinto is preoccupied with the notion of *naka ima* (literally "middle present"), the conception of the eternal flow of time in which the present is the center point, the meeting point between oneself and the eternal course of history.[74] The needs which Shinto confronts and which the *kami* are called upon to alleviate are all squarely placed in the present.

And this, of course, dictates the manner in which "salvation" is understood within Shinto. Since according to Shinto humankind is basically good, there is no need for a radical transformation of the human character. Thus there is nothing resembling the Christian doctrine of regeneration in Shinto. Similarly, salvation is not something to be anticipated in the future; it is rather the state of well-being in the present. As Kazushige Sekioka puts it,

> It is in a healthy life that Shinto finds salvation, as expressed by the fact that [it does not] see any distinction between man as he actually is and man as he should be. When one is healthy, it means that he is already in the state of salvation. Unlike Christianity, which regards man as sinful or sick and as having deviated from what he originally should have been, Shinto assumes that a man

74. Naofusa Hirai, "Shinto," p. 288.

is healthy in his primary condition and that sin or sickness is only secondary.[75]

One of the most remarkable things about Shinto is the fact that, in spite of its being an ancient tradition based upon certain prehistoric myths with no clearly defined creed or canonical scriptures, it nevertheless continues to flourish in the highly technological and sophisticated society of contemporary Japan. Here, as in many other areas, the Japanese exhibit their exceptional capacity for adapting traditional values and ways to the exigencies of modern civilization.

CONCLUSION

We have briefly looked at four religious traditions — Hinduism, Buddhism, Islam, and Shinto — in an effort to see what answers they provide the three questions concerning the religious ultimate, the human predicament, and the nature of salvation. The discussion has hardly been exhaustive; much more can and probably should be said about each tradition. But even in this concise overview it is apparent that the four religions differ sharply among themselves — as well as with orthodox Christianity — over the question of humankind's relation to the religious ultimate.

The religious ultimate. There is no question about what is ultimate in the monotheism of Islam. Allah, the one eternal creator God, is the religious ultimate. Any attempt to blur the clear-cut distinction between the creator and the creation is regarded by Muslims as shirk — idolatry. Islam thus joins monotheistic faiths such as Christianity and Judaism in ascribing ultimacy to the one eternal creator God.

The matter is not so unambiguous, however, in the case of the other three religions. What, for example, are we to say of Buddhism? Theravada Buddhism does not acknowledge anything

75. Kazushige Sekioka, "Soteriology in Shinto," Japanese Religions, 6, January 1970, p. 60.

like a monotheistic God. In the case of Theravada Buddhism, if we must speak in these terms at all, perhaps ultimacy should be identified with *nirvana,* since it alone is said to be unconditioned and permanent. But in doing so, of course, we must be careful not to think of *nirvana* as some kind of ultimate Being with identifiable personal characteristics. Mahayana Buddhists might prefer to speak of the *Dharmakaya,* the ultimate, all-inclusive Law Body of the Buddha essence, as the religious ultimate. Zen Buddhists might ascribe ultimacy to Emptiness or Suchness. And, of course, Pure Land Buddhists will tend to think in quasi-theistic terms of the Amida Buddha, a being with definite personal characteristics, as the religious ultimate. Obviously, there is not just one concept which functions as the religious ultimate for all Buddhists.

Among Hindus too we find a variety of possibilities for religious ultimacy. Followers of monistic Advaita Vedanta will regard the *nirguna* Brahman, an absolutely nondifferentiated Being, as the religious ultimate. Philosophically less sophisticated Hindus might recognize a wide variety of deities, singling out one or more for special reverence and devotion. Thus some Hindus will think of Vishnu, Shiva, or even Krishna in theistic terms, and ultimate devotion and reverence will be accorded these figures. By contrast, rather than identifying ultimacy with any particular deity atheistic Hindus will tend to regard the entire cosmic process as ultimate.

It is not clear that the notion of religious ultimacy is even applicable in the case of Shinto, for the *kami* are not regarded as ontologically distinct from the phenomenal world. Strictly speaking, the *kami* are not transcendent, standing over against the world, but rather exist within the continuum of the phenomenal world. There is no room in Shinto for the monotheistic understanding of an ontologically distinct eternal creator who brought into being from nothing all that exists. In Shinto the religious ultimate is not something located outside of the world but rather is in an important sense continuous with the world of our experience. And yet the difficulty we have in identifying religious ultimacy in Shinto is in itself instructive. For it underscores the great differences in worldview between polytheistic religious traditions such as Shinto and monotheistic faiths such as Christianity and Islam.

The human predicament. The various religions give quite different answers to the question of the human predicament as well. Hinduism and Buddhism largely accept the view that humankind is trapped within *samsara,* the cycle of rebirths through which one transmigrates in accordance with *karma*; and, at least in the case of Buddhism, *samsara* is characterized by *dukkha,* pervasive suffering or dissatisfaction. The root problem of human existence is not sin — deliberate moral rebellion against a holy and righteous God — but rather a profound ignorance, blindness, or confusion regarding the true nature of reality.

Unlike Christianity, Buddhism, or Hinduism, there does not seem to be in Shinto a strong sense that the present order is somehow radically distorted or fallen. The human predicament, if this terminology is even adequate, is more a matter of cosmic imbalance or disharmony brought about through somehow offending the *kami.* Evil is rooted in defilement or contamination from association with what is impure. Contamination does not stem from sin, rebellion against a holy God, but from association with what is undesirable — especially death.

Islam, on the other hand, does have an understanding of sin, although not one as clearly defined as that found in the Christian tradition. The ultimate sin, of course, is *shirk,* associating anything created with Allah. Idolatry is unambiguously condemned. Conspicuously lacking in Islam, however, is the emphasis upon the total depravity of human nature, of the pervasive impact of sin, and the complete inability of humankind to redeem itself from the bondage of sin. Sin is more a weakness, defect, or imperfection than a radical corruption of the nature and will. Thus, although Iblis (Satan) is said to be constantly tempting humans to disobey Allah, it is within their power to resist and to remain faithful to Allah. It is not that humankind stands in need of a savior and redeemer, someone who can transform the corrupted sinful nature into one pleasing to God, but rather that it needs to act in faithfulness and submission to the revealed will of Allah — something held to be within the grasp of disciplined and religiously sensitive persons.

The nature of salvation. Given the various understandings

of the nature of the human predicament, it is to be expected that the four religions would have different perspectives on how one is to attain salvation or liberation from the present predicament. Hindus generally regard the spiritual goal as *moksha,* complete release from the chains of *karma* and the cycle of rebirths. Such deliverance is said to be attainable through a variety of means: *karma marga,* the way of selfless or disinterested action, or the rigorous adherence to moral and ritual prescriptions; *jnana marga,* the way of liberating insight into the nature of reality; or *bhakti marga,* the way of devotion to a personal lord. Some Hindus consider all three ways to be equally legitimate, depending upon one's circumstances and abilities. Others pick out one particular way — say, *bhakti marga* — as the only legitimate way or at least as superior to the others.

For Buddhists release from *samsara* is generally thought of in terms of *nirvana,* the complete elimination of desire and the conditions producing rebirth. According to Theravada Buddhists, through a process of rigorous self-discipline focused upon the Noble Eightfold Path and encompassing numerous lives, one can attain *nirvana.* On the other hand, many Mahayana Buddhists, minimizing the notion of *samsara,* tend to think of salvation more in terms of enlightenment in this life. And Pure Land Buddhists generally equate salvation with rebirth in the Pure Land after death. Also within Buddhism are striking differences between those who insist that salvation/enlightenment is strictly the result of one's own individual efforts (Theravada Buddhists) and those who, calling all self-effort futile, maintain that only faith in the mercy and merit of another will bring about salvation (Jodo-Shinshu Buddhists).

Shinto has no explicit eschatology or soteriology. Salvation in Shinto is largely a matter of achieving a healthy and robust life in the present. A sincere heart that seeks to acknowledge the presence of the *kami* in all of life, carefully maintaining the rituals of ceremonial purity, can expect the blessings of the *kami* in the daily affairs of life.

By contrast, salvation in Islam is primarily eschatological. On the Day of Judgment only those whom Allah declares worthy will be admitted to the delights of Paradise. Salvation is not so much a present reality that finds its culmination in the future as a glorious future awaiting those who prove faithful to the will of Allah.

It is evident, then, that Buddhism, Hinduism, Islam, and Shinto provide quite different answers to the questions concerning the religious ultimate, the human predicament, and the nature of salvation. Significantly, in some cases such as Shinto the three questions themselves do not seem entirely appropriate. Thus, rather than regarding the various religions as providing different answers to certain common questions — still less as providing similar answers to common questions — it is perhaps best to think of them as responding to certain issues that arose within their own particular historical and cultural contexts. And while there may be some overlap in issues addressed (especially in the case of Hinduism and Buddhism), there is also considerable diversity, both in terms of questions posed and answers given.

What implications follow from this? First, while we must recognize that mere difference in perspective in and of itself does not entail opposition of beliefs, there are instances in which the various religions clearly do seem to be making mutually incompatible claims about the nature of reality.[76] Is the religious ultimate personal or nonpersonal? Is there one God, many *kami*, or no higher Being of any kind? Is the human predicament at root caused by human rebellion against a holy and righteous God? Or is it the product of a cosmic illusion or ignorance? Is salvation a matter of the total transformation of one's nature, resulting in a restored relationship with God? Or is it a matter of release from the cycle of rebirths? William Christian suggests that "two doctrines are opposed if they cannot be jointly accepted without absurdity."[77] It is difficult indeed to escape the conclusion that some of the central affirmations of Christianity, Hinduism, Buddhism, Islam, and

76. For an excellent study of the many complex issues involved in identifying instances of conflicting truth claims among various religions see William A. Christian, *Oppositions of Religious Doctrines: A Study in the Logic of Dialogue Among Religions* (London: Macmillan, 1972).

77. Ibid., p. 2.

Shinto are opposed; so long as the meanings of the doctrines within the respective religious communities are preserved, they cannot be jointly accepted without absurdity.

Second, although our concern here is primarily with beliefs we should observe that opposition takes place not only on the level of doctrine but also with respect to courses of action advocated by various religious communities. Fundamental beliefs about the nature of the religious ultimate and the human predicament call for certain appropriate patterns of behavior. Based upon their respectives beliefs about reality, the Advaitin Hindu, Pure Land Buddhist, and Muslim will advocate markedly different courses of action.

Third, the common assumption that all religions ultimately are teaching the same things in their own culturally conditioned ways is prima facie untenable. Not only are they not all saying the same things, but the particular issues addressed in the various religions are not necessarily the same. Christian says that the recently popular views that the beliefs of the major religions are all mutually consistent and that all religions say basically the same thing "seem very implausible, and certainly much current talk in aid of these views is loose and sentimental."[78] Surely the burden of proof rests with those who would maintain the contrary.

78. Ibid., p. 5.

CHAPTER FOUR

Religion and Truth

Christian exclusivism, as defined in chapter 1, contends that where the central claims of Christian faith are incompatible with those of other religious traditions the latter are to be rejected as false. Thus, for example, it has traditionally been said that the Muslim and the orthodox Christian cannot both be correct in their respective beliefs about the identity of Jesus of Nazareth. Christians consider Jesus to have been the unique incarnation of the eternal, infinite God. Jesus was fully God and fully man. Muslims, on the other hand, reject as blasphemous the suggestion that Jesus was God incarnate. Although certainly a great prophet, Jesus was only a man. The disagreement between Christians and Muslims on this point is fundamental, and it would seem that while it is logically possible for both to be wrong about the identity of Jesus (perhaps he was neither God incarnate nor a great prophet), both cannot be correct. At least one view of Jesus must be false. This example presents us with the notorious problem of conflicting truth claims. As we have seen in the previous two chapters, conflicting claims are made by different religions. Which, if any, are correct?

Now while this way of looking at the matter is widespread today and seems perfectly reasonable to many, a growing number of thinkers are deeply dissatisfied with it and suggest that posing the issue in terms of conflicting truth claims is misguided from the start. One of the major charges levelled against exclusivism is that it is dependent upon notions of faith and truth which, while perhaps legitimate in other domains, are inappropriate in religion. Christian exclusivists, it is claimed, assume that the most important aspect of religion is religious belief and that the various religions advance beliefs about reality which are mutually incompatible. However, this assumption is said to be problematic on at least two counts. First, it unduly emphasizes the propositional element in religious faith. And second, it adopts an exclusivist view of truth that is out of place in religion. Even if there is a sense in ordinary life or in science in which truth can be regarded as propositional and exclusive, to think of religious truth in these terms is to indicate that one really does not understand what religious faith and truth are all about. For religious truth is not like ordinary truth; it is unique and thus not necessarily subject to the limitations inherent in ordinary truth.

This is a powerful and influential criticism that must be taken seriously. In this chapter we will examine several variations of this theme as they appear in modern theology, religious studies, and philosophy. Although particular formulations of the criticism may differ, they all have one thing in common: all agree that the notion of propositional and exclusive truth is misleading and inappropriate when applied to religion. So a proper response to these criticisms will involve defending the legitimacy of the concepts of propositional and exclusive truth in religion. I will argue that an adequate understanding of religious faith and belief — one that is epistemologically sound and accurately reflects the actual phenomena of religion — must include the notions of propositional and exclusive truth.

But before looking at specific arguments it is necessary to clarify what is meant by propositional truth. In order to appreciate what propositional truth is we must first be clear on what is meant by "proposition." Most philosophers today make a fundamental distinction between sentences and statements or propositions. The distinction is essentially between "what is said (or written)" and "what is used to say what is said." What is said is said through a sentence or by means of a sentence, but it is not identical with the sentence. Sentences are always in a given language, such as English, German, Spanish, Hindi, etc., whereas what is expressed by the sentence is not. Significantly, the same statement can be expressed in many different languages. Indeed, the same statement can be expressed in different sentences in the same language. For this and other reasons philosophers make a distinction between sentences and statements or propositions. For our purposes we can regard "statements" and "propositions" as virtually synonymous. We can roughly define a proposition as the meaning expressed by a declarative sentence or as "what is conveyed" by a sentence which makes an implicit or explicit assertion.[1] There is considerable debate among philosophers over the ontological status of propositions — just what are they and what is their relation to the mind? There is no need to enter into that rather technical discussion here, although we should emphasize that propositions cannot be identified with mental acts such as believing, judging, asserting, etc. Strictly speaking, propositions are not "in the mind," although the mind does apprehend them.

To say that truth is propositional, then, is to recognize that although "true" and "truth" can be used in a variety of ways, in the logically basic sense truth is a quality or property of propositions. That is, truth is a property of propositions such that a

---

1. Helpful introductory discussions of propositions and their relation to truth can be found in S. Gorovitz, M. Hintikka, D. Provence, and R. G. Williams, *Philosophical Analysis: An Introduction to its Language and Techniques,* 3rd ed. (New York: Random House, 1979), pp. 85-98; and Alan White, *Truth* (London: Macmillan, 1970), chap. 1. More technical discussions can be found in Ramon Lemos, "Propositions, States of Affairs, and Facts," in *The Southern Journal of Philosophy* 24 (1986): 517-30; John T. Kearns, "Sentences and Propositions," in *The Logical Enterprise,* ed. A. R. Anderson, R. B. Marcus, and R. M. Martin (New Haven: Yale University Press, 1975), pp. 61-84; and Simon Blackburn, "The Identity of Propositions," in *Meaning, Reference, and Necessity,* ed. Simon Blackburn (Cambridge: Cambridge University Press, 1975), pp. 182-205; Alonzo Church, "The Need for Abstract Entities in Semantic Analysis," in *Proceedings of the American Academy of Arts and Sciences* 80 (1951), reprinted in *Contemporary Readings in Logical Theory,* ed. Irving M. Copi and James A. Gould (New York: Macmillan, 1967), pp. 194-203.

proposition is true if and only if the state of affairs to which it refers is as the proposition asserts it to be; otherwise it is false. Thus, "John failed the math exam last Tuesday" is true if and only if John did in fact fail the math exam last Tuesday. *All* propositions are either true or false and, strictly speaking, *only* propositions are either true or false. Propositions can thus be thought of as the minimal vehicle of truth. Although this understanding of truth is widely accepted in contemporary philosophy, as we shall see, there are many in religious circles who reject it as inadequate and even misleading in religion.

Rejection of Propositional Truth

The assault upon propositional truth in religion takes a variety of forms and is prompted by a variety of factors. We will consider briefly some representative figures from theology, religious studies, and philosophy who have encouraged the tendency to disparage the notion of propositional truth in religion.

Twentieth-century theology has not looked favorably upon the idea of propositional truth. The rejection of propositional truth in much modern theology is closely related to the widespread debunking of the notion of propositional revelation. The assumption that divine revelation includes communication of propositional truth by God to humankind has been dismissed as naive scholastic rationalism by many theologians. According to a popular dictum, God does not reveal truths or propositions about himself — God reveals himself.[2] Earlier in this century, the attack upon propositional revelation was vigorously pressed by so-called "dialectical theologians," especially the early Karl Barth, Emil Brunner, and Rudolf Bultmann. Revelation, it was claimed, should not be construed in terms of communication of information about God but rather as a dynamic, dialectical encounter between God and humankind. Revelation is

2. See Avery Dulles, *Models of Revelation* (New York: Doubleday, 1983), chap. 6, and Ronald Nash, *The Word of God and the Mind of Man* (Grand Rapids: Zondervan, 1982), chap. 3.

event, the divine-human encounter, not some timeless, impersonal, static propositions about God. Although not necessarily accepting all the views of the dialectical theologians, by and large most nonevangelical theologians of the past fifty years have bought into their fundamental assumption concerning the disjunction between propositional and nonpropositional revelation (either God reveals himself or he reveals a set of propositions) and have concluded that since divine revelation involves a dynamic encounter with God it does not include a propositional dimension. Parallel to the acceptance of the nonpropositional view of revelation has been a reinterpretation of religious truth as well. For religious truth, it is said, is not propositional truth about God but consists rather in the existential encounter with God himself.

Any of a number of modern theologians could be selected to illustrate the reinterpretation of religious truth as encounter with God, but we will consider one of the most influential thinkers in the early decades of this century, the great Swiss theologian Emil Brunner. In his influential work *Truth As Encounter,* Brunner drew a sharp contrast between scientific or philosophical truth and truth in Christian faith. Whereas the former kinds of truth are concerned with propositions, truth in the biblical sense should be understood as "personal encounter."

> Truth as encounter is not truth about something, not even truth about something mental, about ideas. Rather, it is that truth which breaks in pieces the impersonal concept of truth and mind, truth that can be expressed *only* in the I-Thou form. All use of impersonal terms to describe it, the divine, the transcendent, the absolute, is indeed the inadequate way invented by the thinking of the solitary self to speak of it — or, more correctly, of Him.[3]

Truth as encounter is thus something utterly unique to religion and is not to be found in science or philosophy. In *Revelation and Reason* Brunner claimed that the "truth" in God's revelation is "the truth which may be described . . . as the encounter of the human

3. Emil Brunner, *Truth As Encounter,* 2nd ed. (Philadelphia: Westminster, 1964), p. 24. Emphasis in the original.

'I' with God's 'Thou' in Jesus Christ."[4] Although not necessarily following Brunner in all respects, many contemporary theologians accept his basic contention that religious truth is not to be construed in terms of propositional truth but rather in terms of the dynamic relation of personal encounter between the human and the divine.

From a quite different academic perspective, the Harvard historian of religion and Islamics scholar Wilfred Cantwell Smith makes a similar claim. Few scholars have exerted greater influence in the field of religious studies over the past several decades than Wilfred Cantwell Smith. And throughout his many writings Smith has been a vigorous critic of propositional truth in religion.[5] There are two major reasons for his dissatisfaction with propositional truth.

First, Smith distinguishes between what he calls the external "cumulative tradition" of religious communities and the inner faith of the religious believer.[6] The cumulative tradition is formed over a period of time and includes the various external aspects of a religious tradition that give it its peculiar identity. This is what is normally thought of when one thinks of, say, Buddhism or Islam. Smith claims, however, that far more important than this external dimension is the inner faith of the religious believer. Thus, to concentrate upon external factors such as rites, practices, beliefs, institutions, scriptures, and the like is to ignore the real dynamic, the inner essence, of religion. Smith even goes so far as to claim that it is misleading to think in terms of "a religion" (e.g., Christianity or Buddhism) as a distinct entity, since to do so obscures the fact that what really matters is the personal religious faith of believers (regardless of their particular religious affiliation) and not the external trappings of various religious communities.

The second reason for Smith's rejection of propositional

4. Idem, *Revelation and Reason,* trans. Olive Wyon (Philadelphia: Westminster, 1946), p. 171.

5. The Indian theologian Stanley Samartha is also a sharp critic of propositional truth in religion. See Samartha's *Courage for Dialogue* (Maryknoll, N.Y.: Orbis, 1981), pp. 11, 42, 144-57.

6. Cf. Wilfred Cantwell Smith, *The Meaning and End of Religion* (New York: Harper & Row, 1962).

truth in religion follows from the first. If beliefs and doctrines are of only secondary importance and if what really matters in religion is the inner faith of the believer, then it follows that we should not think of religious truth in terms of propositional truth — that is, the truth of beliefs or doctrines — but rather the "personal truth" of the faith of religious persons. Religious truth, then, is not a matter of the beliefs and doctrines of a given religion being objectively true, since in religion "one has to do not with religions, but with religious persons."[7]

Smith is not saying that we cannot speak of truth in religion, that the term "truth" is inapplicable in religion. But he is asserting that religious truth is different from concepts of truth found in ordinary life or in the sciences. And he emphatically rejects the idea that religious truth is propositional truth. "Truth, I submit, is a humane, not an objective, concept. It does not lie in propositions."[8]

> Truth and falsity are often felt in modern times to be properties or functions of statements or propositions; whereas the present proposal is that much is to be gained by seeing them rather, or anyway seeing them also, and primarily, as properties or functions of persons.[9]

If religious truth is not propositional, what is it? The alternative suggested by Smith is personal truth. "Human behaviour, in word or deed, is the nexus between man's inner life and the surrounding world. Truth at the personalistic level is that quality by which both halves of that relationship are chaste and appropriate; are true."[10] Now it is not entirely clear just what is meant by personal truth, but what is intended seems to be something like the following: The locus of truth is not propositions, statements, or beliefs, but rather is in persons. Religious truth does not reflect

7. Ibid., p. 153.
8. Idem, *Towards a World Theology* (Philadelphia: Westminster, 1981), p. 190.
9. Idem, "A Human View of Truth," in *Truth and Dialogue in World Religions,* ed. John H. Hick (Philadelphia: Westminster, 1974), p. 20.
10. Ibid., p. 26.

correspondence with reality so much as it signifies integrity, sincerity, faithfulness, authenticity of life, and existentially appropriating certain beliefs in one's life and conduct. Thus, religious traditions

> can be seen as more or less true in the sense of enabling those who look at life and the universe through their patterns to perceive smaller or larger, less important or more important, areas of reality, to formulate and to ponder less or more significant issues, to act less or more truly, less or more truly to be.[11]

Truth is not a static property of propositions or doctrines but rather a dynamic product of human involvement with what is said to be true. Personal truth is not something detached from actual life; it demands existential appropriation. "No statement might be accepted as true that has not been inwardly appropriated by its author."[12] Thus, personal truth is not an abstract truth which leaves unaffected the moral character and private behavior of those who know it. It is a transforming, life-changing truth.

Furthermore, Smith claims that personal truth is not static and unchanging. Statements, beliefs, and even religious traditions can become true, or they might be "true for me" but "false for you." A religious tradition "becomes more or less true in the case of particular persons as it informs their lives and their groups and shapes and nurtures their faith."[13]

> Christianity, I would suggest, is not true absolutely, impersonally, statically; rather, it can *become* true, if and as you or I appropriate it to ourselves and interiorize it, insofar as we live it out from day to day. It becomes true as we take it off the shelf and personalize it, in actual existence.[14]

Obviously, acceptance of the notion of personal truth will have far-reaching consequences for the way in which we regard the

---

11. *Towards a World Theology,* p. 94.
12. "A Human View of Truth," p. 35.
13. *Towards a World Theology,* p. 187.
14. Idem, *Questions of Religious Truth* (London: Victor Gollancz, 1967), pp. 67-68. Emphasis in the original.

relation among different religions. Instead of considering truth and falsity to be properties of propositions (or beliefs) that are accepted by believers in the respective traditions, truth will be viewed as a changing, dynamic product of the faith of religious individuals. The assumptions that religious beliefs are central to religious traditions, that they have objective truth value, and that on occasion beliefs from different religions conflict with each other — these will have to be discarded as misleading at best. No longer will it make sense to speak of, say, the truth of the doctrine of the Incarnation without also making reference to the personal response of faith to the doctrine. The doctrine could not be said to be true or false in and of itself. We could only say that it is true for someone, and it would only be true to the extent that someone existentially appropriated belief in the doctrine. Thus, while the doctrine of the Incarnation might be "true for Joe" it could simultaneously be "false for Linda" insofar as she failed to existentially appropriate belief in the doctrine. We could no longer speak of a particular religion, such as Christianity, being true in and of itself. It would be "true" only to the extent that individual Christians appropriate its teachings and traditions and are significantly affected in their lives by it. Similarly, it would make little sense to speak of one religion being true and others false, for presumably there are devout believers in all religions who are transformed existentially by their respective traditions. In this sense, all religions could be considered "true" — or at least true for those believers who happen to appropriate the beliefs and practices of the respective religions. It is evident, then, that Smith's proposal is a radical reinterpretation of the concept of truth in religion.

The attack upon propositional truth in religion is to be found in recent analytic philosophy as well. Although there are welcome signs that this is now changing, Anglo-American philosophy of religion during the past forty years or so has been largely preoccupied with questions of the meaning of religious discourse. An influential movement within analytic philosophy has held that, properly understood, religious utterances are not expressions of propositions about objective reality that are either true or false but rather serve other, noncognitive functions. And those who accept this view are generally said to be noncognitivists with respect to religious language.

In his influential 1955 Arthur Stanley Eddington Memorial Lecture, R. B. Braithwaite argued that religious discourse should not be understood as including cognitively meaningful statements about reality that are either true or false.[15] Religious statements, he maintained, should instead be viewed as somewhat analogous to moral statements, or as the expression of an intention to live in a particular manner. For example, the Christian's statement that God is love (agape) should be understood not as an assertion about the ontological nature of reality but as an expression of the Christian's "intention to follow an agapeistic way of life."[16] What is distinctive about religious discourse, as opposed to strictly ethical discourse, is its association with certain "stories" (myths, parables, teachings) that help to inspire and regulate the desired behavior. Braithwaite contends that it is not necessary that these stories be in any sense objectively true — or even thought to be true — since their connection with the believer's behavior is of a purely psychological nature. Thus, for Braithwaite a religious statement is "the assertion of an intention to carry out a certain behavior policy, subsumable under a sufficiently general principle to be a moral one, together with the implicit or explicit statement, but not assertion, of certain stories."[17]

What, then, of the apparent differences between various religions? Are we not to conclude, then, that the differences between the teachings of Christianity and Buddhism are indicative of fundamental disagreements about the nature of reality? Braithwaite considers this problem and suggests that although the Buddhist and the Christian might well advocate virtually identical "ways of life," this does not mean that there is no distinction between Christian statements and Buddhist statements. The difference between the

15. R. B. Braithwaite, "An Empiricist's View of the Nature of Religious Belief," in *The Philosophy of Religion*, ed. Basil Mitchell (Oxford: Oxford University Press, 1971), pp. 72-91.

16. Ibid., p. 81.

17. Ibid., p. 89.

statements is, however, not to be taken as indicative of disagreement about the truth value of certain propositions. Rather, the fundamental difference between the two is that "the intentions to pursue the behavior policies, which may be the same for different religions, are associated with thinking of different *stories* (or sets of stories)."[18] Thus, according to Braithwaite, although the ways of life advocated by Christianity and Buddhism are essentially the same, it is the fact that the intention to follow this way of life is for the Christian associated with Christian stories, and for the Buddhist associated with Buddhist stories, that enables one to distinguish Christian discourse from Buddhist discourse.

The Cambridge philosopher Ludwig Wittgenstein (d. 1951) has had an enormous influence upon recent analytic philosophy. Although he was primarily interested in problems in the philosophy of mind, language, and mathematics, his views have had significant impact upon discussions of religious language.[19] Wittgenstein emphasized the importance of understanding the relevant "form of life" and "language game" in which a particular kind of discourse occurs if we are to understand the discourse in question. There are many kinds of discourse, and one must be sensitive to the context and circumstances in which each kind occurs if one is to understand what is said. For example, the word "strike" will have different meanings depending upon the language game in which it is used. "Strike" means one thing in the language game of baseball; it has an entirely different meaning in the language game of a labor dispute. One can only understand the meaning of "strike" on any given occasion if he or she is sufficiently familiar

18. Ibid., p. 84. Emphasis in original.
19. Particularly influential have been Wittgenstein's posthumously published *Philosophical Investigations,* trans. G. E. M. Anscombe (New York: Macmillan, 1958). Also important are his *Lectures and Conversations on Aesthetics, Psychology, and Religious Belief,* ed. C. Barrett (Oxford: Oxford University Press, 1966) and *Culture and Value,* ed. G. H. von Wright, trans. Peter Winch (Chicago: University of Chicago Press, 1980). For a helpful introduction to Wittgenstein's thought in relation to religion see W. Donald Hudson, *Wittgenstein and Religious Belief* (London: Macmillan, 1975), and Patrick Sherry, *Religion, Truth, and Language Games* (London: Macmillan, 1977), chaps. 1 and 2.

with the language game and the accompanying form of life (relevant practices, beliefs, goals, etc.) in which it occurs. Similarly, in order to understand the meaning of the language of Christian faith one must first become well acquainted with the discourse environment of Christian faith and practice.

There is considerable dispute over just what Wittgenstein's own views on the nature of religious language were, but it is clear that he at least minimizes, and perhaps denies entirely, the cognitive or propositional element in religious discourse. Religious utterances are not to be considered expressions of statements of "fact" or propositions referring to external, objective states of affairs "out there" in the world. Rather, they are to be thought of as "pictures" which regulate the lives of believers. Moreover, he held that it is misleading to think of the dispute between believers and nonbelievers as disagreement over matters of "fact." For example, Wittgenstein considers the Christian belief in the Last Judgment. It is not that the believer and the nonbeliever disagree over the truth value of a particular proposition — "There will be a Last Judgment" — which is understood to refer to an objective, extramental state of affairs. Rather, the disagreement reflects the fact that the two are involved in entirely different forms of life and language games. It is not a disagreement over questions of "fact" but rather the conflict of two different "pictures," resulting in two radically different forms of life. Taking another example, Wittgenstein notes that some people regard illness as a punishment from God, whereas others (including Wittgenstein) do not. Is the dispute here over a question of "fact," with one party holding true beliefs and the other false beliefs? Not so, according to Wittgenstein. The dispute here is not really a disagreement over the nature of reality at all. Wittgenstein says, "you can call it believing the opposite but it is entirely different from what we normally call believing the opposite. I think differently, in a different way. I say different things to myself. I have different pictures."[20]

D. Z. Phillips is one of a number of contemporary philos-

---

20. Wittgenstein, *Lectures and Conversations on Aesthetics, Psychology, and Religious Belief,* p. 55.

ophers who have applied Wittgenstein's notions of forms of life and language games to religion.[21] More so than Wittgenstein, however, Phillips emphasizes the uniqueness and autonomy of the religious form of life. Each language game is said to have its own internal criteria for determining what is true or false within that universe of discourse and cannot be evaluated on the basis of criteria external to that language game. The meanings of terms such as "real," "unreal," "rational," and "irrational" thus differ from context to context. And religious statements cannot be understood or appraised on the basis of criteria external to the religious language game, such as that of philosophy or the sciences. Phillips asserts that "[a] necessary prolegomenon to the philosophy of religion, then, is to show the diversity of criteria of rationality."[22] Not only does religion in general constitute a distinct form of life with its own language game, but various religious traditions can also be regarded as having their own language games. Criteria for assessment are thus internal to each religious tradition; there are no neutral or independent criteria on the basis of which we can say one religion is true and others false.[23]

Phillips would be unhappy with the Christian exclusivist's suggestion that various religions advance mutually conflicting truth claims. For to think in these terms is really to misunderstand the status of religious discourse. Phillips holds that religious statements are not assertions of "fact" or the nature of objective reality. They are not expressions of propositions which can be either true or false. For example, the belief in immortality — central to many religions — should not be understood as a factual assertion about actual life after death, an assertion which, if true, will be confirmed in future experience. Rather, it expresses a particular way of looking at life in the present.

21. See especially D. Z. Phillips, *Death and Immortality* (London: Macmillan, 1970); *The Concept of Prayer* (London: Routledge & Kegan Paul, 1965); *Religion Without Explanation* (Oxford: Basil Blackwell, 1976); *Faith and Philosophical Enquiry* (New York: Schocken Books, 1970).

22. D. Z. Phillips, *Faith and Philosophical Enquiry*, p. 17. As quoted in Patrick Sherry, *Religion, Truth, and Language Games*, p. 27.

23. Ibid., pp. 4, 246.

Eternal life is the reality of goodness, that in terms of which
human life is to be assessed. . . . Questions about the immortality
of the soul are seen not to be questions concerning the extent of
a man's life, and in particular concerning whether that life can
extend beyond the grave, but questions concerning the kind of
life a man is living.[24]

Although neither Wittgenstein nor Phillips is primarily
concerned with questions of religious pluralism, it is easy enough
to draw out the implications of their views for this subject. It
would be consistent with their views to hold that, just as the
believer and the nonbeliever are not in fundamental disagreement over questions of "fact," so Muslims, Hindus, Buddhists,
and Christians are not actually disagreeing over the truth value
of certain propositions. The dispute is not over the truth or
falsity of a statement such as, "Jesus Christ was the eternal creator God incarnate." Rather, the differences between religions are
simply the result of the fact that the various religions accept
different "pictures" which then regulate different forms of life.
Christian exclusivism, then, errs in viewing the differences as
actual disagreements between religions about questions of "fact,"
since in actuality no such claims about reality are being made.
The problem of conflicting truth claims, then, can be dismissed
as a kind of pseudo-problem, for in reality no truth claims are
being made.

  We have looked at some influential criticisms of the assumption that religious truth should be understood in terms of
propositional truth. If these criticisms are sound, then clearly the
traditional understanding of Christian exclusivism is untenable.
But careful consideration of each of the above positions shows
them to be seriously deficient.

  1. We noted that, among theologians, the tendency to understand religious truth as excluding propositional truth was
prompted in part by the move toward a nonpropositional view of
divine revelation. Many contemporary theologians regard the dis-

24. *Death and Immortality*, pp. 48-49.

tinction between propositional and nonpropositional truth as an exclusive disjunction — one must choose either propositional revelation or nonpropositional revelation, but not both. God either reveals himself or he reveals propositions about himself to humankind. But surely, construing the matter in these terms is mistaken. An account of divine revelation that is faithful to Scripture and epistemologically sound will include both propositional and nonpropositional revelation.[25] Clearly, divine revelation cannot be strictly identified with a set of propositions. Jesus is the supreme revelation of God (Heb. 1:1-3; John 1:18; Col. 2:9), yet Jesus is not a proposition. However, insofar as revelation is informative about God — and surely this is the whole point in divine revelation in the first place — it must be capable of being expressed propositionally. It is simply nonsensical to think in terms of knowledge of God that is nonpropositional. If the propositional element is eliminated from divine revelation, whatever else one is left with, it cannot be informative about God.

Once the necessity of including propositional revelation in an adequate account of revelation is recognized, the importance of propositional truth for religion will also be apparent. As we have seen, Brunner's primary concern is with the personal response of the believer to God. Central to his notion of truth as encounter is the dynamic interrelation between God and the believer. However, it is naive and misleading to present the alternatives here as an exclusive disjunction — either one has propositional truth about God or one has an existential encounter with God, but not both. Not only is it possible to have both, one cannot respond appropriately to God without first having some knowledge of God. The believer can only respond personally to God as Lord and Savior if he or she already knows something about what God is like and what he expects from humankind. And the more one knows about God the more one will be able to know God personally and respond appropriately to him. As Nash puts it, "Personal encounter cannot

25. Cf. Nash, *The Word of God*, pp. 46-49, and Paul Helm, *Divine Revelation* (London: Marshall, Morgan, & Scott, 1982), pp. 21-26; and Colin Brown, *History and Faith: A Personal Exploration* (Grand Rapids: Zondervan, 1987), chap. 4.

take place in a cognitive vacuum."[26] To say that God reveals himself in divine revelation, if meant to be informative, is to imply, among other things, that he communicates some knowledge, some truth, about himself. Therefore, to eliminate the notion of propositional truth from divine revelation is to reduce revelation to an epistemologically vacuous concept. Furthermore, we must reject the assumption, implicit in much contemporary theology, that propositional revelation is abstract, detached, cold, and incapable of eliciting more than a bland intellectual response of mental assent from believers. There is no reason why we must suppose that propositions about God cannot prompt powerful and moving personal responses from believers. Propositions may indeed be "response evoking," as Paul Helm puts it, particularly if the propositions have to do with the nature of God (e.g., his love) and what he has graciously done for humankind.[27]

2. Wilfred Cantwell Smith's insistence that we concentrate upon the inner faith of religious believers and not upon the external cumulative tradition is really largely irrelevant to the question of propositional truth in religion. Even if it is granted that the notion of "a religion" as a distinct entity is somehow misguided,[28] the problem of the status of religious beliefs and their truth value remains. For we would still have individuals who accept and propagate certain beliefs, dogmas, and teachings, all presumably accepted by believers as true. We would still have, for example, the Christian theologian Augustine asserting that an omnipotent God created the universe ex nihilo and the Buddhist Vasubandhu maintaining that it is simply the product of karmic effect. So merely shifting the focus from religions as such to the religious faith of believers will not rid us of the question of the truth value of the beliefs endorsed by the various traditions.

3. Although Smith's notion of personal truth is based upon an important insight, if it is meant to exclude the concept of

---

26. Nash, *The Word of God*, pp. 46f.

27. Cf. Helm, *Divine Revelation*, p. 27.

28. But see the incisive critique of Smith's claim by Ninian Smart, "Truth and Religions," in *Truth and Dialogue*, pp. 45-47.

propositional truth it is seriously confused. Certainly the personal
dimension is important in religion. Religion is a complex dynamic
centered upon the experience and religious faith of individual
believers. And Smith correctly emphasizes that religious faith cannot be reduced to mere intellectual assent to a set of propositions.
Integral to religious faith is the idea that one must appropriate
certain beliefs so that one's conduct and character are significantly
altered — we are to be doers of the Word and not hearers only!
From this legitimate insight, however, Smith proceeds to construct
a theory of religious truth that is highly problematic.

It is helpful here to distinguish three frequently conflated
concepts — faith, belief, and truth. "Faith" can be used in two
distinct senses, the difference between the two being indicated by
the Latin words *fiducia* and *fides*, both of which are translated into
English as "faith." *Fiducia* refers to faith as trust in or commitment
to God. *Fides* signifies belief that certain propositions about God
are true.[29] Now it is important to see that faith as *fiducia* is logically
dependent upon faith as *fides*. Faith in *x* (trust in or commitment
to *x*) presupposes acceptance of certain beliefs about *x*.[30] Trust in
God presupposes that certain propositions about God (that he is
reliable, trustworthy, etc.) are true. Although there is some overlap
in the meanings of "faith" and "belief," for our purposes it will be
helpful to restrict use of "faith" to indicate *fiducia* — that is, the
personal response of trust and commitment to God or the appropriate religious ultimate. "Belief" should then be used to mean
faith as *fides* or the acceptance of certain propositions about God
as true. "Truth" should not be used to mean faith in either of these
senses, but, as I argue in this chapter, should be understood primarily as a property of propositions or statements. With these

29. See the discussion by John Hick in *Faith and Knowledge,* 2nd ed.
(London: Macmillan, 1987), pp. 3-4. See also the excellent article by H. H. Price,
"Belief 'In' and Belief 'That,' " in *The Philosophy of Religion,* ed. Basil Mitchell, pp.
143-67.

30. "In any sphere the fact of commitment logically entails certain beliefs
and precludes certain others. One must believe in the truth of what one is committed to." Roger Trigg, *Reason and Commitment* (London: Cambridge University
Press, 1973), p. 44.

distinctions in mind, let us return to Smith's proposal of personal truth.

There is a pervasive ambiguity in Smith's discussions of personal truth which allows for at least three possible interpretations:

(1) Personal truth can legitimately be applied to religion whereas propositional truth cannot.
(2) Both personal truth and propositional truth can be applied to religion, but personal truth is somehow more basic and fundamental than propositional truth.
(3) Both personal truth and propositional truth can be applied to religion, but propositional truth is more basic than personal truth.

Careful reflection shows that only (3) is epistemologically tenable. The major difficulty with both (1) and (2) is the fact that epistemologically the most basic notion of truth in any realm whatsoever is propositional truth. To be sure, "truth" and "true" have a wide variety of meanings in ordinary discourse. We can say "the purse is true alligator," "he is a true Democrat," "Jesus is the Truth," "her music is full of truth," or "his presentation this morning just didn't have the ring of truth." And in religion "truth" is often used to mean something like "ultimate significance," "ultimate meaning or purpose," "that which radically transforms one." Without question, both Smith's notion of "personal truth" and Brunner's concept of "truth as encounter" are based upon important insights about how religious truth affects believers. But as theories about the nature of religious truth, as definitions of religious truth, they are inadequate since they fail to recognize that there is an important sense in which propositional truth is logically basic and is presupposed by all other uses of "truth."

This can be demonstrated as follows. Let us use P to stand for the statement of Smith's theory of personal truth.

P: In religion truth is primarily personal, not propositional, and has its locus in persons who satisfactorily appropriate religious beliefs.

It is crucial to see that if P is offered as something we should accept as true (and surely this is Smith's intention), then it is itself dependent upon the notion of propositional truth. For P expresses a proposition that makes a claim about reality: it asserts that reality is such that truth is primarily personal and has its locus in persons who satisfactorily appropriate religious beliefs. Thus, in proposing P for acceptance Smith is suggesting that we accept it because it is true — that is, that reality actually is as the proposition expressed by P asserts it to be. Now the sense in which P is presumed to be true is not that of personal truth. For if P were said to be true only in the sense of personal truth, then it would be true only insofar as you or I appropriate it and allow it to impact significantly upon our lives. P might then be true for Smith but false for me, or true for me but false for you. But clearly this is not what Smith has in mind. Therefore, in advancing and arguing for his theory he is implicitly assuming that it is true in the logically basic sense of propositional truth.

The inadequacy of the concept of personal truth can be seen from a different perspective. Smith's suggestion that religious beliefs become true to the extent that they are internalized and appropriated — if meant to exclude the notion of propositional truth — is highly confused. For a believer will only appropriate such beliefs if he or she already accepts them as true in a nonpersonalistic or propositional sense. For example, the belief that Allah is a righteous judge will "become true" in a personal sense only if the Muslim first accepts as true the proposition expressed by "Allah is a righteous judge."[31] We can readily admit that "true" can be used to mean something like "authentic," "genuine," "faithful," "sincere," etc. When used in this sense, religious truth would be a quality of life in the believer such that there are no glaring inconsistencies between what one professes and the manner in which one lives. To affirm that "Allah is a righteous judge" is true, on this understanding of "true," would then be to recognize that a particular Muslim's life is congruous with belief that Allah is a righteous

31. I am indebted here to the fine essay by William Wainwright, "Wilfred Cantwell Smith on Faith and Belief," in *Religious Studies* 20 (September 1984).

judge. But this presupposes that the Muslim accepts and appropriates not only a certain set of practices and a manner of life but also a set of beliefs and values which taken together articulate a comprehensive perspective on reality. And such basic beliefs will be accepted in the first place because the Muslim regards them as accurately portraying the way reality actually is. Thus, the fundamental beliefs defining the Muslim's worldview (e.g., "Allah is a righteous judge") are accepted as true, not in a personal but in a propositional sense. But if so, personal truth cannot be regarded as an alternative to propositional truth, for it actually presupposes propositional truth. Philosopher Donald Wiebe has astutely remarked that Wilfred Cantwell Smith confuses the question of truth with that of the believer's response to the truth.[32] But the truth value of a belief and the degree to which one allows that belief to impact one's life are two very different matters.

4. Wittgenstein and later analytic philosophers are correct in pointing out the importance of understanding the relevant forms of life and language games of religion if one is to understand the statements of religious believers. It is ironic, however, that noncognitivists such as Wittgenstein and Phillips appear to have failed to take their own advice sufficiently seriously, for their views give little indication of understanding the ways believers actually use religious language. Certainly some religious language serves noncognitivist functions (e.g., the Bible is full of expressions of praise, worship, questions, and exclamations; religious stories are used to encourage desired patterns of behavior, etc.). But it can hardly be denied that many, if not most, religious believers do indeed intend to make statements about the actual nature of reality that are true. When the Christian speaks of God creating the universe or about eternal life after death, when the Buddhist speaks of release from *samsara* through the Four Noble Truths and the Noble Eightfold Path, or when the Hindu speaks of the effects of *karma*, they normally intend to be making assertions about the nature of reality. That believers in the respective traditions accept

32. Donald Wiebe, *Truth and Religion: Towards an Alternative Paradigm for the Study of Religion* (The Hague: Mouton, 1981), p. 213.

such statements as true is indicated by the fact that if the believer can be convinced that the ultimate reality with which one deals (e.g., God, Allah, Brahman) has no objective existence, then the believer's religious faith usually vanishes. The suggestion that religious believers really do not intend to make truth claims in their statements is indicative of a fundamental failure to understand the religious "language game" on its terms. The noncognitivist theory is not an accurate account of how people do in fact engage in religious discourse but rather a radical proposal for a fresh interpretation of religious language. The comments of philosopher Dorothy Emmet are very much to the point:

> [R]eligious thinking may well have other concerns besides the epistemological question of the relation of our ideas to reality beyond ourselves . . . but . . . [it] loses its nerve when it ceases to believe that it expresses in some way truth about our relation to a reality beyond ourselves which ultimately concerns us.[33]

Believers are not so unconcerned with questions of truth as noncognitivists suggest. Braithwaite, Wittgenstein, and Phillips all speak of certain "stories" or "pictures" that are used within the religious language game to inspire and regulate a particular way of life. Braithwaite explicitly states that the truth or falsity of such stories is irrelevant to the believer. But this is difficult indeed to accept. It is hard to see how religious discourse could have the desired effect upon believers' lives unless the central beliefs associated with such stories and pictures are accepted by the believers as true. One does not normally simply choose to follow a particular way of life and accord it the kind of commitment found in religious faith entirely apart from considerations of the truth or falsity of central beliefs associated with that way of life.[34]

It seems undeniable that beliefs about the nature of reality

---

33. Dorothy Emmet, *The Nature of Metaphysical Thinking* (London: Macmillan, 1966), p. 7.

34. For a more extensive discussion of the inadequacies of the noncognitivist view see Roger Trigg, *Reason and Commitment,* and Patrick Sherry, *Religion, Truth, and Language Games.*

are integral to religious traditions. The various religions advance many different and even conflicting claims about the nature of reality. While undoubtedly such claims do serve a variety of functions, it is crucial to recognize that they are accepted by religious believers within the respective traditions as true. As Donald Wiebe observes, "talk of truth in religion must concern itself primarily with belief."[35] Even in religion one cannot escape the epistemologically basic notion of propositional truth. To be sure, religious discourse differs significantly from, say, scientific discourse or political discourse. And religious faith does include, in some sense, an existential involvement with the object of one's faith. But none of this should obscure the fact that even in religion the notion of propositional truth is ineradicable.

Religious Truth as Ineffable

A possible objection to the assertion that propositional truth is inescapable in religion comes from those who argue that religious beliefs and doctrines are really no more than inadequate attempts to express what is essentially inexpressible — the ineffable core of religious truth. Beliefs and doctrines are really just inadequate pointers toward what cannot be clearly articulated. Religious truth is essentially ineffable; it cannot be expressed in neat propositions but can only be directly intuited. The important thing is not the beliefs themselves but rather what they point toward. It is like the proverbial finger pointing toward the moon. If one concentrates upon the finger itself, instead of what it is pointing at, one will never see the moon. Focusing upon doctrines, then, is like mistaking the finger for the moon.

In his classic work *Das Heilige*, Rudolf Otto suggested that the idea of the holy, of holiness as such, is fundamental to all religious belief and practice. And essential to the idea of the holy is the notion of a verbally and conceptually indefinable "otherness" which Otto signified by the term "numinous." The numinous is

35. Donald Wiebe, *Truth and Religion*, p. 185.

experienced as *mysterium tremendum et fascinans* — that is, as a mystery both awe-inspiring and fascinating, simultaneously the object of both fear and desire. A good example of how one responds when confronted by the numinous is found in Isaiah 6:5, where, after seeing the vision of the exalted Lord, the prophet cries out, "Woe is me! . . . for I am a man of unclean lips!" Otto claimed that too much attention has been given the rational dimension in religion and thus he concentrated upon the nonrational (as opposed to irrational) aspect of religion. According to Otto, the numinous cannot be rationally analyzed or comprehended. Although it can be recognized and identified when encountered, it "completely eludes apprehension in terms of concepts."[36] It can only be experienced through a kind of intuition.

The incomprehensibility of God is, of course, a major theme in the history of Christian thought. God is an infinite Being far exceeding human concepts and language. The following statement by the early church father Chrysostom is typical of many writers through the centuries who have emphasized God's incomprehensibility:

> [W]e call Him the inexpressible, the unthinkable God, the invisible, the inapprehensible; who quells the power of human speech and transcends the grasp of mortal thought; inaccessible to the angels, unbeheld by the Seraphim, unimagined of the Cherubim, invisible to principalities and authorities and powers, and, in a word, to all creation.[37]

Similarly, Gregory of Nyssa stated that God is "incapable of being grasped by any term, or any idea, or any other device of our apprehension."[38]

In thinking about God, there is a long and venerable tradi-

36. Rudolf Otto, *Das Heilige,* trans. by J. Harvey as *The Idea of the Holy* (New York: Oxford University Press, 1950), pp. 5-6.

37. Chrysostom, third discourse of "De Incomprehensibili," as quoted in Otto, *Idea of the Holy,* p. 180.

38. Gregory of Nyssa, "Against Eunomius," bk. 1, sec. 42, in *A Select Library of Nicene and Post-Nicene Fathers of the Christian Church,* ed. P. Schaff, 2nd series, vol. 5 (Grand Rapids: Eerdmans, 1954), p. 99.

tion in Christian theology of the *via negativa,* the negative way. Pseudo-Dionysius (6th century), Meister Eckhart (13th century), and Nicholas of Cusa (15th century), among others, made use of the way of negation in speaking of God. But probably the most sophisticated argument for the *via negativa* is found not in a Christian theologian but in the Jewish philosopher Moses Maimonides (13th century).[39] Maimonides claimed that although we can know of the acts of God no positive statements at all can be made about the nature of God unless the predicate terms (e.g., "wise," "good") are given meanings entirely different from the meanings of the terms when predicated of finite creatures. We cannot speak positively of what God is; we can only speak negatively of what God is not. No human concepts or linguistic terms can be applied to God since God utterly transcends all human categories.

The idea that the religious ultimate is beyond any possible description and cannot be expressed in linguistic terms is a common theme in non-Christian religions as well.[40] The Tao (Way) of Taoism is said to be indescribable, indefinable, incapable of being grasped by human thought. The Taoist classic Tao-te-Ching begins with the enigmatic statement, "The way [Tao] that can be spoken of is not the constant way; The name that can be named is not the constant name."[41] The Tao is said to be "forever nameless."[42] The suspicion of verbal expression is apparent in the warning, "One

39. Cf. Moses Maimonides, *Guide for the Perplexed,* 2nd ed., trans. M. Friedlander (London: George Routledge & Sons, 1940).

40. "Therefore, let every disciple take good heed not to become attached to words as being in perfect conformity with meaning, because Truth is not in the letters. When a man with his finger-tip points to something to somebody, the finger-tip may be mistaken for the thing pointed at; in like manner the ignorant and simple-minded, like children, are unable even to the day of their death to abandon the idea that in the finger-tip of words there is the meaning itself. They cannot realize Ultimate Reality because of their clinging to words which were intended to be no more than a pointing finger." *Self-Realization of Noble Wisdom: The Lankavatara Sutra,* compiled by Dwight Goddard (Clearlake, Cal.: Dawn Horse Press, 1932), p. 92.

41. *Lao Tzu: Tao Te Ching,* translated and with introduction by D. C. Lau (New York: Penguin Books, 1963), p. 57.

42. Ibid., p. 91.

who knows does not speak; one who speaks does not know."[43] Zen Buddhism, heavily influenced by Taoism, similarly rejects the idea that the Buddhist *dharma,* or ultimate Truth, can be expressed in language; it is passed on directly from *roshi* (master) to disciple. The Zen master Daiei claimed that "Zen has no words: when you have *satori* [enlightenment] you have everything."[44] And in Advaita Vedanta Hinduism there is the concept of the *nirguna* Brahman, the totally unqualified Brahman, the absolutely undifferentiated Being which is devoid of all qualities and attributes. Any attempt to ascribe names, qualities, and form to it is the result of ignorance *(avidya)* stemming from illusion *(maya).*

Given this strong tradition which in various religions maintains that the religious ultimate cannot be captured in conceptual and linguistic categories, one might argue that surely it is a serious error to concentrate so much upon matters of belief and doctrine and their alleged truth value. After all, beliefs and doctrines are no more than inadequate pointers toward that which ultimately is inexpressible. Religious truth cannot be neatly expressed in propositions either true or false. Therefore, to focus upon the beliefs of various religions, and especially to be concerned over any apparent conflict between beliefs, indicates a failure to appreciate what religious truth is really all about.

This objection must not be cavalierly dismissed, for it is based upon the legitimate insight that the religious ultimate is transcendent and far exceeds the grasp of the human intellect. The religious ultimate, whether conceived of as God, Allah, or Brahman, is held to be categorially unique and incapable of being identified with objects from the finite world with which we are familiar. The problem here, however, is how to understand the transcendence and uniqueness of the religious ultimate in such a way that both the "otherness" of the religious ultimate is preserved and the possibility of genuine knowledge of this ultimate is maintained. A full treatment of this problem would involve us in some

    43. Ibid., p. 117.
    44. Quoted in D. T. Suzuki, *Essays in Zen Buddhism,* 2nd series, ed. Christmas Humphreys (New York: Samuel Weiser, 1953), p. 31.

of the central issues in the epistemology of religion and thus cannot be pursued here. But several important points should be noted. Although the following discussion deals with the problem within the context of Christian theism, similar points could be made concerning the alleged ineffability of the religious ultimate in other traditions as well.

We should begin by observing that there is a legitimate sense in which God can be said to be "beyond the scope" of human conceptual and linguistic categories. God is transcendent and infinite whereas we are finite creatures. God is utterly unique and categorically distinct. Any attempt to identify him with finite objects or categories with which we are familiar will be misleading and even idolatrous. Thus there is an important sense in which we must think of God as the ultimate Mystery.

It does not follow from this, however, that none of our concepts and linguistic terms can be applied meaningfully to God. The question is how we are to understand God's transcendence. In a seminal study, W. D. Hudson observed that there are two distinct senses in which we can say that God is "wholly other," incomprehensible, and beyond the grasp of our intellect.[45] The difference between the two can be seen in the ways in which they respectively answer the question, "Can God coherently be described in human language as ordinarily used?" On the one hand, one tradition claims that no coherent descriptions of God can be formulated in language. We might call this the ineffability thesis. On the other hand, a different tradition maintains that coherent descriptions of God's nature and activity can be formulated in human language, although such descriptions have their limitations and must be interpreted appropriately. The latter position has been characteristic of most Protestant and Catholic theology.

45. W. D. Hudson, "The Concept of Divine Transcendence," *Religious Studies* 15 (1979): 197. For helpful discussions of some of the epistemological issues involved see also W. A. Alston, "Ineffability," *The Philosophical Review* 65 (1956): 506-22; Keith Yandell, "Some Varieties of Ineffability," *International Journal for the Philosophy of Religion* 6 (1975): 167-79 and "The Ineffability Theme," *International Journal for the Philosophy of Religion* 10 (1979): 209-31; Steven Katz, ed., *Mysticism and Philosophical Analysis* (New York: Oxford University Press, 1978).

The major problem with the ineffability thesis is the difficulty of stating it in such a way that it is coherent (not self-refuting)
and also preserves the possibility of knowledge about God. An
extreme form of the thesis is as follows:

(1) No meaningful and informative statements about God can be
     made.

This is ineffability with a vengeance. But this thesis is clearly inadequate for at least two reasons. First, it rules out the possibility
of any knowledge of God by implying that no true or false statements about God can be made. Not only is this theologically
unacceptable, but we must also ask on what basis such a categorical
denial of knowledge of God can be made. Second, this thesis is
self-refuting. It does express a statement about God — namely,
that the nature of God being what it is no meaningful statements
about him can be made. So the assertion of (1) is actually incompatible with (1) itself.

A modified formulation of the ineffability thesis is that

(2) No concepts at all can be applied to God.

In order to appreciate this statement, we must be clear on what is
meant by "concept." We might say that to have a concept of some
entity x is, roughly, to know the meaning of the word x, to be able
to pick out and recognize an instance of x, and to have a grasp of
the properties which distinguish x. Concepts are essentially linked
to properties, attributes, or qualities. To ascribe a property to an
object (e.g., "The ball is red") is to apply a concept, or collection
of concepts, to that object.

Now if concepts are essentially linked to properties and if
no concepts at all can be applied to God, then it follows that no
properties at all can be ascribed to God. It would follow further
that no truths about God could be known. For to know a truth
about God is to know that some proposition p about God is true.
If p is a true proposition about God it will attribute some property
to God; it will be a statement about God's nature, activities, desires,

relation to creation, and so on. To say "God is merciful" is to ascribe the property of being merciful to God. But according to (2), since no concepts can be applied to God, no properties can be ascribed to him either. It follows, then, that no truths about God can be known.

Paradoxically, if this thesis were true, we could never know that it is true. For if true, it would express a true proposition about God. But as we have seen, (2) entails that no truths about God can be known. Thus, if true, we could never know that it is true. It is possible also to argue that this thesis is self-refuting since it ascribes a concept (the concept of "being unconceptualizable") to God. But if even one concept is applicable to God, then (2) cannot be true. Thus the assertion of this thesis actually falsifies it. If, on the other hand, (2) is interpreted as not applying any concept to God, then it is hard to see how it can be a meaningful and informative statement. So (2) is also unacceptable.

The ineffability thesis can be formulated in terms of the *via negativa:*

(3) No predicate terms signifying positive attributes can be applied to God. Only predicate terms signifying what God is not can be applied to God.

It is important to recognize that the *via negativa* rests upon a significant insight. The transcendence and uniqueness of God are emphasized in the thundering question of Isaiah: "To whom then will you liken God, or what likeness compare with him?" (Isa. 40:18). Certainly one way of clarifying what God is like is to contrast him with finite creatures and thereby point out what he is not.

But it is crucial to see that the *via negativa* must be supplemented with some positive knowledge of God.[46] Negative predication of God can only be informative if there is presupposed some identifiable positive knowledge of God. If we have some positive knowledge of God, or at least what is taken to be knowledge of

46. This was clearly recognized by Thomas Aquinas. Cf. *On the Power of God* VII.5 and *Summa Theologiae* I.q.13.a.2.

God, then we can apply negative predication in order to purify our understanding of God. For example, if we know that God is an incorporeal being, then we can deny that he is tall, short, or even a physical being at all. But if we have absolutely no positive knowledge of God, on what basis could we say that certain properties cannot be ascribed to God? Simply to say that God is not x, y, or z, with no corresponding positive affirmation, is hardly informative. Thus, although the *via negativa* has a legitimate function in theology, it presupposes that at least some positive knowledge of God is available and that at least some positive predication about God is legitimate.

A fourth formulation of the ineffability thesis states:

(4) God is by definition a Being beyond human understanding and comprehension, who cannot be captured by human words and concepts.

This too rests upon an important insight. Obviously there is much about God which must remain mysterious and unknowable to humans. There is an important sense in which God is incomprehensible. But (4) is ambiguous and can be taken in at least two ways. On the one hand, it could mean that no concepts or linguistic terms with which we are familiar can be applied to God. And if so, it faces the same difficulties noted above with respect to (2) and (3).

On the other hand, this fourth thesis could mean that concepts and linguistic terms with which we are familiar cannot exhaustively "capture" God. Such concepts and terms have limitations and must thus be interpreted carefully. In other words, concepts and linguistic terms can be used meaningfully in talk of God but there are some limitations in doing so. The question then is not whether we can apply certain concepts and terms to God but how we are to understand them when we do so. Thus, the possibility of using concepts and terms with which we are familiar in talking of God is recognized, but so are the problems in understanding just what is meant by such terms when they are used of God.[47]

47. There is much helpful literature on the problems of religious dis-

Nor should we be bothered by the fact that (4) rules out exhaustive knowledge of God. Certainly no concepts or terms with which we are familiar will exhaustively convey what God is like. But this should provide no cause for alarm, for our concepts and linguistic terms cannot exhaustively portray what any finite entity is like either. I cannot have exhaustive knowledge about something as trivial as my desk — there are many true propositions about my desk which I do not and cannot know. It is hardly surprising, then, if we should conclude that we cannot have exhaustive knowledge of God.

We have seen that attempts to preserve the majesty, uniqueness, and transcendence of God (or Allah, Brahman, etc.) by claiming that he is ineffable are epistemologically unacceptable. If knowledge of the religious ultimate is possible, then use of concepts and linguistic terms with which we are familiar in thinking and talking about the religious ultimate cannot be ruled out. The difficulties and limitations of doing so should be admitted, but this is quite different from denying outright that concepts and linguistic terms can be applied to God.

Religious Truth as a Higher Form of Truth

In this chapter we have been considering various views which maintain that truth in religion is somehow different from notions of truth found in other disciplines and in ordinary life. We are especially concerned with theories which reject the idea that truth in religion must be propositional and exclusive. We must now consider two views which have recently become increasingly influential. The first simply rejects the applicability of the principle of noncontradiction in religion, whereas the second is a more

---

course. A useful introduction to the issues can be found in C. Stephen Evans, *The Philosophy of Religion* (Downers Grove, Ill.: Inter-Varsity Press, 1985), pp. 141-85. See also *The Logic of God*, ed. Malcolm L. Diamond and Thomas V. Litzenburg (Indianapolis: Bobbs-Merrill, 1975), and Patrick Sherry, *Religion, Truth, and Language Games*. An excellent, but highly technical, study is James Ross' *Portraying Analogy* (Cambridge: Cambridge University Press, 1981).

142   DISSONANT VOICES

elaborate theory calling for two levels of truth, with religious truth
being a higher kind of truth than that found in other realms.

Christian exclusivism is based upon the assumption that
two or more incompatible assertions cannot all be true. Where
there are contradictory claims being advanced by various religions,
not all of them can be true. At least one must be false. This, of
course, is simply an application of the principle of noncontradiction — two contradictory statements cannot both be true.

Although the principle of noncontradiction is unquestioned in ordinary life, there are those who hold that it is inappropriate in religion. In some non-Christian religions there is a long
and deeply rooted tradition of suspecting logical precision in
thinking about religious matters. Zen Buddhism, for example, explicitly rejects any attempt to express ultimate religious insight in
rational and conceptually precise terms. *Satori*, or enlightenment,
is said to be an awakening to that ultimate reality which transcends
all conceptualization and dichotomies. Use of the *koan* (an irrational riddle or theme for meditation) is intended to stimulate
the monk to transcend the rational order and to grasp *satori*
directly. Japanese religion, including Shinto, has characteristically
been highly suspicious of attempts to express ultimate truth in
logically precise, rational categories.

What is disturbing, however, is that opposition to conceptual precision and use of logical principles in religion is not limited
to certain Eastern traditions but is increasingly being found within
the Western Christian community as well. Some theologians and
mission leaders now proclaim that reliance upon the principle of
noncontradiction in religion is a mistake, and that Western (Greek)
notions of truth as either/or and exclusive are unhelpful in religion.
Wilfred Cantwell Smith states that "in all ultimate matters, truth
lies not in an either-or but in a both-and."[48] Similarly, Catholic
theologian Paul Knitter asserts that the understanding of truth as
exclusive, as either/or, is highly problematic in the modern context,
and that today we must recognize the "ongoing, pluralistic nature

48. Wilfred Cantwell Smith, *The Faith of Other Men* (New York: Mentor,
1965), p. 17.

of truth."[49] We must admit that "all religious experience and all religious language must be two-eyed, dipolar, a union of opposites."[50]

The terminology used by Knitter is from the provocative book *Truth is Two-Eyed,*[51] by the late New Testament scholar and theologian John A. T. Robinson. The thesis of Robinson's book is that we must stop looking at religions through an exclusivistic, either/or framework, that we should instead adopt a holistic, dipolar, "two-eyed" approach to religious truth. The traditional one-eyed approach emphasizes just one dominant conception of the religious ultimate and carries with it an implicit or explicit claim to exclusive validity. It maintains that it alone has all the truth about religious matters and that other traditions must simply be rejected as mistaken.

The two-eyed perspective, on the other hand, rejects any such claim to exclusivity and incorporates two different visions of reality that are said to be found in varying degrees within both Hinduism and Christianity — the religious ultimate as personal (Christianity) and nonpersonal (Hinduism). According to Robinson, the one-eyed approach is narrow-minded, negative, and the product of a bigoted ignorance.[52] Religious truth can only be attained by transcending the limitations of an exclusive, either/or perspective. "[T]ruth may come from refusing this either-or and accepting that the best working model of reality may be elliptical or bi-polar, or indeed multi-polar."[53]

Robinson claims that he is not advocating a naive syncretism which adopts partial insights from all religions and then fuses them together. He admits that Islam, Christianity, Hinduism, and Buddhism do say very different things about the nature of the religious ultimate. His concern, however, is to discover how one

49. Paul Knitter, *No Other Name? A Critical Survey of Christian Attitudes Toward the World Religions* (Maryknoll, N.Y.: Orbis, 1985), p. 218.

50. Ibid., p. 221.

51. John A. T. Robinson, *Truth is Two-Eyed* (Philadelphia: Westminster, 1979).

52. Ibid., pp. ix, 16, 24, 54.

53. Ibid., p. 22.

can be faithful to and accept as equally legitimate two very different perspectives on the religious ultimate. Although basic differences in religions should not be minimized, he calls for pushing beyond such differences toward the "unitive pluralism" which, while allowing for differences, admits a "unity of vision" among the varying perspectives.[54]

It is not clear just what Smith, Knitter, and Robinson are proposing in their attacks upon exclusive truth. Much of the language of the discussion is ambiguous and makes use of highly suggestive metaphors. Unfortunately in this case, gains in literary style are made at the expense of perspicuity. It is possible that the attacks upon exclusive truth are meant simply to emphasize the fact that no single religious tradition can have a monopoly on all truth and that members of one religious community should be willing to listen to, and learn from, other traditions. If so, their point is an important one. No religious community can claim to have exhaustive knowledge of God. Properly understood, Christian exclusivism does not entail that all truth worth knowing is to be found within Christianity, although it will hold that all truth, regardless of where it is found, is God's truth and is compatible with God's revelation in Scripture. Christian exclusivism simply affirms that where the beliefs of other religions are incompatible with those of Christian faith the former are to be rejected as false.

But I suspect that considerably more than this is intended in the attack upon exclusive truth. Robinson's and Smith's comments in particular can be interpreted as a rejection of exclusive truth because of its reliance upon the principle of noncontradiction. Smith states, "Modern Western logic, I myself am pretty sure, though serviceable for computers, is in other ways inept and is particularly ill-suited, it seems, for thinking about . . . spiritual matters."[55]

However, even in religion the price of rejecting the principle of noncontradiction is simply too high. The principle can be ex-

54. Ibid., p. 39. See especially chap. 4.
55. Wilfred Cantwell Smith, "An Attempt at Summation," in *Christ's Lordship and Religious Pluralism*, ed. G. H. Anderson and T. F. Stransky (Maryknoll, N.Y.: Orbis, 1981), p. 201.

pressed in both its logical and its ontological forms.[56] The logical principle applies to propositions and maintains that a proposition cannot be both true and false. The ontological principle applies to states of affairs (anything that is or is not the case) and holds that something cannot simultaneously both be and not be in the same respect. Strictly speaking, contradiction is the affirmation and denial of the same meaning. The price of rejecting the principle of noncontradiction is forfeiture of the possibility of meaningful affirmation about anything at all — including any statement about the religious ultimate. One who abandons the principle of non-contradiction is reduced to utter silence, for he or she has rejected a necessary condition for the coherent and meaningful statement of any position whatsoever.

That the principle of noncontradiction is inescapably basic to all thought can be demonstrated as follows. Suppose that some-one were to affirm the position expressed in

> P: In religion one is not limited by the principle of noncontra-diction but can go beyond it to recognize the unitive pluralism of religious truth.

Is this a coherent position? Is it even possibly true? Presumably the person asserting P does so with the assumption that what is ex-pressed by P is true — that is, that the state of affairs to which P refers actually is as P asserts it to be. If this is not the intent behind the assertion of P, then there is little reason to consider it in the first place. But notice that in advancing P as true one will be implicitly rejecting what is incompatible with P as false. For ex-ample, Q below is incompatible with P.

> Q: In religion one is necessarily limited by the principle of non-contradiction.

56. The classic statement of the principle of noncontradiction is found in Aristotle's *Metaphysics*, 1005b, 15-1009a. Cf. *The Basic Works of Aristotle*, ed. Richard McKeon (New York: Random House, 1941), pp. 736-43. For a helpful introductory treatment of the principle see Irving M. Copi, *Introduction to Logic*, 5th ed. (New York: Macmillan, 1978), pp. 306-8.

Now to deny that in asserting P one is implicitly ruling out acceptance of Q is to imply both that in religion one is not limited by the principle of noncontradiction and that in religion one is limited by the principle of noncontradiction. But clearly this is absurd. We can assume, then, that in asserting P one is implicitly rejecting Q as incompatible with P.

But if in asserting P one is implicitly rejecting as false what is incompatible with P, then one is actually appealing to the principle of noncontradiction in the assertion of P. That is, the principle is actually being presupposed in the very denial of the principle. It is impossible to refute the principle of noncontradiction since it is a necessary condition for any coherent, meaningful, or intelligible position whatsoever. Contrary to what many contemporary theologians and missiologists claim, the principle of noncontradiction is not simply a Western presupposition that works well in the West but is not necessarily binding in non-Western contexts. The fact that a Greek (Aristotle) happens to have been the first person to formulate the principle explicitly is entirely irrelevant. The principle is binding upon all humans — Japanese, Chinese, Indians, as well as Europeans and Americans. The principle is irrefutable since any attempt at refutation necessarily makes appeal to the principle itself. Even the Catholic theologian Raimundo Panikkar — hardly an apologist for traditional Christian exclusivism — admits the inescapably exclusive nature of truth in religion.

> A believing member of a religion in one way or another considers his religion to be true. Now, the claim to truth has a certain built-in exclusivity. If a given statement is true, its contradictory cannot also be true. And if a certain human tradition claims to offer a universal context for truth, anything contrary to that "universal truth" will have to be declared false.[57]

Any attempt to resolve the question of the relation among religions by appealing to a higher form of religious "truth" which is not limited by the principle of noncontradiction must be rejected as

57. Raimundo Panikkar, *The Intrareligious Dialogue* (New York: Paulist Press, 1978), p. xiv.

epistemologically untenable. By rejecting the principle one does not attain more profound "truth"; one is reduced to incoherence or utter silence.

Implicit in many of the theories of religious truth considered thus far is the idea that there are two distinct levels of reality and, correspondingly, two distinct levels of truth. On the one hand, it is assumed, there is the level of ordinary reality and truth, the phenomenal world of our ordinary experience. Propositional and exclusive truth, rational analysis, logical principles, and so on, are said to be legitimate and helpful on this level. However, it is claimed, there is a higher level of Reality and Truth transcending the ordinary, mundane realm. Ultimate Truth is to be found on this level and cannot be assessed on the basis of criteria and principles appropriate to the lower level of reality and truth.

Something like this distinction is found in Frithjof Schuon's *The Transcendent Unity of Religions.*[58] Schuon distinguishes between exoteric and esoteric truth in religion. Exoteric truth is that truth which followers of religions generally are able to apprehend. It is subject to rational analysis and can be expressed propositionally. The highest form of religious Truth, however, is esoteric Truth, and it is on this level that one discovers the ultimate unity among religions. Esoteric Truth cannot be expressed propositionally, nor can it be assessed by rational and logical criteria applicable to exoteric truth. It can only be experienced by direct intuition or "faith."

The notion of two distinct levels of reality and truth is particularly characteristic of certain schools of Hinduism and Buddhism. Japanese Zen Buddhism, for example, makes a fundamental distinction between *zokutai* ("relative" truth, which is limited to the phenomenal world of ordinary experience) and *shintai* (absolute Truth, which is identified with ultimate, undifferentiated Reality). Rational analysis, logical distinctions, and ordinary notions of truth

58. Frithjof Schuon, *The Transcendent Unity of Religions,* rev. ed., trans. Peter Townsend (New York: Harper & Row, 1975). Cf. also Aldous Huxley, *The Perennial Philosophy* (New York: Harper & Brothers, 1945), and Huston Smith, *Forgotten Truth: The Primordial Tradition* (New York: Harper & Row, 1976).

and falsity are appropriate with *zokutai.* However, the enlightened or awakened mind, the person who has attained *satori,* will recognize the inadequacy of this level. For the enlightened one directly perceives *shintai,* the ultimately undifferentiated Reality in which no distinctions of any kind are appropriate.

Similarly, the Hindu scripture Mundaka Upanishad states, "There are two knowledges to be known — as indeed the knowers of Brahman are wont to say: a higher [*para*] and also a lower [*apara*]."[59] The distinction between two levels of reality and two levels of truth is fundamental to Advaita Vedanta Hinduism. Shankara (A.D. 788- 820),[60] the outstanding philosopher of Advaita Vedanta, accepted the distinction between the realm of ordinary phenomenal reality and that of Brahman, absolute, undifferentiated Being. Truth on the ordinary phenomenal level is important — the reality of the empirical world is not to be denied. However, there is a higher Reality, that of absolutely undifferentiated Being. For the person who has transcended the ordinary realm and has realized that he or she is in fact identical with Brahman, the truth of ordinary reality cannot be regarded as ultimate. From the perspective of ultimate Truth or the highest Reality, ordinary reality must be considered illusion *(maya)* and the "truth" attained on this level no more than cosmic ignorance *(avidya).* The highest form of spiritual knowledge or Truth *(para vidya)* relegates all other kinds of knowledge and truth to lower levels of reality. Such Truth is entirely self-certifying; no criteria, principles, or experience from the lower level of reality and truth can confirm or refute it.

As outlined above, the doctrine of two levels of truth ini-

59. Mundaka Upanishad I.1.4, as quoted in *A Source Book in Indian Philosophy,* ed. Sarvepalli Radhakrishnan and Charles A. Moore (Princeton: Princeton University Press, 1957), p. 51.

60. Helpful introductory discussions of Shankara's subtle thought can be found in Eliot Deutsch's *Advaita Vedanta* (Honolulu: University of Hawaii Press, 1969), and Stuart Hackett's *Oriental Philosophy* (Madison: University of Wisconsin Press, 1979), pp. 145-54. Sophisticated defense of the notion of two levels of truth goes back at least to the influential second-century Mahayana Buddhist Nagarjuna and the Madhyamika school. It can also be found in the thought of the sixth-century Chinese Buddhist Chi-tsang, who was heavily influenced by Nagarjuna.

tially appears to be quite impregnable and immune to criticism. After all, it can be claimed, only the person who has transcended the ordinary realm and has perceived ultimate Reality directly, who has grasped the unity of ultimate Truth, is in any position to pronounce judgment upon the validity of the distinction. Any attempt to refute the doctrine of two levels of truth can be casually dismissed as irrelevant since it will involve rational and logical principles, criteria, and categories which are said to be appropriate only on the lower level of reality. Thus, simply demonstrating that the doctrine is problematic on rational grounds — or even that it is logically incoherent — need not be troublesome to the believer.

Closer examination, however, indicates that the doctrine is not so invincible after all. First, if the doctrine of two levels of truth is taken to mean that logical principles such as the principle of noncontradiction do not apply to the highest level of truth, then the doctrine faces the same difficulties noted earlier with respect to the views of Robinson and Smith. Any attempt to state the distinction itself will necessarily appeal to the principle of noncontradiction. The very postulation of a higher level of truth implicitly makes use of the principle. Either there is such a thing as a higher level of truth or there is not. It is nonsensical to affirm both that there is and that there is not a higher level of truth. So it cannot be maintained that the higher level of truth in religion — if there is such a thing — is utterly beyond all distinctions and logical principles.

Second, we must ask why we should accept the doctrine of two levels of truth in the first place. Is there compelling reason to do so? If consistent, the advocate of the doctrine will not present carefully reasoned arguments for the distinction. For to do so would be to appeal to rational and logical criteria in support of a doctrine which holds that such criteria are only legitimate on the lower level of reality. It would be blatantly inconsistent to appeal to such criteria in order to justify the assertion that ultimate Truth transcends ordinary reality and truth.

Advocates of the doctrine might respond by saying that the distinction is somehow self-evident or self-certifying. The person who is fortunate enough to have the experience of grasping the nature of ultimate Reality simply knows that the distinction is legitimate. Those who do not have this experience cannot be persuaded by rational argument that the distinction is sound. It would seem, then, that those without the experience must simply accept the testimony of the one claiming to have had the experience. His or her authority justifies accepting the distinction.

But why should we accept the word of someone claiming to have had such an experience? The simple claim to have had such an experience, in and of itself, cannot be regarded as determinative. Appeal to authority in and of itself settles nothing. There are always competing claims based upon authority, and the question then becomes which (if any) authority or testimony is to be accepted, and on what basis. Nor will it help here to appeal to the sacred scripture of some tradition, for one can always ask why those particular writings should be accepted as divinely revealed truth.

Advocates of the doctrine of two truths thus face a dilemma: any attempt to provide reasons for accepting the testimony of someone claiming to have had the experience will make appeal to criteria and principles which are said to be applicable only on the lower level of reality and truth. And one cannot consistently appeal to such criteria in an effort to justify the basic distinction between levels of truth. However, failure to provide such reasons for accepting the testimony of the one claiming to have had the experience results in a vicious irrationalism in which one simply makes an arbitrary choice to accept, or not to accept, the testimony. It would seem that the one without the experience, then, could never be in a position in which the most reasonable thing to do is to accept the testimony.

Conclusion

In this chapter we have examined various attempts to formulate theories of religious truth that do not include the notions of propositional and exclusive truth. We have seen that there are serious problems with each of the formulations. Any epistemologically acceptable theory of religious truth must recognize that beliefs are integral to religion and that truth in religion, just as in other domains, must include the notions of propositional and exclusive truth.

CHAPTER FIVE

Evaluating Religious Traditions

Orthodox Christians have traditionally held that other religions are false to the extent that they embrace truth claims incompatible with central Christian beliefs. In so doing, Christians make an evaluation about the truth or adequacy of other religions. But the fact that Christians make such judgments about other religions (and by implication, about followers of other religions) is highly offensive to many today. Dismissing other religions as false while regarding one's own tradition as true is often regarded as presumptuous arrogance and intolerance of the worse kind.

Consideration of the question of intolerance must be postponed until chapter 8 (see section on tolerance, pp. 301ff.). What does concern us here, however, is a more fundamental reason for the current dissatisfaction with Christians' evaluations of other religions. The assumption is widely accepted today that the exclusivist's negative evaluation of other religions is really no more than the product of his or her own subjective and limited perspective and thus cannot be considered binding or authoritative in any objective sense. Of course, it is said, the Christian can be critical of Hindu beliefs, but we must recognize that in so doing she is simply making a value judgment from within the perspective of Christian beliefs and values and not an objective assessment of the truth or falsity of Hindu beliefs. Conversely, the Hindu too can be critical of Christian beliefs and practices, but in so doing he will simply be making a value judgment based upon the Hindu perspective. All of our evaluations are necessarily perspectival. Thus, for the Christian to pretend that he or she has access to some neutral vantage point from which to make objective judgments about the truth or falsity of other religions is gross naïveté.

Are there any objective, nonarbitrary criteria for evaluating religious traditions? Or are all evaluations necessarily no more than the product of one's own limited, culture-bound perspective? Can a Christian legitimately conclude that religious beliefs incompatible with Christian faith are false? These are pressing questions demanding careful treatment by theologians and missiologists. Although they cannot here be treated in the comprehensive manner they deserve, they must be addressed — even if briefly — in a study of this nature. I will argue that, contrary to the emerging consensus in certain theological and missiological circles, some nonarbitrary criteria exist to evaluate various religious traditions, and that it is indeed legitimate for a Christian to conclude that other religions which embrace basic beliefs incompatible with central tenets of Christian faith are false.

Evaluation and Religion

Implicit in much thinking on religious pluralism today is the rather simplistic notion that the most civil manner in which to respond to other religious traditions is the complete suspension of judgment of any kind: don't make value judgments of any kind, positive or negative; simply allow the other religions to carry on in their own way. Now, to be sure, there is an important truth here about the importance of respecting followers of other faiths and not infringing upon their rights to believe and practice their faith. And undoubtedly we could all benefit from exerting greater caution in making evaluations of beliefs and practices of other traditions. Moreover, in the phenomenological study of religions there is a significant sense in which a temporary suspension of one's own values and beliefs, insofar as this is possible, is surely desirable.

But the total elimination of value judgments concerning other religious traditions is neither desirable nor possible. Clearly people do make judgments about other religions. The orthodox Christian, while perhaps recognizing many admirable things in Buddhism, ordinarily concludes that the fundamental teachings of Buddhism are mistaken. The Theravada Buddhist, on the other hand, will probably respond by saying that the Christian claim that the universe was created ex nihilo by an eternal, omnipotent creator God is unacceptable. The Jehovah's Witness and the Muslim both reject the Christian teaching on the divine Trinity. And atheists, agnostics, and religious believers of many persuasions will disagree among themselves on the proper way to respond to the Rev. Sun Myung Moon.

Not only is it a fact that ordinary people today make judgments about religious traditions but, as John Hick points out, the great religious figures of the past, the founders of the major religious movements, also made critical judgments about the religious beliefs and practices around them.[1] Gautama Buddha, the founder of Buddhism, unambiguously rejected the idea of the eternal *atman* or soul which was accepted in the religious thought of sixth century B.C. India. The Hebrew prophets scorned the practices of the popular Baal cult, rejecting them as idolatrous. Jesus vigorously attacked the legalism and formalism of Jewish religious practices of his time. Muhammad denounced the polytheism of contemporary Arabian society. If we are to accept in principle the religious insights of the great religious figures, then we must also accept the legitimacy of their critical evaluations of surrounding beliefs and practices. Or as Hick puts it, "some kind of assessing of religious phenomena seems a corollary of deep religious seriousness and openness to the divine."[2] I am not suggesting here that all, or even any, of the criticisms of prevailing religious prac-

---

1. Cf. John Hick, *Problems of Religious Pluralism* (New York: St. Martin's Press, 1985), p. 67.
2. Ibid.

tices by the great religious leaders should be accepted as valid, but am merely pointing out that, regardless of our own religious affiliation, if we recognize that in criticizing surrounding beliefs and practices the founders and reformers were not simply expressing arbitrary personal opinions but were possibly making legitimate criticisms, then we are implicitly admitting that there are some legitimate, nonarbitrary criteria upon which evaluation of religious phenomena can be based.

The suggestion that one can and perhaps should withhold judgment about a given religion is misleading at best. For in reality, some evaluative stance with respect to religion is unavoidable. It is simply impossible for the person who has undergone a normal education in developed or developing countries not to make at least some implicit value judgments about religion in general as well as about particular religious traditions. The person who converts to Christianity, for example, who freely chooses to be baptized and to participate in the Christian community, probably does so at least in part because of a favorable view of basic Christian teachings and practices. Similarly, the person who, having been exposed to the Bible and the Christian community, chooses to have nothing to do with Christian faith and explicitly claims to be an atheist, can be said to have an unfavorable view of Christianity. Both cases involve persons who, for whatever reasons, have made judgments about the adequacy, truth, or desirability of religion. The person embracing Christianity has a positive view of Christian faith. Perhaps he regards the central claims of Christianity as true, or possibly he is primarily attracted by what he sees as the benefits of becoming a Christian — warm fellowship with other believers, feelings of peace, security, and acceptance in the midst of perplexing problems. By contrast, the person rejecting Christian faith probably has a largely negative view of Christian teachings and practices. Perhaps she is convinced that the assertions of Christianity are simply mistaken. Or possibly she believes that Christianity is irrelevant to modern life or is actually a hindrance to coping effectively in the modern world.

It is important to see, however, that value judgments about religion cannot be limited to those who explicitly accept or reject the claims of a particular faith. The person who claims utter indifference and who professes to have neither a positive nor a negative view of religion cannot escape making at least some implicit value judgments about religion. For in making such a claim to indifference he or she implicitly accepts at least one value judgment — namely, that participation in a given religious tradition is (for whatever reason) an activity not worthy one's involvement. For it is precisely because being a Christian or a Buddhist is not regarded as particularly worthwhile that he or she can maintain an attitude of indifference toward such religions. Thus, irrespective of whether one adopts a favorable, unfavorable, or even an indifferent attitude toward religion, one cannot escape at least implicitly making some judgments about the desirability or propriety of belonging to particular religious traditions. Having views about the acceptability of other religions, then, is not something unique to Christian exclusivists; it is inevitable for anyone aware of the fact that there are various religious traditions. The question, then, is not whether we should make judgments about other religions but rather on what basis we should do so. Are such evaluations simply the result of one's particular perspective, the cumulative influences of one's upbringing and culture? Or are there objective, nonarbitrary criteria which can be applied in making such judgments?

Functionalist Interpretations of Religion

How a person evaluates a given religion will depend largely upon his or her views on the nature, purpose, and distinctives of religion. The criteria applied in evaluating a religion will be determined significantly by one's view of religion.[3] Many people today — both scholars

---

3. We should note here the notorious problem of trying to define what is meant by "religion." Attempts at definition run the risk of being too narrow and thus eliminating certain traditions and institutions widely accepted as religious, or being too broad, and thereby becoming vacuous by including too much. Obviously Christianity and Islam are religions. Is Zen Buddhism a religion? Confucianism? Marxism? Secular humanism? Fortunately we need not resolve such issues here. We can assume that the reader has a good working understanding of what is meant by "religion" and would agree that Christianity, Islam, Buddhism, and Hinduism

and laity alike — regard religion in highly pragmatic and functionalist terms. Donald Crosby defines a functionalist theory about the nature of religion as one that seeks to characterize what religion is by providing an account of what it does.[4] Religions are thought of as complex institutions which serve a variety of social and psychological functions. Max Weber, Emile Durkheim, and Sigmund Freud, pioneers in the attempt to explain religion in social and psychological terms entirely apart from appeal to a transcendent order, have exerted an enormous influence upon Western academic treatment of religion. This is especially evident in the social sciences. A pragmatic view of religion is clearly reflected in Frederick Streng's definition of religion as "a means to ultimate transformation."[5] Streng elaborates by further defining ultimate transformation as "a fundamental change from being caught up in the troubles of common existence (sin, ignorance) to living in such a way that one can cope at the deepest level with those troubles."[6] From a similar perspective anthropologist Clifford Geertz defines religion as

(1) a system of symbols which acts to (2) establish powerful, pervasive, and long-lasting moods and motivations in men by (3) formulating conceptions of a general order of existence and (4) clothing these conceptions with such an aura of factuality that (5) the moods and motivations seem uniquely realistic.[7]

We are not concerned here with the accuracy of the definitions proposed by Streng and Geertz. The point is simply to call attention

---

are paradigmatic examples of religious traditions. For a good introductory discussion of problems of definition see Donald Wiebe, *Religion and Truth: Towards an Alternative Paradigm for the Study of Religion* (New York: Mouton, 1981), chap. 1.

4. Cf. Donald A. Crosby, *Interpretive Theories of Religion* (The Hague and New York: Mouton, 1981), p. 37.

5. Frederick Streng, *Understanding Religious Life*, 3rd ed. (Belmont, Cal.: Wadsworth Publishing Company, 1985), p. 2.

6. Ibid.

7. Clifford Geertz, "Religion as a Cultural System," in *Anthropological Approaches to the Study of Religion*, ed. M. Banton (London: Tavistock Publications, 1966), p. 5, as quoted in W. Richard Comstock, "The Study of Religion and Primitive Religions," in *Religion and Man: An Introduction*, ed. W. Richard Comstock (New York: Harper & Row, 1971), p. 27.

to the fact that the definitions are functionalist in the sense that they are primarily about what religion does for the religious believer. The focus is upon the ends served by religion.

It is not uncommon to encounter functionalist views of religion on a more popular level as well. For example, it is assumed by many that the purpose of religion is to help to cultivate a sense of moral values and responsibility — that is, to make decent citizens out of people. Others regard religion as primarily a refuge for those who face crises or traumatic upheavals. Religion is supposed to help provide the inner resources — peace, tranquillity, confidence, security — necessary for coping in our perplexing world. Some look to religion to provide a prophetic voice for justice in a world marked by injustice and oppression. Religion is said to be the champion of the oppressed and persecuted; its raison d'être is to work for a more just and equitable society.

Now if such functionalist or pragmatic views of religion are adopted, then one's evaluation of any given religious tradition will depend upon the manner and extent to which it serves the desired ends. The criteria applied in evaluation will be pragmatic in nature. How well does Christianity (or Buddhism or Hinduism) provide the necessary inner resources for people in times of crisis? Do they find peace, meaning, hope? Does Christianity really help to preserve moral values in society? Does it speak out clearly on behalf of the oppressed? Does it tend to produce greater justice and equality?

Functionalist Criteria for Evaluating Religion

In his seminal article "On Grading Religions,"[8] John Hick considers the problem of criteria for evaluating religious traditions and suggests a pragmatic criterion for evaluation. Hick begins his dis-

8. John Hick, "On Grading Religions," *Religious Studies* 17 (1982), reprinted in John Hick, *Problems of Religious Pluralism*, pp. 67-87. Hick's recent treatment of the problem of criteria, in his *An Interpretation of Religion* (New Haven: Yale University Press, 1988), is considered in chap. 6.

cussion by admitting that some assessment of religious phenomena is unavoidable. Not only do we regularly make judgments
about religious beliefs and practices, we cannot avoid doing so. He
then claims that, although the major religions have different views
of the nature of salvation/enlightenment/liberation, they do share
a common soteriological structure — namely, a "transition from
a radically unsatisfactory state to a limitlessly better one." In each
case "salvation/liberation consists in a new and limitlessly better
quality of existence which comes about in the transition from
self-centredness to Reality-centredness."[9]

Hick initially suggests two general criteria by which we
might evaluate religious traditions: moral and rational adequacy.[10] However, while allowing the theoretical possibility of
judging religious traditions on the basis of a moral criterion, Hick
argues that, due to our limited knowledge and the complexity of
religious traditions, in practice we are not able to rank religions
on moral grounds.[11] So although there is in principle a legitimate
moral criterion, it is of little use in the actual evaluation of
religions. Similarly, Hick contends that although rational analysis
can be useful in evaluating theological systems or formulations
within particular religious traditions, it is not adequate to discriminate between competing religious traditions taken as comprehensive, religiocultural totalities.[12] That is, the criterion of
internal consistency, for example, can be applied to particular
theological systems — such as those of Aquinas or Shankara —
within the respective religious traditions. But rational analysis
cannot establish the superiority or greater truth of one tradition
over against another one. Curiously, no argument or reason is
given for this claim about the inadequacy of reason to make such
judgments. The closest we come to a reason is Hick's statement
that comprehensive religious worldviews are all-encompassing
"linguistic pictures" or "maps" of the universe whose function it

9. Ibid., p. 69.
10. Ibid., pp. 79f.
11. Ibid., p. 84.
12. Ibid., pp. 80f.

is to "enable us to find salvation/liberation, the limitlessly better quality of existence that the nature of reality is said to make possible."[13]

Given that although moral and rational criteria are legitimate in principle but in practice prove to be of little value, are we to conclude that there are no criteria that can be applied in the evaluation of alternative religious traditions? Hick is not so pessimistic. He asserts that there is one criterion — a pragmatic one — which can be applied to comprehensive religious traditions or worldviews. The pragmatic criterion grades religions on the basis of "their success or failure in fulfilling the soteriological function. . . . [S]uch a test can only be pragmatic: Is this complex of religious experience, belief, and behavior soteriologically effective? Does it make possible the transformation of human existence from self-centredness to Reality-centredness?"[14] He states, "religious phenomena — patterns of behavior, experiences, beliefs, myths, theologies, cultic acts, liturgies, scriptures, and so forth — can in principle be assessed and graded; and the basic criterion is the extent to which they promote or hinder the great religious aim of salvation/liberation."[15]

Is such a pragmatic criterion adequate? Can it by itself serve as a neutral, nonarbitrary basis upon which to evaluate competing religious claims? In spite of its undeniable appeal, a strictly pragmatic criterion, which makes no appeal to other considerations, cannot effectively be used to assess various religious traditions. Careful scrutiny of Hick's criterion reveals the inherent deficiency of any strictly pragmatic criterion. For if Hick's criterion is to work at all, we must first be able to settle questions of the truth or falsity of certain basic beliefs within the respective religious worldviews.

We might begin by questioning Hick's assumption that there is one great religious aim of salvation/liberation/enlightenment common to all religions. Certainly the major religions are all concerned in some sense with the theme of "salvation" — that is,

13. Ibid., p. 80.
14. Ibid.
15. Ibid., p. 86.

the "transition from a radically unsatisfactory state to a limitlessly better one."[16] Structurally, perhaps, this is a common element. But Hick minimizes differences in conceptions of salvation by speaking as if all religions share a common soteriological goal and a common understanding of what constitutes salvation. His characterization of salvation as the transition from self-centeredness to Reality-centeredness (whatever this means) strikes one as little more than a kind of "lowest common denominator" soteriology of religions. This depiction of salvation may be acceptable to adherents of various religions, but only if they each understand very different things by it. For, as we saw earlier, the major religions offer very different answers to two fundamental questions: What is the nature of the human predicament? and What is the nature of salvation/enlightenment? Is the human predicament brought on by sin against a righteous and holy God, or is it due to *maya* (illusion) and *avidya* (ignorance)? Is salvation to be thought of in terms of justification before God or in terms of liberation from *samsara*? It is highly misleading to speak as if all religions share a common soteriological goal and simply differ on the means to reach it. Since the analyses of the human predicament in the major religions differ, it is only to be expected that the soteriological goals in the respective religions will differ as well.

So Hick's pragmatic criterion cannot be understood as asking, "How well do the various religions provide for the attainment of the one common goal of salvation?" but rather, "How well do the various religions provide for the attainment of salvation/liberation/enlightenment as this is understood in the respective traditions?" That is, how effective is Christianity in providing justification of sinners before a righteous God? How effective is Hinduism in providing *moksha,* or release from *samsara?* How effective is Zen in providing *satori,* or enlightenment?

But in raising these questions we are ineluctably confronted by the question of truth. Christianity can only be considered effective in providing salvation as justification if the human predicament is in fact characterized by alienation from God due to

16. Ibid., p. 69.

human sin and if God has in fact made possible through Jesus Christ justification of sinful humanity. Similarly, Theravada Buddhism can only be said to be effective in providing liberation if the human condition is in fact one of ignorance concerning the true nature of reality combined with a bondage to craving and desire, and if strictly following the Noble Eightfold Path will indeed bring the elimination of craving and thus *nirvana*. In other words, a given religion can be regarded as soteriologically effective only if its diagnosis of the human condition is accurate and if its proposed way for achieving the intended soteriological goal will indeed bring about the desired effect. The question of the truth of basic beliefs about the human predicament, and ways of release from that predicament, cannot be avoided. To be able to apply the pragmatic criterion, then, and to determine that, for example, Buddhism is soteriologically more effective than Christianity, we must first be able to tell whether Buddhism's or Christianity's analysis of the human predicament is true, and then to determine which of the proposed ways of salvation/enlightenment in the respective religions will indeed be effective.

It is interesting that Hick concludes his article by stating,

> We can, I suggest, only acknowledge, and indeed rejoice in the fact, that the Real, the Ultimate, the Divine, is known and responded to within each of these vast historical complexes, so that within each of them the gradual transformation of human existence from self-centredness to Reality-centredness is taking place.[17]

We can leave aside for now the question how Hick knows that the same divine reality is indeed being known and responded to in each of the major religions, as this will be pursued in the following chapter. But what is significant here is that in making the judgment that in each religion there is the gradual transformation from self-centeredness to Reality-centeredness (salvation), Hick is assuming that the different analyses of the human condition in the

17. Ibid., p. 87.

various religions are all true and that the ways of salvation proposed by the various religions are basically effective. We need not be concerned here with the question whether he is right in doing so. The point is simply that his pragmatic criterion cannot function without at least implicit appeal to considerations of the truth or falsity of basic beliefs in the major religions.

A similar pragmatic criterion for evaluating religious traditions is proposed by Paul Knitter.[18] After pointing out the convergence of interests in liberation theology and the theology of religions, Knitter suggests that those engaged in the debate over religious pluralism might profit from the concerns of liberation theologies. He states,

> In light of the present state of our world, therefore, both basic humanitarian concerns as well as the soteriologies of most religions would seem to dictate that *a preferential option for the poor and the nonperson* constitutes both the *necessity* and the *primary purpose* of interreligious dialogue. Religions must speak and act together because only so can they make their crucially important contribution to removing the oppression that contaminates our globe.[19]

The overriding concern of religion is identified with the struggle for justice and the elimination of oppression, inequality, and poverty. Knitter argues that Christian attitudes toward other religions should be governed by a "kingdom centrism" or "soteriocentrism" which holds that the major religions share common soteriological ground in their respective concerns for liberation.[20] He suggests that the soteriocentric understanding of religions — the preferential option for the poor and nonpersons — can provide a criterion for assessing various religions.[21] The soteriocentric criterion is used to evaluate a given religious tradition in terms of

18. Paul Knitter, "Toward a Liberation Theology of Religions," in *The Myth of Christian Uniqueness*, ed. John H. Hick and Paul F. Knitter (Maryknoll, N.Y.: Orbis, 1987), pp. 181f.

19. Ibid., p. 181. Emphasis in the original.

20. Ibid., p. 187.

21. Ibid., p. 189.

its effectiveness in promoting justice and equality and the elimination of oppression. Those religions which have a proven track record of working for "the kingdom and its justice" can be regarded as superior to those which do not, for "from their ethical, soteriological fruits we shall know them — we shall be able to judge whether and how much other religious paths and their mediators are salvific."[22]

> [B]y applying the criteria of liberating praxis, by asking, for example, how a particular Hindu belief or Christian ritual or Buddhist practice promotes human welfare and leads to the removal of poverty and to the promotion of liberation, we might be able to arrive at communal judgments concerning what is true or false, or what is preferable, among different religious claims or practices.[23]

But Knitter's soteriocentric criterion for the evaluation of religions, if taken by itself, is also highly problematic. Surely his claim regarding a common soteriological concern in the major religions which finds expression in the "preferential option for the poor and the nonperson" is open to question. One cannot escape the suspicion that he has simply taken the emphasis within the Judeo-Christian tradition upon justice and concern for the oppressed and read it back into other religious traditions as well. This is particularly evident in his repeated use of the term "the kingdom" in reference to the alleged soteriological common ground between religions. But, it must be asked, whose kingdom? The kingdom of God as articulated by Jesus? The theocratic society envisioned by Islam? Does Buddhism, Hinduism, or Shinto even have a concept of the kingdom — with the accompanying principles of justice, righteousness, and individual as well as social well-being — which warrants use of the term in this manner? Knitter, like Hick, seems to be reading more into the "common soteriological structure" than is actually there.

More importantly for our present purposes, Knitter's crite-

22. Ibid., p. 193.
23. Ibid., p. 190.

rion — like Hick's — is entirely useless apart from first settling the question of truth. For the soteriocentric criterion presupposes a particular view about the human predicament and the proper way of overcoming this undesirable condition. Curiously, the human predicament is depicted in largely "this-worldly" terms — social inequality, oppression, injustice, and poverty experienced in this life. Indeed, Knitter's discussion is remarkably reductionistic in its careful avoidance of transcendent categories to explain the human predicament.[24] But clearly the soteriocentric criterion, as discussed by Knitter, will be acceptable only if in fact the human predicament is primarily characterized by such this-worldly concerns as poverty and oppression. On the other hand, if the human predicament is ultimately due to human rebellion against a righteous God and if such rebellion will have profound ramifications for the individual beyond the present life, or if it is primarily due to *samsara* and *karma* and thus will affect the individual in numerous lives to come, then obviously a soteriocentric criterion that addresses simply the promotion of justice and the elimination of oppression in this life will be inadequate. The adequacy of Knitter's soteriocentric criterion, then, is partially a function of the adequacy of his implicit views on the nature of the human predicament and the proper way to achieve release from that condition. We see again that the question of truth is inescapable: What is the ultimate nature of the human predicament and how can one attain release from it?

To be sure, a functionalist approach to religion is not without merit. Any adequate understanding of religion must take into account how a given religion affects its adherents. And surely there is an important sense in which religions can be evaluated on pragmatic grounds. Certainly, if various religious traditions did not have a transforming effect upon believers and did not exert a positive influence upon society there would be little appeal to them and they would likely die out. But it is crucial to see that func-

24. One is tempted to ask what is distinctly religious about soteriology as discussed by Knitter. Is not the struggle against injustice and oppression something all moral persons, atheists and agnostics included, should embrace? What distinguishes religious soteriology from common morality? As we shall see in the following chapter, this is a criticism to which Hick is also vulnerable.

tionalist accounts of religion which attempt to explain religion solely in terms of what religion does for the believer are not only reductionistic and thus distort the actual phenomena of religion; they also cannot provide adequate criteria for making judgments about religious phenomena. Something more than a strictly pragmatic or functionalist criterion is necessary.[25]

How then should we evaluate religious traditions? It would seem that, depending upon the purposes of the evaluation, different religions can be assessed on a variety of grounds. We might, for example, consider them on the basis of their historical record in contributing toward promotion of literacy or health care, or their struggle against injustice. Or they could be evaluated in terms of their tendency to promote social cohesion and stability. On a more subjective note, religions might be appraised in terms of their capacity to produce peace, hope, serenity, and security in their adherents. Although admittedly difficult to do, such evaluations of various religions are in principle possible and, if properly conducted, could be informative and helpful.

However, I suggest that the most important question is not what a given religion does for society at large or for any of its members, but rather whether what it affirms, explicitly and implicitly, about reality is in fact true. The most significant question we can ask of any religion is whether its fundamental claims are true.[26]

25. In his article "Ranking Religions," *Religious Studies* 22 (1986), Dan Cohn-Sherbok argues that although it is impossible to determine criteria which will establish the truth or falsity of religions, it is possible to evaluate various religions on the basis of their "viability," that is, their "capacity to satisfy the spiritual demands and animate the lives of adherents" (p. 382). On this criterion no judgment is made about the truth or falsity of various religions. Evaluation is strictly on the basis of whether a given religion is still perceived by adherents as spiritually satisfying. But while such a criterion may have limited value in assessing the psychological and social effects of a religion, it can hardly be regarded as an adequate criterion for determining which religion — if any — one should follow.

26. See the comments of Ninian Smart, *Worldviews* (New York: Charles Scribner's Sons, 1983), pp. 35-36. Donald Wiebe, in his important work *Religion and Truth*, incisively criticizes the strictly descriptivist approach to the study of religion for evading the question of truth. Genuine understanding of religious pluralism will inevitably confront the question of truth.

Many, of course, object to this emphasis upon truth. Stanley Samartha, for example, makes the curious statement that "the question of truth is indeed important, but God's love is even more important. . . . Love takes precedence over truth."[27] Certainly one must not minimize the significance of God's love. But, as it stands, Samartha's statement is confused. Important as it is, the concept of God's love would have no relevance for anyone apart from the truth of certain basic propositions: that there is in fact a God, that God loves all persons, that God's love is supremely manifested in the Incarnation, and so on. We conclude, then, that the most important basis upon which to evaluate various religions is the question of truth.

Relativism

Any suggestion that there are nonarbitrary criteria which can be used to assess differing worldviews must confront the challenge of relativism. The influence of relativism upon contemporary society is enormous. Philosophers Jack Meiland and Michael Krausz note that "relativism is one of the chief intellectual and social issues of our time."[28] Especially disturbing is the fact that relativism is not only gaining greater acceptance within the academic community, but it is increasingly becoming the creed of those outside academia as well.[29]

27. Stanley Samartha, "Reply," in *Christ's Lordship and Religious Pluralism*, ed. Gerald H. Anderson and Thomas F. Stransky (Maryknoll, N.Y.: Orbis, 1981), pp. 54-55.

28. Jack Meiland and Michael Krausz, "Introduction," *Relativism: Cognitive and Moral*, ed. J. Meiland and M. Krausz (Notre Dame: University of Notre Dame Press, 1982), p. 4.

29. In an important article the distinguished anthropologist Clifford Geertz dismisses critics of relativism as "anti-relativist" alarmists. See "Anti Anti-Relativism," in *American Anthropology* 86 (June 1984): 263-78. Unfortunately, however, Geertz gives little evidence of grasping the fundamental epistemological issues in the debate over cognitive and moral relativism. For a penetrating analysis of the place of relativism in anthropology, see Elvin Hatch's *Culture and Morality: The Relativity of Values in Anthropology* (New York: Columbia University Press, 1983).

Although relativism in some form is as old as philosophy,[30] it was not particularly influential in Western thought until the nineteenth century. There are of course many reasons for the emergence of relativism at this time: increased contact with other, often radically different, cultures and nations; the development of sociology, anthropology, and comparative religion as distinct disciplines which emphasize the differences between peoples and cultures; a strong intellectual reaction against the Enlightenment focus upon reason and universal principles, etc. In the intellectual realm the seeds of modern relativism can be traced to the thought of Giambattista Vico, J. G. Herder, and the great German philosopher Immanuel Kant.[31] Although Kant himself was certainly no relativist, his critical philosophy has had a profound impact upon modern thought — in particular, his thesis that the mind plays a determinative role in organizing sensory data by imposing concepts or categories upon the raw data, thereby determining the form taken by our experience, and that all we can know are the phenomena (or appearances) and never the noumena themselves. Kant had assumed that the categorial scheme imposed by the mind was the same for all rational beings. However, those who followed him did not necessarily share this assumption; they were more impressed by the essential part played by the mind in ordering our experience and in creating frameworks of concepts and principles according to which judgments about reality are made. Given this emphasis upon the creative interpretive activity of the mind, it was natural to assume that there are many alternative ways of interpreting experience, each of which is legitimate, and that there are no neutral or nonarbitrary criteria by which to choose between competing conceptual schemes.

Relativism is prompted by the observation of diversity. But it is helpful here to distinguish between what we might call descriptive

30. Several of the fifth century B.C. Sophists seem to have espoused various forms of relativism. Plato portrays Protagoras as a relativist in the *Theaetetus* 152A, where he states that man is the measure of all things. Cf. *Plato: Collected Dialogues,* ed. Edith Hamilton and Huntington Cairns (Princeton: Princeton University Press, 1961), p. 856.

31. See the excellent essay by Patrick Gardiner, "German Philosophy and the Rise of Relativism," in *The Monist* 64 (1981): 138-54.

relativism and normative relativism. Descriptive relativism simply recognizes the great diversity among peoples and cultures. In ethics, for example, descriptive relativism attempts to describe accurately the different ethical values, principles, and practices of different peoples or cultures. Certain actions accepted as morally right in one culture may not be regarded as morally acceptable in another. Cannibalism, polygamy, widow burning, and infanticide are morally acceptable in some cultures but not in others. That different cultures have different practices and beliefs is undeniable. What is not so obvious, however, is whether such differences in practice are due to the fact that different cultures actually have different basic moral values and principles, or whether the various cultures share similar basic values and principles but simply apply them in very different ways. At any rate, descriptive relativism is merely the recognition of diversity in values, beliefs, and practices in various cultures. It describes the way cultures are without making any value judgments about the cultures themselves.

Frequently in anthropology, the terms "cultural validity" or "cultural relativism" are used to mean something similar to what I mean by descriptive relativism.[32] Cultural relativism is then taken to mean that each culture has a certain validity in it that meets (to some extent) the needs of its members, and that each culture's values, beliefs, and practices should be understood and appreciated within the total context of that culture. As Charles Kraft puts it, cultural validity or cultural relativism "maintains that an observer should be careful to evaluate a culture first in terms of its own values, goals, and focuses before venturing to compare it (either positively or negatively) with any other culture."[33] Certainly there is nothing in this which is objectionable in itself, although it is regrettable that the loaded term "cultural relativism" is used to refer to this quite legitimate activity. The need today for appreciating the great diversity among cultures and for understanding other cultures on their own terms can hardly be exaggerated.

Unfortunately, however, many people — including many

32. See Charles Kraft, *Christianity in Culture* (Maryknoll, N.Y.: Orbis, 1979), pp. 49f., and Melville Herskovits, *Man and His Works* (New York: Knopf, 1948), p. 77.

33. Kraft, *Christianity in Culture*, p. 49.

cultural anthropologists and sociologists — go well beyond mere descriptive relativism to embrace a form of normative relativism. Taking ethics as an example again, normative relativism maintains that what is actually morally right and wrong depends upon the views of the culture in question. What is actually morally right in one culture might be morally wrong in another. If polygamy is considered morally acceptable in one culture, then it actually is morally acceptable for that culture. On the other hand, if another culture regards polygamy as morally wrong, then it actually is morally wrong in that culture. Polygamy can thus be simultaneously right and wrong, depending upon the prevailing views of different cultures. In other words, basic moral values and principles are not universally valid for all people in all cultures but relative to a particular cultural context. There are no neutral, non-arbitrary criteria for identifying the correct moral code from among the many different moral codes in our world.

For our purposes, far more significant than ethical relativism is what is often called cognitive relativism, or the view that truth, knowledge, and basic rationality norms are relative to particular contexts.[34] Different relativists emphasize different contexts: truth and knowledge may be said to be relative to particular conceptual schemes, conceptual frameworks, linguistic frameworks, forms of life, language games, modes of thought, Weltanschauungen, systems of thought, paradigms, points of view, worldviews, etc. In each case, however, what counts as truth, knowledge, or rationality is dependent upon factors internal to the context itself. There is no truth, knowledge, or rationality norm independent of particular contexts. Thus, the basic assumptions and values of a given conceptual scheme cannot be evaluated on the basis of anything independent of or higher than what is internal to the context itself.[35]

---

34. See Roger Trigg, *Reason and Commitment* (Cambridge: Cambridge University Press, 1973), chap. 1, for a good discussion of cognitive relativism.

35. Cognitive relativism should be distinguished from skepticism, although the end result of both is the same. Skepticism does not deny that there is objective truth or knowledge. It simply maintains that, for whatever reasons, we do not or cannot have access to such knowledge. Relativism, on the other hand, does deny that there is any objective truth or knowledge which is not ultimately

Relativism enters the debate over religious pluralism in a variety of forms. Gordon Kaufman, among others, emphasizes the historical relativity of all of our knowledge.

> But there really is no such universally human position available to us; every religious (or secular) understanding and way of life we might uncover is a *particular* one, that has grown up in a particular history, makes particular claims, is accompanied by particular practices and injunctions, and hence is to be distinguished from all other particular religious and secular orientations. . . . [I]t seems undeniable that every position to which we might turn is itself historically specific. A universal frame of orientation for human understanding and life is no more available to us than is a universal language. . . . Instead of searching for a single "universal position" that sets forth, supposedly, the "essence" of the human or of human religiousness, I want to acknowledge immediately that in my view it is impossible simply to move out of and leave behind the particular symbolic, linguistic, and conceptual frames of reference within which one does all one's thinking and living.[36]

> If we understand human historicity in the sense I am urging here, Christian faith (like every other faith) will be seen as one perspective, one worldview, which has developed in and through a long history alongside other traditions, many of which are vying for the attention and loyalty of us all today. . . . We now see the great theologians of Christian history, for example, not simply as setting out the truth that is ultimately salvific for all humanity (as they have often been understood in the past), but rather as essentially engaged in discerning and articulating one particular perspective on life among many others.[37]

---

dependent upon a particular context. Either way, the result is the same: we have no knowledge of objective truth which is universal in the sense that it is not dependent upon a particular context or conceptual scheme.

36. Gordon Kaufman, "Religious Diversity, Historical Consciousness, and Christian Theology," in *The Myth of Christian Uniqueness*, p. 5. Emphasis in the original.

37. Ibid., p. 9.

Similarly, Catholic theologian Paul Knitter calls for "a new 'historical consciousness' of the relativity of all cultures."[38] He claims that if Christians are to make any sense out of religious pluralism "they are going to have to become part of the historical culture of the world of today and recognize the reality of historical relativism."[39] And Cambridge theologian Don Cupitt states that "all our thinking is historically conditioned."[40] He embraces what he calls "perspectivism":

> The main doctrines of perspectivism are as follows. There isn't any pure or quite neutral experience or knowledge of reality. In order to have any experience or knowledge at all, you must have a practical slant, an interest, an angle or a perspective which, so-to-say, makes certain things stand out and become noticeable. To take the simplest possible example, acute hunger may give you an interest in dividing up the world in such a way that the edible stands out from its inedible background. There are indefinitely many such perspectives or angles upon the world — and they are all of them historically-occasioned, human and contingent. Some, like certain branches of our natural sciences, are very highly refined. But even the most advanced scientific theories are still human, perspectival, historically-evolved and subject to future revision. . . . We can say only how things currently *seem* to us from our point of view; we cannot say how they are absolutely.[41]

> [T]here is no sense in trying to step outside the changing human debate and fix realities, meanings, and truths absolutely. We have to live and act without absolutes. To take just one example, I personally am prepared to fight tooth and nail for modern evolutionary biology against creationism. But I cannot claim that current evolutionary theory is, in any part of it, objectively,

38. Paul Knitter, *No Other Name? A Critical Survey of Christian Attitudes Toward the World Religions* (Maryknoll, N.Y.: Orbis, 1985), p. 173.

39. Ibid., p. 32.

40. Don Cupitt, "Anti-Realist Faith," p. 1. Unpublished paper delivered at the 1988 Philosophy of Religion Conference held at Claremont Graduate School, January 29-30, 1988.

41. Ibid., p. 2. Quoted with the permission of the author. Emphasis in the original.

dogmatically and perennially just true. On the contrary, over the generations to come I expect that every bit of current evolutionary theory will be replaced by something different. In this shifting relativistic world of ours, we can still choose our values and fight for them, but our beliefs won't have the old kind of permanent anchorage in an unchanging ideal order.[42]

Behind such contemporary expressions of historical relativism lurks the specter of Ernst Troeltsch (1865-1923), one of the first Western thinkers to grapple seriously with problems of religious pluralism. Toward the end of his life, Troeltsch maintained a radical historical relativism that considered all religions as different concrete, culturally and historically conditioned manifestations of the Absolute at work within humankind.[43] All religions reflect the work of the divine, but since they are all historically conditioned they are necessarily limited and relative. No particular religion can legitimately claim to be absolute. The relativity of history means that ultimately no single religion can be regarded as definitive. There are no objective criteria by which one can determine that one religion is superior to all others.

In our own day, philosopher Peter Winch has been much concerned with notions of intelligibility and rationality in various social and cultural contexts. Winch rejects the suggestion that there are universally valid norms, irrespective of their relation to particular contexts.

[C]riteria of logic are not a direct gift of God, but arise out of, and are only intelligible in the context of, ways of living or modes of social life as such. For instance, science is one such mode and religion is another; and each has criteria of intelligibility peculiar to itself. So within science or religion actions can be logical or illogical; in science, for example, it would be illogical to refuse to

42. Ibid., p. 5.
43. See his posthumously published "The Place of Christianity Among the World Religions," in *Christianity and Other Religions*, ed. John H. Hick and Brian Hebblethwaite (Philadelphia: Fortress Press, 1980), pp. 11-31. His earlier views are found in *The Absoluteness of Christianity and the History of Religions* (Richmond: John Knox Press, 1971).

be bound by results of a properly carried out experiment; in religion it would be illogical to suppose that one could pit one's own strength against God's; and so on. But we cannot sensibly say that either the practice of science itself or that of religion is either illogical or logical; both are non-logical.[44]

It is not clear just what is meant by "criteria of logic," but Winch seems to have in mind what are often called basic rationality norms — principles which regulate what is to be accepted as rational or reasonable. In a later much-discussed essay, Winch turns to the problem of understanding key practices and concepts of an alien society, such as the difficulty of modern Western persons understanding the practice of magic and witchcraft among the Azande of Africa.[45] He argues that the meanings of key concepts and practices, as well as the criteria for determining what is rational and irrational, are internal to the culture in question and cannot be imposed from outside. This theme has found wide acceptance among some theologians and philosophers as well as cultural anthropologists. That it can be carried to absurd lengths is apparent in the following statement by D. Z. Phillips.

> If I hear that one of my neighbours has killed another neighbour's child, given that he is sane, my condemnation is immediate. . . . But if I hear that some remote tribe practices child sacrifice, what then? I do not know what sacrifice means for the tribe in question. What would it mean to say that I condemned it when the "it" refers to something I know nothing about? If I did condemn it, I would be condemning murder. But murder is not child sacrifice.[46]

It is indeed a vicious form of relativism that refuses to condemn child sacrifice on the grounds that we allegedly cannot know what the practice means to the participants. But Phillips is simply taking

44. Peter Winch, *The Idea of a Social Science and Its Relation to Philosophy* (London: Routledge & Kegan Paul, 1958), pp. 100-101.

45. "Understanding a Primitive Society," in *American Philosophical Quarterly* 1 (1964): 307-24. Reprinted in *Rationality*, ed. Bryan Wilson (Oxford: Basil Blackwell, 1970), pp. 78-111.

46. D. Z. Phillips, *Faith and Philosophical Enquiry* (London, 1970), p. 237.

to its logical conclusion the thesis that criteria for appraising beliefs and practices are strictly internal to the particular form of life in which they appear.

Theologian Langdon Gilkey also accepts the limitations of relativism, but unlike some others he is well aware of the troubling implications which follow:

> There seems here no firm ground to stand on, either in a given tradition and its symbols, or in religious experience and its various aspects. And note, this is *real* relativism: if they are relativized, God, Christ, grace, and salvation, higher consciousness, *dharma, nirvana,* and *mukti* alike begin to recede in authority, to take on the aspect of mere projections relative to the cultural and individual subjectivity of the projectors, and so in the end they vanish like bloodless ghosts. We have no grounds for speaking of salvation at all, a situation of relativity far beyond asking about the salvation of *all.* A drift toward radical relativity has come to light, and any theological basis we might suggest for stopping that drift also begins itself to drift. The rough parity of religions, by removing the absolute starting point of each, seems to drain each of whatever it has to say and give to us, and so to leave us empty — and incapable of moving to some other more solid ground. Ecumenical tolerance represents an impressive moral and religious gain, a step toward love and understanding. But it has its own deep risks, and one of them is this specter of relativity, this loss of any place to stand, this elimination of the very heart of the religious as ultimate concern.[47]

47. Langdon Gilkey, "Plurality and Its Theological Implications," in *The Myth of Christian Uniqueness,* pp. 43-44. Emphasis in the original. Gilkey does, however, recognize that even relativists must condemn certain values and actions as "demonic" and thus "intolerable." He specifically identifies "a virulently nationalistic Shinto," Nazism, aspects of Stalinism and Maoism, and Shi'ite fundamentalism as representing "intolerable forms of religion." Thus, even in the midst of relativity, "we must assert some sort of ultimate values" and embrace a "relative absoluteness." "Paradoxically, plurality, precisely by its own ambiguity, implies both relativity and absoluteness, a juxtaposition or synthesis of the relative and the absolute that is frustrating intellectually and yet necessary practically." Ibid., pp. 45-46. It is very difficult indeed to make any clear sense out of Gilkey's call for "relative absoluteness." It seems a classic case of having one's cake and eating it too!

Although we cannot here launch into a full treatment of the difficulties faced by various forms of relativism, the inadequacy of any position which rules out the possibility of nonarbitrary criteria for assessment which transcend particular contexts can be seen from the following considerations.

1. Undoubtedly, the major difficulty with relativism is the problem of incoherence. Ever since the time of Plato it has repeatedly been demonstrated that it is difficult, if not impossible, to state the thesis of relativism without thereby engaging in self-refutation. That is, any statement of relativism, regardless of whether it be formulated in terms of historical, linguistic, or cultural relativism, implicitly appeals to the falsity of the central thesis of relativism.[48] We might take cultural relativism as an example. Cultural relativism holds that truth and basic principles of rationality are internal or relative to a given culture; they are determined by factors within the culture and not by reference to anything external to the culture. The incoherence of this can be demonstrated in two ways. First, if cultural relativism is true, then the statement of cultural relativism itself must be true only within the context of the culture of the person asserting it. It cannot be regarded as true in any universal, transcultural sense. But then why should anyone who is not a member of that culture bother to accept the thesis of cultural relativism as true? Cultural relativism would only be "relatively true." Second, the one advancing the thesis of cultural relativism usually presents evidence and reasons for accepting relativism as true. But if cultural relativism is true, then the statements expressing evidence for it can be no more than "relatively true." Such evidence may be compelling within the context of the culture of the person asserting relativism but not necessarily binding for the outsider. But then why should an outsider accept cultural relativism? Similar difficulties vitiate any attempt to restrict truth and rationality norms to a particular con-

48. See the fine essay by Maurice Mandelbaum, "Subjective, Objective, and Conceptual Relativisms," in *The Monist* 62, 4 (1979): 403-23. Reprinted in *Relativism: Cognitive and Moral*, pp. 34-61.

text, whether that context be cultural, lingustic, historical, or religious. Any attempt to state that truth is not objective but relative to a particular context, if intended as a true statement, faces the embarrassment of self-refutation. For we can always ask whether the statement of relativism itself is a truth about objective reality. If so, then relativism is false. If not, then it is hard to see why it should be accepted.

2. We noted earlier that relativism is often prompted by observing the fact of cultural diversity and human disagreement. The fact that there are many different and conflicting beliefs, values, and practices in various cultures prompts many to conclude that there is no universally valid, objective truth in religion or ethics, or at least that we have no access to nonarbitrary criteria by which to determine which of the beliefs (if any) are true.

But, as Roger Trigg points out, the question of what is believed by various groups is logically distinct from that of what should be accepted and believed. "What they do in fact accept or reject ought to be a different question from what is worthy of acceptance or rejection."[49] Simply because people in different cultures happen to accept different religious beliefs, it does not necessarily follow that all of these beliefs are correct or equally valid. Ultimately, truth is not dependent upon what people happen to accept; it is defined by what is in fact the case. Philosopher William Alston correctly observes that "truth is independent of epistemic considerations, of what is recognized in one or another language-game as constituting justification, rationality, or acceptability."[50] History provides ample proof that a false belief can be widely accepted and fervently believed. Up until the seventeenth century, for example, the geocentric theory of the universe was virtually unquestioned, although it later proved to be false.

3. The theory that notions of truth, rationality, and intelligibility are strictly internal to a particular social context does not

49. Trigg, *Reason and Commitment*, pp. 123f.

50. W. P. Alston, "The Christian Language Game," in *The Autonomy of Religious Belief*, ed. Frederick Crosson (Notre Dame: University of Notre Dame Press, 1981), p. 138.

account for the fact that such criteria often change and develop over a period of time within a given context.[51] What is acceptable, and the way in which such acceptability is determined in contemporary liberal Protestantism is quite different from what it was in eighteenth-century European Protestantism. What was widely accepted as true and relatively nonproblematic in medieval Europe is generally looked upon with incredulity in contemporary Western society (e.g., the Virgin Birth). Given that within a particular social or cultural context beliefs as well as criteria for determining the acceptability of beliefs change dramatically, if truth and rationality norms are internal to the social context, on what basis is one to affirm that, say, the beliefs and criteria of the twentieth century are preferable to those of the twelfth century? Any such judgment would seem arbitrary. Once it is admitted that different people within a society believe different things, or that over a period of time they have believed different things, truth cannot be defined in terms of what is accepted in that society.

4. The price of accepting relativism is forfeiture of the right to make any judgments about worldviews, positive or negative. If truth and rationality norms are relative to particular social or cultural contexts, then clearly one cannot appeal to such factors to make judgments about one's own worldview or the worldviews of others. Criteria determined by factors internal to a given worldview cannot be appealed to in assessing the truth or adequacy of various other worldviews. All we would be able to say is that from our own relative perspective worldview A is to be preferred to worldview B. But this, of course, amounts to no more than a statement of preference. It follows that a relativist cannot make judgments about the objective truth of any particular religion, or indeed about the superiority of a religious worldview to a secular worldview. As Trigg puts it,

> Once the notion of there being a justification for accepting one religion rather than another is discarded, all questions of objective

51. See Alasdair MacIntyre, "Is Understanding Religion Compatible With Believing?" in *Rationality*, pp. 66f.

truth and falsity, and all distinctions between genuine religion and superstition, have to be swept aside. Commitments to different religions have each to be regarded as ultimate.[52]

A relativist can have preferences and commitments and can recommend that others join him or her in accepting a particular worldview. But no reasons for such preferences or commitments can be offered; least of all could the relativist argue that his or her perspective is in any sense objectively true or superior to alternative perspectives. For any attempt to present reasons for being committed to a particular perspective will implicitly involve denial of the fundamental tenets of relativism.

It is a remarkable irony that some of the staunchest critics of relativism — theological fideists — embrace a view that faces precisely the same logical difficulties as relativism. Fideists hold that each person's worldview is ultimately based upon certain basic faith postulates and that there are no neutral or "autonomous" rationality norms by which to evaluate competing perspectives. The Christian believer has her set of fundamental assumptions which must be accepted by faith; so does the atheistic materialist and the pantheistic Taoist. Appeal to rational considerations alone cannot settle questions of the relative adequacy of competing perspectives. Nevertheless, while maintaining that one's most basic assumptions are ultimately the product of a faith commitment, theological fideists hold that, based upon such commitments, Christians are to judge every other worldview on the basis of God's self-revelation in Jesus Christ and Holy Scripture.

Theological fideism occasionally manifests itself in discussions of religious pluralism. In his otherwise fine book *The Open Secret*, Lesslie Newbigin, for example, makes unnecessary concessions to fideism.

> It is understandable that anyone faced with the clashing diversity of religious commitments should seek some basis for unity among them, or at least some agreed common framework. The difficulty is that we are here dealing with *ultimate* commitments, and the

52. Trigg, *Reason and Commitment*, p. 61.

basis which I accept can only be *my* commitment. . . . The framework which I devise or discern is my ultimate commitment or
else it cannot function in the way intended. As such a commitment, it must defend its claim to truth over against other claims
to truth. I have no standpoint except the point where I stand. The
claim that I have is simply the claim that mine is the standpoint
from which it is possible to discern the truth that relativizes all
truth. That claim is the expression of the ultimate commitment
which is my real religion. . . . I must repeat the simple truth that
no standpoint is available to any man except the point where he
stands; that there is no platform from which one can claim to
have an "objective" view which supersedes all the "subjective"
faith-commitments of the world's faiths; that every man must take
his stand on the floor of the arena, on the same level with every
other, and there engage in the real encounter of ultimate commitment with those who, like him, have staked their lives on their
vision of the truth.[53]

Curiously, Newbigin follows this by stating that "Jesus is for the
believer the source from whom his understanding of the totality
of experience is drawn and therefore the criterion by which other
ways of understanding are judged."[54]

Despite the commendable intention of safeguarding the
priority of Jesus as the norm by which all other perspectives are
to be judged, Newbigin's statement faces the same epistemological
difficulties noted with relativism. The Christian claims epistemic
priority for God's self-revelation in Jesus. The Zen Buddhist claims
ultimacy for *satori*, the direct, unmediated apprehension of ultimate reality. The Hindu appeals to *para vidya*, the highest form of
knowledge and truth, which is allegedly entirely self-certifying.
Obviously, simply appealing to what is held to be the self-certifying
nature of one's own faith commitments as the proper criterion by
which to evaluate other perspectives is inadequate for settling the
question of truth. Why should Jesus be the norm by which to judge

53. Lesslie Newbigin, *The Open Secret* (Grand Rapids: Eerdmans, 1978),
pp. 184-85, 190.
54. Ibid., p. 191.

other traditions? If indeed, as Newbigin suggests, there are no
neutral norms or criteria and all perspectives reduce to certain
fundamental faith postulates, it is hard to see how the Christian
can, in Newbigin's terms, "defend [his] claim to truth over against
other claims to truth" or how there can be any "real encounter of
ultimate commitment" with those of other faiths. And like relativism, fideism not only forfeits the right to reject competing perspectives as false, but it too faces the charge of self-refutation. For
the mere thesis of fideism appeals to rationality norms, such as the
principle of noncontradiction, which logically cannot be merely
faith postulates.[55]

Criteria for Appraising Worldviews

If, as I have argued, relativism is epistemologically unacceptable, then it follows that at least some criteria are not context-
dependent or relative to worldviews and, at least in principle,
can be used to appraise various competing religious worldviews.
However, recognizing that there are such criteria is one thing;
identifying and applying them to particular religious traditions
is an entirely different matter. Highly technical and complex
issues are involved in any appraisal of worldviews; the difficulty
of the task should not be minimized. On the other hand, we
must not fall into the opposite error of supposing that unless
one can spell out clearly and defend all criteria used in evaluating
religions we are not justified in making any such judgments.
Philosopher Roderick Chisholm reminds us that we can and do
know many things without our necessarily being able to specify
criteria justifying such claims to knowledge.[56] I suggest, however,
that there are some criteria which can be identified and, in
principle, can be applied to the evaluation of religious world-

55. For an incisive critique of theological fideism see Mark M. Hanna,
Crucial Questions in Apologetics (Grand Rapids: Baker, 1981), pp. 33-39, 95-106,
109-14.

56. See Roderick Chisholm, *The Problem of the Criterion* (Milwaukee:
Marquette University Press, 1973).

views, although in any given situation it might prove to be very difficult to do so.

In evaluating a religious worldview we are concerned ultimately with the question of its truth. But what do we mean by this? We saw earlier that, in its logically most basic sense, truth is a property of propositions such that a proposition is true if and only if the state of affairs to which it refers is as the proposition asserts it to be. Otherwise it is false. We can also think in terms of beliefs being true or false, although strictly speaking it is the believed proposition that is true or false. But what can it mean to speak of a religion, or religious worldview, as true or false?

Here it is helpful to recall our earlier discussion of defining beliefs of a religious worldview.[57] The degree to which religious beliefs can be said to be essential to the religious worldview of which they are a part varies. Some beliefs are clearly of a more peripheral nature. Acceptance or rejection of belief in baptism by immersion as opposed to, say, sprinkling, does not alter substantially the nature of the Christian worldview. On the other hand, acceptance of belief in the existence of an eternal creator God is clearly essential to Christian faith. Although there are some Christian theologians today who would dispute even this, most Christians would not hesitate to affirm that belief in God is indispensable; it is a defining belief of Christianity.

Let us think of a defining belief of a religion R as follows:

D1: p is a defining belief of R if and only if being an active participant in good standing within the religious community of R entails acceptance of p.

It seems clear that each religious tradition does have a set of defining beliefs, although there may be considerable debate over just what is to be included in this set. With this definition of defining beliefs we can then proceed to define what is meant by a true religion.

57. See p. 40.

D2: A religion R is true if and only if all of its defining beliefs are true; if any of its defining beliefs are false, then R is false.[58]

But how are we to determine whether the defining beliefs of a given religious tradition are true? There is no simple answer to this question. In asking it we confront some of the knottiest problems in contemporary epistemology, and unfortunately there is no clear consensus on how some fundamental epistemological questions should be answered.[59] What constitutes knowledge? Under what conditions is one justified in accepting a particular belief? Must one be able to provide sufficient grounds for, say, belief in God in order to be justified in believing in God? What would constitute such grounds? What kind of contrary evidence would falsify belief in God? Recent discussions indicate that these questions are considerably more complex than might initially be supposed.[60]

Fortunately, there is no need for us to try to resolve these issues here. For our purposes it is sufficient simply to indicate in rather broad terms some principles that can be appealed to in

58. On this definition a religion can have some true defining beliefs and still be regarded as false. There is no entirely satisfactory way to classify religions which have defining beliefs of mixed truth value. If, say, a religion R has ten defining beliefs, eight being true and two false, we might be tempted to call R true because most of its defining beliefs are true. But what if R is orthodox Christianity and one of the two false propositions concerns the deity of Christ? Would we still wish to speak of orthodox Christianity as true? Can we really speak of a true religion which has at least one false belief among its defining beliefs? It seems best to restrict the notion of a true religion, and to recognize that in labelling a given religion as false we do not necessarily imply that all of its defining beliefs are false.

59. For an excellent overview of the current status of epistemological theory see John L. Pollock, *Contemporary Theories of Knowledge* (Totowa, N.J.: Rowman & Littlefield, 1986).

60. Helpful discussions of these issues as they pertain to Christian faith can be found in Keith Yandell, *Christianity and Philosophy* (Grand Rapids: Eerdmans, 1984); Basil Mitchell, *The Justification of Religious Belief* (New York: Macmillan, 1973); George Mavrodes, *Belief in God* (New York: Random House, 1970); C. F. Delaney, ed., *Rationality and Religious Belief* (Notre Dame: University of Notre Dame Press, 1979); and Alvin Plantinga and Nicholas Wolterstorff, eds., *Faith and Rationality: Reason and Belief in God* (Notre Dame: University of Notre Dame Press, 1983).

trying to determine the truth or falsity of competing religious worldviews. The actual application of these principles in evaluating various religious worldviews is a task we cannot pursue here. I hardly need to point out that the following discussion of criteria is not exhaustive. Undoubtedly there are other significant principles which have not been mentioned here, and much more could and should be said about each of those listed below. What follows is meant merely to indicate that there are some principles which can be applied legitimately in the evaluation of competing religious worldviews.[61]

1. Basic logical principles. The three basic principles of classical logic are the principles of identity, noncontradiction, and excluded middle. The principle of identity, when applied to statements, holds that if a statement is true, then it is true. The principle of noncontradiction maintains that a statement cannot be both true and false. The principle of excluded middle affirms that any statement is either true or false.[62] The three principles are important in that they provide necessary conditions for meaningful and intelligible thinking and discourse on any subject whatsoever. They are not merely assumptions that have been adopted because they prove useful; they are among the necessary conditions for making any assumption in the first place. Nor are they simply descriptive of the way people reason. They are normative or prescriptive in being among the rules which dictate the conditions under which one can have meaningful and intelligible thinking and discourse.

A statement or belief that is self-contradictory is necessarily false. Two or more statements or beliefs that are mutually contradictory cannot all be true. At least one must be false. This suggests the following principles for evaluating worldviews:

61. In the following discussion of criteria I am indebted to the very fine treatment of the subject by Yandell, *Christianity and Philosophy,* chap. 8. He, of course, is in no way responsible for my formulation of the principles.

62. For more on these principles see Irving M. Copi, *Introduction to Logic,* 5th ed. (New York: Macmillan, 1978), pp. 306-8. On the objectivity of logical relations and principles see Dallas Willard, *Logic and the Objectivity of Knowledge* (Athens, Ohio: Ohio University Press, 1984), especially pp. 143-66.

P1: If a defining belief p of a religion R is self-contradictory then p is false.

P2: If two or more defining beliefs of R are mutually contradictory at least one of them must be false.

And, of course, if a defining belief of R is false, then R is to be regarded as false as well. These requirements can be formulated in terms of consistency: for a set of defining beliefs of R to be all true they must be consistent. This is a necessary, but not a sufficient, condition for their truth. Lack of consistency entails that not all the defining beliefs are true; at least one is false. But lack of inconsistency in itself does not guarantee that all the beliefs are true, for a set of false beliefs can also be internally consistent.

Obviously, if it can be shown that the defining beliefs of a religion are contradictory, then there is good reason for rejecting that religion as false. Not surprisingly, charges of self-contradiction have been levelled at various traditions. The Christian doctrine of the Trinity, for example, is frequently dismissed by non-Christians as entailing contradictions, whereas orthodox Christians vigorously defend the doctrine as noncontradictory, although admittedly it is a mystery. Similarly, some philosophers claim that the notions of *satori* and *nirvana* in Buddhism entail contradictions. Now if the doctrine of the Trinity is indeed contradictory, then orthodox Christianity must be rejected as false. Likewise, if *satori* or *nirvana* is contradictory, then the traditions which accept either of these notions as defining beliefs are falsified. Whether any of these doctrines is indeed self-contradictory is of course a separate and complex question.

2. Self-defeating statements. Some statements cannot be true because they provide the grounds for their own refutation. There are various kinds of self-defeating statements. For example, as we saw in the discussion of relativism, the affirmation of thoroughgoing relativism is self-refuting. That is, the statement "All truth is relative to a particular cultural context" cannot be regarded as a universal truth. For if true, there would be at least one truth not relative to cultural contexts — namely, the truth of the thesis of cultural relativism. And as we saw in an earlier chapter, it is difficult, if not impossible, to formulate the ineffability thesis without its being self-refuting. In a slightly different sense, the statements "Nothing exists" and "There are no conscious beings" can be regarded as self-defeating in that if they are true no one could know that they are true.[63] Thus, we might formulate another principle as follows:

P3: If a defining belief p of R is self-defeating it cannot reasonably be accepted as true.

And if R includes a self-defeating defining belief, then R cannot reasonably be accepted as true. Thus, for example, there are good grounds for rejecting as false religious worldviews which essentially include a version of relativism or the ineffability thesis.

3. *Coherence of worldview.* For a given religious worldview to be accepted as true it is not sufficient merely that its defining beliefs all be internally consistent. The defining beliefs must also be properly related to each other. We might use the term "coherence" to indicate this proper relationship among defining beliefs.[64] For a worldview to be coherent in this sense, the defining beliefs of the worldview must combine to form a system in which some significant phenomena concerning human existence are explained, or some fundamental problem is solved, or a unified view of the world is presented. As Keith Yandell observes, "A supposed system which lacks mutual coherence among its propositional constituents provides a poor explanation, solution, or perspective, or none at all, and so, short of revision, is a weak candidate for truth."[65]

For example, the following statements are all not only mutually consistent but also true, and yet they can hardly be said to form a coherent system: "September follows August"; "Richard Nixon resigned as president of the United States"; "Two plus two

63. The examples are from Keith Yandell, *Christianity and Philosophy,* pp. 278f.

64. "Coherence" is sometimes used to mean "consistency" or "lack of contradiction." This, however, is not the sense in which it is being used here.

65. Ibid., p. 274.

equals four"; "Christians believe in an eternal creator God." There
is no obvious relationship among the statements and no unified
perspective on any particular problem is presented. It would be
ludicrous to suggest that these statements form the set of defining
beliefs of a true religion. Thus, a further principle might be:

P4: If the defining beliefs of R are not coherent in the sense of
     providing a unified perspective on the world, then R cannot
     plausibly be regarded as true.

Coherence of a worldview in and of itself is not sufficient to
guarantee truth of the worldview, but lack of coherence does provide good reason for its rejection.

4. Adequacy of explanation within reference range. Following
Yandell, we might think of the reference range of a theory as the
range of data which, given its nature, the theory should be able to
account for or explain.[66] A theory about the nature of morality
should be able to account for all the relevant data concerning
morality. Likewise, a theory about the nature of religion should be
able to explain satisfactorily the relevant religious phenomena. In
particular, a religious worldview should be able to provide adequate answers to the basic questions that lie at the heart of the
religious orientation: Where did I come from? What is the nature
of the religious ultimate? What is my relation to the religious
ultimate? Why is there evil, suffering, and moral failure? How can
one escape the human predicament? Is there life after death? And
so on. This suggests P5:

P5: Any religious worldview which is unable to account for fun-
     damental phenomena associated with a religious orientation
     or which cannot provide adequate answers to central ques-
     tions in religion should not be accepted as true.

P5 initially seems noncontroversial enough. On both popular and
more academic levels religious believers expect their religious

66. Ibid., p. 282.

worldview to provide satisfactory answers to basic questions about human existence. Failure to find adequate answers within a given religion often results in withdrawal from that religious tradition. And yet, despite its obvious legitimacy as a general principle, the actual application of P5 to particular religions is notoriously controversial and provides much philosophical grist for the mill. For there is not always agreement concerning just what phenomena fall within the reference range of a religious worldview and what constitutes a satisfactory answer to the basic questions of religion. This fact, however, does not call into question the legitimacy of the criterion itself but simply indicates the difficulty of applying it to particular religious worldviews.

    5. Consistency with knowledge in other fields. Since ultimately there is unity and consistency to truth, we would expect that what is true in religion is consistent with what is true in other domains such as science, history, and archeology. Glaring inconsistency between what is asserted in a given religious worldview and what has been established in, say, history indicates that either the religious claim or the conclusion from history is in error. If the inconsistency is in fact a contradiction, clearly both claims cannot be true. The assertion to be rejected as false is a matter which cannot be stipulated in advance but which must carefully be determined on the basis of a variety of factors, such as the degree of evidential support enjoyed by the historical claim and the relation of the religious claim to other well-supported propositions (both religious and nonreligious) which might in turn provide it with compelling support. In general, however, we might say that if the historical claim is well established and widely accepted, barring other considerations, the religious claim should be rejected as false. The belief of many Muslims, for example, that Jesus did not in fact die on the cross but that someone else was crucified in his place is inconsistent with the widely accepted and well-established fact of his crucifixion on the cross. If this belief is indeed central to Islam — and ultimately only Muslims can answer this question — then, unless it can be justified on other grounds, we have good reason for rejecting a central tenet of Islam as probably false. Thus we have:

P6: If a defining belief p of R contradicts well-established conclu-
     sions in other domains and if R cannot justify doing so, then
     p should be rejected as probably false.

Often there may not be an explicit inconsistency between a religious belief and a truth in another domain, but there is a relation
between a given religious belief and a conclusion in another field
which nevertheless calls into question the religious belief.
Frequently, for example, a religious belief depends upon a truth in
history. The statement "Muhammad is the Messenger of Allah"
can plausibly be said to depend upon the truth of "Muhammad
recited the surahs of the Qur'an." If it could be demonstrated that
Muhammad never did recite the surahs of the Qur'an, then there
would be prima facie evidence against accepting "Muhammad is
the Messenger of Allah" as true.[67] Or the statement "Jesus arose
bodily from the dead on the third day" can be said to depend upon
the historical statement "The tomb did not contain Jesus' corpse
on the third day." If it could somehow be demonstrated that the
latter historical statement is false — that Jesus' corpse was indeed
in the tomb on the third day — then the religious statement about
Jesus' bodily resurrection would be falsified. It is not that the
historical statement entails the corresponding religious statement.
But the truth of the religious statement nevertheless depends upon
the truth of the historical statement. That is, the historical statement would have to be included, along with other statements, in
any list of premises from which the religious statement would
follow. This suggests

P7: If a defining belief p of R depends upon a belief in another
     domain (e.g., history) which there is good reason to reject as
     false, then there is good reason to reject p as probably false.

     6. *Moral assessment.* Although the precise nature of the
relation may not be clear, most of the major religions suggest a

_____

67. The example is from William A. Christian's helpful article, "Domains
of Truth," *American Philosophical Quarterly* 12 (January 1975): 62.

close connection between the religious ultimate and basic moral values and principles. On a popular level as well, the idea that moral indicators can be used to evaluate religious leaders and traditions finds ready acceptance. John Hick correctly observes that it was not simply what Jesus said that attracted his followers and convinced them that he was from God; it was the combination of what he said and did, of his teachings as well as his morally impeccable life, which marked him as sent from God.[68] Conversely, part of the reason for the widespread condemnation of the charismatic cult leader Jim Jones after the 1978 Jonestown tragedy was the fact that what he said and did was at variance with fundamental moral values and principles. He was perceived — particularly after the Jonestown tragedy — as an evil and immoral man. Religious leaders are expected to lead morally exemplary lives and the authentication of a religious leader's message rests partially upon the moral quality of that leader's life.

Furthermore, most religious traditions seem to accept the objectivity of moral values and principles. Basic moral values and principles are held to be binding upon all persons and are not dependent upon, or merely reflections of, the prevailing norms of particular social or cultural contexts. If we are justified in accepting the objectivity of basic moral values and principles[69] and in believing that we can know at least some of these values and principles, then we can formulate two general moral principles by which to evaluate religious worldviews:

P8: If one or more defining beliefs of R are incompatible with widely accepted and well-established moral values and principles; or if R includes among its essential practices or rites activities which are incompatible with basic moral values and practices, then there is good reason for rejecting R as false.

P9: If the defining beliefs of R entail the denial of the objectivity of basic moral values and principles; or if they entail the denial

---

68. John Hick, *Problems of Religious Pluralism*, p. 76.

69. On the objectivity of moral values see Richard Swinburne, "The Objectivity of Morality," *Philosophy* 51 (1976): 5-20.

of the objective distinction between right and wrong, good and evil, then there is good reason for rejecting R as false.

Now in applying P8 it will not suffice simply to examine the historical record of a given religious tradition. It is a sad fact that immoral practices and evils can be enumerated from the history of each of the major religious traditions. And while there is surely a sense in which the actual track record of a religion is relevant to questions of its truth — a religion which has consistently failed to exemplify fundamental moral values and principles should not be taken seriously — the more important question concerns the essential beliefs and values of the religion. Each religion should be evaluated primarily on the basis of its best ideals, not its failures in practice. But if its fundamental tenets are at odds with basic moral values, then there is good reason for rejecting it. Thus, a religious worldview which includes child sacrifice or cannibalism as an essential rite or adopts as a basic tenet the inherent superiority of whites over blacks should, for this reason, be rejected as probably false.

Moreover, if basic moral principles and values are objective in the sense specified above, then clearly any worldview incompatible with moral objectivity should be rejected as false. P9, then, provides an interesting test for certain forms of Hinduism and Buddhism. A strong case can be made for the view that Advaita Vedanta Hinduism and Zen Buddhism — insofar as they make a fundamental ontological distinction between levels of reality and truth and maintain that the highest Reality and Truth is absolutely undifferentiated unity, allowing no distinctions whatever — are incompatible with moral objectivity. It is hard to see how Advaita Vedanta or Zen can accommodate an objective distinction between good and evil, right and wrong. For such distinctions are explicitly relegated to the lower level of reality and truth *(zokutai)* and are said to be transcended by the absolute unity of ultimate Reality and Truth *(shintai)*. This is unambiguously expressed in an ancient Zen poem from the sixth century attributed to Seng Ts'an:

> If you want to get the plain truth
> Be not concerned with right and wrong.
> The conflict between right and wrong
> Is the sickness of the mind.[70]

Arthur Koestler tells of a fascinating interview he had with a Japanese Zen scholar who, when pressed by Koestler for Zen's response to the atrocities of Hitler and Nazism, merely replied that what Hitler had done to the Jews was "very silly." Although repeatedly pressed by Koestler, the Zen scholar refused to call Hitler evil, saying that such distinctions between good and evil were alien to Zen.[71] Surely this is eloquent testimony which, according to P9, counts significantly against accepting the Zen worldview as true.[72]

Not only must a given religious tradition be compatible with basic moral values and principles, but, given the intimate connection between morality and religion, it must also satisfactorily account for and explain the phenomena of morality: Why is it that humans are aware of the distinction between right and wrong? Why does doing what is wrong produce a sense of guilt and moral failure? Why is it that although one desires to do what is right one often cannot help doing what is wrong? Why is the human person regarded as having particular dignity and value? If we are to accept a given religious tradition as true, these questions should receive adequate answers. This suggests a further principle:

70. Quoted in Alan Watts, *The Way of Zen* (Harmondsworth, Eng.: Penguin, 1957), p. 135.

71. Arthur Koestler, *The Lotus and the Robot* (New York: Harper & Row, 1960), p. 274.

72. The notion of *nirvana* in Buddhism faces similar difficulties. The Buddhist scholar Walpola Rahula claims, "*Nirvana* is beyond all terms of duality and relativity. It is therefore beyond our conceptions of good and evil, right and wrong, existence and non-existence." Rahula, *What the Buddha Taught*, 2nd ed. (New York: Grove Press, 1974), p. 43. Speaking of *nirvana*, the Buddha is reported to have said, "Here the four elements of solidity, fluidity, heat and motion have no place; the notions of length and breadth, the subtle and the gross, good and evil, name and form are altogether destroyed; neither this world nor the other, nor coming, going or standing, neither death nor birth, nor sense-objects are to be found" (as quoted in Rahula, p. 37).

P10: If R is unable to provide adequate answers to basic questions about the phenomena of moral awareness, this provides good reason for rejecting R as false.

Before leaving the subject of moral criteria, we should take note of an assumption implicit in some recent writings on religious pluralism. Frequently there is the suggestion that the "saintly" or morally exemplary life of a religious leader such as Gandhi or Gautama Buddha in and of itself provides sufficient grounds for accepting that figure as being from God and his teachings as true. Obviously, there is a connection between one's conduct and the corroboration of any religious claims that are made. Lack of moral integrity will detract from the credibility of one's claim to be a prophet. Nevertheless, it cannot be maintained that a morally exemplary life in and of itself validates either one's claims to be from God or the truth of one's teachings. For if this were the case, the truth of atheism could be established simply by pointing to an atheist who lived a compelling, morally exemplary life — and surely there are morally exemplary atheists! While we readily admit that there are many morally outstanding religious leaders in non-Christian religions and that there is a sense in which a morally exemplary life, when combined with other relevant factors, does help to corroborate the claims made by a religious teacher, we must recognize that moral considerations are only part of a broader constellation of factors that are relevant to the determination of truth or falsity of an individual's teachings.

It might be helpful to summarize the preceding discussion by listing the definitions and principles proposed above:

D1: p is a defining belief of R if and only if being an active participant in good standing within the religious community of R entails acceptance of p.

D2: A religion R is true if and only if all of its defining beliefs are true; if any of its defining beliefs are false, then R is false.

P1: If a defining belief p of a religion R is self-contradictory then p is false.

P2: If two or more defining beliefs of R are mutually contradictory at least one of them must be false.

P3: If a defining belief p of R is self-defeating it cannot reasonably be accepted as true.

P4: If the defining beliefs of R are not coherent in the sense of providing a unified perspective on the world, then R cannot plausibly be regarded as true.

P5: Any religious worldview which is unable to account for fundamental phenomena associated with a religious orientation or which cannot provide adequate answers to central questions in religion should not be accepted as true.

P6: If a defining belief p of R contradicts well-established conclusions in other domains, and if R cannot justify doing so, then p should be rejected as probably false.

P7: If a defining belief p of R depends upon a belief in another domain (e.g., history) which there is good reason to reject as false, then there is good reason to reject p as probably false.

P8: If one or more defining beliefs of R are incompatible with widely accepted and well-established moral values and principles; or if R includes among its essential practices or rites activities which are incompatible with basic moral values and practices, then there is good reason for rejecting R as false.

P9: If the defining beliefs of R entail the denial of the objectivity of basic moral values and principles; or if they entail the denial of the objective distinction between right and wrong, good and evil, then there is good reason for rejecting R as false.

P10: If R is unable to provide adequate answers to basic questions about the phenomena of moral awareness this provides good reason for rejecting R as false.

Although this cannot be argued here, I should state that the reason I believe one is justified in accepting the Christian faith as true is because it is the only worldview that satisfies the requirements of all the above criteria.

To this point we have been concerned with criteria which are "neutral" in the sense that they are logically independent of one's religious commitments; they are criteria which, if valid, are applicable for all persons regardless of religious orientation. But an obvious question is whether it can be legitimate to evaluate other religions on the basis of one's own religious convictions. Can a Christian legitimately make judgments about other religions on the basis of Christian values and teachings? Can an evangelical, for example, reject the Shinto understanding of *kami* (the divine) as false simply because it is incompatible with the biblical understanding of the eternal creator God? Or can a Christian reject the Buddhist understanding of the human predicament as inadequate because it has no place for the biblical teaching on sin as human rebellion before a holy and righteous creator God?

There is a sense in which it is understandable and even to be expected that the follower of a given religious tradition will reject as false any claims that are incompatible with defining beliefs of his or her own tradition. Certainly there is a sense in which a Christian can reject other competing beliefs, practices, or values simply because they are incompatible with basic Christian tenets. On this understanding, a Christian can reject as false the Buddhist teaching on rebirth because he or she regards it as incompatible with biblical teaching on the afterlife. But, of course, this general principle also holds for adherents of other religions. There is a sense in which the Buddhist too is entitled to reject as false Christian teaching conflicting with basic Buddhist beliefs. One's religious worldview articulates one's deepest commitments. And it would be absurd to suppose that someone embracing a particular religious worldview could not reject alternative beliefs and practices which conflict with his or her own basic beliefs.

This notion of what might be called "weak entitlement," however, must be clearly distinguished from the much stronger concept of epistemic justification. Simply because it is admitted that there is a sense in which a Buddhist, for example, can reject Christian teaching on God the creator because it conflicts with fundamental Buddhist dogma, it does not follow that the Buddhist is justified in doing so. Epistemic justification has to do with the justification or warrant for one's beliefs — the question whether there are sufficient grounds for one's beliefs. Ultimately, the question of the justification for making judgments about alternative religious beliefs on the basis of one's own religious commitments hangs upon the logically prior question of the justification for accepting one's basic religious beliefs in the first place. Thus, a Christian is justified in making judgments about other religious beliefs on the basis of Christian teaching only if he or she is justified in accepting the fundamental tenets of the Christian faith as true. If indeed one is justified in accepting the Christian faith as true — as I am convinced is the case — then one is also justified in making judgments about other religious traditions on the basis of Christian teaching, and in rejecting as false those beliefs from other traditions that are incompatible with Christian faith.

CHAPTER SIX

All Roads Lead to . . .

There is today growing acceptance of the view that, whatever the differences in practice and belief, all religious traditions can be regarded as culturally and historically conditioned human responses to the same divine reality. All religions are mediators of salvation and can be said to be true. A traditional Japanese saying, "Although the paths to the summit may differ, from the top one sees the same moon," when applied to religion suggests that although there are different religious paths, ultimately each way is in touch with the same divine reality and will reach the same goal. And this, of course, is a prominent theme in Hindu thought as well. In the Bhagavad Gita Krishna proclaims, "Whatever path men travel is my path; No matter where they walk it leads to Me" (4.11).[1] Commenting on this verse, Hindu philosopher Sarvepalli Radhakrishnan says, "The same God is worshipped by all. The differences of conception and approach are determined by local colouring and social adaptations. All manifestations belong to the same Supreme."[2] And Kshiti Mohan Sen states:

1. *Bhagavad Gita* 4.11, trans. Swami Prabhavananda and Christopher Isherwood (New York: Mentor, 1972), p. 51.
2. *The Bhagavadgita: With an Introductory Essay, Sanskrit Text, English*

As the age old *Mahimna-Stotra* puts it: "All these paths, O Lord, *Veda, Samkhya, Yoga, Pasupata, Vaishnava*, lead but to Thee, like the winding river that at last merges into the sea." This, in fact, is the message of Hinduism, if it has one. He is infinite, omniscient, omnipresent, but He may appear different to different people. There are various ways of reaching Him, each as valid as every other. Apparently conflicting views of God may be nothing more than the infinite aspects of the same Supreme.[3]

That various religions are different ways of encountering the same divine reality is readily accepted by many who do not have extensive contact with more than one religious tradition. But it is increasingly embraced by scholars who are familiar with the great diversity among religious traditions. The distinguished sociologist Peter Berger, for example, who is well acquainted with non-Christian religions, says:

> I cannot believe, looking at India, looking at Hinduism particularly, that millennia of human experience and thought are simply a mistake. I think there is a particular access to reality here, and *mutatis mutandis*, I think the same is true of Buddhism, and the same is true of every other major religious tradition.[4]

Some scholars have argued that, despite the many obvious external differences between religious traditions, there is a common core or unity to all religions. Frequently a distinction is made between the inessential external trappings of various religions and the essential core said to be common to all major religions. One thinks here of the writings of Rudolf Otto, Friedrich Heiler, Ernest Hocking, Sarvepalli Radhakrishnan, Arnold Toynbee, Aldous Huxley, Frithjof Schuon, and Wilfred Cantwell Smith.[5] Unfortunately,

---

Translation and Notes, by S. Radhakrishnan (New York: Harper Colophon Books, 1973), p. 159.

3. K. M. Sen, *Hinduism* (New York: Penguin, 1961), pp. 39-40.

4. Peter Berger, "The Pluralistic Situation and the Coming Dialogue Between the World Religions," *Buddhist-Christian Studies* 1 (1981): 41.

5. See Friedrich Heiler, "The History of Religions as a Preparation for the Cooperation of Religions," in *The History of Religions: Essays in Methodology*, ed.

advocates of this position do not all agree on just what is essential
and inessential in religion and how we are to characterize this
alleged unity of religions. Critics are quick to point out that those
championing the alleged essential unity of all religions tend to
distort or ignore significant data from the religious traditions that
do not neatly fit their hypothesis.[6]

Other scholars carefully emphasize the diversity among religious traditions but nevertheless maintain that we can think of
the various religions as different culturally and historically conditioned responses to the one divine reality. In recent years this
perspective has been especially associated with John Hick, Dan-
forth Professor of Philosophy and Religion at Claremont Graduate
School. In a number of recent writings, culminating in *An Interpretation of Religion* (New Haven: Yale University Press, 1988),
which is based upon his 1986-87 Gifford Lectures, Hick has presented a bold theory of religious pluralism accounting for the fact
of religious diversity by appealing to a comprehensive understanding of the nature of religious experience.[7] In 400 pages of
careful argument, Hick defends the thesis that

Mircea Eliade and Joseph M. Kitagawa (Chicago: The University of Chicago Press,
1959), pp. 132-60; Ernest Hocking, "The Way of Reconception," in *Attitudes
Toward Other Religions*, ed. Owen C. Thomas (London: SCM Press, 1969), pp.
133-49; Rudolf Otto, *The Idea of the Holy*, trans. J. W. Harvey (London: Oxford
University Press, 1957); Sarvepalli Radhakrishnan, *Eastern Religions and Western
Thought* (London: Oxford University Press, 1969); Arnold Toynbee, "What Should
Be the Christian Approach to the Contemporary Non-Christian Faiths?" in *Atti-
tudes Toward Other Religions*, pp. 151-71, and *An Historian's Approach to Religion*
(New York: Oxford University Press, 1956); Frithjof Schuon, *The Transcendent
Unity of Religions* (New York: Harper & Row, 1975); Wilfred Cantwell Smith, *The
Meaning and End of Religion* (New York: Harper & Row, 1978), and *Towards a
World Theology* (Philadelphia: Westminster, 1980); and Aldous Huxley, *The Peren-
nial Philosophy* (London: Triad Grafton, 1989 [1945]). For a helpful discussion of
this view see Paul Knitter, *No Other Name? A Critical Survey of Christian Attitudes
Toward the World Religions* (Maryknoll, N.Y.: Orbis, 1985), chap. 3.

    6. See Keith E. Yandell, "On the Alleged Unity of All Religions," *Christian
Scholars' Review* 6 (1976): 140-55.

    7. Other important works by Hick dealing with religious pluralism include
God and the Universe of Faiths (London: Macmillan, 1973), *God Has Many Names*
(Philadelphia: Westminster, 1982), and *Problems of Religious Pluralism* (New York:
St. Martin's Press, 1985).

the great world faiths embody different perceptions and conceptions of, and correspondingly different responses to, the Real from
within the major variant ways of being human; and that within
each of them the transformation of human existence from self-
centredness to Reality-centredness is taking place. These traditions are accordingly to be regarded as alternative soteriological
"spaces" within which, or "ways" along which, men and women
find salvation/liberation/ultimate fulfilment.[8]

Hick's thesis is provocative and, if accurate, would require radical
modification of many accepted beliefs about the relations among
major religious traditions. In developing his argument, Hick
traverses over many of the familiar problems of recent analytic
philosophy of religion and demonstrates familiarity with the
major non-Christian religions, particularly Hinduism and Buddhism. His writing is lucid, as usual, and even discussion of
familiar problems (religious language, problem of evil, God's
existence) is fresh and innovative, since throughout he is concerned with problem solving from the broader perspective of
religious pluralism. Hick's recent book is, to date, the most
sophisticated and persuasive articulation of the pluralist position, and it will undoubtedly exert considerable influence over
theologians, philosophers, and missiologists in coming decades.
As such, it demands close scrutiny. The brief discussion in this
chapter cannot hope to capture the rigor and subtlety with which
Hick develops his thesis, but the central tenets can be isolated
and considered in their own right.[9] I will argue that, despite its
considerable appeal, Hick's thesis is seriously flawed.

---

8. *An Interpretation of Religion*, p. 240.
9. Quite apart from Hick's central thesis on religious pluralism, *An Interpretation of Religion* provides much philosophical meat to chew on. His treatment
of the probability arguments for God's existence (chap. 6), realism and nonrealism
in religion (chaps. 11-12), and the rationality of religious belief (chap. 13) is
especially stimulating.

Hick's Theory of Religious Pluralism

Even a rudimentary exposure to various religions makes it apparent that quite different beliefs are advanced by different religious traditions.[10] Orthodox Christians, Jews, and Muslims believe in the existence of one eternal creator God, the sovereign Lord of all there is. On the other hand, many Theravada Buddhists do not regard the religious ultimate as an ontologically distinct creator at all, and Jainas are explicitly atheistic. Many Hindus believe that the religious ultimate is monistic — the *nirguna* Brahman. Others are theistic, ascribing ultimacy to Vishnu, Shiva, or even Krishna. Many Buddhists identify the religious ultimate with *nirvana,* the *Dharmakaya,* or *Sunyata.* Others look to quasi-theistic figures such as the Amida Buddha. And Shintoists see *kami* (the divine) in almost anything — a waterfall, mountain, deceased ancestors, living heroes, etc.

Christians hold that the one eternal God has revealed himself definitively in the Incarnation in Jesus of Nazareth, the long-awaited Messiah. Many Jews deny that Jesus is the Messiah, and Muslims reject as blasphemous any suggestion that Jesus was God incarnate.

Christians assert that only by responding appropriately to the person and work of Jesus Christ can one be brought into a saving relationship with God. Pure Land Buddhists, on the other hand, claim that salvation (rebirth in the Pure Land) is attainable simply through exercising faith in the Amida Buddha and proper recitation of the *nembutsu.* And Zen Buddhists, rejecting as illusory any worldview that implies dualism, hold that *satori* is to be attained solely through rigorous self-discipline. Clearly, very different conceptions of the universe, the religious ultimate, and the human predicament are operative in the different religions.

Traditionally, Christians have responded to this plurality of claims by maintaining that not all of them can be true. At least some must be false. This traditional perspective — which Hick labels the "Ptolemaic view" of other religions[11] — is said to be no

10. See chaps. 2 and 3.
11. *God Has Many Names,* p. 32.

longer acceptable. Hick, who admits to having accepted a Christian faith "of a strongly evangelical and indeed fundamentalist kind" at one time,[12] began in 1973 to call for a "Copernican revolution" in our thinking about religions.[13] The revolution he advocates involves a shift from the view that Christianity, or even Jesus Christ, should be at the center of religious commitment to the perspective that there is one divine reality at the center of all religious belief and practice and that all the major religions are historically and culturally conditioned human responses to this reality. The proposal is that "the great religions are all, at their experiential roots, in contact with the same ultimate divine reality."[14]

But if the various religions all are "in contact" with the same divine reality, why the bewildering diversity among the conceptions of this reality? Why is there not greater uniformity of belief among the many religions? Hick is fully aware of the great diversity in belief and practice among religious traditions. Unlike some, he does not presume that such differences are merely various ways of expressing the same basic insight. He recognizes that the differences in perspective are fundamental. The Buddhist conception of the cosmos and the human predicament is not the same as that of the orthodox Christian. The Taoist and the Muslim do not share common views on the nature of the religious ultimate. Recognizing this, Hick presents a comprehensive theory that accounts for diversity in belief and practice by appealing to historical and cultural factors, and which holds that, within this diversity, there is a fundamental unity in that the varying religious expressions are conditioned human responses to the same ultimate reality — the Real. In what follows we will examine Hick's theory in some detail and in relation to three basic categories: epistemology, ontology, and soteriology.

Epistemology. Hick maintains that historical and cultural factors play a major role in shaping the particular doctrines of a

---

12. Ibid., p. 14.

13. Idem, *God and the Universe of Faiths*, chap. 9.

14. Idem, "The Outcome: Dialogue Into Truth," in *Truth and Dialogue in World Religions: Conflicting Truth-Claims,* ed. John Hick (Philadelphia: Westminster, 1974), p. 151.

given religious community. The various conceptions of the religious ultimate in the major religious traditions are said to be culturally and historically conditioned human responses to the one divine reality.

> The basic hypothesis which suggests itself is that the different streams of religious experience represent diverse awarenesses of the same transcendent reality, which is perceived in characteristically different ways by different human mentalities, formed by and forming different cultural histories. . . . One then sees the great world religions as different human responses to the one divine Reality, embodying different perceptions which have been formed in different historical and cultural circumstances.[15]

While the major religions can be regarded as different responses to the same religious ultimate,

> we always perceive the transcendent through the lens of a particular religious culture with its distinctive set of concepts, myths, historical exemplars and devotional or meditational techniques. And it is this inexpungible human contribution to religious awareness that accounts for the fascinating variations of religious thought, experience, and practice around the globe and down through the centuries, in all their rational and irrational, profound and shallow, impressive and absurd, morally admirable and morally reprehensible features.[16]

In part, this is simply an extension of Hick's earlier views on epistemology to the problem of religious pluralism.[17] Hick holds

15. *God Has Many Names*, pp. 83, 11.

16. *An Interpretation of Religion*, p. 8. In an earlier work Hick states, "The divine presence is the presence of the Eternal One to our finite human consciousness, and the human projections are the culturally conditioned images and symbols in terms of which we concretize the basic concept of deity." *God Has Many Names*, p. 53.

17. For Hick's epistemology see his *Faith and Knowledge*, 2nd ed. reissued (London: Macmillan, 1987) (originally published by Cornell University Press, 1957); "Religious Faith as Experiencing-As," in *Talk of God*, ed. G. N. A. Vesey (New York: Macmillan, 1969); M. Goulder and J. Hick, *Why Believe In God?* (London: SCM Press, 1983); and *An Interpretation of Religion*, chaps. 5-13.

that religious experience is basic to religious epistemology. Furthermore, the universe is "religiously ambiguous" in that it is not possible, on the basis of careful analysis of the universe and experience alone, to settle definitively the question whether there is or is not a God. The universe can reasonably be interpreted in either religious or nonreligious ways. And if interpreted religiously, one cannot, by philosophical analysis alone, determine whether the religious ultimate is the monotheistic God of the Semitic tradition or the monistic *nirguna* Brahman of Hinduism. Persuasive arguments and counterarguments can be produced for each position. After reviewing traditional arguments used to support religious and nonreligious interpretations of the data, Hick concludes:

> It seems, then, that the universe maintains its inscrutable ambiguity. In some aspects it invites whilst in others it repels a religious response. It permits both a religious and a naturalistic faith, but haunted in each case by a contrary possibility that can never be exorcised. Any realistic analysis of religious belief and experience, and any realistic defence of the rationality of religious conviction, must therefore start from this situation of systematic ambiguity.[18]

Nevertheless, we are not left simply with choosing arbitrarily among alternative interpretations. It is rational to interpret the universe religiously, and the decisive element in the epistemological equation is the phenomenon of religious experience. "It is as reasonable for those who experience their lives as being lived in the presence of God, to believe in the reality of God, as for all of us to form beliefs about our environment on the basis of our experience of it."[19] Thus, although philosophical reflection alone cannot settle the question of the reality of God (or any other conception of the divine ultimate), it is rational for those who experience the universe religiously — who undergo religious experiences — to believe in the reality of God.

Borrowing insights from Immanuel Kant and Ludwig Wittgenstein, Hick contends that all experience — including religious

18. *An Interpretation of Religion*, p. 124.
19. Ibid., p. 210.

experience — is inherently interpretive. All conscious experiencing is "experiencing-as."[20] But religious experience is distinctive in that the interpretive element in religious experience is faith. Religious faith "is that uncompelled subjective contribution to conscious experience which is responsible for its distinctively religious character."[21] As an "uncompelled interpretive activity," religious faith is an exercise of "cognitive freedom." The data of the universe are ambiguous and can be interpreted in either a religious or a nonreligious manner. On the religious level, then, there is a significant element of cognitive freedom operative in one's worldview. Those who interpret the universe religiously are rationally entitled to do so; but those who, lacking the requisite religious experience, do not interpret religiously might be equally justified in so doing.

Ontology. Although ultimately it is the same divine reality that is encountered in the various religious traditions, both the awareness of and the response to this reality are conditioned by historical and cultural factors — hence the tremendous diversity in belief and practice. Historical, cultural, and conceptual factors form a kind of grid or filter through which the reality of the religious ultimate is perceived and understood.

Drawing upon Immanuel Kant's famous distinction between the noumenon and the phenomenon in the epistemology of perception, Hick distinguishes between the religious ultimate as it is in itself and the religious ultimate as experienced by historically and culturally conditioned persons. The former is referred to by the term "the Real." But the Real as it is in itself is never the direct object of religious experience. Rather, it is experienced by finite humankind in one of any number of historically and culturally conditioned manifestations of the Real — either as personal (e.g., Yahweh, Allah, Krishna) or as nonpersonal (*Dharmakaya, Sunyata, nirguna* Brahman). The various conceptions or manifestations of the Real as personal are called *personae* of the Real; conceptions of the Real as nonpersonal are referred to as *impersonae* of the Real. Hick is worth quoting at length on this point:

20. Ibid., pp. 140f.
21. Ibid., p. 160.

And so Kant distinguished between noumenon and phenomenon, or between a *Ding an sich* and that thing as it appears to human consciousness. . . . In this strand of Kant's thought — not the only strand, but the one which I am seeking to press into service in the epistemology of religion — the noumenal world is that same world as it appears to human consciousness. The world as it appears is thus entirely real: in being a "transcendental idealist" Kant is, as he says, "an empirical realist". . . . Analogously, I want to say that the noumenal Real is experienced and thought by different human mentalities, forming and formed by different religious traditions, as the range of gods and absolutes which the phenomenology of religion reports. And these divine *personae* and metaphysical *impersonae*, as I shall call them, are not illusory but are empirically, that is experientially, real as authentic manifestations of the Real. . . . But for Kant God is postulated, not experienced. In partial agreement but also partial disagreement with him, I want to say that the Real *an sich* is postulated by us as a pre-supposition, not of the moral life, but of religious experience and the religious life, whilst the gods, as also the mystically known Brahman, Sunyata and so on, are phenomenal manifestations of the Real occurring within the realm of religious experience. Conflating these two theses one can say that the Real is experienced by human beings, but experienced in a manner analogous to that in which, according to Kant, we experience the world: namely by informational input from external reality being interpreted by the mind in terms of its own categorial scheme and thus coming to consciousness as meaningful phenomenal experience. All that we are entitled to say about the noumenal source of this information is that it is the reality whose influence produces, in collaboration with the human mind, the phenomenal world of our experience.[22]

The Real, then, is the "divine noumenon" which is experienced and thought within the various religious traditions as the range of "divine phenomena" exemplified in the religious history of humankind.

We have, then, the Real as it is in itself, the postulated ground of all religious experience, and the Real as it is perceived

22. *An Interpretation of Religion*, pp. 241-43.

by finite humankind — the *personae* of the theistic faiths and the *impersonae* of Hinduism, Buddhism, and Taoism. The distinction is intended to enable affirmation of both the undeniable diversity in conceptions of the religious ultimate so apparent in the various traditions and the essential unity of religions in their varying responses to the same religious ultimate. Whether it is in fact able to do so depends largely upon the manner in which the relation between the Real *an sich* and the various *personae/impersonae* is formulated — a question to which we shall turn shortly.

Soteriology. Given the clear differences in conceptions of the religious ultimate found in the religions, it may be tempting to ask why one should postulate the existence of the Real as the common ground of the varying religious perspectives. Hick responds that the main motivation for a comprehensive interpretation embracing conceptions of the religious ultimate as both personal and nonpersonal comes from "the perception that the personal deities and the non-personal absolutes have a common effect" upon believers in the respective traditions.[23] This alleged common effect is the "transformation from self-centredness to Reality-centredness." Hick argues that there is a common soteriological structure to the major religions. The teachings of the various religions concerning the human predicament and the nature of salvation/ liberation/enlightenment constitute

> variations within different conceptual schemes on a single fundamental theme: the sudden or gradual change of the individual from an absorbing self-concern to a new centring in the supposed unity-of-reality-and-value that is thought of as God, Brahman, the Dharma, Sunyata or the Tao. Thus the generic concept of salvation/liberation, which takes a different specific form in each of the great traditions, is that of the transformation of human existence from self-centredness to Reality-centredness.[24]

Understood as the transformation from self-centeredness to Reality-centeredness, salvation is said to be an evident reality in all the

23. Ibid., p. 278.
24. Ibid., p. 36.

major religions. All religions provide effective paths of salvation. But from our present perspective, it is impossible to rank religions according to their soteriological effectiveness.

> It may be that one [religion] facilitates human liberation/salvation more than the others, but if so this is not evident to human vision. So far as we can tell, they are equally productive of that transition from self to Reality which we see in the saints of all traditions. . . . We can, I suggest, only acknowledge, and indeed rejoice in the fact, that the Real, the Ultimate, the Divine is known and responded to within each of these vast historical complexes, so that within each of them the gradual transformation of human existence from self-centredness to Reality-centredness is taking place.[25]

Not only does what Hick sees as a common soteriological structure in the great religions provide the impetus for postulating the existence of the Real as the transcendent ground of varying religious images, but it also provides the criterion for discriminating between authentic manifestations of the Real and what might be mistaken for manifestations of the Real. No one supposes that all religious leaders, all religious teachings, are equally valid or equally "in touch" with the Real. There is a substantial difference between, say, a Jim Jones and a St. Francis of Assisi, or between the teachings of Mahatma Gandhi and those of Bhagwan Shree Rajneesh, or between child sacrifice to Moloch and the Muslim practice of *zakat* (giving alms). How is one to discriminate between what is and what is not an authentic response to the Real? Hick contends that "the basic criterion must be soteriological." Religious traditions "have greater or less value according as they promote or hinder the salvific transformation."[26]

But how do we know when such transformation has taken place? This too requires some identifiable criteria. And Hick suggests that the criteria for making that judgment lie in the spiritual

25. *Problems of Religious Pluralism,* pp. 86-87. Cf. *An Interpretation of Religion,* pp. 307, 337.
26. *An Interpretation of Religion,* p. 300.

and moral fruits found in the lives of exemplary believers within
the respective traditions. Those whose lives have been authentically
transformed, who no longer are controlled by "self-centredness"
but live according to "Reality-centredness" — the "saints" of the
great traditions — manifest certain qualities in their lives. Among
these qualities are compassion and love for all humankind —
indeed, for all of life—strength of soul, purity, charity, inner peace
and serenity, and radiant joy.[27]

> The production of saints, both contemplative and practical, in-
> dividualistic and political, is thus one valid criterion by which to
> identify a religious tradition as a salvific human response to the
> Real. In the light of this criterion we can readily see that each of
> the great world faiths constitutes a context for salvation/libera-
> tion: for each has produced its own harvest of saints. . . . The
> salvation/liberation which it is the function of religion to facilitate
> is a human transformation which we see most conspicuously in
> the saints of all traditions. It consists, as one of its aspects, in
> moral goodness, a goodness which is latent in the solitary con-
> templative and active in the saint who lives in society, serving his
> or her fellows either in works of mercy or, more characteristically
> in our modern sociologically-conscious age, in political activity
> as well, seeking to change the structures within which human life
> is lived.[28]

The presence of saints in each of the major religions, then, is held
to be compelling evidence of the religions being authentic responses to the one divine reality — the Real.

An Evaluation of Hick's Thesis

In a world torn apart by strife, bigotry, and aggressive competition among religions for the souls of humankind, Hick's suggestion that the major traditions are all culturally and historically

27. Ibid., pp. 301-2.
28. Ibid., pp. 307 and 309.

conditioned human responses to the same ultimate Reality has an undeniable attraction. With the exception of certain aberrant forms of religious expression which are condemned by all morally sensitive persons, all religions are to be accepted and affirmed, for all provide effective paths in which the transition from self-centeredness to Reality-centeredness takes place. There is no one true religion. All religions are true in that they provide authentic channels for salvation. One is left with a parity among religions that removes the possibility of any one tradition being definitive or normative. For many today this is indeed an enticing proposal.

The issue, however, is not whether Hick's thesis is attractive, but rather whether it is plausible — specifically, whether it is warranted by the data from the various religious traditions. In spite of its considerable intuitive appeal, I find Hick's proposal implausible on several grounds.

Evaluation of Hick's thesis is complicated by the uncertainty about the intent behind his theory. Is Hick intending to offer a comprehensive theory about the nature of actual religious traditions, a kind of "meta-religious" or second-order theory about existing first-order religions? Or is he proposing a fresh religious perspective, an alternative to present and past religious worldviews? If the former, then Hick is basically offering a descriptive theory about the nature of existing religions. The adequacy of his theory would depend largely upon two factors: (1) the accuracy with which his theory reflects and the ease with which it can accommodate the data from various religious traditions, and (2) the internal consistency of the theory itself.

But if Hick is not so much attempting an interpretation of existing religions as he is pointing the way toward what he sees as a more adequate religious perspective — a preferred alternative to existing traditions — then somewhat different criteria for evaluation would come into play. For the adequacy of his theory would then depend upon demonstration of its superiority to existing religious worldviews. Hick would need to show that present religious traditions are, for one reason or another, seriously deficient in their understanding of the religious ultimate, the human predicament, and the nature of salvation, and that his proposal more accurately reflects the actual state of affairs.

Perhaps it is best to understand Hick's theory as including both intentions mentioned above. Certainly he intends to present an account of religious experience that is faithful to the data of the various religions. For throughout his argument he is careful to provide appropriate illustrations from different traditions. But clearly Hick is not satisfied with descriptive analysis alone. He is also calling for a radical reinterpretation of our understanding of religious phenomena — that is, a fresh alternative to existing paradigms for understanding the relation among religions. And in so doing, at key points he engages in significant reinterpretation of certain troublesome doctrines of the major religions in an effort to forge a more synthetic perspective.

Hick's theory can be challenged at several key points. One might well question certain epistemological views — for example, the suggestion that all experience, including religious experience, is "experiencing-as"; or that the universe is as "religiously ambiguous" as Hick contends; or that religious experience, as construed by Hick, is epistemologically determinative. Here, however, I will concentrate upon some significant epistemological difficulties which fall broadly into two categories: (1) the relation between the Real *an sich* and the *personae/impersonae* of the many religions, and (2) the reductionism resulting from Hick's reinterpretation of major elements of the religions.

The Relation of the Real *an sich* and the Various *Personae/Impersonae*

A host of interesting epistemological issues stem from Hick's distinction between the religious ultimate as it is in itself and the religious ultimate as it is experienced by humankind.[29] The Real

29. Mention should also be made here of another, relatively minor, matter. Hick argues that religious experience in general cannot be dismissed as delusory, and that it is rational to believe in God on the basis of such experience. The details

an sich is said to be the divine noumenon, the ground of all authentic religious experience and perception, with the various culturally conditioned conceptions of the religious ultimate being the divine phenomena. Thus, conceptions of the religious ultimate in personal terms — Yahweh, Allah, Krishna, Shiva, Ahura Mazda — are the divine *personae,* and images of the religious ultimate in nonpersonal terms — the Tao, *niruna* Brahman, *Sunyata, Nirvana, Dharmakaya* — are the divine *impersonae* through which the Real is manifest.

Now Hick correctly observes that the distinction between the divine reality as it is in itself and the divine reality as it is perceived by humans has a long and distinguished history. Ex-

---

of this argument need not detain us here, but what is of concern is a claim which is alleged to follow from this. Hick seems to hold that if a Christian, for example, can justifiably believe in God on the basis of religious experiences within the Christian tradition, then correspondingly, religious experiences from other religions substantiate the claims of these other traditions. Speaking of his argument for the reliability of religious experience, Hick asserts, "But if such an argument holds for the Christian experience of the divine, it must also hold for the Jewish, the Muslim, the Hindu, the Buddhist, and other experiences of the divine. One must follow the Golden Rule and grant to religious experiences within the other great traditions the same presumption of cognitive veridicality that one quite properly claims for one's own" (*God Has Many Names,* p. 24. Virtually the same statement is found in *An Interpretation of Religion,* p. 235). There is a curious ambiguity here. Certainly one must extend to adherents of other faiths the same courtesies that one expects from them. If Hick's point is simply that once it is demonstrated that the veridicality of religious experience in general cannot be ruled out a priori then religious experience from any given tradition can in principle be regarded as veridical (provided, of course, that there are no compelling reasons to suppose otherwise), then his point is well taken. One cannot dismiss classes of experience as delusory simply because they do not come from within one's own tradition. But his comments can also be taken to mean that if it is shown to be reasonable to accept as veridical religious experiences from a particular tradition, then the religious experiences of the other great traditions must also be accepted as veridical. But this hardly follows. From the fact that religious experience in general cannot be ruled out as delusory it does not follow that any particular experience is in fact veridical. Nor can we assume that simply because experiences within one tradition have been shown to be veridical any given experience within any other tradition is veridical. Even if it is granted that religious experience cannot be ruled out a priori as delusory, surely reports of religious experiences should be carefully evaluated on their own merits.

amples of the distinction can be found in the major traditions.[30] Within the Christian tradition alone variations on this theme are found in Augustine, Aquinas, Calvin, Luther, Barth, and others. And if the transcendence of God and the finitude of humankind are to be maintained it seems that some such distinction is inevitable.

But there is a danger here which many theologians take too lightly. For in emphasizing this distinction one runs the risk of eliminating the informative nature of religious discourse and of being reduced to religious agnosticism. This seems particularly to be so with Hick's treatment of the distinction. The problem can be seen by looking at two possible ways of interpreting the distinction between the Real *an sich* and the various *personae/impersonae*.

1. On the one hand it is possible to maintain a strong element of continuity between the Real *an sich* and the various manifestations of the Real. The *personae* and *impersonae* do authentically manifest and inform us of the Real. Thus in their experiences of Yahweh, Allah, *Sunyata,* or Brahman the great religious figures were indeed experiencing the Real, but always as mediated through a particular *persona* or *impersona.* Some of Hick's statements lend themselves to this interpretation.

> I want to say that the noumenal Real is experienced and thought by different human mentalities, forming and formed by different religious traditions, as the range of gods and absolutes which the phenomenology of religion reports. And these divine *personae* and metaphysical *impersonae,* as I shall call them, are not illusory but are empirically, that is experientially, real as authentic manifestations of the Real.[31]

The *personae* of the theistic and polytheistic traditions and the *impersonae* of the monistic traditions are the manifestations of the Real to culturally and historically conditioned humans. They are the "images" or "grids" through which the Real is perceived and experienced.

30. See *An Interpretation of Religion,* pp. 236-38.
31. Ibid., p. 242.

Now if these images — the *personae* and *impersonae* — are accurate reflections of the Real there must be significant continuity between them and the religious ultimate which they reflect. One way to put this is to say that the set of true propositions about a given image (Amida, Allah, *Nirvana*) must form a subset of the set of all true propositions about the Real *an sich*. If this were not the case it is difficult to see how the various *personae/impersonae* could be regarded as genuinely informative of the Real. Indeed, there would seem to be little reason for referring to them as images of the Real at all.

But the view that posits significant continuity between the Real *an sich* and the various *personae/impersonae* runs into serious difficulty due to the undeniable differences among such images of the religious ultimate. Indeed, the use of two terms — *personae* and *impersonae* — to refer to the images of the religious ultimate in the religions is Hick's way of acknowledging that there are fundamental differences between those traditions which regard the religious ultimate as personal and those which regard it as non-personal. On this interpretation, it is crucial to Hick's thesis that the Real can accurately be thought of in both personal and non-personal categories. Images from both traditions can legitimately be applied to the Real. As Hick says in an earlier work, "the divine nature is infinite, exceeding the scope of all human concepts, and is capable of being experienced both as personal Lord and as nonpersonal ground or depth of being."[32]

Now it is not just a question of whether the Real can be experienced as personal and nonpersonal; it is a question of whether its ontological status is such that it can correctly be described as both personal and nonpersonal. For it may be possible for the Real to be experienced as personal and nonpersonal without necessarily being both. Perhaps the Real is able to present itself in certain situations as a personal Lord and in others as a nonpersonal ground of being. But since in talking about Brahman or Allah, for example, Hindus or Muslims are not simply talking about their respective experiences but fully intend to make significant onto-

32. *God Has Many Names,* p. 38.

logical claims about the nature of reality, it seems that on Hick's thesis the Real must actually be both personal and nonpersonal.

Thus, if Hick's thesis is correct it should be possible to speak informatively of the Real as Yahweh, Jesus Christ, Allah, Brahman, *Sunyata*, the Amida Buddha, the *Dharmakaya*, etc., as these designations are understood within the respective traditions. But is this plausible? Does it make sense to speak of the Real in personal and nonpersonal categories as these are understood within the various traditions? Several of the designations seem to have clearly incompatible ontological implications: Can one seriously maintain that the ontological implications of the Judeo-Christian understanding of the divine as Yahweh, the ontologically independent, personal creator and righteous judge are compatible with the monistic implications of the Hindu notion of *nirguna* Brahman or with the ontologically ultimate image of Nothingness in Zen?

On this interpretation terms such as "Yahweh," "Allah," "Shiva," "*nirguna* Brahman," "Nothingness," and "the Tao" should all ultimately have the same referent. To be sure, in one sense the terms do have different meanings; they do not all share the same connotations and they can be paraphrased in different ways. Perhaps here a distinction should be made between what we can call the direct or penultimate referent of a term and its ultimate referent. Thus, the direct referent of "Allah" is not the same as that of "*Sunyata*." On Hick's thesis, then, they refer to different manifestations of the Real. But if indeed such *personae* and *impersonae* are all reflections of the one religious ultimate, then it seems that they should all have the same ultimate referent — they should all denote the same Reality.

It may be tempting at this point to recall mathematician and philosopher Gottlob Frege's classic discussion of identity statements and his distinction between *Sinn* (sense) and *Bedeutung* (reference) in an effort to clarify Hick's thesis.[33] Frege observed that although both of the following are similar identity statements they differ in an important respect:

33. Cf. Gottlob Frege, "Uber Sinn und Bedeutung," trans. by M. Black as "On Sense and Reference," in *Translations From the Philosophical Writings of Gottlob Frege*, ed. M. Black and P. Geach (Oxford: Oxford University Press, 1952).

    (A) The Morning Star is identical with the Morning Star.
    (B) The Morning Star is identical with the Evening Star.

Although we now know that both (A) and (B) are true and that in
both cases it is the planet Venus that is being referred to, there is a
significant difference between the two statements. For (A) expresses
a tautology and is obviously and necessarily true, whereas (B) enun-
ciates an astronomical discovery. In an important sense, then, the
meanings of (A) and (B) are the same, but they are clearly different
as well. Frege's solution to the puzzle was the well-known distinction
between sense and reference. "The Morning Star" means the same
thing as "The Evening Star" in that both expressions refer to the same
thing: they both denote the planet Venus. But the two expressions
mean different things in that they each have a different sense: their
connotations differ and they can be paraphrased differently.

    Similarly, it may be suggested that terms such as "Allah,"
"Yahweh," "Brahman," and "*Sunyata*" all have the same *referent* (the
Real) although they have different *senses*. It seems that some such
distinction is inevitable if Hick's thesis is to have any plausibility. But
an important difference between Frege's example and the current
discussion must not be overlooked. Frege's example only has the
force and charm that it does because relevant astronomical data have
already made it plausible to believe that the referents of "the Morning Star" and "the Evening Star" are identical. But this identity of
referents is precisely what is at issue in the debate over religious
pluralism. Given the undeniable differences in connotation of terms
such as "Shiva," "Allah," "the Tao," "Yahweh," and "Brahman," it
does not seem plausible to maintain that they all denote the same
reality. Surely the burden of proof rests with anyone claiming that
the ultimate referent of each is the same.

    2. But although there are statements which, if taken by
themselves, indicate that Hick sees a strong element of continuity
between the Real *an sich* and the various *personae/impersonae*,
careful reading of *An Interpretation of Religion* indicates that Hick
rejects this interpretation in favor of one minimizing continuity
between the Real and the *personae/impersonae*. The object of religious experience is not the Real *an sich* but always some particular

image or manifestation of the Real.[34] The distinction between the Real and the *personae/impersonae* takes on a strong Kantian tone: The religious experience of humankind is said to be limited to culturally conditioned experiences of certain images of the Real *an sich*. The Real — much like the noumenon in Kant's epistemology of perception — is never the direct object of experience but is a postulate posited in order to make sense of the fact of religious experience in general.[35]

Hick does not hesitate to draw the obvious implications from such a radical disjunction between the direct objects of religious experience and the Real *an sich*.

> The distinction between the Real as it is in itself and as it is thought and experienced through our human religious concepts entails . . . that we cannot apply to the Real *an sich* the characteristics encountered in its *personae* and *impersonae*. Thus it cannot be said to be one or many, person or thing, conscious or unconscious, purposive or non-purposive, substance or process, good or evil, loving or hating. None of the descriptive terms that apply within the realm of human experience can apply literally to the unexperienceable reality that underlies that realm.[36]

The Real is said to be "the ultimate ground, transcending human conceptuality, of the range of *personae* and *impersonae* through which humans are related to it."[37] But is the Real *an sich* personal or nonpersonal, or somehow both? Hick explicitly rules out the possibility that it is personal. "[T]he Real *an sich* cannot be said to be personal."[38] Personality is not a category applicable to the Real in itself, although there is a sense in which in its relation to humans, conceptualized as, say, Krishna or Yahweh, the Real can be said to be personal. But neither can one say that the Real *an sich* is nonpersonal. For Hick claims that the Real transcends both the *per-*

34. *An Interpretation of Religion*, p. 294.
35. Ibid., pp. 243f.
36. Ibid., p. 350. Cf. p. 246.
37. Ibid., p. 266.
38. Ibid., p. 264.

sonae and the *impersonae,* and that none of the characteristics encountered in either the *personae* or the *impersonae* can be attributed to the Real.[39] It seems, then, that although the Real is the ground of both personal and nonpersonal conceptions of the religious ultimate, in itself the Real is neither personal nor nonpersonal. It transcends such distinctions.

And it is here that the religious agnosticism inherent in Hick's proposal becomes most apparent. For the ontological hiatus between the Real *an sich* and the *personae/impersonae* severely restricts what can be said informatively about the Real. It comes as no surprise, then, that Hick accepts a modified version of the ineffability thesis with respect to the Real *an sich.* On the one hand, he affirms that "the noumenal Real is such as to be authentically experienced as a range of both theistic and non-theistic phenomena." Yet he quickly qualifies this by adding, "We cannot, as we have seen, say that the Real *an sich* has the characteristics displayed by its manifestations, such as (in the case of the heavenly Father) love and justice or (in the case of Brahman) consciousness and bliss." Thus, "whilst there is a noumenal ground for the phenomenal divine attributes, this does not enable us to trace each attribute separately upwards into the Godhead or the Real."[40] Hick recognizes that a strong ineffability thesis, which maintains that no concepts at all can be applied to the Real, lapses into incoherence. What he does maintain, however, is that "substantial properties"[41] — properties such as being good, being powerful, having knowledge, being loving, etc. — cannot be applied to the Real *an sich.* It

---

39. Ibid., p. 246; cf. p. 350. Curiously, in spite of his contention that the Real transcends both personal and nonpersonal conceptions of the religious ultimate, in places Hick does seem to equate the Real *an sich* with certain nonpersonal images such as the *nirguna* Brahman and *Sunyata* (cf. pp. 283 and 291). Identification of the Real *an sich* with, say, *nirguna* Brahman would imply that the various *personae* such as Yahweh, Allah, or Krishna are manifestations of *nirguna* Brahman. Although this might be acceptable to Hindus, it will certainly be rejected by orthodox Jews, Christians, and Muslims.

40. Ibid., pp. 246-47.

41. Substantial properties are contrasted with "purely formal properties" — such as the property of being the referent of a term, or the property of being such that no concepts apply to it.

is hardly an exaggeration, then, for Hick to state that "the Real *an sich* is the ultimate Mystery."[42]

Are we then reduced to utter silence concerning the religious ultimate? Not necessarily, for Hick suggests that in line with the great mystics of both theistic and nontheistic traditions, we can effectively apply the *via negativa,* the way of negation, to the Real.[43] We can say what the Real is not, although we cannot positively affirm what it is. Now the way of negation has a long history in religious thought. And there is an important sense in which we can clarify our understanding of the religious ultimate through purging it of erroneous and misleading ideas. This was recognized by St. Thomas Aquinas over seven centuries ago.

> For, by its immensity the divine substance surpasses every form that our intellect reaches. Thus we are unable to apprehend it by knowing what *it is.* Yet we are able to have some knowledge of it by knowing what *it is not.*[44]

However, it is important to see that negative predication can only be informative if there is presupposed some identifiable positive knowledge of the subject. Simply to assert that some entity S does not have properties x, y, and z is hardly informative of S unless there is presupposed some positive knowledge of S. Aquinas clearly recognized this as well.

> The idea of negation is always based upon an affirmation; as is evidenced by the fact that every negative proposition is proved by an affirmative: wherefore unless the human mind knew something positive about God, it would be unable to deny anything about Him.[45]

If we already know that God is a being with consciousness who is capable of acting intentionally, then it can be helpful to clarify our

42. Ibid., p. 349.
43. Ibid., pp. 239f.
44. St. Thomas Aquinas, *Summa Contra Gentiles,* I.14, trans. Anton Pegis (Notre Dame: University of Notre Dame, 1975), p. 96. Emphasis in the original.
45. Idem, *On the Power of God,* VII.5, trans. English Dominican Fathers (Westminster: Newman Press, 1952).

understanding by saying that nevertheless God does not have a physical body, is not limited in knowledge as finite creatures are, and does not act in precisely the same way that humans do. Similarly, if one first has some positive knowledge about the Real, then it makes good sense to apply the *via negativa* and thereby eliminate any misconceptions that might be present. But the way of negation by itself will not be informative about the Real.

Hick also suggests that, although we cannot use predicate terms literally, we can nevertheless employ mythological language about the Real. A myth is defined as "a story or statement that is not literally true but which tends to evoke an appropriate dispositional attitude to its subject matter." And "true religious myths" are defined by Hick as "those that evoke in us attitudes and modes of behaviour which are appropriate to our situation in relation to the Real."[46] On this understanding, the doctrines concerning various *personae* or *impersonae* in the religious traditions, while not applying literally to the Real, can be said to express mythological truth about the Real insofar as they evoke in the believers appropriate dispositional responses. Literal truth and mythological truth are contrasted:

> The literal truth or falsity of a factual assertion (as distinguished from the truth or falsity of an analytic proposition) consists in its conformity or lack of conformity to fact: "it is raining here now" is literally true if and only if it is raining here now. But in addition to literal truth there is also mythological truth. A statement or set of statements about X is mythologically true if it is not literally true but nevertheless tends to evoke an appropriate dispositional attitude to X. Thus mythological truth is practical or, in one sense of this much abused word, existential. For the conformity of myth to reality does not consist in a literal conformity of what is said to the facts but in the appropriateness to the myth's referent of the behavioural dispositions that it tends to evoke in the hearer.[47]

Thus, the biblical story of the fall of Adam and Eve, the story of the flight of the Buddha through the sky to Sri Lanka, and the

46. *An Interpretation of Religion,* p. 248.
47. Ibid., p. 348.

belief that the Qur'an was dictated by the archangel Gabriel are all examples of "true myths" in that, although not literally true, they tend to evoke in Christians, Buddhists, and Muslims appropriate dispositional responses to the Real. Hick holds that "we can identify the various systems of religious thought as complex myths whose truth or untruth consists in the appropriateness or inappropriateness of the practical dispositions which they tend to evoke."[48]

But an obvious question here is what it means for human attitudes, emotions, modes of behavior, or patterns of life to be "appropriate dispositional responses to the Real." Hick responds by saying:

> We can only answer within the circle of the hypothesis. It is for the god or the absolute to which we relate ourselves to be an authentic manifestation of the Real and for our practical response to be appropriate to that manifestation. Insofar as this is so, that *persona* or *impersona* can be said to be in soteriological alignment with the Real.[49]

To love God and one's fellow human beings is an appropriate response to the awareness of God as understood within the Christian tradition. And thus to the extent that the Christian understanding of God is an authentic *persona* of the Real, constituting the form in which the Real is experienced within the Christian strand of religious history, then to that extent loving God and one's fellow human beings is an appropriate response to the Real. To the extent that they tend to evoke this dispositional response in Christians, Christian doctrines and stories can be regarded as "true myths." And, as noted earlier, it is the soteriological criterion — the evidence for the transformation from self-centeredness to Reality-centeredness — which discriminates between authentic and inauthentic manifestations of the Real.

The question of religious discourse is as fascinating as it is complex. We cannot here pursue the question whether talk of the

---

48. Ibid., p. 353.
49. Ibid.

religious ultimate can be literal or must be mythological.[50] But two brief comments should be made concerning Hick's attempt to interpret religious beliefs and doctrines in mythological terms. First, it is clear that Hick's suggestion runs counter to the understanding of religious discourse held by many ordinary believers. Most Buddhists, Muslims, Hindus, and Christians do intend to make factual claims about the nature of reality. (This point will be taken up again below.) And second, mythological statements about the Real are only informative to the extent that they are parasitic upon nonmythological — literal — truth. For the question whether any given behavior or pattern of life (loving one's neighbor, fasting regularly, sacrificing children to Moloch) is to be regarded as an appropriate response to the Real will depend upon our ability to formulate clearly certain propositions about the nature of the Real and our relationship to the Real.

Reinterpretation of Major Elements of Various Religions

It was observed earlier that insofar as Hick's theory of religious pluralism is intended to be a comprehensive theory about the nature of various religious traditions its adequacy will be a function of (1) the accuracy with which it reflects, and the ease with which it accommodates, the data from different religions, and (2) the internal consistency and plausibility of the theory itself. Some epistemological tensions within the theory itself have been noted above. But perhaps the vulnerability of the theory is most apparent in its failure to account satisfactorily for significant elements of major religions. Hick's treatment of various beliefs is frequently reductionistic and he freely reinterprets troublesome doctrines so as to accommodate them within his theory. But to the extent that

50. For helpful discussions of the issues see Patrick Sherry, *Religion, Truth, and Language Games* (London: Macmillan, 1977); and William Alston, *Divine Nature and Human Language: Essays in Philosophical Theology* (Ithaca: Cornell University Press, 1989). An important, but rather technical, discussion of religious discourse can be found in James Ross, *Portraying Analogy* (Cambridge: Cambridge University Press, 1981).

major religious traditions do not find their beliefs — as they are understood within the respective traditions — adequately accounted for on Hick's analysis, his theory is called into question. Now in such cases it may be that, as Hick occasionally charges, certain religious beliefs are simply not true and that traditions embracing them should amend some cherished beliefs. But this is largely beside the point. Given that his proposal is (among other things) a second-order theory about existing religious traditions, purporting to offer an explanation of their distinctive beliefs and practices, the adequacy of his theory is partially a function of its ability to account for the central beliefs of major traditions as they are understood within the respective religions. Thus, if there are significant elements of religions which clash with Hick's analysis, this prima facie counts against his theory.

1. Hick's theory fails to account satisfactorily for the fact that each tradition ascribes ultimacy to its own particular conception of the religious ultimate. Now Hick is well aware that the various *personae* and *impersonae* within the religions hold the place of religious ultimacy for their respective devotees.[51] Thus, the notion of Yahweh is ontologically ultimate for the Christian, as is Allah for the Muslim, Brahman for the Hindu, the Tao for the Taoist, the *Dharmakaya* for the Mahayana Buddhist, and so on. Orthodox followers of each of these traditions would vigorously resist the suggestion that their particular conception of the religious ultimate is in fact not ultimate but merely a penultimate manifestation of what is truly ultimate — the Real. Nevertheless, this is precisely what Hick suggests. As humanly experienced *personae* of the Real, images such as Yahweh, Allah, Shiva, Vishnu, or Amida are not themselves the religious ultimate but are merely penultimate images, or manifestations, of the Real. The same holds for *impersonae* such as the *Dharmakaya, Sunyata,* or Brahman. Yet careful attention to what Jews, Christians, or Muslims mean when they speak of Yahweh or Allah, or what Buddhists, Hindus, or Taoists mean when they refer to the *Dharmakaya,* Brahman, or the Tao reveals that in each case religious and ontological ultimacy is

51. Ibid., pp. 269-71.

accorded the referent of the particular concept. It would be inconceivable for an Orthodox Jew or Christian to concede that there is something ontologically more ultimate than Yahweh; similarly, an Advaita Vedantin Hindu would reject the suggestion that something more ultimate than Brahman exists. (A Hindu might, of course, admit that Yahweh or Jesus Christ can be regarded as a lesser manifestation of Brahman — a concession hardly welcomed by Christians — but he or she is not likely to grant the converse.)

Furthermore, the ontological status of the *personae/impersonae* on Hick's theory is not clear. Although he does not rule out the possibility, Hick clearly does not wish to suggest that all of the *personae* of the various traditions throughout history (Agni, Mitra, Indra, Baal, Poseidon, Nabongo, Yahweh, Shiva, Allah, etc.) exist as independent beings.[52] This would result in a polytheism of amazing proportions. While technically possible, this would necessitate each of the "divinities" existing as immense but nevertheless finite beings. But neither does he wish to say that they are simply illusions or that they have no extramental existence. For a divine *persona* is the product of both human projection and the manifestation of the Real and "arises at the interface between the Real and the human spirit, and is thus a joint product of transcendent presence and earthly imagination, of divine revelation and human seeking."[53] While Hick claims that his thesis is compatible with both a view which ascribes separate ontological existence to the various *personae* — each existing as a limited, penultimate manifestation of the Real — and one which regards the *personae* as merely different manifestations or "faces" of the single divine Reality, it would seem that his general theory is more amenable to the latter. Either way, the understanding of the *personae* and *impersonae* as penultimate manifestations of the Real, and not as having ontological ultimacy on their own, will be strongly resisted from many within the major traditions.

2. Central to Hick's thesis is the contention that religious experience is never direct experience of the Real *an sich* but is

52. Ibid.
53. Ibid., p. 266.

always experience of one of the *personae/impersonae.* There is no direct, unmediated experience of the Real. Many would immediately object that mysticism in its varying forms presents an obvious counterexample to Hick's assertion. Particularly illuminating examples come from the traditions of Advaita Vedanta Hinduism and Zen Buddhism. Advaita Vedanta distinguishes between two levels of knowledge — *apara vidya,* lower knowledge about the phenomenal world, and *para vidya,* or higher knowledge of Brahman. The higher knowledge is direct, unmediated, intuitive knowledge of the actual nature of Brahman. Similarly, the Zen notion of *satori,* "awakening," is held to be an immediate, direct, unmediated apprehension of ultimate reality transcending all duality and dichotomies. It is significant that both Advaita Vedanta and Zen claim direct, unmediated access to the ultimate nature of reality, although their respective understandings of this reality are quite different.

Although Hick is well aware of claims by Zen and Advaita Vedanta to a direct perception of ultimate reality, he nevertheless argues that even in these cases there is no direct, unmediated awareness of reality and suggests to the contrary that "that which is being directly experienced is not the Real *an sich* but the Real manifested respectively as *Sunyata* and Brahman."[54] In other words, even mystical experience involves interpretive activity and thus does not provide privileged, direct access to ultimate reality. Now I suspect that Hick is basically correct in his analysis of mystical experience. It is far from clear that the notion of *satori,* for example, is even coherent. But again, this is beside the point. The problem here is that the notions of *satori* and *para vidya,* as they are understood in Zen and Advaita Vedanta, cannot be accounted for neatly on Hick's thesis, and thus they are significantly reinterpreted and regarded as highly unusual cases of "experiencing-as."

---

54. Ibid., p. 294. On the epistemological status of mystical experience see the fine article by Steven Katz, "Language, Epistemology, and Mysticism," in *Mysticism and Philosophical Analysis,* ed. Steven Katz (New York: Oxford University Press, 1978), pp. 22-74.

Further examples of Hick's reinterpretation of troublesome doctrines include the notions of the Incarnation in orthodox Christianity and the divine inspiration of the Qur'an in Islam. It is also remarkable that the notion of God's special revelation to humankind — a central tenet in orthodox Judaism, Christianity, and Islam, and present in varying forms in certain streams of Hinduism, Baha'i, and Sikhism — is virtually ignored in Hick's discussion. To be sure, the idea that God has definitively revealed himself in any one tradition is ruled out on Hick's theory. But again, the fact that a significant aspect of major traditions must be ruled out or radically reinterpreted to fit his theory prima facie counts against the theory as a comprehensive explanation for religious phenomena.

3. Perhaps nowhere is Hick's reinterpretation of key doctrines more evident than in his treatment of soteriology. Hick correctly observes that the major traditions are all concerned in some sense with the theme of salvation/liberation/enlightenment. He uses the term "salvation/liberation" to refer to what is regarded as a common soteriological structure within the great religions — "the transformation of our human situation from a state of alienation from the true structure of reality to a radically better state in harmony with reality."[55] The various doctrines of the different religions are historically and culturally conditioned variations on the central theme of "the transformation of human existence from self-centredness to Reality-centredness."[56] Several things need to be said about Hick's treatment of soteriology.

First, it may well be that "the transformation from self-centeredness to Reality-centeredness" is part of the soteriological structure of the great religions. But as it stands this is largely a formal formula lacking specific content, and each religious tradition would contribute strikingly different content to the formula. What does it mean to be transformed from self-centeredness to Reality-centeredness? What does "self-centeredness" mean? The mistaken belief in a substantial, enduring ego, as Buddhists argue?

55. *An Interpretation of Religion*, p. 10.
56. Ibid., p. 36.

Or the sinful tendency of individual human beings to regard themselves — and not God — as the object of ultimate concern, as
Christians maintain? What does "Reality-centeredness" mean?
Again, each religion will interpret this phrase differently, depending upon their respective beliefs about the nature of the religious
ultimate. For Advaita Vedantins this will mean recognizing one's
own essential identity with Brahman; for Theravada Buddhists it
will mean attaining liberation from rebirth through carefully following the Noble Eightfold Path; for Jodo Shinshu Buddhists it
will mean responding appropriately to Amida Buddha by proper
recitation of the *nembutsu;* for orthodox Christians it will mean
coming to the one righteous God and Savior, Jesus Christ, in
repentance, seeking forgiveness and new life. Hick greatly minimizes differences in conceptions of salvation by speaking as if all
religions share a common soteriological goal and understanding
of the nature of salvation. But this is seriously misleading. Can the
great Pauline theme of justification by faith, or the Hindu understanding of *moksha,* or the Zen notion of *satori* be reduced to "the
transition from self-centeredness to Reality-centeredness"? As
noted in the previous chapter, it appears that Hick is adopting a
kind of "lowest common denominator" soteriology, resulting in a
strictly formal formula that ignores central aspects of the soteriology of the various religions.

When Hick spells out what is meant by the "transition from
self-centeredness to Reality-centeredness," it is clear that he has in
mind primarily a moral transformation of the person. As he puts
it, "the transformation of human existence which is called salvation
or liberation shows itself in its spiritual and moral fruits."[57] The
result of such transformation is the production of saints, who are
characterized by moral purity, charity, strength of soul, compassion, and inner peace and radiant joy. Their lives are marked by
selfless giving of themselves for others, working to promote peace
and justice. But, we are tempted to ask, what is distinctively religious about this transformation? Is this not a goal any morally
sensitive person would readily embrace? Is this transformation not

57. Ibid., p. 301.

also a reality among those who are explicitly not religious — agnostics and atheists? It would seem so, for Hick admits that

> from a religious point of view the basic intent of the Marxist-Leninist, Trotskyist, Maoist, and broader socialist movements, as also of "liberation theology" and the contemporary drive for racial and gender equality, has to be interpreted as a dispositional response of the modern sociologically conditioned consciousness to the Real.[58]

But if so, then what is it about the Real, as the postulated ground of different forms of religious experience, which distinguishes "Reality-centeredness" from, say, "morally acceptable behavior"? One suspects that soteriology comes close here to being reduced to common morality; but this is something that a host of religious figures from many traditions would emphatically reject.[59]

4. As we have seen, the different religions seem to be making quite different and even incompatible claims about the nature of the religious ultimate, the human condition, and the nature of salvation/liberation. It would seem that not all can be correct. Does this not mean that at least some are incorrect? And if so, how can one seriously maintain that all religious traditions constitute authentic human responses to the one divine Reality?

One way to avoid the conclusion that some religious tradi-

---

58. Ibid., p. 306.

59. We noted earlier that Hick has offered an ethical criterion — the spiritual and moral fruits in the lives of believers — for determining when the transformation from self-centeredness to Reality-centeredness takes place. And it is this transformation within a given religious tradition which serves as a soteriological criterion, distinguishing authentic manifestations of the Real from what are mistakenly taken to be such. But can Hick consistently apply such an ethical criterion? Given Hick's contention that the Real *an sich* transcends even distinctions between good and evil, right and wrong (cf. *An Interpretation of Religion*, pp. 246, 350), what sense does it make to speak of an ethical criterion for distinguishing appropriate from inappropriate dispositional responses to the Real? The criterion would not seem to be indicative of any ontological relation to the Real *an sich*, but merely a reflection of our human values and principles. This conclusion is reinforced by Hick's understanding of ethics and morality as the product of the inherently social nature of human beings (ibid., pp. 97f.).

tions are mistaken is to maintain that ultimately there is no real conflict between the truth claims of the various religions. There are undeniable differences in belief, it might be said, but these differences are complementary and are not indicative of mutually incompatible claims. Christians and Muslims think of the religious ultimate in personal categories, whereas many Hindus and Buddhists regard the religious ultimate as nonpersonal. Occasionally Hick makes statements suggesting that such differences should be thought of as complementary rather than as strictly incompatible claims.

> The relation between these two very different ways of conceiving and experiencing the Real, as personal and as non-personal, is perhaps a complementarity analogous (as has been suggested by Ian Barbour) to that between the two ways of conceiving and registering light, namely as waves and as particles.[60]

What seem to be major differences in belief, then, are ultimately not mutually incompatible but simply very different ways of conceiving and expressing the same reality. Ultimately, the central claims of the major religions are all mutually consistent.

Now it is very difficult to maintain this hypothesis if one accepts that religious believers do intend to make actual truth claims about the nature of reality and if the understandings of the beliefs within the respective traditions are preserved. It is very difficult indeed, for example, not to conclude that an orthodox Muslim and an orthodox Christian hold mutually incompatible beliefs about the person of Jesus Christ, or that the Christian and the Shinto understandings of divine reality are mutually incompatible, or that Muslim and Theravada Buddhist views on the afterlife cannot both be true. Hick recognizes that so long as different religions are regarded as making truth claims about the nature of reality which might literally be true or false, the problem of conflicting truth claims is inescapable. He delineates three levels of such disagreements and in so doing offers his resolution of the problem of conflicting truth claims.[61]

60. *An Interpretation of Religion*, p. 245.
61. Ibid., pp. 363f.

First, there are disagreements about what are in principle straightforward matters of historical fact which carry significant theological ramifications. Was it Ishmael or Isaac who was almost sacrificed by Abraham? Did Jesus have a human father or not? Did Jesus in fact die on the cross or did he merely appear to die? Hick notes that the dispute between Muslims and Christians over the death of Jesus is perhaps the major example of disagreement concerning a factual matter. Such disputes are in principle open to careful investigation and, given sufficient data, capable of resolution, although in reality we may never be in a position to settle the question one way or another.

The second level of disagreement concerns what Hick calls "trans-historical" differences in belief. These have to do with questions to which there are in principle true answers, but the answers cannot be established by historical or other empirical evidence. Hick suggests as an example of this kind of dispute the debate over reincarnation: Are we continually reborn in a succession of lives or not? Presumably there is a true answer to this question, but Hick contends that we are not now nor are we likely in the future to be able to settle this dispute. Accordingly, taking a cue from the Buddha's unwillingness to answer certain metaphysical questions since they are not relevant to attaining liberation, Hick urges that we leave aside such conflicts of transhistorical fact since they are not important for salvation. He claims

> that both correct and incorrect trans-historical beliefs, like correct and incorrect historical and scientific beliefs, can form part of a religious totality that mediates the Real to human beings, constituting an effective context within which the salvific process occurs. My far from original suggestion, then, concerning issues of trans-historical fact is (a) that they should be fully and freely recognised as matters on which directly opposed views are often held; (b) that — although by no means everyone ranged on either side of these disagreements will be able to accept this — the questions are ones to which humanity does not at present know the answers; (c) that this ignorance does not hinder the process of salvation/liberation; and (d) that we should therefore learn to live with these differ-

ences, tolerating contrary convictions even when we suspect them to be mistaken.[62]

Since knowledge of such matters is not necessary for salvation, there is little point in concentrating upon disputes which, in all likelihood, will not be settled definitively one way or another.

Hick also suggests that many transhistorical doctrines from the major religions should not be regarded as assertions that are actually true or false but should be reinterpreted mythologically and treated as "true myths." "Thus the pluralistic hypothesis suggests that a number of trans-historical beliefs, which are at present unverifiable and unfalsifiable, may well be true or false myths rather than true or false factual assertions."[63] Among the candidates mentioned for such mythological reinterpretation are these: within Hinduism, the Vedic stories of the gods and reincarnation; within Judaism, the notion of Israel as God's chosen people, the "numerous anthropomorphic rabbinic stories about the Lord," and the "idea of the ups and downs of Jewish history as divine rewards and punishments"; within Buddhism, the idea of rebirth, the tales of the Buddha's previous lives, and discourse about the heavenly Buddhas; within Christianity, the stories of Jesus' virgin birth, bodily resurrection, and ascension, the doctrines of divine incarnation, the satisfaction and penal-substitutionary conceptions of atonement, and the ontological doctrine of the Holy Trinity.[64] Such reinterpretation of central beliefs in various religions would, of course, dispose of the problem of conflicting truth claims, since religious believers would no longer be regarded as making ontological claims about the nature of reality which are true or false but merely expressing mythological statements which tend to evoke appropriate responses to the Real.

Third, there are disagreements concerning ultimate questions about the nature of the religious ultimate and the source and destiny of the universe. Is the Real personal or nonpersonal? Is the universe eternal or did it have a beginning? Are there eternal souls that are ontologically distinct from the religious ultimate, or ulti-

62. Ibid., p. 370.
63. Ibid., p. 371.
64. Ibid.

mately do all perceived "selves" merge into the sole reality —
Brahman? Here, too, Hick's proposal is that we think of such
conflicting beliefs not in terms of mutually incompatible claims
about the nature of reality which are in fact either true or false but
rather as sophisticated mythological expressions which are "true"
in the sense that they tend to evoke in the believers appropriate
dispositional responses to the Real. In particular, Hick speaks of
"eschatological myths" — beliefs about the afterlife in various
traditions — as "imaginative pictures of the ultimate state" which
"can be said to be true in so far as dispositional responses which
they tend to evoke are appropriate to our actual present situation
as beings on the way towards salvation/liberation."[65]

There is considerable irony in the fact that Hick is calling
for such extensive reinterpretation in mythological terms of religious belief and discourse, since among his earlier writings are
highly influential arguments for the "factually informative" status
of religious discourse in the face of attacks by logical positivism.[66]
It is difficult to escape the conclusion that his resolute desire to
resolve the problem of conflicting truth claims without admitting
that some beliefs of some traditions are false has driven him to a
radical reinterpretation of religious beliefs and doctrines in mythological terms. The price for resolving the problem in this manner,
however, is that Hick's theory must be called into question as a
general explanation of the nature of religious experience. For his
understanding of religious beliefs bears little resemblance to that
of most believers in the major traditions and consequently will be
vigorously resisted by all within the mainstream of these traditions.

It can hardly be denied that most believers do intend to
make significant ontological claims about reality which are true:
Most Theravada Buddhists do believe that we are locked in a
succession of rebirths and that liberation (whatever else it involves)
is release from this cycle of rebirths; most Christians do believe
that there is in fact an eternal creator God who, two thousand years

65. Ibid., p. 355.
66. See Hick's "Theology and Verification," in *Theology Today* 17 (1960),
and "Eschatological Verification Reconsidered," in *Religious Studies* 13 (1971).

ago, became incarnate in the man Jesus Christ; most Muslims do believe that the Qur'an is the very Word of God dictated to Muhammad. Hick, of course, is free to reinterpret such doctrines in mythological terms, but it must be recognized that in so doing he is parting company with the vast majority of religious believers in the major traditions.

Furthermore, the suggestion must be rejected that many disagreements over doctrinal belief are unimportant since they are irrelevant to salvation. That correct belief (among other things) is essential for salvation is accepted in most religions. The New Testament shows Paul telling the Philippian jailor, "Believe in the Lord Jesus, and you will be saved, you and your household" (Acts 16:31). John's Gospel states that "whoever believes in [Jesus] should not perish but have eternal life" (John 3:16). Even Shankara, the architect of Advaita Vedanta Hinduism, placed priority upon correct insight and belief: "If the soul . . . is not considered to possess fundamental unity with Brahman — an identity to be realized by knowledge — there is not any chance of its obtaining final release."[67] And the Buddhist Pali canon says the following of the Buddha and his liberation/enlightenment:

> The Tathagata [the Buddha] knows the nature of form, and how form arises, and how form perishes; the nature of sensation, how sensation arises, and how sensation perishes; the nature of predispositions, and how the predispositions arise, and how the predispositions perish; the nature of consciousness, and how consciousness arises, and how consciousness perishes. *Therefore* I say that the Tathagata has attained deliverance.[68]

Salvation/enlightenment/liberation — however this is understood — is seen to be partially dependent upon having a correct view of

---

67. G. Thibaut, *The Vedanta Sutras of Badarayana with the Commentary of Sankara*, vol. II (New York: Dover, 1962), p. 399, as quoted in K. Yandell, "On the Alleged Unity of All Religions," p. 141.

68. H. C. Warren, *Buddhism in Translations* (New York: Atheneum Press, 1969), p. 122; as quoted in Yandell, "On the Alleged Unity of All Religions," p. 141. My emphasis.

the nature of the human predicament and, upon this basis, responding appropriately to the actual nature of reality. Only on a very different understanding of salvation than is found in the actual religions can one maintain that doctrinal belief is not essential to salvation.

The suggestion that despite obvious differences in belief and practice the major religions are all different historically and culturally conditioned human responses to the same divine reality has considerable intuitive appeal, but, as we have seen, it is highly problematic when carefully considered. If we are to have a comprehensive understanding of the religious traditions of humankind that takes seriously both the varied data of the religions and is epistemologically sound, it is very difficult to escape the conclusion that at least some of the central claims of some religions must be false.

CHAPTER SEVEN

No Other Name: The Question of Jesus

In his recent work *Many Mansions,* Harvey Cox offers some fascinating observations about the place of Jesus in contemporary interreligious dialogue. Speaking from years of experience in dialogue with those of other faiths, Cox chides fellow ecumenists who
play down the figure of Jesus Christ in interfaith discussions. Many
Christians presume that since the question of Jesus will prove so
divisive, interreligious dialogue should begin by dealing first with
less controversial issues, seeking for areas of mutual agreement,
and that only after having carefully constructed a proper foundation should the subject of Jesus be introduced. The result is that
often the issue of Jesus is not broached at all — or if it is, it is
mentioned with some embarrassment, almost as an afterthought.

But Cox correctly points out two problems with this approach. First, to ignore or set aside the question of Jesus is to be
less than honest in one's encounter with those of other faiths.

> For the vast majority of Christians, including those most energeti-
> cally engaged in dialogue, Jesus is not merely a background figure.
> He is central to Christian faith. Not only do the Christian dia-
> loguers recognize this, but so do their Muslim, Buddhist, Shinto,
> Hindu, and Jewish conversation partners. Wherever one starts . . .

any honest dialogue between Christians and others will sooner or later — and in my experience it is usually sooner — have to deal with the figure of Jesus.[1]

And second, Cox notes that in his experience whereas some Christians are reluctant to bring up Jesus for discussion, frequently it is precisely the question of Jesus that non-Christian participants seem most eager to get to. Cox admits that in the past he too, in an effort to stay clear of controversy and any appearance of insensitivity to others, avoided "talking about Jesus too quickly." But, he continues, "I soon discovered my interlocutors wanted me to, and their bearing sometimes suggested that they did not believe they were really engaged in a brass-tacks conversation with a Christian until that happened."[2]

Such interest in the person of Jesus by followers of other faiths should not be surprising. For as historian Jaroslav Pelikan remarks, "Regardless of what anyone may personally believe about him, Jesus of Nazareth has been the dominant figure in the history of Western culture for almost twenty centuries."[3] No serious discussion of the relation of Christianity to other faiths can proceed very far without coming to grips with the towering figure of Jesus. Sooner or later, the blunt question put by Jesus to his followers — "Who do people say I am?" (Mark 8:27, NIV) — must be confronted. For Christian faith includes, above all else, commitment to the Lordship of Jesus Christ.

But who is this Jesus whom Christians worship as Lord and Savior and what are the implications of commitment to Jesus for those who claim other lords and saviors? Is it theologically and morally permissible to hold today that Jesus of Nazareth was indeed God incarnate, that salvation is mediated exclusively through him, and that adherents of other religions too must recognize him as their personal Lord and Savior? What of those who,

1. Harvey Cox, *Many Mansions: A Christian's Encounter With Other Faiths* (Boston: Beacon Press, 1988), pp. 7-8.
2. Ibid., pp. 8-9.
3. Jaroslav Pelikan, *Jesus Through the Centuries: His Place in the History of Culture* (New Haven: Yale University Press, 1985), p. 1.

through no fault of their own, have no opportunity to hear and respond to the gospel of Jesus Christ? Are they to be denied salvation simply because of the "accidents" of history? These are perplexing questions which must trouble all thoughtful Christians who maintain the uniqueness and normativity of Jesus Christ for salvation.

The challenge of pluralism has prompted many theologians today to grope for fresh, alternative Christologies not bound by the perceived limitations of the traditional understanding of the uniqueness and normativity of Jesus Christ. Christology is today an enormously complex and controversial subject, and we cannot hope here to settle definitively technical questions of New Testament interpretation. In any event, I am hardly qualified to attempt to do so. But we will examine briefly the views of John Hick and Paul Knitter, two leading critics of traditional Christology who have presented alternative interpretations portraying Jesus as one of many lords and saviors. And we will conclude the chapter by looking at current evangelical thinking on the question of the implications of traditional Christology for those who have never heard of the gospel of Jesus Christ — an increasingly controversial question among evangelicals. But first a brief word about the traditional understanding of Jesus.

Chalcedonian Christology

Orthodox Christianity has historically maintained that Jesus of Nazareth was not simply a great religious and moral teacher in first-century Palestine, but that, in an admittedly mysterious sense, he was the eternal creator God who became man. Jesus was God incarnate. But during the past century the orthodox view has come under increasingly sharp criticism, both from those calling themselves Christians and from those outside the Church. And yet, the vigorous attack upon the orthodox understanding of the Incarnation today should not be allowed to obscure the fact that for centuries it has been the dominant — indeed, virtually unquestioned — view of Christ within the Christian community, one clearly reflected in the great historic creeds of the Christian faith. Regardless of one's own personal views concerning Jesus, it can hardly be denied that the orthodox understanding of the Incarnation — which sees Jesus as both fully God and fully man, the only Savior of humankind — has been historically the accepted paradigm within the Christian community.

For example, the Creed of Nicea (A.D. 325), formulated as a response to the question of Christ's deity raised by Arius, affirmed belief in

> one Lord Jesus Christ, the Son of God, begotten of the Father as only begotten, that is, from the essence of the Father, God from God, Light from Light, true God from true God, begotten not created, of the same essence as the Father, through whom all things came into being, both in heaven and in earth; who for us men and for our salvation came down and was incarnate, becoming human.[4]

The classic definition of orthodox Christology is found in the Chalcedonian definition, formulated by the Council of Chalcedon in 451. The Council did not wish to amend or replace the earlier Nicene Creed but simply to clarify what is meant by the affirmation that Jesus was both God and man. Thus Jesus was said to be

> perfect both in deity and also in humanness; this selfsame one is also actually God and actually man. . . . He is of the same reality as God as far as his deity is concerned and of the same reality as we ourselves as far as his humanness is concerned. . . . one and only Christ — Son, Lord, only begotten — in two natures.[5]

The Chalcedonian definition is usually associated with "two-nature" Christology in that it affirms that Jesus is God undiminished, is man undiminished, was sinless in his life, that there were two distinct natures in the Incarnation, and that in the union

---

4. Cited in *Creeds of the Churches*, ed. John H. Leith, 3rd ed. (Atlanta: John Knox Press, 1982), pp. 30-31.
   5. Ibid., pp. 35-36.

of the two natures there was "no confusion, no change, no division, and no separation." Thus the Chalcedonian definition is often taken as the classic expression of orthodox Christology, and while we can certainly accept this, the limitations of the definition must also be recognized. It was never meant to be an explanation of the Incarnation — that is, an explanation as to how one being could be both fully God and fully man. It is rather an unambiguous affirmation of both the deity and humanity of Jesus which serves to set the boundaries within which proper speculation about the person of Christ is to take place.[6] The profound mystery of the Incarnation is in no way removed.

Orthodox two-nature Christology is reaffirmed in later creeds, such as the Lutheran Augsburg Confession (1530), which states that "God the Son became man, born of the Virgin Mary, and that the two natures, divine and human, are so inseparably united in one person that there is one Christ, true God and true man, who was truly born, suffered, was crucified, died, and was buried in order to be a sacrifice not only for original sin but also for all other sins."[7] Similarly, the Thirty-nine Articles (1563) speak of Jesus as "the Son, . . . the very and eternal God . . . [who] took Man's nature in the womb of the blessed Virgin . . . so that the two whole and perfect Natures, that is to say, the Godhead and Manhood, were joined together in one Person . . . to reconcile his Father to us."[8] And the influential Westminster Confession of Faith (1646) affirms that Jesus "is very God and very man, yet one Christ, the only mediator between God and man."[9] The Articles of Religion (1784) of Methodism speak of "one Christ, very God and very man, who truly suffered, was crucified, dead, and buried, to reconcile his Father to us."[10]

In the Roman Catholic tradition, from the Council of Trent (1563), the Decree Concerning the Symbol of Faith enjoins belief

6. Cf. Bernard Ramm, *An Evangelical Christology: Ecumenic and Historic* (Nashville: Thomas Nelson, 1985), p. 36.
7. Leith, *Creeds of the Church*, p. 68.
8. Ibid., p. 267.
9. Ibid., pp. 203-4.
10. Ibid., p. 354.

in "one Lord Jesus Christ, the only begotten Son of God and born of the Father before all ages; God of God, light of light, true God of true God . . . who for us men and for our salvation descended from heaven, and was incarnate by the Holy Ghost of the Virgin Mary, and was made man."[11] And from the Second Vatican Council (1965), the Decree on the Church's Missionary Activity, *Ad Gentes*, declares, "Jesus Christ was sent into the world as the true Mediator between God and men. Since he is God, all the fullness of the divine nature dwells in him bodily (Col. 2:9); as man he is the new Adam, full of grace and truth (John 1:14), who has been constituted head of a restored humanity."[12]

The confessional statement of the World Council of Churches states unambiguously that the Council is "a fellowship of churches which confess the Lord Jesus Christ as God and Saviour according to the Scriptures."[13] And the Lausanne Covenant (1974) affirms belief in "one eternal God, Creator and Lord of the world, Father, Son and Holy Spirit" and that "Jesus Christ, being himself the only God-man, who gave himself as the only ransom for sinners, is the only mediator between God and man."[14]

The fact that the two-nature Christology of Chalcedon has been the dominant understanding of the person of Jesus Christ throughout the history of the Church does not, of course, in and of itself guarantee its correctness. The creeds themselves are not inspired.[15] At best they are carefully formulated prescriptions that clarify the explicit and implicit teaching of Scripture

---

11. Ibid., p. 401.

12. *Documents of Vatican II*, ed. Austin P. Flannery (Grand Rapids: Eerdmans, 1975), p. 814.

13. *The New Delhi Report*, ed. W. A. Visser 't Hooft (New York: Association, 1962), p. 152.

14. *Let the Earth Hear His Voice: International Congress on World Evangelization, Lausanne, Switzerland*, ed. J. D. Douglas (Minneapolis: World Wide Publications, 1975), pp. 3-4.

15. "Belief in historic Christology does not mean that every line of a creed is beyond criticism, nor that the original creeds resolve all problems, nor that the creeds end Christological reflection. It is the belief that the creeds reflect in their way the materials found here and there in the New Testament." Bernard Ramm, *Evangelical Christology*, p. 16.

and stake out the acceptable parameters within which further
thinking about the person and work of Christ should take place.
Although expressing universal, unchanging truth, they are formulated out of a concern to address certain issues and challenges
to the biblical teaching on Christ current at the time. The contexts in which the great historic creeds were formulated are in
some respects significantly different from those of today. Thus,
we should not expect the historic creeds of yesterday to settle
every question the Church encounters today. While the historic
creeds are highly relevant to the contemporary questions posed
by religious pluralism and no informed Christian response to
pluralism dare ignore them, there is a critical need today for
Christians to articulate in a fresh way a genuinely biblical response to the challenges presented by other religions. However,
although its expression will be fresh, relevant to current issues,
and couched in currently acceptable terminology, even today a
genuinely biblical response to pluralism must rest upon an understanding of the person and work of Jesus Christ that is clearly
within the parameters marked out by Chalcedon.

John Hick's Inspiration Christology

One of the more distressing developments in modern theology is
the fact that Chalcedonian Christology has been increasingly attacked not only by hostile critics outside the faith, but also by
prominent Roman Catholic and Protestant theologians on the
inside. A growing number of Christian theologians explicitly reject
the traditional understanding of the Incarnation. There are, of
course, many reasons for current dissatisfaction with orthodox
Christology. But an increasingly influential factor is the widespread
perception today that traditional Christology — which sees Jesus
as fully God and fully man, absolutely unique among religious
figures and the only Lord and Savior for all humankind — simply
cannot be maintained in light of our more adequate understanding
today both of the New Testament data and the other great religious
traditions. This view is clearly reflected in the thought of John

Hick, one of the more influential contemporary critics of Chalce-donian Christology.

Hick is well aware of the implications of Chalcedonian Christology for followers of other religions.

> If Jesus was literally God incarnate, and if it is by his death alone that men can be saved, and by their response to him alone that they can appropriate that salvation, then the only doorway to eternal life is Christian faith. It would follow from this that the large majority of the human race so far have not been saved.[16]

Hick is understandably deeply troubled by these implications, and, for this and other reasons, rejects the traditional, orthodox view of the Incarnation. He contends that the Incarnation should not be understood in a literal sense to be affirming that the first-cen-tury Jew, Jesus of Nazareth, was actually God become man, but rather that it is a profound myth[17] or figure of speech which communicates that Jesus is "our sufficient, effective, and saving point of contact with God."[18] Jesus is not, then, literally God incarnate but rather simply a human being who was open to the presence and reality of God to such an unprecedented degree that he dramatically impacted everyone with whom he came in contact.

> I see the Nazarene, then, as intensely and overwhelmingly con-scious of the reality of God. He was a man of God, living in the unseen presence of God, and addressing God as *abba*, father. His spirit was open to God and his life a continuous response to the divine love as both utterly gracious and demanding. He was so powerfully God conscious that his life vibrated, as it were, to the divine life; and as a result his hands could heal the sick, and the

16. John Hick, "Jesus and the World Religions," in *The Myth of God Incarnate,* ed. John Hick (London: SCM, 1977), p. 180.

17. Myth is defined by Hick as "a story which is told but which is not literally true, or an idea or image which is applied to someone or something but which does not literally apply, but which invites a particular attitude in its hearers." "Jesus and the World Religions," p. 178. Cf. Hick's *An Interpretation of Religion* (New Haven: Yale University Press, 1989), chap. 19.

18. John Hick, *God Has Many Names* (Philadelphia: Westminster, 1982), p. 75.

"poor in spirit" were kindled to new life in his presence. . . . Thus
in Jesus' presence, we should have felt that we are in the presence
of God — not in the sense that the man Jesus literally *is* God, but
in the sense that he was so totally conscious of God that we could
catch something of that consciousness by spiritual contagion.[19]

We must not misunderstand Hick by supposing that he is
calling for Christians to abandon their ultimate loyalty and commitment to Christ. He allows that it is entirely appropriate for
Christians to have an absolute commitment to Jesus Christ and to
regard him as their Lord and Savior, so long as they recognize that
followers of other religious traditions have their own equally legitimate objects of ultimate devotion and commitment. Jesus may be
the Savior for Christians, but he is not necessarily Lord and Savior
for all persons in all cultures.

There seem to be three main reasons for Hick's rejection of
the traditional understanding of the Incarnation. First, Hick is
clearly very much bothered by what he sees as implications of the
orthodox doctrine: If Jesus really was in fact the eternal creator
God become man, then it becomes very difficult indeed to treat
Jesus, the New Testament, and Christian faith as being on the same
level as phenomena from other religious traditions. There would
seem to be something inherently superior and normative, to say
the least, about Jesus and the Christian faith. The way to a restored
relationship with God would then lie solely with Jesus Christ. Hick
assumes that this entails that the vast majority of humankind
throughout history have not been saved, and that this in and of
itself is sufficient to discredit the traditional interpretation.[20]

A second reason for rejecting the orthodox view is what
Hick regards as the failure of orthodoxy to give any specific meaning to the formula "truly God and truly man." "That Jesus was

19. "Jesus and the World Religions," p. 172. See also Hick's "An Inspiration Christology for a Religiously Plural World," in *Encountering Jesus,* ed.
Stephen T. Davis (Atlanta: John Knox, 1988), pp. 5-38.
20. Cf. "Jesus and the World Religions," p. 180; "Religious Pluralism," in
The World's Religious Traditions, ed. Frank Whaling (New York: Crossroads, 1986),
pp. 150-51; *God Has Many Names,* pp. 29-31.

God the Son incarnate is not literally true," he maintains, "since it has no literal meaning."[21] To affirm that the historical Jesus of Nazareth was also literally God "is as devoid of meaning as to say that this circle drawn with a pencil on paper is also a square."[22] It is not clear whether Hick believes that the traditional formula actually entails a logical contradiction, so that it is logically impossible for it to be true, or whether it simply is so muddled and unclear that there is no significant identifiable meaning which it conveys.[23] Either way, there would be little reason for its adoption.

Furthermore, Hick's treatment of Christology relies heavily upon the more radical wing of New Testament scholarship. He agrees with those who hold that, whereas Jesus did not regard himself as in any sense divine, over a period of time the early Church came to interpret his significance in such categories. Hick is remarkably skeptical about the possibility of our having significant knowledge of the historical Jesus of first-century Palestine. For example, he begins his essay "Jesus and the World Religions" by pointing to what he sees as the "confusion and uncertainty which assail us when we try to speak of Jesus. For New Testament scholarship has shown how fragmentary and ambiguous are the data available to us as we try to look back across nineteen and a half centuries, and at the same time how large and how variable is the contribution of the imagination to our 'pictures' of Jesus."[24] Given this perspective it is hardly surprising that he later refers to Jesus as "the largely unknown man of Nazareth."[25]

Hick explicitly rejects the suggestion that Jesus thought of himself as in any sense divine — certainly Jesus did not regard himself as literally God incarnate.[26] He argues that the title "Son

---

21. "Jesus and the World Religions," p. 178.

22. Ibid.; cf. also idem, *The Center of Christianity* (New York: Harper & Row, 1978), p. 31.

23. See the exchange between John Hick and Stephen Davis in *Encountering Jesus;* S. Davis, "Critique of John Hick," pp. 23-24; J. Hick, "Hick's Response to Critiques," pp. 34-35; idem, "Critique of Stephen Davis," pp. 66-69.

24. "Jesus and the World Religions," p. 167.

25. Ibid., p. 168.

26. Cf. *God Has Many Names,* pp. 28, 72-73, 125; "Jesus and the World Religions," pp. 171-73; "The Non-Absoluteness of Christianity," in *The Myth of*

of God," a title often used in reference to the Messiah, could be used of any extraordinary religious figure. It connoted uniqueness but not necessarily exclusivity and certainly not deity. It was the early church, because of the compelling manner in which Jesus mediated the presence of God, the tremendous impact of the mysterious resurrection experience,[27] and the influence of the surrounding Greco-Roman culture, which came to think of Jesus first as the Messiah, then as a metaphorical "Son of God," and eventually as literally a metaphysical Son of God — God the Son.[28] Hick claims that ideas of divinity embodied in human form were widespread in the ancient world, "so that there is nothing in the least surprising in the deification of Jesus in that cultural environment."[29]

Few issues in contemporary theology are as controversial as questions of New Testament interpretation. Although the distinction is undoubtedly somewhat simplistic, contemporary interpreters of the New Testament can be very broadly divided into two categories: (1) those who, while fully aware of the various critical problems involved, nevertheless accept the New Testament documents as authentic, historically reliable material describing what Jesus said and did, and (2) those who hold that the documents are primarily the creations of the early Christian community; although they inform us of the experiences and beliefs of the early church, the task of trying to uncover what the actual historical Jesus of Nazareth said and did is, at best, highly problematic. Hick falls clearly within the second camp.

It is obvious that the presuppositions with which one approaches the New Testament data dramatically affect one's view of

---

Christian Uniqueness, ed. John H. Hick and Paul F. Knitter (Maryknoll, N.Y.: Orbis, 1987), p. 31.

27. "That there was some kind of experience of seeing Jesus after his death, an appearance or appearances which came to be known as his resurrection, seems virtually certain in view of the survival and growth of the tiny original Jesus movement. But we cannot ascertain today in what this resurrection-event consisted." "Jesus and the World Religions," p. 170.

28. Ibid., pp. 172-76.

29. Ibid., p. 174.

the person of Jesus. While recognizing that there are significant critical problems involved in New Testament interpretation, and in no way denying the important part played by the early Christian communities in the formation of the New Testament documents, I see no reason for concluding that the New Testament is not a reliable source for the sayings and deeds of Jesus.[30]

There has been no lack of critics of Hick's Christology, most of whom charge that Hick has seriously distorted the New Testament data and relies upon certain dubious assumptions concerning the allegedly evolutionary development of early Christian beliefs which, although popular in the earlier part of the century, have been shown in more recent literature to be untenable. The 1977 symposium *The Myth of God Incarnate*, edited by Hick, provoked a vigorous debate over Christology which exposed the tenu-

---

30. There is an enormous amount of technical literature on the question of the historical reliability of the New Testament. A good introduction to the issues can be found in Donald Guthrie's *New Testament Introduction* (Downers Grove, Ill.: Inter-Varsity Press, 1970). Also helpful as introductions are F. F. Bruce's classic *The New Testament Documents: Are They Reliable?*, 5th ed. (Grand Rapids: Eerdmans, 1982); R. T. France, *The Evidence for Jesus* (Downers Grove, Ill.: Inter-Varsity Press, 1986); and I. Howard Marshall, *I Believe in the Historical Jesus* (Grand Rapids: Eerdmans, 1979). On a more technical level is the work of the Gospels Research Project of Tyndale House, Cambridge, which resulted in the six-volume series *Gospel Perspectives*, published by Sheffield University's JSOT Press: vol. 1 — *Gospel Perspectives: Studies of History and Tradition in the Four Gospels*, ed. R. T. France and David Wenham (Sheffield: JSOT Press, 1980); vol. 2 — *Gospel Perspectives: Studies of History and Tradition in the Four Gospels*, ed. R. T. France and David Wenham (Sheffield: JSOT Press, 1981); vol. 3 — *Gospel Perspectives: Studies in Midrash and Historiography*, ed. R. T. France and David Wenham (Sheffield: JSOT Press, 1983); vol. 4 — David Wenham, *The Rediscovery of Jesus' Eschatological Discourse* (Sheffield: JSOT Press, 1984); vol. 5 — *Gospel Perspectives: The Jesus Tradition Outside the Gospels*, ed. David Wenham (Sheffield: JSOT Press, 1985); vol. 6 — *Gospel Perspectives: The Miracles of Jesus*, ed. David Wenham and Craig L. Blomberg (Sheffield: JSOT Press, 1986). The results of the Gospels Research Project are summarized in Craig Blomberg's *The Historical Reliability of the Gospels* (Downers Grove, Ill.: Inter-Varsity Press, 1987). Also helpful are C. F. D. Moule, *The Phenomenon of the New Testament* (London: SCM Press, 1967); Joachim Jeremias, *New Testament Theology*, trans. John Bowden (New York: Scribner's & Macmillan, 1971), especially chap. 1; and Oscar Cullmann, *The Christology of the New Testament*, rev. ed., trans. Shirley C. Guthrie and Charles A. M. Hall (Philadelphia: Westminster, 1963).

ous nature of the evidence for the main theses of the contributors.[31] In particular, Hick's fundamental assumptions — for instance, that early Christological understanding evolved in a linear
fashion from a primitive devotion to Jesus as Master and Messiah
into a more metaphysical conception of him as Son of God, God
the Son, and eventually into the sophisticated trinitarian formula
of the Second Person of the Trinity, and that neither Jesus himself
nor his first followers thought of him as in any sense divine —
have been shown by C. F. D. Moule of Cambridge, among others,
to be highly problematic.[32] Moule persuasively argues that an evolutionary model which holds that a "high" Christology evolved
from a primitive "low" Christology by a process of borrowing from
extraneous sources over a period of time, and that these Christologies can be arranged in an evolutionary sequence from "low" to
"high," does not fit the data of the New Testament. To the contrary,
he maintains that the transition from invoking Jesus as a revered
Master to the acclamation of him as divine Lord is better understood in terms of a model of development, according to which
"the various estimates of Jesus reflected in the New Testament
[are], in essence, only attempts to describe what was already there
from the beginning. They are not successive additions of something new, but only the drawing out and articulating of what is
there."[33] Moule argues that "Jesus was, *from the beginning,* such a
one as appropriately to be described in the ways in which, sooner
or later, he did come to be described in the New Testament period
— for instance, as 'Lord' and even, in some sense, as 'God'."[34] He
contends that some of the most elevated Christology in the New

31. See especially *The Truth of God Incarnate,* ed. Michael Green (Grand
Rapids: Eerdmans, 1977); *Incarnation and Myth: The Debate Continued,* ed. Mi-
chael Goulder (Grand Rapids: Eerdmans, 1979); and A. Heron's review article in
Scottish Journal of Theology 31 (1978): 51-71.
32. Cf. C. F. D. Moule, *The Origin of Christology* (Cambridge: Cambridge
University Press, 1977). See also R. N. Longenecker, *The Christology of Early Jewish
Christianity* (London: SCM, 1970); I. Howard Marshall, *The Origins of New Testament Christology* (Downers Grove, Ill.: Inter-Varsity Press, 1976); and *Christ the
Lord,* ed. H. H. Rowdon (Leicester, Eng.: InterVarsity Press, 1982).
33. Moule, *Origin of Christology,* pp. 2-3.
34. Ibid., p. 4. Emphasis in the original.

Testament is present, either explicitly or implicitly, in the Pauline epistles — widely accepted as the earliest documents in the New Testament.[35] Moule and Martin Hengel of Tübingen have demonstrated that the Christological titles are not later innovations but can be traced back to very early usage. Hengel, for example, holds that the title "Son of God" was applied to Jesus between A.D. 30 and 50.[36] Similarly, after a short but judicious summary of the New Testament data, I. Howard Marshall concludes, "We have found that the concept of incarnation, i.e., that Jesus Christ is the Son of God made flesh, is the principle of Christological explanation in the writings of John, the writings of Paul including the Pastoral Epistles, the Epistle to the Hebrews, and 1 Peter. The view that it is found merely on the fringe of the New Testament is a complete travesty of the facts."[37] And in his classic study of Christology Oscar Cullmann observes, "Our investigation of the Christological utilization of *Kyrios,* 'Logos', and 'Son of God' has already shown that on the basis of the Christological views connected with these titles the New Testament *could* designate Jesus as 'God'. . . . The fundamental answer to the question whether the New Testament teaches Christ's 'deity' is therefore 'Yes.'"[38]

Moreover, Sir Norman Anderson correctly points out that Hick "greatly exaggerates the paucity of positive evidence we have about the one to whom he refers as the 'largely unknown man of Nazareth.'"[39] Curiously, in spite of his professed skepticism concerning the possibility of knowledge about the historical Jesus, Hick proceeds to make some rather specific claims about what

35. Ibid., pp. 2-7; cf. also Moule's "Three Points of Conflict in the Christological Debate," in *Incarnation and Myth,* p. 137.

36. Martin Hengel, *The Son of God: The Origin of Christology and the History of Jewish-Hellenistic Religion* (Philadelphia: Fortress, 1976), pp. 2, 10.

37. I. Howard Marshall, "Incarnational Christology in the New Testament," in *Christ the Lord,* p. 13.

38. Oscar Cullmann, *Christology of the New Testament,* p. 306. A significant, but neglected, dimension in the Christological debate is the implicit claims of Jesus to deity found in the parables. For a good discussion of this see Philip B. Payne, "Jesus' Implicit Claim to Deity in His Parables," *Trinity Journal* 2 (1981): 3-23.

39. Norman Anderson, *The Mystery of the Incarnation* (London: Hodder & Stoughton, 1978), p. 64.

Jesus was like and his relation to God and his immeuiate followers.
Consider, for example, the following statement:

> It was the experience of the disciples that God's fatherly love was
> revealed in the life of Christ. Jesus told men that God loves and
> cares for each of them with an infinitely gracious, tender, and wise
> love; and the assertion was credible on his lips because this su-
> pernatural agape was apparent in his own dealings with them. . . .
> The will and power of love which flowered out from him in
> healing to men's bodies and renewal of their spirits was manifestly
> continuous with the eternal heavenly love of which he spoke.[40]

It would seem that Hick does have access, after all, to considerable
information about the person of Jesus of Nazareth and knows
more than a little about what Jesus was like, the impact he had
upon his followers, and his relation to God.

Hick, of course, is not the first to question the intelligibility
of the Chalcedonian formulation. And if he is correct in charging
that the formula "truly God and truly man" is incoherent —
whether this be construed in terms of logical inconsistency or
merely the absence of any significant identifiable meaning — it
follows that the orthodox understanding of the Incarnation cannot
stand.

But is the doctrine really incoherent? No one would deny
that it is mysterious, even paradoxical. But it is far from obvious
that it is logically inconsistent or devoid of any significant meaning.
As Stephen Davis reminds us, millions of people throughout history have regarded the claims made by Chalcedon as not only
coherent and meaningful but true.[41] Some recent philosophers
have devoted careful attention to the question of the logical consistency of the two-natures doctrine and have concluded that there
are no clear logical inconsistencies in the formula.[42] Certainly the

40. John Hick, *Faith and Knowledge,* 2nd ed. (London: Macmillan, 1988),
p. 225.

41. Stephen Davis, "Critique of John Hick," in *Encountering Jesus,* p. 23.

42. Idem, *Logic and the Nature of God* (Grand Rapids: Eerdmans, 1983),
chap. 8; Thomas V. Morris, *The Logic of God Incarnate* (Ithaca: Cornell University
Press, 1986).

Chalcedonian formula does not explain how it is that Jesus can be both God and man and, given the limitations of human finitude, any attempt at such explanation inevitably runs into difficulty. Chalcedon simply defines the acceptable parameters within which we are to think of the person of Christ if we are to be faithful to the witness of the New Testament.

Paul Knitter's Theocentric Christology

Paul Knitter, a contemporary Roman Catholic theologian and articulate spokesman for pluralism, devotes a chapter of his influential book *No Other Name?* to what he calls "theocentric Christology."[43] Knitter admits "that Jesus *is* unique, but with a uniqueness defined by its ability to relate to — that is, to include and be included by — other unique religious figures." He views Jesus "not as exclusive or even as normative, but as *theocentric,* as a universally relevant manifestation (sacrament, incarnation) of divine revelation and salvation."[44]

Knitter takes the New Testament data very seriously and does not share Hick's general skepticism concerning the possibility of knowledge about the historical Jesus. Furthermore, he is concerned to show that his model of theocentric Christology is faithful to the central witness of the New Testament. Unlike many pluralists, he does attempt to marshal biblical support for his thesis.

Knitter claims that Jesus was theocentric, or, in other words, that his mission and person were profoundly kingdom-centered, or God-centered. "All his powers were to serve this God and this kingdom; all else took second place. 'Thy kingdom come; thy will

43. Paul Knitter, *No Other Name? A Critical Survey of Christian Attitudes Toward the World Religions* (Maryknoll, N.Y.: Orbis, 1985). Knitter's views on Christology have changed somewhat since the publication of the book. See his "Toward a Liberation Theology of Religions," in *The Myth of Christian Uniqueness,* ed. John Hick and Paul F. Knitter (Maryknoll, N.Y.: Orbis, 1987), and "Theocentric Christology: Defended and Transcended," in *Journal of Ecumenical Studies* 24 (Winter 1987): 41-52.

44. *No Other Name?* pp. 171-72. Emphasis in the original.

be done', was the content of his prayer and his work."[45] Knitter agrees with Hick that Jesus probably did not think of himself as divine.[46] He does, however, hold that the data indicate that Jesus was aware of a special, unique relationship with God and his role in God's plan (perhaps as the eschatological prophet?), although we cannot be certain of the precise nature of this relationship. But although the original message of Jesus was theocentric and focused upon God and his kingdom, after Jesus' death and resurrection a significant change occurred and the message of the early church became strongly christocentric. The proclaimer became the proclaimed.

How did Jesus' original message of the kingdom of God come to be transformed into the early Christian community's proclamation of Jesus as Messiah, Lord, Christ, Word, Savior, Son of God, and eventually, God the Son? Like Hick, Knitter accepts the hypothesis of an evolutionary transition in the early Christian understanding of Jesus. He explicitly rejects C. F. D. Moule's contention that development is a more accurate model than evolution for understanding early progression in Christological thinking. Whereas Jesus almost certainly did not have any consciousness of divine status himself, and the early followers did not think of him in divine terms, by the time of the second generation of Christianity, under various Jewish and Gentile influences, the Christian communities came to identify Jesus with the Logos or with Wisdom and to think of him as a preexistent Being, the Son of God. What we see in the New Testament, then, is an "evolution from a predominantly functional, eschatological understanding of Jesus as Son of God to an incarnational, even ontological, proclamation of his divinity."[47]

Knitter further rejects the idea that any one New Testament trajectory or image of Christ should be taken as definitive or normative for all time. Just as the early Christian community witnessed an evolution in their understanding of Jesus, an evolution

45. Ibid., p. 173.
46. Ibid., p. 174.
47. Ibid., p. 180.

partly inspired by interaction with other religious and cultural influences, so today, while remaining in fundamental continuity with the essential witness of the New Testament, there is need for an ongoing evolution in Christological understanding that fully takes into account the contemporary challenge of religious pluralism.[48]

One of the more interesting aspects of Knitter's discussion is his treatment of the problem of exclusivism in the New Testament. He readily admits that "much of what the New Testament says about Jesus is . . . *exclusive*, or at least *normative*."[49] There is an inescapable exclusivism in such texts as 1 Timothy 2:5, Acts 4:12, John 1:14, 14:6, and Hebrews 9:12. Moreover, he notes that "it is also either dishonest or naive to argue that the early Christians really did not mean or believe what they were saying. . . . When the early Jesus-followers announced to the world that Jesus was 'one and only', they meant it."[50]

Does it not follow, then, that if we are to be faithful to the New Testament we must admit that Jesus is after all the only mediator between God and humankind, the Way, the Truth, and the Life, the only One through whom one can receive salvation? Knitter does not think so and he offers two reasons for this. The first has to do with the nature of Christological language in the New Testament. He echoes Hick in saying that the various interpretations or images of Jesus in the New Testament must not be taken literally. They should be understood more as "impressionistic paintings" than as "photographs."[51] Christological language is mythical or figurative, not literal.

The distinctiveness of Christological language is further seen in the exclusive statements in the texts noted above. We are told that when Peter states that salvation is found in no one else,

48. "Through such an open and critical dialogue with Hinduism, Buddhism, and Islam, theologians of the theocentric model are open to new images of Jesus that will make him more meaningful to them as well as to persons of other faiths." Ibid., p. 181.

49. Ibid., p. 182. Emphasis in the original.

50. Ibid.

51. Ibid., p. 180.

"for there is no other name . . . by which we must be saved" (Acts 4:12), or when Jesus is called the "one mediator between God and men" (1 Tim. 2:5), we should not suppose that the intention here is to make an all-embracing metaphysical claim which categorically rules out the possibility of there being any other saviors. For this is not the language of "philosophy, science, or dogmatics" but of "confession and testimony."[52] In the words of Krister Stendahl, whom Knitter quotes approvingly, this is "love language, caressing language."[53] Exclusivist Christological language is thus much like the language an adoring husband might use in speaking of his wife: "She is the most beautiful woman in the world. She is the most wonderful person alive." It would be ludicrous to assume that the husband who says this means to assert that his wife could actually win any beauty contest she entered, or that absolutely no one on earth is as wonderful as she. The point is simply that *for him* she has no rivals; he is absolutely committed to her. Similarly, "in describing Jesus as 'the only' Christians were not trying to elaborate a metaphysical principle but a personal relationship and a commitment that defined what it meant to belong to this community."[54] Thus Acts 4:12 "is abused when used as a starting point for evaluating other religions."[55] Such exclusive language should not be understood as making ontological claims which rule out all rivals, but as "love language" which expresses one's absolute devotion and commitment to Jesus Christ.

Second, Knitter claims that we must make a fundamental distinction between the essential core message of the New Testament and the medium used to communicate this message. And all of the "one and only" qualifiers to the various Christological titles must be seen as pertaining more to the medium used by the New Testament writers than to its core message.[56] Such exclusivistic

52. Ibid., p. 185.
53. Cf. Krister Stendahl, "Notes for Three Bible Studies," in *Christ's Lordship and Religious Pluralism*, ed. Gerald H. Anderson and Thomas F. Stransky (Maryknoll, N.Y.: Orbis, 1981), p. 14.
54. Knitter, *No Other Name?* p. 185.
55. Ibid.
56. Ibid., p. 182.

formulations did not belong to the "main content" of what the early church experienced and believed.

Knitter suggests that it was inevitable that the early Christians who belonged to "classicist culture" couch their expressions in highly exclusive categories.

> [C]lassicist culture, in distinction from contemporary *historical* culture, took it for granted that truth was one, certain, unchanging, normative. For anything to be true, to be reliable, it had to bear these qualities. Certainly the early Christians were aware that there were many truth-claims in the world around them. For the most part, however, they felt that if any one of these claims really were true, it had to either conquer or absorb the others. That is what truth did. Unavoidably, then, when they encountered the overwhelming truth of Jesus, they would *have* to describe it as the only or the final truth. Today, however, in the world of historical consciousness, coupled with a new experience of pluralism, it seems possible for Christians to feel and announce the saving truth about Jesus and his message without the requirements of classicist culture — that is, without having to insist that Jesus' truth is either exclusive or inclusive of all other truth.[57]

The early Christians, then, were captives of their classicist culture and could not help expressing their commitments in exclusive categories. Fortunately, we know better today and can avoid the pitfalls of exclusivism inherent in classicist culture.

In sum, Knitter argues that we are today in need of a fresh understanding of the person of Jesus, one in substantial continuity with the central message of the early Christians but which also is sensitive to and informed by extensive interaction with other religious traditions. Christians can and should maintain that Jesus is, for them, absolute and normative, so long as it is recognized that there are other saviors and lords who are, for their followers, equally unique and normative. One can be totally committed to Jesus Christ, says Knitter, and simultaneously open to the possibility of other saviors and lords. "When a Christian experiences

57. Ibid., p. 183. Emphasis in the original.

Jesus Christ to be 'my savior' and 'savior for all', that does not
necessarily mean 'only savior'."[58] Christocentrism — an excessive
focus upon the person and work of Jesus — leads to a narrow,
divisive, exclusivism. But by following Jesus' own example and
setting our sights ultimately upon God we can remain fully committed to the lordship of Jesus without supposing that God's revealing and saving activity is limited to Jesus. Knitter's proposal

> will allow [Christians] to affirm the *uniqueness* and the universal
> significance of what God has done in Jesus; but at the same time
> it will require them to recognize and be challenged by the *unique-
> ness* and universal significance of what the divine mystery may
> have revealed through others. In boldly proclaiming that God has
> indeed been defined in Jesus, Christians will also humbly admit
> that God has not been confined to Jesus.[59]

It is difficult to know where to begin in evaluating Knitter's
theocentric Christology.[60] Since he assumes that the "high" Christology of much of the New Testament is the product of an evolutionary development away from the primitive, original understanding
held by the earliest followers of Jesus, one might begin by criticizing
him at this point. We have already seen that some of the leading New
Testament scholars today reject this assumption. Similarly, we should
observe that it has not been established that Jesus did not have any
consciousness of his own deity. But rather than focus here upon such
technical questions of New Testament interpretation, I will raise
several other, more epistemological, problems with his Christology.

1. Orthodox Christians have traditionally maintained that in
a very real sense to know and to follow God is to know and follow
Jesus Christ. While we know some truths about God through his
general revelation, Jesus is the definitive self-revelation of God. We

---

58. Ibid., p. 143. Cf. pp. 201f.
59. Ibid., pp. 203-4. Emphasis in the original.
60. Mark Heim provides a trenchant critique of Knitter's Christology in
his "Thinking About Theocentric Christology," *Journal of Ecumenical Studies* 24
(Winter 1987): 1-16. See also the responses to Heim by Carl Braaten, John B. Cobb,
Jr., Thomas Dean, Elouise Renich Fraser, and Kosuke Koyama, as well as the final
response by Paul Knitter, in the same issue.

know what God is like by observing what Jesus is like (cf. John 1:1, 14, 18; 14:9-10; Heb. 1:1-3). Thus in order to know and follow God more adequately we are to model our lives after Christ.

But in advocating a shift from christocentrism to theocentrism, Knitter in effect is negating the epistemological priority traditionally given the person of Christ. For in his theocentric Christology it is no longer possible simply to "read off" what God is like from observing what Jesus is like. Instead, Christ himself is now to be judged by what we know about God. It is God who is normative, and our understanding of Christ must be shaped by reference to what we know of God's nature and works.

But here is the problem: Knitter's theocentrism presupposes that we have significant knowledge of God — what he is like and what he expects from humankind — apart from any reference to Jesus Christ. For God is now said to be the norm by which we judge the significance of Jesus. But what then is the source of this other knowledge of God? As Mark Heim puts it, for there to be a theocentric Christology there must first be a theocentric theology.[61] Yet Knitter offers no clue as to the epistemological source of theocentric theology. Are we to construct it inductively on the basis of a synthesis of all the beliefs and practices of the various religions? The formidable problems associated with such a project were noted in the previous chapter. Why should we assume that such an inclusive picture of God, based upon the collective data of all religious traditions, is at all accurate? On the other hand, if we are selective in our use of the data — perhaps we accept the Hindu or Buddhist understandings of the religious ultimate but we reject those of the Mormons or the Unification Church — on what basis are such decisions made? If Christ no longer defines what we mean by God, then where do theocentrists get their idea of God? It is difficult to escape the impression that Knitter's God, while ostensibly severed ontologically from the person of Jesus and

61. Cf. Mark Heim, "Thinking About Theocentric Christology," pp. 5-7. This objection is also posed by Carl Braaten in his essay "Christocentric Trinitarianism vs. Unitarian Theocentrism: A Response to S. Mark Heim," in *Journal of Ecumenical Studies*, pp. 17-18.

functioning as an independent norm by which we are to understand Jesus, is actually in significant measure derived from the New Testament picture of Jesus.

In response to this criticism, Knitter suggests that the fundamental source from which we draw our idea of God is "our personal and societal *experience* of ourselves and our world."[62] More specifically, he admits two sources of knowledge of God — human experience and the person and message of Jesus. Both are "genuine sources of revelation" and neither can be held up as in any way epistemologically determinative over the other. Furthermore, the person of Jesus is normative revelation because "he so speaks to [Christians'] lives, to their experience." But Jesus is by no means unique in this respect. Thus, "if in interreligious dialogue [Christians] might find other voices so speaking to their experience (even as that experience has been illumined and transformed in Christ), they might also come to recognize other 'normative' expressions or lures of truth and infinite Mystery."[63] Where then do theocentrists get their idea of God? According to Knitter, "From Christ *and* from our dialogue with others. Theocentrism argues that it can never be *only* from Christ."[64]

Yet this hardly clarifies the matter. For if Christ is not God,[65] then there must be some independent norm by which one is able to

62. Paul F. Knitter, "Theocentric Christology: Defended and Transcended," p. 43. Emphasis in the original.

63. Ibid., p. 44.

64. Ibid., p. 45. Emphasis in the original.

65. It is not at all clear just what Knitter's views on the deity of Christ are. Carl Braaten accuses him of being a unitarian — a charge Knitter denies. (See Braaten, "A Response to S. Mark Heim," p. 21, and Knitter, "Theocentric Christology," p. 52.) He does reject, however, any view of Jesus' relation to God which would place him in an absolutely unique and unrivalled category. Jesus' "divinity" cannot, in principle, set him apart from other saviors and lords in whom God can also be said to be present. "So I follow the Logos Christology and trinitarian perspective of Raimundo Panikkar, who suggests that, while we Christians surely must affirm that Jesus is the Logos/Christ, we cannot so neatly or exclusively affirm that the Logos/Christ is Jesus. The 'incarnating' activity of the Logos is actualized in but not restricted to Jesus. The God manifested in and as Jesus of Nazareth is the only true God (so I am not an Arian), but there is more to that God than Jesus." Knitter, "Theocentric Christology," p. 52.

determine that basic values and teachings of Jesus are congruent with the nature and works of God. But what is this norm? Furthermore, it hardly suffices to say that Jesus is normative revelation because he "so speaks to [Christians'] lives, to their experience." Hitler spoke in a deeply moving manner to the experiences and needs of the German people, but surely this does not qualify him for revelatory status. What is it about human experience that is revelatory? Is all of experience revelatory? If not, which experiences, and why? How is it that dialogue with other religious traditions is informative about the nature of God? Given the vastly conflicting data from the various traditions, how could one possibly arrive at a coherent understanding of God on this basis? Are all the various religious traditions equally informative about God? If not, what criterion serves to discriminate between the genuinely informative and those which are not? Why accept that particular criterion? The central question thus remains: Where do theocentrists get their idea of God?

2. It is not clear whether or in what sense Scripture is normative for Knitter's Christology. On the one hand, he seems to be very much concerned to demonstrate that the theocentric view of Jesus is consistent with the "core message" of the early believers and with the New Testament data, including such problematic texts as Acts 4:12 and John 14:6. (Unfortunately, Knitter never explains how one is to distinguish between the "core message" and the extraneous medium through which the message is communicated.) On the other hand, he also emphasizes that the evolution in Christological understanding is not yet complete, that there must continually be fresh interpretations of the text, and that central to theology's task today is reinterpretation of the significance of Jesus in light of our awareness of other great religious figures. Presumably there must be some substantial continuity between our new, reinterpreted understanding of Jesus today and the picture of Jesus we find in the New Testament. But Knitter leaves us wondering when he states that "we don't have to lay out an explicit, material legitimization from the New Testament for every new christological move today."[66] Thus, the question Knitter

66. Ibid., p. 51. Cf. also *No Other Name?* pp. 172-73.

leaves unanswered is whether, and on what basis, the New Testament exercises any control over the continuing evolution in Christological understanding.

3. One must also object to Knitter's claim that the exclusive understanding of truth operative in the New Testament was due to the "classicist" culture in which the New Testament was born and that our more enlightened "historical" culture today need not be bound by such primitive views. It seems that it is Knitter, and not the first-century Christians, who is confused on this point. For as was demonstrated in chapter 4, truth is inescapably exclusive: a true proposition necessarily excludes its contradictory as false. To try to remove the exclusive element from the concept of truth, as Knitter does, is hardly enlightened. It simply demonstrates deep epistemological confusion.

4. Similarly, Knitter's suggestion that such exclusive statements were inevitable given the classicist culture of which the New Testament writers were a part is surely unacceptable. As Carl Braaten points out, exclusive statements about the person and work of Christ were no more palatable in the first century than they are today.[67] They were foolishness to the Greeks and scandalous to the Jews. Far from being dictated by the dominant thought patterns of the surrounding culture, they were in fact strongly countercultural. Historian John Ferguson reminds us that the first-century Mediterranean world was highly relativistic and syncretistic and very accommodating to divergent religious beliefs and practices, so long as they did not become exclusive and parochial.[68] It was precisely the uncompromising exclusivism of the early Christians that provoked the antagonism of the surrounding culture.

Moreover, the assumption that one and the same God could be called by different names or take on different forms in different cultures — a central tenet of Hick's and Knitter's pluralism — was widely accepted in the first-century Mediterranean world. If the

67. Braaten, "A Response to S. Mark Heim," p. 18.
68. See John Ferguson, *Religions of the Roman Empire* (Ithaca: Cornell University Press, 1970), chap. 12.

writers of the New Testament were indeed as influenced by the prevailing assumptions of the surrounding culture as Knitter suggests, one would expect to find in the New Testament not the exclusive statements about Christ one does find, but precisely the opposite. One would expect to find greater openness to alternative images and religious figures. Perhaps Jesus could have been identified with Apollo, or Mithras, or Asclepius. The fact that such syncretistic accommodations are absent is therefore highly significant. The early Christians surely were aware of such options but rejected them as inappropriate for communicating what they wished to say about Jesus' relation to God.

5. Knitter would have us believe that when the New Testament writers said "salvation is found in no one else" (Acts 4:12, NIV), or that Jesus is the "one mediator" between God and humankind, or that he is "the One and only Son, who came from the Father" (John 1:14, NIV), that they did not intend to make any exclusive metaphysical claims about Jesus with respect to other possible saviors or lords but simply to express their complete devotion and commitment to him. This, we are told, is the language of the heart, of lovers, and not of analytic philosophy. So we misinterpret such texts when we take them to mean that only in Jesus is there salvation.

We can agree with Knitter that the early Christians were not necessarily addressing precisely the same issues we are concerned with today. And certainly we must recognize that the New Testament is full of expressions of adoration and commitment to the lordship of Jesus. But Knitter draws a misleading dichotomy between expressions of commitment and devotion ("love language") and statements with exclusive ontological implications. There is no reason why a statement cannot be both an expression of adoration and also make significant ontological claims. Even if we grant that the statements in Acts 4:12 or 1 Timothy 2:5 are, among other things, expressions of one's adoration for and commitment to Jesus, it hardly follows that the authors of these statements did not intend to make ontologically exclusive claims about Jesus or that we are not entitled to draw any such ontological implications from them.

Curiously, Knitter provides no argument from the biblical text itself to support his contention that Acts 4:12 and 1 Timothy 2:5 were not intended to rule out the possibility of there being other saviors and lords apart from Jesus. Not only is Knitter's suggestion lacking in evidential support from the biblical text, but logically it seems he is committed to the position that such exclusive statements are not cognitively meaningful. That is, they cannot be regarded as factually informative statements that are true or false but simply as emotive utterances or expressions of one's feelings or commitment. But why should we regard them in this manner? Is there any indication in the text that this is how they were intended to be understood? Is all religious language to be regarded in noncognitivist categories? If not, why just the exclusivist statements which Knitter finds so objectionable? It is difficult to escape the conclusion that the major reason for regarding such statements as noncognitive expressions of one's devotion and not as true-or-false assertions about actual states of affairs is a resolute unwillingness to accept the perceived undesirable ontological implications which follow if they are taken in their most normal, straightforward sense.

The Uniqueness of Jesus

We return, then, to the question Jesus put to his disciples: "Who do people say that I am?" Pluralists such as Hick and Knitter would answer that Jesus, while a great — perhaps even the greatest — religious leader, is ultimately in the same category as other great religious figures. Certainly God (or, as Hick prefers, the Real) was present and active in Jesus. But the same can also be said of Gautama Buddha, Shinran, Muhammad, or Confucius. Each can be regarded as an authentic prophet, savior, or lord for his respective followers. None can claim to be universally normative for all peoples in all cultures.

But this view is far removed from what evangelicals understand the New Testament to be asserting about Jesus Christ. Scripture declares that all of the fulness of the Godhead was present in the human person of Jesus (Col. 1:19). In Jesus the eternal God became a man (John 1:1, 14). Jesus is thus the definitive self-revelation of God (John 14:9-10; Heb. 1:1-3). He is the one and only Savior, the unique mediator between God and humankind (1 Tim. 2:5). There is no other name, no other person, through whom one can find salvation (Acts 4:12). Jesus himself claims to be the way, the truth, and the life; access to the one God is through him alone (John 14:6). Jesus' atoning death, a once-for-all event, makes possible reconciliation with God (1 Pet. 3:18). It is the atoning death of Jesus that redeems fallen humanity from sin and justifies us before God (Rom. 3:21-26). And it is only through the person and work of Jesus Christ that God's forgiveness and justification are available (Rom. 5:12-21). Therefore, the day is coming when "at the name of Jesus every knee [shall] bow, in heaven and on earth and under the earth, and every tongue confess that Jesus Christ is Lord" (Phil. 2:10-11).

Certainly there is no cause for treating other religious figures in a disparaging manner. We can admire the tenacity with which Muhammad, in a highly polytheistic environment, condemned idolatry and called for worship of the one God. And surely we must be impressed with the great compassion and sensitivity to human suffering evident in the Gautama Buddha. One cannot help but be struck by the keen insight into human nature and interpersonal relationships found in the teachings of Confucius. But when all is said and done the dissimilarities between Jesus and other religious figures far outstrip any possible similarities. Jesus was a strict monotheist. The Buddha, and most likely also Confucius, was at best agnostic about the existence of any God(s). Certainly no other founder of a major religion ever claimed to be the eternal creator God. Jesus located the source of the human predicament in human sin. No other religious figure spoke in quite these terms, choosing instead, like Confucius or the Buddha, to identify the human problem with deep-rooted ignorance or various social influences. No other figure claimed to be able to forgive sin. Nor does any other major religious figure call all people to believe on himself and to find salvation in his person, as does Jesus. The Buddha, Confucius, Muhammad, and Jesus all died, but there is no reliable historical record of any of the others, apart from

Jesus, being resurrected after death. To suggest, then, that Jesus and the other religious leaders are essentially in the same category is to play fast and loose with what the New Testament says about Jesus. The eloquent statement on the uniqueness of Christ by the late Bishop Stephen Neill — who was well acquainted with other religions — sums up the matter well:

> [Christian faith] maintains that in Jesus the one thing that needed to happen has happened in such a way that it need never happen again in the same way. The universe has been reconciled to its God. Through the perfect obedience of one man a new and permanent relationship has been established between God and the whole human race. The bridge has been built. There is room on it for all the needed traffic in both directions, from God to man and from man to God. Why look for any other? . . . For the human sickness there is one specific remedy, and this is it. There is no other. Therefore the Gospel must be proclaimed to the ends of the earth and to the end of time. The church cannot compromise on its missionary task without ceasing to be the church. If it fails to see and to accept this responsibility, it is changing the Gospel into something other than itself.[69]

What of Those Who Have Never Heard?

The exclusivity and uniqueness of Jesus Christ is unambiguously affirmed in the Lausanne Covenant of 1974:

> We affirm that there is only one Savior and only one Gospel, although there is a wide diversity of evangelistic approaches. . . . We also reject as derogatory to Christ and the Gospel every kind of syncretism and dialogue which implies that Christ speaks equally through all religions and ideologies. Jesus Christ, being himself the only God-man, who gave himself as the only ransom for sinners, is the only mediator between God and man. There is

69. Stephen Neill, *Crises of Belief* (London: Hodder & Stoughton, 1984), p. 31. First printed as *Christian Faith and Other Faiths* (London: Oxford University Press, 1961).

no other name by which we must be saved. All men are perishing because of sin, but God loves all men, not wishing that any should perish but that all should repent. Yet those who reject Christ repudiate the joy of salvation and condemn themselves to eternal separation from God. To proclaim Jesus as "the Savior of the world" is not to affirm that all men are either automatically or ultimately saved, still less to affirm that all religions offer salvation in Christ. Rather it is to proclaim God's love for a world of sinners and to invite all men to respond to him as Savior and Lord in the wholehearted personal commitment of repentance and faith. Jesus Christ has been exalted above every other name; we long for the day when every knee shall bow to him and every tongue shall confess him Lord.[70]

The exclusivism of the statement is offensive to many today. What is particularly repulsive is the apparent implication that all those who, through no fault of their own, have never had an opportunity to hear the gospel of Jesus Christ are eternally lost. Carl E. Braaten, for example, hardly a radical theologian, sharply criticizes the Lausanne Covenant for its explicit rejection of soteriological universalism.

They [evangelicals] now teach as dogmatic truth and as a criterion for being faithful to the gospel of Jesus Christ that all those who die or who have died without conscious faith in Jesus Christ are damned to eternal hell. If people have never heard the gospel and have never had a chance to believe, they are lost anyway. The logic of this position is that children who die in infancy are lost. The mentally retarded are lost. All those who have never heard of Christ are lost. Nevertheless, evangelicals cling to this view as the heart of the gospel and the incentive to mission.[71]

Gavin D'Costa, an Indian Roman Catholic largely sympathetic to the evangelical emphasis upon the uniqueness and normativity of

---

70. J. D. Douglas, *Let the Earth Hear His Voice*, pp. 3-4.
71. Carl E. Braaten, "The Uniqueness and Universality of Jesus Christ," in *Mission Trends No. 5: Faith Meets Faith*, ed. Gerald H. Anderson and Thomas F. Stransky (Grand Rapids: Eerdmans, 1981), p. 73.

Jesus Christ, pointedly asks, "Can we really accept that the God revealed in Christ, a loving father of 'generous, unlimited Divine love,' has denied so many millions the means to salvation — through no fault of their own?"[72]

Are those who, through no fault of their own, have never heard the gospel of Jesus Christ necessarily condemned to hell? Is there no possibility of salvation apart from explicitly responding to the gospel of Jesus Christ? These are deeply troublesome questions for all Christians who accept the uniqueness and normativity of Jesus Christ. No sensitive Christian who holds that salvation is available solely through the person and work of Jesus and who has been exposed to sincere followers of other religious traditions can fail to be distressed by the problem of those who have never heard.

There is a common perception among those outside the evangelical camp that evangelicals are agreed on all matters of doctrine, that in evangelical theology every question is definitively settled, and that there is no room for ambiguity or mystery. This, of course, is hardly the case. It is becoming increasingly evident that one issue upon which there is considerable disagreement among evangelicals is the question of the fate of those who have never been exposed to the gospel of Jesus Christ.[73] And there are strong indications that this will be an even more controversial and divisive issue among evangelicals in the years to come. All evangelicals agree that ultimately this question is to be settled solely on the basis of the clear teaching of Scripture, which they agree is that all humankind stands condemned before God for its sin, that not all persons will ultimately be saved, and that God is entirely just and fair in his dealings with humankind. Evangelicals further agree that those who are saved are saved strictly on the basis of the person and work of Jesus Christ — salvation comes only through Jesus Christ.

72. Gavin D'Costa, *Theology and Religious Pluralism* (Oxford: Basil Blackwell, 1986), p. 67.

73. See Malcolm J. McVeigh, "The Fate of Those Who've Never Heard? It Depends," in *Evangelical Missions Quarterly* 21 (October 1985): 370-79; John E. Sanders, "Is Belief in Christ Necessary for Salvation?" *Evangelical Quarterly* 60 (July 1988): 241-59. See also the discussion of the views of younger evangelicals on salvation and hell in James Davison Hunter's *Evangelicalism: The Coming Generation* (Chicago: University of Chicago Press, 1987), pp. 34-40.

But must one actually be confronted with the gospel of Jesus Christ and explicitly respond in faith to Christ in order to be saved? Or is it possible for some who have never heard of Jesus Christ nevertheless to benefit from the work of Christ and be saved? A variety of answers have been suggested. Without attempting here to settle the question, in the coming pages we will examine briefly some of the answers suggested by leading evangelicals. The responses fall into four general categories. Significantly, the Lausanne Covenant was framed in such a manner as to allow for some diversity of opinion on this point, and each of the positions outlined below could claim to be faithful to the parameters set by the Covenant.

First, some evangelicals maintain that only by consciously and explicitly responding to the proclaimed gospel of Jesus Christ can one be saved. The following statement by Harold Lindsell is representative of this position:

> Regeneration is the real need of man. But man may not be regenerated either because he has never heard the Gospel without which regeneration is impossible or because he has refused to avail himself of the benefits of the Gospel when he has heard it. Whichever it may be, the end is the same. He is permanently separated from God. Heaven and hell, then, are the competing options which unredeemed man faces. The knowledge that the man who has never heard of Christ is separated from God is a prime factor in stimulating conservative missionary zeal. Knowing that his only hope lies within the Gospel, it follows that man must be given the opportunity to make a rational choice.[74]

Lindsell's statement suggests that ultimately there is no significant distinction between those who have heard the gospel and rejected it and those who have never had the opportunity of hearing it. Both face eternal condemnation. The only hope for the unevangelized today is to be presented with the opportunity to respond

74. Harold Lindsell, "Fundamentals for a Philosophy of the Christian Mission," in *The Theology of the Christian Mission,* ed. Gerald H. Anderson (New York: McGraw-Hill, 1961), p. 246.

in faith to Jesus Christ. The implications of this for the missionary movement are unmistakable: unless someone brings the gospel to the unevangelized in this life they face eternal condemnation and separation from God.

Similarly, in his short but incisive book *The Christian's Attitude Toward World Religions,* Sri Lankan evangelical Ajith Fernando asserts that "apart from faith in Christ, there is no hope for salvation for anyone."[75] Although Scripture indicates that people will be held accountable and judged on the basis of their response to the light they have received, "it also shows that no one lives according to the light he receives, and that no one can be saved without the gospel."[76] Fernando does, however, allow that Scripture teaches that there will be degrees of punishment and that the criteria by which the severity of punishment will be determined are the light one has received through general revelation and the degree to which one has lived in accordance with what he or she knew to be the truth. "Sin is such a terrible thing that no one deserves to be saved. In his mercy God saves some. Others will be punished. But those who try to live up to the light they had will receive less punishment."[77]

An obvious objection to a position which strictly limits salvation to those who explicitly accept Jesus as Lord and Savior is that not only does it cut off those today who have never heard of Jesus, but it also eliminates the possibility of salvation for those in the Old Testament era. Surely no Christian would deny that great Old Testament figures such as Abraham, Moses, Samuel, David, Isaiah, and Jeremiah, as well as a host of ordinary persons, were indeed saved. Yet it can hardly be maintained that they were saved on the basis of their explicit acceptance of Jesus Christ as Lord and Savior. Apparently, then, it is possible to be saved apart

75. Ajith Fernando, *The Christian's Attitude Toward World Religions* (Wheaton: Tyndale, 1987), p. 129.

76. Ibid., p. 120. For similar views see also J. Robertson McQuilkin, "The Narrow Way," in *Perspectives on the World Christian Movement: A Reader,* ed. Ralph D. Winter and Steven C. Hawthorne (Pasadena, Cal.: William Carey Library, 1981), pp. 127-34.

77. Ibid., pp. 131-32.

from explicit faith in Jesus Christ. Might it not also be that those today who are without the gospel of Jesus Christ can be saved apart from explicit faith in Christ?

Fernando acknowledges the force of this objection, but rejects it since Old Testament salvation included two central features that are lacking in the case of those today who are without the gospel. First, those saved in the Old Testament received a special revelation of God and his ways, a revelation which "presents a covenant relationship between God and his people, which is mercifully initiated by God and received by man through faith."[78] Second, it was necessary that there be, in the words of Carl F. H. Henry, "a divinely approved sacrifice . . . which focuses on the Mediator-Messiah . . . if only in an elementary and preparatory sense."[79] The Old Testament sacrificial system anticipated and foreshadowed the perfect sacrifice of Christ and thus propitiated God. Fernando concludes that "salvation in the Old Testament, then, involved a covenant relationship with God, which required accepting God's special revelation of himself and his ways and also required the offering of sacrifices of atonement to God. These two requirements could not be fulfilled by the so-called 'B.C. non-Christians' of today who have not yet heard the gospel."[80]

While still holding that the unevangelized today need to respond in faith to the gospel of Jesus Christ in order to be saved, some evangelicals also suggest that in his sovereign mercy God will see to it that those who genuinely seek after him will have an opportunity in this life to hear the good news. In his important book *What of Those Who Have Never Heard?*, the distinguished

---

78. Ibid., p. 136.
79. Ibid.
80. Ibid., p. 137. Respected New Testament scholar Robert H. Gundry concurs. "The Bible is our only source of information concerning the status of the unevangelized heathen. The notions of salvation through general revelation or after death find no solid footing in Scripture. In fact the Bible indicates that apart from hearing and believing the Gospel the heathen are hopeless. . . . Apart from our preaching to them the word of Christ, they have no hope." Robert H. Gundry, "Salvation According to Scripture: No Middle Ground," *Christianity Today*, December 9, 1977, p. 16.

missionary statesman J. Oswald Sanders cites a number of cases in which missionaries tell of having encountered in remote areas individuals who, although not knowing about Jesus or the Bible, nevertheless had been seeking after God and whose hearts had been specially prepared by the Holy Spirit to receive the message the missionaries brought. After examining the biblical examples of Cornelius and the Ethiopian eunuch, Sanders concludes, "These cases encourage us to believe that God will always respect sincerity where it exists, and will grant further light and lead those who respond to the impulses of the Holy Spirit to a knowledge of Christ."[81]

A second position can be distinguished which, unlike the first, is willing to allow the theoretical possibility that some who have never heard the gospel of Jesus Christ might be saved, although it refuses to speculate on the matter, choosing rather to leave the question in the mystery of God's sovereign justice. Missiologist Donald McGavran, for example, echoes Lindsell and Fernando in his assertion that "only as people of every race, culture, language, condition, and economic status believe on Jesus Christ is it possible for them to be reconciled to God."[82] However, he goes beyond the other two in allowing the possibility that God might have ways of dealing with the unevangelized of which we are not aware.

> Evangelicals believe that, according to the teaching of the Bible, those who do not believe in Christ are lost. Evangelicals also believe that God is sovereign. Should He so choose, He can bring those who know nothing of Jesus Christ back into fellowship with himself. But the means by which he might do this (and whether in point of fact he ever does do it) remains hidden. God has not chosen to reveal this in Scripture.[83]

81. J. Oswald Sanders, *What of Those Who Have Never Heard?* (Crowborough, East Sussex: Highland Books, 1986), p. 120. Cf. J. Robertson McQuilkin, "The Narrow Way," p. 133.

82. Donald McGavran, "Contemporary Evangelical Theology of Mission," in *Contemporary Theologies of Mission,* ed. Arthur F. Glasser and Donald A. McGavran (Grand Rapids: Baker, 1983), p. 103.

83. Ibid.

And the late J. Herbert Kane, in a careful and judicious discussion of the problem, argues that not all persons will be judged by God on the same basis.[84] Romans 2 makes it clear that each one will be judged according to the light he or she had. No person will be judged on the basis of light that was unavailable. "Every man possesses *some* form of light and he will be judged by that light and by no other."[85] Those without access to the gospel of Jesus Christ nevertheless have some light available to them. The unevangelized has the "light of creation, providence, and conscience and will be judged by that light. If he is finally condemned it will not be because he refused to believe the gospel, but because he failed to live up to the little light he had."[86] Do any of the unevangelized in fact live up to the light they have? Kane maintains that the biblical testimony leaves little room for hope in this regard. "Moral failure is a universal phenomenon."[87] And yet, in an important paragraph, Kane leaves the door slightly open, choosing to leave the final resolution of the problem in the mystery of the sovereign justice of God.

> Nevertheless, in the light of Romans 2:6-7 we must not completely rule out the possibility, however remote, that here and there throughout history there may have been the odd person who got to heaven without the full light of the gospel. In that case *God* is the sole Judge. He is the sovereign in the exercise of His grace. We are not called on to pass judgement in such cases — if indeed they ever occurred. Here, as in many other instances, we must fall back on the sovereignty of God and say with Abraham, "Shall not the Judge of all the earth do right?" (Genesis 18:25).[88]

Kane emphasizes that if any are saved apart from explicit faith in Christ, it would not be on the basis of works but solely by grace through faith. "But how could he exercise faith? In only one way — by acknowledging his utter and complete spiritual bankruptcy

---

84. J. Herbert Kane, *Understanding Christian Missions*, 4th ed. (Grand Rapids: Baker, 1986), pp. 135f.
85. Ibid. Emphasis in original.
86. Ibid.
87. Ibid., p. 134.
88. Ibid., p. 137. Emphasis in original.

and casting himself unreservedly on the mercy of God."[89] Thus, the theoretical possibility that some may be saved without explicitly hearing and responding to the gospel of Jesus Christ is maintained, although whether this occurs at all, and, if so, how they are saved, is left untouched. Ultimately, such questions must be left unresolved as we trust in the sovereignty and justice of God.

A third position is very similar to that of Kane, but those who adopt it demonstrate greater willingness to speculate on the possibility of salvation apart from explicit faith in Christ. This position is generally identified with British Islamics scholar Sir Norman Anderson, although a significant number of other leading evangelicals have also endorsed it. Advocates suggest that although there are undeniably major differences between the two groups, there are also important parallels between people living in Old Testament times (chronologically B.C.) and those today who, through no fault of their own, have not yet heard of the gospel of Jesus Christ (informationally B.C.). These parallels, it is suggested, provide possible hints as to how God might deal with those today who have never heard the gospel.

Millard Erickson is a contemporary evangelical Baptist theologian who has carefully considered the question of the fate of those who have never heard the gospel. After an analysis of texts such as Romans 1:19-20; 2:12-16; 10:14-18; and Psalm 19:4, Erickson concludes that Scripture indicates that "the essential nature of saving faith can be arrived at without the special revelation.... Perhaps, in other words, it is possible to receive the benefits of Christ's death without conscious knowledge-belief in the name of Jesus."[90] Erickson suggests that there are five elements which constitute "the essential nature of the gospel message" and which are available through general revelation. These are

89. Ibid. Bruce A. Demarest accepts a similar position. See his *General Revelation* (Grand Rapids: Zondervan, 1982), pp. 260f.
90. Millard Erickson, "Hope for Those Who Haven't Heard? Yes, but . . ." in *Evangelical Missions Quarterly* 11 (April 1975): 124. See also Stuart C. Hackett, *The Reconstruction of the Christian Revelation Claim* (Grand Rapids: Baker, 1984), pp. 243-46. Similar views are found in the earlier Baptist theologian Augustus Strong, *Systematic Theology*, vol. III (Philadelphia: Judson Press, 1909), pp. 842-43.

(1) The belief in one good powerful God. (2) The belief that he (man) owes this God perfect obedience to his law. (3) The consciousness that he does not meet this standard, and therefore is guilty and condemned. (4) The realization that nothing he can offer God can compensate him (or atone) for this sin and guilt. (5) The belief that God is merciful, and will forgive and accept those who cast themselves upon his mercy.[91]

Erickson then asks,

May it not be that if a man believes and acts on this set of tenets he is redemptively related to God and receives the benefits of Christ's death, whether he consciously knows and understands the details of that provision or not? Presumably that was the case with the Old Testament believers. Their salvation was not based upon works. It was, as with all who are saved, a matter of grace. The grace, in turn, was manifested and made available through the death of Jesus Christ. The Old Testament saints, however, did not know the identity of the Redeemer or the details of the accomplishment of salvation.[92]

Is it possible, then, that the person who has never heard the gospel of Jesus Christ is in an analogous position to the people of Old Testament times?

Now if the God known in nature is the same as the God of Abraham, Isaac, and Jacob (as Paul seems to assert in Acts 17:23), then it would seem that a person who comes to a belief in a single powerful God, who despairs of any works righteousness to please this holy God, and who throws himself upon the mercy of this good God, would be accepted as were the Old Testament believers. The basis of acceptance would be the work of Jesus Christ, even though the person involved is not conscious that this is how provision has been made for his salvation. We should note that the basis of salvation was apparently the same in the Old Testament as in the New. Salvation has always been appropriated by

91. Erickson, "Hope for Those Who Haven't Heard?" p. 125.
92. Ibid.

faith (Gal. 3:6-9); this salvation rests upon Christ's deliverance of us from the law (vv. 10-14, 19-29). Nothing has been changed in that respect.[93]

Thus Erickson claims that Scripture allows for the "theoretical possibility" of salvation apart from contact with God's special revelation in Jesus Christ.[94] However, he is quick to emphasize that this is only a theoretical possibility and should not in any way diminish the imperative of evangelism. "It is highly questionable how many, if any, actually experience salvation without having special revelation. Paul suggests in Romans 3 that no one does. And in chapter 10 he urges the necessity of preaching the gospel (the special revelation) so that men may believe."[95] In allowing for an "essential nature of the gospel message" which is in principle available to all persons through general revelation, and on the basis of which, at least in principle, one can come into a saving relationship with God, Erickson maintains that one can have and exercise a "minimum content" of belief necessary for saving faith entirely apart from contact with the gospel of Jesus Christ.

Sir Norman Anderson is another leading evangelical who draws a parallel between the people of Old Testament times and those today who have not had the opportunity to hear the gospel. Anderson observes that believing Jews in Old Testament times enjoyed forgiveness and salvation through the saving work of Jesus Christ, although most of them had no understanding of this.[96] He further emphasizes that the Old Testament saints were saved by grace through faith, and not by works. He also rejects the notion that anyone today can be saved merely by "living up to the light that is available to him." For just as no Jew succeeded in keeping all of the Mosaic Law, so "no non-Jew has ever succeeded in living up to the standard of the moral and ethical

93. Millard Erickson, *Christian Theology*, vol. 1 (Grand Rapids: Baker, 1983), p. 172.

94. Ibid., p. 173.

95. Ibid.

96. Norman Anderson, *Christianity and World Religions* (Downers Grove, Ill.: Inter-Varsity Press, 1984), p. 144.

principles according to which he knows that he ought to regulate his conduct."[97]

However, he does suggest that there is an important parallel between salvation for Old Testament believers and possible salvation for those today without access to the gospel.

> My suggestion is that we can, perhaps, find a ray of light by going back to what we have already said about those multitudes of Jews who, in Old Testament times, turned to God in repentance, brought the prescribed sacrifice (where such was provided) and threw themselves on [God's] mercy. It was not that they *earned* that mercy by their repentance or obedience, or that animal sacrifice could ever avail to atone for human sin. It was that their repentance and faith (themselves, of course, the result of God's work in their hearts) opened the gate, as it were, to the grace, mercy and forgiveness which he always longed to extend to them, and which was to be made forever available at the cross on which Christ "gave himself a ransom for all, to be testified in due time" (1 Tim. 2:6 AV). It is true that they had a special divine revelation in which to put their trust. But might it not be true of the follower of some other religion that the God of all mercy had worked in his heart by his spirit, bringing him in some measure to realize his sin and need for forgiveness, and enabling him, in the twilight, as it were, to throw himself on God's mercy? . . . I myself cannot doubt that there may be those who, while never hearing the gospel here on earth, will wake up, as it were, on the other side of the grave to worship the One in whom, without understanding it at the time, they found the mercy of God.[98]

John Stott has also given careful consideration to this problem. Stott treats the subject at length in his response to the probing questions of David L. Edwards in the interesting book *Evangelical Essentials: A Liberal-Evangelical Dialogue.* He begins by putting forward three propositions accepted by all evangelicals.[99] First, all

---

97. Ibid., p. 146.
98. Ibid., pp. 148-49, 154. Emphasis in the original.
99. David L. Edwards, with a response from John Stott, *Evangelical Essen-*

human beings, apart from the intervention and mercy of God, are perishing. All humankind stands guilty and without excuse before God. Second, human beings cannot save themselves by any religious or righteous acts. Whenever it occurs, salvation is the product of God's grace alone. And third, Jesus Christ is the only Savior.

But can we go beyond this? What of the millions who die without ever hearing the gospel of Jesus Christ? Stott is cautious here, recognizing that anything beyond the three propositions above must involve a certain amount of speculation. He states, "I believe the most Christian stance is to remain agnostic on this question. . . . The fact is that God, alongside the most solemn warnings about our responsibility to respond to the gospel, has not revealed how he will deal with those who have never heard it."[100] But in an earlier discussion of the problem Stott is less reticent, and like Erickson and Anderson affirms that

> Jesus Christ is the only Saviour, and that salvation is by God's grace alone, on the ground of Christ's cross alone, and by faith alone. The only question, therefore, is how much knowledge and understanding of the gospel people need before they can cry to God for mercy and be saved. In the Old Testament people were "justified by faith" even though they had little knowledge or expectation of Christ. Perhaps there are others today in a similar position, who know that they are guilty before God and that they cannot do anything to win his favour, but who in self-despair call upon the God they dimly perceive to save them. If God does save such, as many evangelical Christians believe, their salvation is still only by grace, only through Christ, only by faith.[101]

It is important to bear in mind that while Erickson, Anderson, and Stott all allow the theoretical possibility of salvation for those who have never heard the gospel, all are agreed that this in no way detracts from the responsibility of the believer to spread

---

tials: *A Liberal-Evangelical Dialogue* (Downers Grove, Ill.: Inter-Varsity Press, 1988), pp. 320-29.

100. Ibid., p. 327.

101. John Stott, *The Authentic Jesus* (London: Marshall, Morgan & Scott, 1985), p. 83.

the gospel of Jesus Christ to all peoples. The missionary mandate remains intact. For although the possibility of salvation apart from explicit acceptance of Christ as Lord and Savior is admitted, all maintain that we are in no position to know how many — if indeed any — are actually saved in this way. Furthermore, all would remind us that world evangelization should be motivated not simply out of compassion for those who have never heard the gospel (significant as this motivating factor is) but also out of obedience to the clear command of our Lord (Matt. 28:18-20) and a burning desire that God be honored and glorified throughout all the earth (Ps. 67).

Mention should also be made of a fourth position, comprising those evangelicals who hold that those who die without having had an opportunity to hear the gospel of Jesus Christ might be given a future chance — at death or immediately after death — to make a decision for Christ. In a controversial article in 1976, for example, theologian Clark Pinnock stated, "Of one thing we can be certain: God will not abandon in hell those who have not known and therefore have not declined His offer of grace. Though He has not told us the nature of His arrangements, we cannot doubt the existence and goodness of them."[102] On the basis of 1 Peter 3:19 and 4:6, Pinnock then left open the possibility that "death is the occasion when the unevangelized have an opportunity to make a decision about Jesus Christ."[103] Pinnock clearly and emphatically rejects soteriological universalism. Not all will ultimately be saved. But in an important — and highly controversial — recent article Pinnock argues that "everyone will have an opportunity to be saved so that the possibility of salvation is universally accessible."[104] Pinnock proposes that "God takes account of

102. Clark Pinnock, "Is Jesus the Only Way?" *Eternity* 27 (December 1976): 34.
103. Ibid.
104. Clark Pinnock, "The Finality of Jesus Christ in a World of Religions," in *Christian Faith and Practice in the Modern World*, ed. Mark A. Noll and David F. Wells (Grand Rapids: Eerdmans, 1988), p. 167. Pinnock's article was controversial not only for putting forward the possibility of responding to Christ after death, but also for its very open and positive posture toward other religions. The article

faith in [the person who has never had opportunity to hear the gospel] even if it occurs in the context of general revelation, and always sees to it that those responding to the light they have encounter Jesus Christ, whether before or after death."[105]

Theologian Donald Bloesch seems to hold a position similar to Pinnock's. In *Essentials of Evangelical Theology,* after stating that "God's love goes out to all, that his atonement is intended for all, but that at the same time . . . not all accept the atonement," Bloesch says, "We can affirm salvation on the other side of the grave, since this has scriptural warrant (cf. Isa. 26:19; John 5:25-29; Eph. 4:8, 9; 1 Peter 3:19, 20, 4:6)."[106]

---

was the subject of vigorous debate at the 41st annual meeting of the Evangelical Theological Society in November 1989. See also Pinnock's "Toward an Evangelical Theology of Religions," *Journal of the Evangelical Theological Society* 33 (Sept. 1990): 359-68.

105. "The Finality of Jesus Christ," p. 163.

i06. Donald Bloesch, *Essentials of Evangelical Theology,* vol. 2 (San Francisco: Harper & Row, 1978), pp. 224, 227. A related, but logically distinct, issue concerns the nature and duration of hell, particularly whether the final destiny of the impenitent is eternal conscious torment or the total annihilation of their being. Traditional Christian orthodoxy has maintained the former, and undoubtedly this is the view held by most evangelical leaders today. But a significant and growing group of evangelicals are rejecting the traditional view in favor of annihilationism — the view that the souls of the unsaved cease to exist at death or after a temporary period of punishment after death. John Stott, for example, after presenting a lengthy argument against the traditional interpretation, urges "that the ultimate annihilation of the wicked should at least be accepted as a legitimate, Biblically founded alternative to their eternal conscious torment" (Stott, *Evangelical Essentials: A Liberal-Evangelical Dialogue,* p. 320). Clark Pinnock charges that the traditional view of eternal torment in hell is "morally and scripturally flawed" and ought to be rejected. Pinnock contends that the fire of God's judgment consumes the lost (Clark Pinnock, "Fire, Then Nothing," in the Christianity Today Institute discussion, "Universalism: Will Everyone Be Saved?" in *Christianity Today,* March 20, 1987, p. 40). And John Wenham calls for careful consideration of the biblical support for annihilationism (cf. John W. Wenham, *The Enigma of Evil* [Grand Rapids: Zondervan, 1985], pp. 34-41). And yet, although in some respects clearly more agreeable to modern tastes than the traditional view, annihilationism is vulnerable to criticism on biblical grounds and is not accepted by the majority of evangelical biblical scholars (see, for example, David Wells' incisive critique of Pinnock in "Everlasting Punishment," in the same issue of *Christianity Today,* pp. 41-42).

Our purpose here has not been to settle the thorny question of the fate of those who have never heard the gospel of Jesus Christ but merely to illustrate the diversity of opinion among evangelicals on this troublesome issue. As awareness of other religions increases and as growing numbers of Protestant and Catholic theologians embrace universalism and question the uniqueness of Jesus Christ, it is only to be expected that this issue will become more prominent and controversial among evangelicals as well. Since evangelicals accept all of Scripture as God's written and thus divinely inspired and fully authoritative revelation, this question must be grappled with through careful and rigorous investigation of Scripture. For ultimately it is what Scripture affirms that is definitive, and not simply what we might wish to be the case or what seems most palatable to modern tastes. But consideration of this topic must never sink to the level of mere academic exercise or a comfortable in-house theological debate. The implications of this question are staggering. The subject should always be approached in a spirit of genuine humility, sorrow for those who will spend an eternity apart from God, and repentance over our own sin and lack of compassion that so often prevents the gospel of Jesus Christ from reaching all peoples.

CHAPTER EIGHT

Evangelism, Dialogue, and Tolerance

Evangelicals are well known for their insistence upon the priority of evangelism in Christian mission. This, of course, does not mean that evangelicals believe Christians ought only to be involved in evangelism or that the whole of the Christian mission can be reduced to evangelism. But while admitting that there are other important and legitimate dimensions to Christian mission, most evangelicals vigorously insist upon the priority of evangelism.

However, the emphasis upon the priority of evangelism has not gone unchallenged. Protestants and Catholics alike are in the midst of a profound rethinking of the nature of Christian mission.[1] Many competing voices clamor for attention, arguing vehemently that Christian mission ought today to be identified not with evangelism but with the struggles for justice and liberation among the many peoples of our world who suffer social, political, or economic oppression; or with pursuit of global peace and the elimination of the nuclear threat; or with a fresh understanding of other religions which recognizes that all faiths are in their own ways bearers of

---

1. Cf. David J. Bosch, "Evangelism: Theological Currents and Cross-Currents Today," in *International Bulletin of Missionary Research* 11 (July 1987): 98-103.

divine revelation and salvation, and which, rather than seeking converts, encourages each person to be more faithful to that particular tradition in which he or she happens to be placed. Preoccupation with evangelism is regarded by growing numbers of Roman Catholics and conciliar Protestants as not only obscurantist but also morally indefensible. In an era of unprecedented contact with those of other faiths, our task, it is said, is not to proselytize but rather humbly to recognize and cooperate with God's presence and work through the other great religions.

Any defense of exclusivism today must come to grips with the increasingly vigorous attacks levelled against the notion that evangelism is a legitimate (to say nothing of its being the overriding) concern of Christian mission. Such a defense could follow one of two routes. First, it could demonstrate, through responsible treatment of the biblical data, that involvement in evangelism with a view toward conversion of non-Christians is obligatory for all Christians. For it is the conviction that the commands of our Lord, the clear teaching of Scripture on the lostness of humankind, and the examples of the apostles all demand our ongoing involvement in evangelism which prompts evangelicals to hold on so tenaciously to its priority in the Christian mission.

Yet a second way to defend evangelism today is to show that commonly raised arguments against it are defective and thus ought not to be accepted. While fully convinced that the priority of evangelism is indeed demanded by Scripture, in this chapter I will be primarily concerned to follow the second of the two routes. For much of the contemporary attack upon Christian exclusivism (and its corollary, evangelism) concerns the moral propriety of exclusivism. Two words in particular figure prominently in such criticism — "dialogue" and "tolerance." It is asserted by many today that dialogue with those of other faiths should replace the traditional emphasis upon evangelism and conversion. This claim is frequently supported by the charge that exclusivism, with its attendant stress upon the need for evangelism and conversion, is inherently intolerant and thus morally unacceptable. In response I will argue that while evangelism must be given priority, properly understood there is a legitimate place for dialogue in Christian mission. Furthermore, the assertion that exclusivism is inherently intolerant will be shown to rest upon significant confusion over the meaning of tolerance. Properly construed, Christian exclusivism need not be intolerant of those of other faiths.

Evangelism

The definition found in the Lausanne Covenant provides a useful point of departure for our consideration of evangelism:

> To evangelize is to spread the good news that Jesus Christ died for our sins and was raised from the dead according to the Scriptures, and that as the reigning Lord he now offers the forgiveness of sins and the liberating gift of the Spirit to all who repent and believe. Our Christian presence in the world is indispensable to evangelism, and so is that kind of dialogue whose purpose is to listen sensitively in order to understand. But evangelism itself is the proclamation of the historical biblical Christ as Savior and Lord, with a view to persuading people to come to him personally and so be reconciled to God.[2]

Evangelism, from the Greek *euangelizomai,* means to bring or announce the good news, the *euangelion.*[3] Evangelism thus is the communication of a message, the "good news." And what is the message to be communicated? A very concise answer would be that evangelism is the communication of the good news about Jesus as Lord and Savior. Surely this reflects the thrust of the preaching of the apostles. The focus of Peter's proclamation was that in the death, resurrection, and exaltation of Jesus of Nazareth "God has made this Jesus, whom you crucified, both Lord and Christ" (Acts 2:36, NIV). This in turn demands proper response

---

2. *Let the Earth Hear His Voice,* ed. J. D. Douglas (Minneapolis: World Wide Publications, 1975), p. 4.

3. For a helpful discussion of the meaning of "evangelism," see John R. W. Stott, *Christian Mission in the Modern World* (Downers Grove, Ill.: Inter-Varsity Press, 1975), pp. 37-57.

on the part of sinful humankind. Thus Peter commands, "Repent, and be baptized, every one of you, in the name of Jesus Christ for the forgiveness of your sins" (2:38). And similarly Paul announced to the Jews that "through Jesus the forgiveness of sins is proclaimed to you. Through him everyone who believes is justified from everything you could not be justified from by the law of Moses" (13:38-39, NIV). To the Gentiles Paul declared that God "commands all people everywhere to repent" (17:30, NIV). Elsewhere, Paul wrote that if we confess with our lips that Jesus is Lord, and believe in our heart that God raised him from the dead, we will be saved (Romans 10:9, NIV).

The good news proclaimed in evangelism, then, is that Jesus is Savior and Lord, that in his name we can have forgiveness of sin, a new life through the indwelling power of the Holy Spirit, and ultimately, everlasting fellowship with God himself. It should not be presumed that what is in view here is an "easy believism." For to confess Christ as Lord in the genuinely biblical sense is to acknowledge his absolute sovereignty over all areas of life. It is to submit to his demands regardless of the cost. It is to make his values, his concerns, his agenda, our own. Nor can this be regarded as an entirely private affair between the individual and God. For submission to the Lordship of Jesus Christ, with all that this entails, will revolutionize one's relations with others. There is thus a horizontal as well as a vertical dimension to salvation.

If we understand by evangelism the proclamation of the good news concerning Jesus Christ as Lord and Savior, then it follows that, strictly speaking, evangelism cannot be defined in terms of results. Many popular views of evangelism include within their definition the actual conversion of non-Christians. Evangelism is thus held to be winning unbelievers to faith in Jesus Christ. Now there is no question that the objective of evangelism is the conversion of unbelievers, and in engaging in evangelism Christians ought to take great care to proclaim the message in such a way as to elicit a favorable response. But we must not confuse the objective of evangelism with the nature of the task itself. As Stott observes, "To 'evangelize' in New Testament usage does not mean to win converts, as it usually does when we use the word. Evange-

lism is the announcement of the good news, irrespective of results."[4] Evangelism, then, is simply the communication, by
whatever means, of the good news about Jesus Christ. The objective
of evangelism is, of course, the conversion of unbelievers. But
evangelism can and does occur even when no conversion results.

We should also emphasize that evangelism is not the only
thing that Christians are to be doing in the world. The mission of
the Church is broader than simply evangelism. Accordingly,
Donald McGavran defines the Church's mission as

> carrying the gospel across cultural boundaries to those who owe
> no allegiance to Jesus Christ, and encouraging them to accept Him
> as Lord and Savior and to become responsible members of His
> church, working as the Holy Spirit leads, at both evangelism and
> justice, at making God's will done on earth as it is done in heaven.[5]

Although it obviously includes evangelism, the Church's mission
cannot simply be reduced to evangelism. Also included are the
ministries that contribute toward the nurture and maturation of
young believers, helping them to organize and develop into responsible members of local assemblies, as well as the important
ministries of compassion which help to alleviate human suffering
and promote justice. And yet, although mission must be understood as including more than simply evangelism, priority of place
must be given to evangelism in the mission of the Church. If in
fact the fundamental problem confronting humankind is not
political or social but spiritual — sin; if in fact one's eternal destiny
is determined by choices made in this life; and if in fact over two
billion people today have no real opportunity to hear the gospel
of Jesus Christ, then surely there can be no greater priority for the

4. Ibid., p. 38. Similarly, J. I. Packer states, "The way to tell whether in fact
you are evangelizing is not to ask whether conversions are known to have resulted
from your witness. It is to ask whether you are faithfully making known the gospel
message." J. I. Packer, *Evangelism and the Sovereignty of God* (Downers Grove, Ill.:
Inter-Varsity Press, 1961), p. 41.

5. Donald McGavran, "What is Mission?" in *Contemporary Theologies of
Mission*, ed. Arthur F. Glasser and Donald A. McGavran (Grand Rapids: Baker,
1983), p. 26.

Church than communicating the message of forgiveness and eternal salvation to those who have never heard.

The urgency of evangelism, then, is based upon a particular view of the nature of the human person and its relation to the religious ultimate. The question of the legitimacy of evangelism cannot be treated in isolation from broader considerations of the correctness of the underlying worldview. If, for example, atheistic humanists such as Bertrand Russell are correct and there is no God, and when we die we "shall rot, and nothing of [our egos] will survive,"[6] then there is little point in exerting great effort to evangelize the world. Or if certain forms of Hinduism are correct in characterizing the human predicament as *samsara* — the wearisome cycle of deaths and rebirths—and liberation from *samsara* comes only through rigorous self-discipline and control of one's mental faculties, then preaching salvation in Jesus is useless. But if in fact, as the Bible claims, the fundamental cause of our predicament is human rebellion against a holy and righteous God, and if the only remedy for this ailment is to be found in the salvation available through Jesus Christ, then clearly evangelism — communication of the good news of salvation through Jesus — is not only a legitimate option but an inescapable imperative. As the apostle Paul put it, "Woe to me if I do not preach the gospel!" (1 Cor. 9:16).

Dialogue

Even a cursory survey of the missiological literature of the past several decades indicates that the question of dialogue is very much at the center of the current redefinition of Christian mission. The emphasis upon dialogue cannot casually be dismissed as merely the latest missiological fad. Dialogue with other religions is here to stay and the questions it stimulates concern fundamental assumptions about God's revelation to humankind, salvation, and

---

6. Bertrand Russell, "What I Believe," in *Why I Am Not a Christian* (New York: George Allen & Unwin, 1957), p. 54.

the nature and purpose of Christian mission in the world today. Evangelicals dare not ignore the current debate in the misguided hope that current fascination with dialogue will eventually quietly pass from the scene.

Recent interest in dialogue has been largely limited to Roman Catholics and conciliar Protestants, although, as we shall see, some prominent evangelicals have also given careful attention to the subject. It is perhaps significant that much of the impetus for interreligious dialogue has come from the initiative of Christian individuals and institutions. Although there are of course exceptions, Richard Wentz seems correct in claiming that the openness to "new levels of religious understanding" and motivation for interreligious dialogue is primarily a Western-inspired phenomenon.[7] Whereas some Christian theologians seem remarkably eager to be transformed by Buddhism or Hinduism, Buddhists and Hindus often do not appear to be nearly as interested in being influenced by Christian faith!

Among those actively involved in dialogue there has been a growing consensus that dialogue is a good thing and ought to be vigorously promoted, although precisely why this is so is usually left unexpressed. Implicitly, and sometimes explicitly, dialogue is often identified with such positive attributes as open-mindedness, tolerance, courtesy, lack of dogmatism, and moral and cultural sensitivity. Rejection of dialogue is often viewed as at least implicit endorsement of the corresponding negative qualities. And since no sensitive Christian wishes to be thought of as a narrow-minded, culturally and morally insensitive, intolerant bigot, dialogue is "in," and it is incumbent upon any critic of dialogue to demonstrate that he or she is not thereby morally or culturally deficient.

Why then have evangelicals been so hesitant to jump aboard the dialogue bandwagon? What are their concerns, and are they legitimate? Is there a place for dialogue in a genuinely biblical

7. Richard E. Wentz, "The Prospective Eye of Interreligious Dialogue," *Japanese Journal of Religious Studies* 14 (1987): 7f.

understanding of Christian mission? We cannot hope to settle these questions here, but they must be given at least brief attention, since the issues they raise go to the very heart of the evangelical understanding of the relation of Christian faith to other faiths.

We might begin by observing that there is no general agreement today on just what is meant by dialogue. Undoubtedly this is because any proposed definition of dialogue reflects one's underlying assumptions about basic theological issues as well as the purpose of dialogue itself, and this is precisely what the current controversy over dialogue is all about. We might, however, take Leonard Swidler's definition as sufficiently representative for our purposes: "Dialogue is a conversation on a common subject between two or more persons with differing views, the primary purpose of which is for each participant to learn from the other so that he or she can change and grow."[8] Unstated but implicit is the understanding that the participants are adherents of different religious traditions and that the conversation concerns common religious issues.[9] That one's understanding of the nature and purpose of dialogue is closely linked to underlying theological assumptions is evident in the second part of Swidler's definition, in which the primary purpose of dialogue is said to be learning from other participants so that one might "change and grow." Significantly, no clue is given as to how we are to understand these crucial verbs. It is in part just this kind of ambiguity, characteristic of much recent literature on dialogue and allowing as it does for varying interpretations depending upon one's own agenda, that causes such uneasiness among evangelicals about the current emphasis on dialogue in Christian mission.

In an important article, Eric Sharpe helps clarify the current debate by delineating four major kinds of dialogue: discursive

8. Leonard Swidler, "The Dialogue Decalogue: Ground Rules for Interreligious Dialogue," *Journal of Ecumenical Studies* 20 (Winter 1983): 1.
9. A distinction should be made between interreligious dialogue, or dialogue between different religious traditions, and interconfessional dialogue, or dialogue between different Christian traditions. We are here concerned only with the former.

dialogue, human dialogue, secular dialogue, and interior dialogue.[10] The four kinds are not necessarily mutually exclusive. In
any given case of interreligious dialogue two or more kinds of
dialogue might well be operative. But the distinctions help to clarify
the kinds of dialogue which are in use and show how different
understandings of the purpose of dialogue in turn affect the nature
of dialogue itself.

Discursive dialogue is that kind of dialogue primarily concerned with learning about other religious traditions. It involves
meeting together with adherents of one or more religions, listening, discussing common questions, and clarifying any misconceptions that might emerge. In order to be effective, participants must
be intellectually competent and must conduct the dialogue in an
atmosphere of mutual respect, trust, and scrupulous honesty. The
purpose of discursive dialogue is enhanced understanding of the
religious tradition of the other participant.

Obviously, discursive dialogue is important in its own right.
And Sharpe observes that effective dialogue of any kind must
include, at least initially, discursive dialogue. An accurate understanding of the beliefs and practices of the other tradition is indispensable. But few participants in interreligious dialogue today
are content to remain strictly within discursive dialogue.

Human dialogue draws a sharp contrast between mere
knowledge about beliefs and practices of other religious traditions
and actually knowing — in a personal, intimate sense — followers
of other religions. To understand Hinduism, for example, it is not
sufficient simply to know all of the relevant facts about Hinduism
— its history, beliefs, practices, etc. One must penetrate to the
point where an "I-Thou" relationship is established with a Hindu,
where the humanity and intrinsic dignity of the other person as a
Hindu is experienced. Doctrines divide, humanity unites. Genuine
understanding of religion is not a matter of apprehending certain
truths about a given tradition. As Wilfred Cantwell Smith, a leading

---

10. Eric J. Sharpe, "The Goals of Inter-Religious Dialogue," in *Truth and
Dialogue in World Religions,* ed. John H. Hick (Philadelphia: Westminster, 1974),
pp. 77-95.

apologist for dialogue, puts it, "True religion is a relation between man and man: a living relation; an actual relation, new every morning, among particular, real men in concrete, changing situations."[11] The purpose of human dialogue, then, is to pass beyond preoccupation with beliefs and doctrines to the point where one genuinely listens to the other participant as a fellow human being and an "I-Thou" relationship of mutual trust and acceptance is established.

Certainly, if one is to participate in dialogue, the importance of genuinely accepting the other participant as a fellow human being and establishing a relationship of mutual trust and acceptance cannot be exaggerated. Swidler suggests "ten commandments" for successful dialogue, and, not surprisingly, eight of them have to do with developing relationships of trust and acceptance within which effective dialogue can occur.[12] On the other hand, if human dialogue entails, as it often seems to, that religious beliefs — in particular divisive beliefs — are relatively unimportant and should not be emphasized, then it is clearly unacceptable. To suggest that one's religious convictions — one's fundamental worldview and most basic commitments — are less important than establishing a strong interpersonal relationship of trust and acceptance demonstrates failure to appreciate the significant question of the truth of one's beliefs. More than that, it also demonstrates failure to understand the religiousness of the other participant. For the Hindu is, among many other things, one who accepts a particular worldview and holds certain basic beliefs about, for example, the soul, *karma,* and rebirth. To ignore or minimize these basic beliefs is to fail to take seriously the religious worldview of the Hindu.

A third kind of dialogue Sharpe calls *secular dialogue.* This is the kind of dialogue that concentrates entirely upon the situation of humankind in the world. The agenda for secular dialogue is very much "this-worldly": concern for social, political, and economic justice; the struggle against world hunger; the elimina-

11. Wilfred Cantwell Smith, *Questions of Religious Truth* (London: V. Gollancz, 1967), p. 115; as cited in Sharpe, "Inter-Religious Dialogue," p. 84.
12. Leonard Swidler, "Dialogue Decalogue," pp. 1-4.

tion of the nuclear arms race; and so on. Stanley Samartha, for ten years the director of the World Council of Churches' unit on Dialogue with People of Living Faiths and Ideologies, states, "It is agreed that the most helpful relationship between persons of different faiths in the world today must be one of cooperation in pursuing common purposes like justice, peace, and human rights."[13] And Catholic theologian Paul Knitter claims that "a *preferential option for the poor and the nonperson* constitutes both the *necessity* and the *primary purpose* of interreligious dialogue. Religions must speak and act together because only so can they make their crucially important contribution to removing the oppression that contaminates our globe."[14] Rather than search for some elusive "common essence" to all religions or try to determine which one of many competing perspectives is ultimately correct, those engaged in religious dialogue today should "recognize a shared locus of religious experience" in the common struggle for justice and liberation throughout the world. *Soteria*, the concept of the kingdom and its justice, is held by Knitter to be the theological basis and goal of interreligious dialogue.

Surely no one would deny that religions should be actively involved in promoting justice and working to alleviate the many pressing problems facing our world today. And although the theoretical and practical problems with doing so should not be minimized, it could well be that in some significant enterprises various religions could work cooperatively together. In democracies that maintain in principle a clear distinction between religion and state, for example, in the face of increasing infringement upon religious liberties, it could be advantageous to have a cooperative effort by a broad coalition of religious traditions to safeguard the rights and freedoms of all parties. Or again, cooperation among various traditions in a common struggle against a particular moral evil — such as prostitution or abortion on demand — can be

13. Stanley Samartha, *Courage for Dialogue* (Maryknoll, N.Y.: Orbis, 1982), p. 30.
14. Paul Knitter, "Toward a Liberation Theology of Religions," in *The Myth of Christian Uniqueness*, ed. John Hick and Paul F. Knitter (Maryknoll, N.Y.: Orbis, 1987), p. 181. Emphasis in the original.

much more effective than the isolated, fragmented efforts of individual groups. But there are important questions here which need to be explored fully before participating in such joint projects. Particular care would need to be exercised to ensure that cooperation in certain carefully defined areas is not taken as implicit endorsement of the beliefs and practices of the various cooperating traditions. There must be no hidden agenda. And certainly such limited cooperation must in no way serve to shift the religious focus from the transcendent realm to the world of strictly social, political, and economic concerns. Interreligious cooperation on social issues may have its place but it cannot be used to conceal more fundamental questions about the truth value of the worldviews of the respective religions themselves.

The fourth kind of dialogue mentioned by Sharpe is *interior dialogue*. This is perhaps the most controversial form of dialogue, since it seems to involve primacy of experience over any kind of conceptualization, doctrinal or otherwise. Its locus is the mystical, contemplative tradition. Dom Bede Griffiths expresses well a central concern of this kind of dialogue:

> What is required is a meeting of the different religious traditions at the deepest level of their experience of God. Hinduism is based on a deep mystical experience and everywhere seeks not simply to know "about" God, but to "know God," that is to experience the reality of God in the depths of the soul. It is at this level that Christian and Hindu have to meet.[15]

Often there is the presupposition that on the deepest level of shared experience a common divine reality, which cannot be conceptually grasped but must simply be intuited, can be uncovered. God (or the religious ultimate, however understood) is one and reveals himself in every religious tradition. The essence of religion is to be found in an ineffable, mystical experience of the divine, and interreligious dialogue can be an effective way of penetrating to this level of experience. Thus interreligious dialogue can even be revelatory, helping participants to uncover more "truth" and to

15. As cited in Sharpe, "Inter-Religious Dialogue," p. 88.

grasp fuller dimensions of the divine. Swidler distinguishes between three levels of dialogue, the third being roughly synonymous
with what Sharpe calls interior dialogue.

If we are serious, persistent, and sensitive enough in the
dialogue, we may at times

> enter into phase three. Here we together begin to explore new
> areas of reality, of meaning, and of truth, of which neither of us
> had even been aware before. We are brought face to face with this
> new, as-yet-unknown-to-us dimension of reality only because of
> questions, insights, probings produced in the dialogue. We may
> thus dare to say that patiently pursued dialogue can become an
> instrument of new "revelation," a further "un-veiling" of reality
> — on which we must then act.[16]

The purpose of interior dialogue, then, is to rise above the level of
fixation with explicit beliefs and doctrines and to introduce the
participants to new horizons of truth and reality through a deep
experience of the divine reality. It is not unusual for those participating in interior dialogue to dispense with verbal dialogue entirely
and to "dialogue" through joint contemplative and meditative
practice. Dialogue here is often thought of as a common quest for
Truth. It is generally taken for granted that God — or the religious
ultimate — has revealed himself in all religions, that all persons
can be "saved" and related to God through their own religious
traditions, and that not only is there no need for conversion to
Christ, but attempts to persuade non-Christians to accept Christ
as Lord and Savior are theologically and morally unacceptable.
Sacred scriptures of all religions can be regarded as revelatory. The
Bible has no privileged status.

Evangelical dissatisfaction with dialogue stems from certain
assumptions generally associated with interior dialogue, although
they may be more or less present in either human dialogue or
secular dialogue. Among these problematic assumptions are the
following:

  1. God has revealed himself in and through all major re-

16. Swidler, "Dialogue Decalogue," p. 4.

ligious traditions. There is nothing in principle about God's revelation in the Judeo-Christian tradition which makes it definitive or normative. There is thus an inescapable relativity of all religions. Wilfred Cantwell Smith says,

> I myself — after studying the history of the Islamic and the Christian movements and having friends in both groups — am not able to think of any reason that one might reasonably have for denying that God has played in human history a role in and through the Qur'an, in the Muslim case, comparable to the role in the Christian case in and through Christ.[17]

And Stanley Samartha states,

> A particular religion can claim to be decisive for some people, and some people can claim that a particular religion is decisive for them, but no religion is justified in claiming that it is decisive for all. The Hindu and the Christian have their own particularly distinctive contributions to make to the common quest for truth.[18]

2. Christians thus cannot enter into dialogue with the assumption that they have any definitive truth about God and the human predicament which is absolute and nonnegotiable. Christian beliefs, while perhaps authoritative for Christians, are but one among many perspectives on fundamental religious issues. Paul Knitter asserts that "dialogue is not possible if any partners enter it with the claim that they possess the final, definitive, irreformable truth."[19] Donald Swearer claims that "if we believe that our particular perception of religious truth is the *only* correct one, then genuine dialogue does not take place at all."[20] And Peter Berger, himself highly sympathetic to interreligious dialogue, very candidly admits,

17. Wilfred Cantwell Smith, "Idolatry," in *The Myth of Christian Uniqueness,* p. 64.

18. Samartha, *Courage for Dialogue,* p. 153.

19. Paul Knitter, *No Other Name? A Critical Survey of Christian Attitudes Toward the World Religions* (Maryknoll, N.Y.: Orbis, 1985), p. 211.

20. Donald K. Swearer, *Dialogue: The Key to Understanding Other Religions* (Philadelphia: Westminster, 1977), p. 41. Emphasis in original.

Interreligious dialogue takes place today in a context of uncertainty, not in a context of traditional authority. It takes
place, very largely, between people who are very unsure of
their position rather than people who are firmly committed to
their traditions. I think this is something that should be
honestly put on the table. . . . We should admit our nakedness,
if you will.[21]

3. Interreligious dialogue thus can be regarded as a common
search for religious truth. Berger suggests that those engaging in
interreligious dialogue think of dialogue as "the *common search for
truth by people who are not safely grounded in any tradition.*"[22]
Similarly, Samartha observes "that dialogue becomes one of the
means of the quest for truth."[23]

4. The most profound religious Truth, which is uncovered
through interreligious dialogue, is not propositional truth but
rather is a symbolic, all-encompassing Truth transcending particular doctrinal formulations. In spite of clear surface differences
between religions, ultimately there is a common unifying center.
Consider the words of Paul Knitter:

Dialogue must be based on the recognition of the possible truth
in all religions; the ability to recognize this truth must be
grounded in the hypothesis of a common ground and goal for all
religions. . . . The deepest level of dialogue cannot be a matter of
"apples and oranges." To try to formulate what this means, we
can say that there must be the same ultimate reality, the same
divine presence, the same fullness and emptiness — in Christian
terms, the same God — animating all religions and providing the
ultimate ground and goal of dialogue.[24]

5. Since God has revealed himself in all religious traditions
and Christians cannot claim to enter into dialogue with any defini-

21. Peter Berger, "The Pluralistic Situation and the Coming Dialogue
Between the World Religions," *Buddhist-Christian Studies* 1 (1981): 36.
22. Ibid., p. 39. Emphasis in original.
23. Samartha, *Courage for Dialogue*, p. 11.
24. Paul Knitter, *No Other Name?* p. 209.

tive truth, it follows that God can speak to Christians through adherents of other religions. Thus Harvey Cox claims that, based upon his experience in interreligious dialogue, "God can and does speak to us through people of other faiths, changing our viewpoint."[25]

6. Adherents of other religions are not to be regarded as spiritually lost, in need of salvation through the atoning death of Jesus Christ, but rather as already enjoying a saving relationship with God. As Wesley Ariarajah puts it, in encounters with followers of other faiths I should recognize that "the other person is as much a child of God as I am and that should form the basis of our relationship with our neighbors."[26] Wilfred Cantwell Smith concurs, asserting that "as far as actual observation goes, the evidence would seem overwhelming that in fact individual Buddhists, Hindus, Muslims, and others have known, and do know, God."[27]

7. Since there is no need for followers of other traditions to accept Jesus Christ as Lord and Savior for salvation, dialogue in an attempt to persuade others to accept Jesus Christ as Lord and Savior has no place. To be sure, as Christians we must be faithful to our commitment to Jesus Christ and must engage in "witness" concerning our fundamental beliefs. But such witness should not have as its goal the conversion of the other person. Samartha thus argues that the time has come for restating the meaning of mission in multireligious contexts, taking into account the integrity of other faiths.[28] And Donald Swearer observes,

> One of my Sinhalese Christian friends . . . has said that part of the mission of the Christian church in Sri Lanka should be to make Buddhists better Buddhists. Such a suggestion may sound like nonsense or even heresy. Yet, in terms of the dialogical ap-

25. Harvey Cox, "Many Mansions or One Way? The Crisis in Interfaith Dialogue," in *Christian Century,* August 17-24, 1988, p. 735.

26. As quoted in Paul Schrotenboer, "Inter-Religious Dialogue," in *Evangelical Review of Theology* 12 (July 1988): 219.

27. Wilfred Cantwell Smith, "The Christian in a Religiously Plural World," in *Christianity and Other Religions,* ed. John Hick and Brian Hebblethwaite (Philadelphia: Fortress, 1980), p. 102.

28. Stanley Samartha, *Courage for Dialogue,* p. 30.

proach where religious men with deep conviction encounter one
another with the openness to be moved to new dimensions of
faith, such a proposal makes perfectly good sense.[29]

Insofar as these assumptions are integral to accepted understandings of interreligious dialogue, evangelicals must unequivocally reject dialogue as inimical to a genuinely biblical understanding of Christian mission. Evangelicals hold certain things
to be nonnegotiable. While fully recognizing that God has revealed
himself significantly through the created natural order and the
moral conscience (Ps. 19; Acts 14:15-17; Rom. 1:18-32, 2:14-15),
evangelicals maintain that God has revealed himself definitively in
the Incarnation in Jesus (John 1:1, 14, 18; Heb. 1:1-3) and that the
Scriptures are the inspired, fully authoritative written revelation of
God. All that is necessary for salvation and holy living is available
in the special written revelation of God. No informed evangelical
would suggest that Christians have a monopoly on truth. Certainly
there are elements of truth within other religious traditions and
evangelicals should humbly recognize that there is always more
that can be learned from those in other faiths. But evangelicals
emphatically maintain that God has revealed unambiguous truths
about himself and salvation in the Scriptures, truths that are absolutely unique and nonnegotiable. Among these truths, of course,
is the central evangelical tenet that salvation is available only
through the person and work of Jesus Christ, and the accompanying corollary is that the good news of salvation in Christ must be
proclaimed to all peoples in all cultures, regardless of their religious
affiliation. Adherents of other religions, no less than secularists and
atheists, need humbly to acknowledge Jesus Christ as Lord and
Savior. Any understanding of interreligious dialogue that threatens
this perspective must be rejected by evangelicals as an incipient
movement away from the biblical view of the relation between God
and humankind.

Having sounded this warning, however, should we conclude
that there is no place in interreligious dialogue for evangelicals?

29. Donald Swearer, *Dialogue*, pp. 43-44.

Not at all. Evangelicals have made some initial, tentative efforts toward exploring a legitimate place for dialogue. On the interconfessional level, mention should be made of the report of the Evangelical-Roman Catholic Dialogue on Mission, the product of three international meetings between leading evangelicals and Roman Catholics from 1977 to 1984.[30] And on the interreligious level we should note the significant dialogues between evangelicals and Jews that have been held between 1975 and 1984. Leading evangelical and Jewish scholars met on three occasions and frankly discussed such controversial subjects as the Messiah, the meaning of Israel, interpretation of Scripture, current evangelical-Jewish relations, and the question of proselytism.[31] Whether such dialogue will expand in the future to include Buddhists, Hindus, or Muslims remains to be seen. And several prominent evangelicals have in recent writings also given a qualified endorsement to dialogue, so long as it is conducted within carefully prescribed parameters.[32]

In considering the question of evangelical participation in interreligious dialogue it is helpful to distinguish between what might be called *formal* and *informal* dialogue. *Formal* dialogue consists of an organized gathering of representatives from two or more religious traditions in which well-defined procedures are followed in

30. For the text of the report see "The Evangelical-Roman Catholic Dialogue on Mission, 1977-1984: A Report," in *International Bulletin of Missionary Research* 10 (January 1986): 2-21.

31. For texts of the papers read at the three conferences, see *Evangelicals and Jews in Conversation on Scripture, Theology, and History,* ed. Marc H. Tanenbaum, Marvin R. Wilson, and A. James Rudin (Grand Rapids: Baker, 1978); *Evangelicals and Jews in an Age of Pluralism,* ed. Marc H. Tanenbaum, Marvin R. Wilson, and A. James Rudin (Grand Rapids: Baker, 1984); and *A Time to Speak: The Evangelical-Jewish Encounter,* ed. A. James Rudin and Marvin R. Wilson (Grand Rapids: Eerdmans, and Austin, Tex.: Center for Judaic-Christian Studies, 1987).

32. See David J. Hesselgrave, "Interreligious Dialogue — Biblical and Contemporary Perspectives," in *Theology and Mission: Papers Given at Trinity Consultation No. 1,* ed. David J. Hessselgrave (Grand Rapids: Baker, 1978), pp. 227-40; John Stott, *Christian Mission,* pp. 58-81; Paul Schrotenboer, "Inter-Religious Dialogue," pp. 208-25; and Vinay Samuel and Chris Sugden, "Dialogue With Other Religions: An Evangelical View," in *Sharing Jesus in the Two-Thirds World,* ed. Vinay Samuel and Chris Sugden (Grand Rapids: Eerdmans, 1984), pp. 122-40. Much of the discussion which follows builds upon the helpful studies by Hesselgrave and Stott.

the pursuit of agreed-upon objectives. The various consultations on interreligious dialogue sponsored by the WCC unit on Dialogue with People of Living Faiths and Ideologies, as well as the dialogue between evangelicals and Jews noted above, would fall into this category. *Informal* dialogue occurs whenever two or more followers of different religious traditions discuss together, in an informal setting, certain issues pertaining to their respective religious commitments. I suggest that informal dialogue is not only an option for evangelicals but is essential if the proclamation of the good news of salvation in Jesus Christ is to be carried out effectively. Furthermore, it would seem that there are certain kinds of formal dialogue in which evangelicals can and should participate.

In order to appreciate the importance of *informal dialogue* it is helpful to recall the examples of our Lord and the apostles in the New Testament. John Stott correctly observes that Jesus frequently engaged in dialogue, or two-way conversation, with others. "He seldom if ever spoke in a declamatory, take-it-or-leave-it style. Instead, whether explicitly or implicitly, he was constantly addressing questions to his hearers' minds and consciences."[33] One thinks here of Jesus' conversations with Nicodemus, the Samaritan woman, and the Jewish religious leaders (cf. Luke 14:1-23; John 3:1-21; 4:1-26).

The word "dialogue" is derived from the Greek noun *dialogos* (vb. *dialegomai*), and in the New Testament this term is associated most with the apostle Paul. The term, often translated in the New International Version as "reasoned," is used of Paul's activity in the synagogues (Acts 17:2, 17; 18:4, 19), in the marketplace (17:17), in the school of Tyrannus (19:9), and in the church at Troas (20:7, 9). Bauer, Arndt, and Gingrich define *dialegomai* as "discuss, conduct a discussion" and note its use in connection with "lectures which were likely to end in disputations."[34] Similarly, Liddell and Scott give its meaning as "to converse, reason, talk with

33. Stott, *Christian Mission*, p. 61.

34. Walter Bauer, *A Greek-English Lexicon of the New Testament and Other Early Christian Literature,* translated and adapted by William F. Arndt and F. Wilbur Gingrich, 2nd ed. (Chicago: University of Chicago Press, 1979), p. 185.

... to discourse, argue."[35] A careful study of Paul's encounters with Jews and Gentiles alike indicates that he often engaged in informal dialogue — arguing, reasoning, clarifying misunderstandings, persuading, responding to questions and challenges. And yet, as Stott points out, such dialogue was for Paul always a part of and subordinate to proclamation of the gospel. Moreover, "the subject of his dialogue with the world was one which he always chose himself, namely Jesus Christ, and its object was always conversion to Jesus Christ."[36] There is no suggestion in the New Testament that Paul was interested in dialogue with others — whether with polytheists as in Acts 14 or with Stoics and Epicureans in Acts 17 — merely to enhance his understanding of other traditions or even simply to establish better interreligious relationships. His concern throughout was proclamation of the gospel in such a way that others were converted to Jesus Christ.

At least four reasons can be cited for evangelical participation in informal dialogue with persons of other faiths. First, to do so is to follow the model of encounter and proclamation we find in our Lord and in Paul. Neither Jesus nor Paul merely lectured in monologue fashion about the truths of salvation. Both demonstrate evidence of understanding well the contexts of the target audiences, sensing their needs, establishing common ground, using questions to prompt interest and understanding, and proclaiming in a clear and sensitive manner truth that needed to be shared.

Second, informal dialogue can be a demonstration of one's willingness to take the other person seriously as a fellow human being. As Christopher J. H. Wright reminds us,

> Our fellow human being is first, foremost and essentially one in the image of God, and only secondarily a Hindu, Muslim, or secular pagan. So, inasmuch as his religion is part of his humanity, whenever we meet one whom we call "an adherent of another religion," we meet someone who, in his religion as in all else, has

35. *Greek-English Lexicon*, abridged from *Liddell and Scott's Greek-English Lexicon* (Oxford: Oxford University Press, 1977), p. 163.
36. Stott, *Christian Mission*, p. 63.

some relationship to the Creator God, a relationship within which
he is addressable and accountable.[37]

To be sure, the follower of another religion is not yet in a saving
relationship with God, and indeed, like all persons who have not
responded to God's grace in Jesus, lives in a state of rebellion and
disobedience. But this should not obscure the fact that even here
there is a fundamental relationship of the creator to the creation,
the human creature being made in the image of the creator.
Genuine respect for the integrity and dignity of the other person
as a human being in God's image demands a willingness to listen
and to take seriously his or her most basic religious commitments.

Third, informal dialogue is essential for effective evangelism. We have already noted that for evangelicals, proclamation of
the gospel, with the conversion of the other person as its objective,
cannot be divorced from dialogue. To deny this is to separate
oneself from the biblical understanding of mission. And yet we
must also stress that effective evangelism will occur only when the
proclamation of the gospel is accompanied by proper informal
dialogue with the other person. It is widely accepted today that
effective communication of the gospel to those with an alien religious and cultural worldview depends upon adequately understanding the basic assumptions and values of the worldview in
question and then making use of forms which will effectively and
faithfully communicate the message to the target audience. One
cannot communicate the good news of Jesus Christ effectively to
an animist without understanding well the worldview of the animist. The same holds for Buddhists, Hindus, Muslims, or even
members of the Unification Church. And it is difficult, if not
impossible, to understand the worldviews of, say, Buddhists or
Hindus without listening carefully to what they have to say, asking
pointed questions for clarification, and contrasting their answers
with basic Christian beliefs. In this sense, informal dialogue is an
essential part of effective evangelism.

37. Christopher J. H. Wright, "The Christian and Other Religions: The
Biblical Evidence," in *Themelios* 9 (January 1984): 5. Emphasis in original.

Fourth, informal dialogue can be a mark of humility, sensitivity, and common courtesy to followers of other faiths. If we expect the Muslim or Hindu to listen carefully to our proclamation of Jesus as Lord and Savior, surely we owe them the same courtesy and respect we expect from them. How can a Christian expect Buddhists, for example, to take his or her assertions seriously if there is no evidence of willingness on the Christian's part to listen carefully and to consider the claims of the Buddhist?

Evangelicals who recognize the importance of participation in informal dialogue may nevertheless hesitate when the focus shifts to *formal dialogue*. Is there a legitimate place for evangelicals in formal dialogue? Although he does not make the same distinction between formal and informal dialogue, evangelical missiologist David Hesselgrave suggests that evangelicals can and should be involved in five kinds of interreligious dialogue. Significantly, what he has in mind seems to include formal dialogue.[38] Hesselgrave's proposal will be given in some detail, as it provides a helpful framework for evangelical participation in interreligious dialogue.

The first kind of dialogue in which evangelicals should participate is discussion of the nature of interreligious dialogue itself. There is no clear consensus today on just what is meant by dialogue and what the proper objectives of dialogue should be. Hesselgrave calls for evangelicals to join the debate over dialogue in an effort to bring about a more biblical understanding of the objectives of dialogue and its compatibility with concern for evangelism. The current debate on interreligious dialogue is vitiated by confusion over fundamental theological issues concerning the nature of divine revelation, sin, and salvation. Thoughtful treatment of these themes in the light of pluralism, based upon rigorous and responsible exegesis of all relevant biblical texts, is imperative. Evangelicals can and should make a contribution to this debate.

The second kind of dialogue in which evangelicals should become involved is what Hesselgrave calls "interreligious dialogue that promotes freedom of worship and witness."[39] Freedom of

---

38. Hesselgrave, "Interreligious Dialogue," pp. 235-37.
39. Ibid., p. 236.

worship is being challenged today not only in totalitarian societies, but also, in some cases, in secular democracies as well. Evangelicals should enter into dialogue with adherents of other faiths on how best to preserve religious liberties for all.

Third, Hesselgrave also advocates evangelical participation in interreligious dialogue concerned with meeting human physical and social needs. This would seem to correspond roughly with Sharpe's secular dialogue. Presumably this would include dialogue concerning proper responses to such common threats as nuclear proliferation, environmental abuse, hunger and starvation, natural disasters, and so on.

Fourth is that kind of dialogue designed to break down barriers of prejudice, distrust, and hatred in the religious world. No religious tradition can claim to be free of religious prejudice or bigotry. The history of religions provides ample evidence of mutual suspicion, hatred, and ill will between religious traditions. Even today many Christians continue to harbor misleading and erroneous assumptions about Hindus, Buddhists, or Muslims which in turn fuel the fires of suspicion and distrust. Surely evangelicals should encourage dialogue with others that can contribute to more accurate understanding and appreciation of followers of other religions.

Closely related is that kind of dialogue which has as its objective the "mutual comprehension of conflicting truth claims."[40] This, of course, is similar to Sharpe's discursive dialogue. The objective here is more accurate understanding of the basic beliefs of the other party and clarification of any similarities or differences between these beliefs and central claims of the Christian faith.[41] Greater understanding of other faiths is certainly important

---

40. Ibid., p. 237.

41. The importance of this is recognized by Julius Lipner, when he says that "the purpose of dialogue today seems to me best fulfilled when participants redefine the limits and areas of facticity in their traditional truth-claims: on the one hand, clearing away as lucidly as possible the tangled undergrowth of hitherto sacrosanct and untouched 'factual truths', and on the other, seeking new insights of convergent understanding in the reinterpretation of these 'facts'." Julius Lipner, "Truth-Claims and Inter-religious Dialogue," *Religious Studies* 12 (1976): 230.

and legitimate in its own right. But the significance of this for evangelicals engaged in communicating the gospel in different religious and cultural contexts can hardly be exaggerated.

It should be clear, then, that, properly defined, dialogue is not incompatible with a commitment to evangelism. Evangelicals can and should become actively involved in certain kinds of inter-religious dialogue, both on the informal and the formal level. The overriding concern throughout, however, must be that the gospel of Jesus Christ is effectively communicated in a sensitive and gracious manner to followers of other religions. In concluding this section we can do no better than to quote the late Bishop Stephen Neill:

> Anyone brought up in the Platonic tradition of dialogue knows well the intense seriousness involved; Socrates and his interlocutors are concerned about one thing only — that the truth should emerge. This is the concern of the Christian partner in dialogue. If Christ is the Truth, then the only thing that matters is that Christ should emerge, but Christ as the Truth makes categorical demands on the individual for total, unconditional and exclusive commitment to himself.[42]

Tolerance

Evangelicals maintain that God has revealed himself definitively in the Incarnation in Jesus of Nazareth, that the Bible is the unique, divinely inspired written revelation of God, that salvation is available only through the person and work of Jesus Christ, and that where the claims of other religions conflict with those of biblical Christianity the former are to be rejected as false. Not surprisingly, then, evangelicals place a high priority upon evangelism. Those who have never heard the gospel of Jesus Christ must be given an opportunity to respond to him as their Lord and Savior.

We have seen, however, that there is today growing dissatis-

42. As quoted in Stott, *Christian Mission*, pp. 72-73.

faction with this perspective. And while theological factors cannot be dismissed as irrelevant, perhaps the major motivating factor for this dissatisfaction is not theological or philosophical but moral. For many today assume that there is something morally blame-worthy about Christian exclusivism. This finds expression most often in the claim that Christian exclusivism is intolerant and thus morally deficient. On a popular level it is held that we should simply accept that people have different religious beliefs (religious "preferences") and not try to determine which particular religion is true or otherwise preferred above the rest. Certainly we should not seek to change one's religious orientation. Proselytism is out. Rather, we should be tolerant and open-minded, accepting the beliefs of others. Asserting that one's own religious perspective is somehow "uniquely true" and normative and that those who hap-pen to disagree with you are wrong is insufferably narrow-minded and intolerant.

Recent literature on religious pluralism is replete with con-demnations of the alleged intolerance of exclusivism. The follow-ing statements may be taken as representative:

> Exclusivism strikes more and more Christians as immoral. If the head proves it true, while the heart sees it as wicked, un-Christian, then should Christians not follow the heart? Maybe this is the crux of our dilemna.[43]

> The conservative Evangelical declaration that there can be authen-tic, reliable revelation only in Christ simply does not hold up in the light of the faith, dedication, love, and peace that Christians find in the teachings and especially in the followers of other religions.[44]

> But if we restrict our attention to the great world traditions, the only criterion by which any of these could be judged to be the one and only true religion, with all others dismissed as false, would

43. Wilfred Cantwell Smith, "An Attempt at Summation," in *Christ's Lordship and Religious Pluralism*, ed. G. H. Anderson and T. F. Stransky (Mary-knoll, N.Y.: Orbis, 1981), p. 202.
44. Paul Knitter, *No Other Name?* p. 93.

be its own dogmatic assertion, in its more chauvinistic moments, to this effect.[45]

At a time when the histories of different nations are increasingly being drawn together, when different communities of faith are in dialogue with each other as never before, and when people of the world, for good or bad, share a common future, the exclusive claims of particular communities generate tensions and lead to clashes.[46]

The exclusive attitude of the past which regarded its own opinions as supreme and others as not worth discussing is no longer useful, if ever it was.[47]

Similarly, the historian Arnold Toynbee, a vigorous critic of exclusivism, asserted that the only way to purge Christianity of the "sinful state of mind" of exclusive-mindedness and its accompanying spirit of intolerance is to shed the traditional belief that Christianity is unique.[48]

These are harsh words indeed, and if accurate would require the rejection of Christian exclusivism by all morally sensitive persons. But is Christian exclusivism necessarily intolerant of followers of other faiths? Is the evangelical who maintains that Jesus alone is the Way, the Truth, and the Life necessarily guilty of arrogance, pride, and narrow-mindedness? Is exclusivism necessarily an obstacle to greater global understanding, cooperation, and peace? While recognizing that — to our shame — Christian exclusivists have indeed on many occasions been arrogant and intolerant, I will argue that there is no necessary connection between Christian exclusivism and intolerance and that the widespread

45. John Hick, *God Has Many Names* (Philadelphia: Westminster, 1982), p. 90.

46. Stanley Samartha, "The Lordship of Jesus Christ and Religious Pluralism," in *Christ's Lordship and Religious Pluralism*, p. 22.

47. Geoffrey Parrinder, *Comparative Religion* (London: Sheldon Press, 1976), p. 32.

48. Arnold Toynbee, *Christianity Among the Religions of the World* (New York: Charles Scribner's Sons, 1957), pp. 95f.

perception of the intolerance of exclusivism rests largely upon confusion over the meaning of tolerance. While fully holding to the nonnegotiables of biblical faith in their relations with those of other religions, evangelicals should be models of gracious tolerance and humble open-mindedness.

Any discussion of the relation between tolerance and religious beliefs must begin by recognizing the shameful fact that history is full of examples of brutal wars and fighting between various religious communities. Christians slaughtered Muslims and Jews. Muslims in turn massacred Christians and Jews. Muslims and Hindus fought bitterly in the Indian subcontinent. Baha'is have faced systematic persecution from Muslims. Even Buddhists, widely regarded as paragons of compassion, tolerance, and serenity, have had their bloody internal feuds with fellow Buddhists. There is no denying that religious communities have indeed often acted in highly barbarous and intolerant ways toward followers of other traditions. And as Parrinder demonstrates, this is not simply so in Christianity, but is true also of Islam, Hinduism, and Buddhism.[49] Contemporary examples of religious persecution and intolerance are not hard to find. Cardinal Newman's apt comment is unfortunately all too accurate in depicting a long tradition of persecution and intolerance in religious history: "Oh, how we hate one another for the love of God!"

Our concern here, however, is not with the historical record itself. Surely no religious tradition is without fault and there is little point in throwing stones at others. Nor would it be particularly helpful to try to determine whose record is most tainted — if such a task were even possible! Rather, our concern here is with the concepts of exclusivism and intolerance themselves: Is there anything in the concept of Christian exclusivism itself which demands such arrogance and intolerance of others?

In order to answer this question we must analyze the concept of tolerance more closely in an effort to see just what is, and what is not, included within it. Clearly tolerance is not simply acceptance of anything and everything. There are limits to toler-

49. Parrinder, *Comparative Religion*, chap. 3.

ance. In the moral realm, the man who passively watches while several other men gang rape a helpless woman will, if it is within his power to assist her, hardly be praised for demonstrating the virtue of tolerance. On the contrary, one could argue that he is morally culpable for failing to do what he could to assist the victim. Similarly, to never disagree with anyone, even when the statements of others are known to be false, is not a mark of tolerance but rather an indication of intellectual suicide. Some things are to be tolerated, others are not.

It might be helpful here to distinguish between three distinct contexts in which the notion of tolerance is applicable.[50] First, there is what we might call the legal context. In modern Western democracies, for example, a kind of legal tolerance is often explicitly written into the constitution of the country, guaranteeing legal protection of basic rights for all persons regardless of sex or religious affiliation. Frequently there is an explicit guarantee of religious freedom: the government is not to prohibit the free exercise of religious beliefs and practices, nor is it to act so as to favor any particular religious tradition. Each person is to have complete legal freedom in pursuit of his or her religious objectives.

This notion of legal tolerance of religious pluralism is essentially a formal recognition of the basic human right of each individual to choose which religious tradition to become a part of (if any at all) and to participate freely in the practices of that tradition. This right is often taken for granted in the democracies of the West, and it is easy to forget that in many countries today there is no, or at best very restricted, legal tolerance of religious pluralism. In Nepal, for example, Hinduism is the state religion and it is illegal to try to convert anyone from the religion of his or her parents. Open Christian evangelism is illegal. Similarly, Saudi Arabia is an officially Islamic state prohibiting attempts to convert Muslims to any other faith. Even in the modern democratic nation of India there have been moves recently to restrict the freedom of

50. The threefold distinction was suggested by John Stott's discussion of religious pluralism in his *The Authentic Jesus* (London: Marshall, Morgan & Scott, 1985), pp. 69f.

Christians (and others) attempting to persuade Hindus to change their religion.[51] Surely evangelicals are to support the notion of legal toleration of religious pluralism. It is right that each person be guaranteed the freedom to pursue his or her religious beliefs and practices.

Tolerance of religious pluralism is also important in the social context. Here tolerance dictates that we treat other persons, regardless of their religious views, with dignity and respect. Any kind of social discrimination on the basis of religious perspective is unacceptable. For Christians, social tolerance stems from the fact that others, even with different religious views, are made in the image of God and thus have inherent dignity and worth. Needless to say, social tolerance is a very difficult ideal to achieve. In societies that have long been dominated by one or two major religious traditions, genuine social acceptance of those with minority views is rare. But even in highly pluralistic societies, with many different traditions represented, social tolerance is more often the exception than the rule. In our increasingly pluralistic Western societies, evangelicals must take the lead in cultivating social tolerance for those with differing religious views.

Certainly the most controversial context for tolerance of pluralism is what might be called the intellectual context. For here we are dealing not simply with people's actions but with fundamental beliefs. In his important book *Foundations of Religious Tolerance*, philosopher Jay Newman observes that it is widely — and mistakenly — held that tolerating a belief is primarily a matter of making a judgment about the content of that belief.[52] Thus there is the widespread assumption today that being genuinely tolerant of another religion means that one will not say anything negative about its basic beliefs. Raimundo Panikkar, for example, implies that if one is truly tolerant of others he or she will not judge or

51. See C. V. Matthew, "The Church and Militant Hinduism," *Asia Theological News* 14 (1988): 12-13; and Stanley Samartha, "Dialogue and the Politicization of Religions in India," *International Bulletin of Missionary Research* 8 (July 1984): 104-7.

52. Jay Newman, *Foundations of Religious Tolerance* (Toronto: University of Toronto Press, 1982), p. 7.

critically evaluate other religions.[53] On this assumption, the evangelical Christian who maintains that Buddhists or Hindus embrace false beliefs is grossly intolerant, whereas the tolerant person is willing to say that the claims of all religions are in some sense true.

There is an important insight here, but an equally important confusion as well. Clearly, in tolerating some entity x I am in some sense accepting x, or displaying a positive attitude toward x. And conversely, by not being tolerant of x I am refusing to accept x. But what must not be overlooked is that in tolerating x there is an important sense in which I am *not* approving of x. Tolerance involves, in one sense, acceptance of something toward which one has a negative estimation. It hardly makes sense to speak of tolerating something of which one heartily approves. If one thoroughly enjoys Mozart we do not speak of him tolerating Mozart. Thus, Maurice Cranston defines toleration as "a policy of patient forbearance in the presence of something which is disliked and disapproved of."[54] Toleration thus has an element of disapproval built into its meaning.

Religious tolerance, then, involves acceptance in some sense of something (e.g., a belief) toward which one has a less than positive view. Let us use p to stand for a particular religious belief. If one tolerates p, then one in some sense accepts p while still not necessarily endorsing the content of p. One can tolerate p while still regarding p as false. (It simply is nonsensical to speak of tolerating a belief that one already accepts as true!) A fundamental distinction emerges here: It is one thing to accept someone's holding a particular belief but quite another matter to accept the content of the belief itself. Religious tolerance does imply the former, but not the latter. As Newman puts it, "Tolerating a religious belief, then, does not involve a half-hearted acceptance or endurance of the belief *in itself,* but rather it involves acceptance or endurance of *someone's holding* that belief, that is, of a certain case of believing."[55]

53. Raimundo Panikkar, *The Intrareligious Dialogue* (New York: Paulist Press, 1978), p. xviii.

54. Maurice Cranston, "Toleration," *The Encyclopedia of Philosophy*, vol. 8, ed. Paul Edwards (New York: Macmillan, 1967), p. 143.

55. Newman, *Religious Tolerance*, p. 8. Emphasis in original.

An example might help to clarify the point. The August 10, 1986 edition of the *Japan Times* contains a fascinating letter to the editor from a Jodo-Shinshu Buddhist priest. In it the priest complains about a particular Christian missionary who regularly drives past the Buddhist temple during funerals and other services, blaring over his loudspeakers, "You heathens had better consider the afterlife and repent, or else you will all roast in hell!"

Undoubtedly, few would hesitate to call this highly intolerant behavior, and it is a reproach to the cause of Christ that such activity occurs at all. But notice why we call this behavior intolerant. It is not the fact that the missionary happens to disagree with the teachings of Jodo-Shinshu Buddhism that marks him as intolerant. Nor is it the fact that he believes that the priest and fellow Buddhists are on their way to hell — distasteful as that conviction may be — that makes him intolerant. Rather, it is the highly insensitive and morally repugnant manner in which he expresses his views and seeks to persuade others that compels us to call him intolerant. For intolerance involves the refusal to accept something that one can and morally ought to accept. The missionary, then, is intolerant because he refuses to recognize the right of the temple to conduct religious rites and services in peace, without interference from outside.

In tolerating a religious belief *p* one is not adopting a special attitude toward the content of *p* itself. One can still regard *p* as false. Rather, one is adopting a certain acceptance of someone's believing in *p*; one is accepting the right of that individual to believe that *p*. It is one thing to recognize that someone has a right to believe *p*. It is an entirely different matter to believe that *p* is in fact true. It would seem, then, that simply maintaining that the beliefs of, say, Buddhism or Islam are false in and of themselves is not intolerant. This is not to deny, of course, that one can be intolerant in one's treatment of Buddhists or Muslims or that the belief in the falsity of the views of others can lead to highly intolerant treatment of others.

The point is simply that such intolerance is not demanded by the view that basic beliefs of other religions are false. There is no necessary connection between holding the beliefs of a particular group to be false and the radical mistreatment of members of that group.[56] Certainly, one can consider the beliefs of another to be false and yet treat that person with dignity and respect. For to deny this is to suggest that we can only respect and treat properly those with whom we happen to agree. But surely this is nonsense! Is it not rather a mark of maturity to be able to live peaceably and cooperate with and act properly toward those with whom we might profoundly disagree? Being tolerant of others in different religious traditions, then, does not entail accepting their basic beliefs as true, or even the refusal to make any kind of judgment about the content of their basic beliefs. It is perfectly compatible with holding that at least some of their beliefs are false.

Some who may agree with the discussion to this point and grant that holding the basic beliefs of others to be false in and of itself is not necessarily intolerant will still maintain that evangelicals are in other respects intolerant of followers of other faiths. Surely, it might be argued, the evangelical emphasis upon evangelism and conversion, the desire to make Christians out of Buddhists, Hindus, Muslims, and Jews, is highly intolerant. Christians may believe that they are correct and all others who disagree with them are wrong — that is their prerogative. But to try to change the religious views and commitments of others and have them accept your particular perspective — surely this is a clear case of arrogance and intolerance. For example, in his otherwise fine book Jay Newman states, "There is something inherently intolerant about the missionary, the proselytizer. . . . We do not like the people who come to convert us. We often find them arrogant, ignorant, hypocritical, meddlesome."[57]

We must readily admit that, to our shame, Christian missionaries have in the past on occasion resorted to immoral methods in an attempt to convert the "heathen." Missionaries have not always shown other cultures and religious traditions the respect

56. On this see the comments of Paul Griffiths and Delmas Lewis, "On Grading Religions, Seeking Truth, and Being Nice to People — A Reply to Professor Hick," *Religious Studies* 19 (March 1983): 77f.

57. Newman, *Religious Tolerance*, pp. 88-89.

they deserve. The Hindu philosopher and statesman Sarvepalli Radhakrishnan, reflecting upon his early experiences with missionaries in mission schools, observed, "I was somewhat annoyed that truly religious people — as many Christian missionaries undoubtedly were — could treat as subjects for derision doctrines that others held in deepest reverence."[58] Similarly, the great Mahatma Gandhi, architect of Indian independence and spiritual guide for millions, tells of his early experiences with Christian missionaries:

> In those days Christian missionaries used to stand in a corner near the high school and hold forth, pouring abuse on Hindus and their gods. I could not endure this. I must have stood there to hear them only once, but that was enough to dissuade me from repeating the experiment. About the same time, I heard of a well-known Hindu having been converted to Christianity. It was the talk of town that, when he was baptized, he had to eat beef and drink liquor, that he also had to change his clothes, and that thenceforth he began to go about in European costume including a hat. These things got on my nerves. Surely, I thought, a religion that compelled one to eat beef, drink liquor, and change one's own clothes did not deserve the name. I also heard that the new convert had already begun abusing the religion of his ancestors, their customs and their country. All these things created in me a dislike for Christianity.[59]

And the example, already mentioned, of the missionary who harassed the Jodo-Shinshu Buddhist temple demonstrates that there are indeed — even today — obnoxious, arrogant, narrow-minded, and intolerant missionaries. There is no sense in denying the record of Christian insensitivity and disrespect for other traditions, although an objective assessment would no doubt confirm that such insensitivity is more the exception than the rule. Again,

58. S. Radhakrishnan, "My Search for Truth," in *Radhakrishnan: Selected Writings on Philosophy, Religion, and Culture,* ed. Robert A. McDermott (New York: E. P. Dutton & Company, 1970), p. 39.

59. M. K. Gandhi, *An Autobiography: The Story of My Experiments With Truth,* trans. by Mahadev Desai (New York: Viking Penguin, 1985), pp. 46-47.

however, our concern here is not with the historical record itself, but with the relation between the concepts of evangelism and tolerance. Is there anything in the concept of evangelism and the accompanying desire to see followers of other faiths converted to faith in Jesus Christ which is necessarily morally unacceptable?

With this question we launch into the highly volatile issue of proselytism. Is there a distinction between evangelism and proselytism? Is evangelism theologically and morally acceptable in today's pluralistic world? These are controversial questions, and thorough treatment of them must include careful attention to the relevant historical, sociological, and political factors that have shaped the perspectives of the various religious communities. The suggestion that it is morally right for Christians to engage in evangelism seems inevitably to provoke protests of spiritual and cultural imperialism from Jews and Muslims, who have suffered greatly under "Christian" attempts to convert them in the past. While fully recognizing the immensely complex web of social and religious factors involved, I will be concerned here merely with the concepts of evangelism and intolerance themselves. The much more difficult question of how, given the atrocities of the past, Christian evangelism should be conducted among groups such as Jews and Muslims, who have suffered much at the hands of Christendom, must be left for another occasion.

Any responsible treatment of the subject must begin by making a sharp distinction between evangelism and proselytism. Evangelism, as noted above, is simply the proclamation of the good news of salvation in Jesus Christ. The objective of evangelism, of course, is that the recipient of the message will respond in faith and accept Jesus as Lord and Savior. But evangelism itself is simply the communication of the message. Evangelism itself is thus morally neutral in the sense that there can be proper and improper, morally acceptable and morally unacceptable, methods of evangelism. Morally unacceptable methods of evangelism fall into the category of proselytism. Any means of evangelism including practices which are coercive, dishonest, manipulative, or otherwise infringe upon the dignity of the target audience must be rejected by Christians as morally unacceptable. In this respect, we can endorse

the following statement from the World Council of Churches'
Consultation on the Church and the Jewish People (1977):

> Proselytism embraces whatever violates the right of the human
> person, Christian or non-Christian, to be free from external coer-
> cion in religious matters, or whatever, in the proclamation of the
> Gospel, does not conform to the ways God draws free men to
> himself in response to his calls to serve in spirit and in truth.[60]

Proselytism, as defined here, is to be unequivocally rejected by
evangelicals. All persons are created in God's image and are granted
by God the freedom to choose their ultimate commitments. The
one who comes in the name of Jesus Christ and shares with a
Buddhist, or Hindu, or Muslim, or Jew the good news of salvation
in Jesus must do so with great humility, sensitivity, and gracious-
ness, always careful to ensure that socially unacceptable or morally
questionable methods are not employed. The dignity of the listener
must be preserved.

Having said this, however, we must add that, if properly
conducted, there does not seem to be any reason why Christians
should not engage in evangelism. Evangelism itself need not be
intolerant. We must disagree with Blu Greenberg's charge that the
evangelical insistence upon the exclusivity of salvation in and
through Jesus Christ reduces evangelical mission to proselytism,
and that only if such exclusivism is abandoned can Christian witness be morally acceptable.[61] Proselytism is not a matter of the
content of one's beliefs but rather of the means one adopts in trying
to persuade others to accept particular beliefs. The evangelical
conviction that all persons are in need of God's gracious forgiveness, that this is available only through Jesus Christ, and that out
of obedience and love Christians are to spread the gospel of Jesus
Christ to all who have never heard, in and of itself is not intolerant.

---

60. From "Christian Witness, Proselytism, and the Jews," in *Mission
Trends No. 5: Faith Meets Faith,* ed. Gerald H. Anderson and Thomas F. Stransky
(Grand Rapids: Eerdmans, 1981), p. 190.

61. Blu Greenberg, "Mission, Witness, and Proselytism," in *Evangelicals
and Jews in an Age of Pluralism,* pp. 232-33.

It is the methods used to communicate this conviction that can be said to be tolerant or intolerant.

To repeat, there need not be anything about attempting to persuade others to accept one's viewpoint, in and of itself, which is intolerant. Admittedly, there are moral and immoral means of persuasion. But when conducted properly, when no social or moral norms are violated, attempting to persuade a person to abandon certain beliefs in favor of alternative beliefs is not intolerant. Notice that if we do not accept this view of tolerance, the implication is that any time people engage in discussion in order to overcome some fundamental disagreement they are being intolerant of each other. Nor can it be maintained that religious beliefs constitute an exception to this understanding of tolerance, and that, whereas persuasion in other areas is legitimate, trying to persuade someone to change basic religious beliefs is somehow intolerant. The question thus is not evangelism itself, nor even the attempt to persuade others to accept Jesus Christ. Rather, the question about tolerance revolves around the methods employed in proclaiming Christ and seeking to persuade.

In considering the question of tolerance and evangelism, we come again, as we have repeatedly in this study, to confront the fundamental question of truth. What kind of universe do we live in? What is the relation of humankind to the religious ultimate? The evangelical is convinced, on the basis of Scripture, that humankind lives in deliberate rebellion against a holy and righteous God, that all persons are guilty of sin and face eternal separation from God unless restored to a saving relationship with him, that such salvation is available only through the person and work of Jesus Christ. If these theological propositions are true, then clearly the message of salvation in Jesus Christ is something that must be made available to all persons. To deny anyone the opportunity of a restored relationship with God by deliberately withholding the gospel would be morally unconscionable. One could well argue that Christians have a moral obligation to share the good news.

I suspect that much of the reason behind the common charge that evangelism is intolerant lies in a pervasive epistemological skepticism that finds the evangelical insistence upon the truth of certain theological propositions simply incredible. To those who take it for granted that one cannot have certainty about basic religious questions, the evangelical proclamation of Jesus Christ as the Way, the Truth, and the Life cannot help but sound arrogant, naive, and intolerant. In such a climate, then, it is incumbent upon evangelicals not only to proclaim the message of the gospel with humility and sensitivity, but also to demonstrate to a skeptical and relativistic culture why it is that it can claim to have certainty concerning ultimate religious questions.

Bibliography

General Works on Religion and Philosophy

Christian, William A., Sr. *Doctrines of Religious Communities: A Philosophical Study.* New Haven: Yale University Press, 1987.

———. *Meaning and Truth in Religion.* Princeton: Princeton University Press, 1964.

———. *Oppositions of Religious Doctrines: A Study in the Logic of Dialogue Among Religions.* London: Macmillan, 1972.

Comstock, W. Richard, ed. *Religion and Man: An Introduction.* New York: Harper & Row, 1971.

Crosby, Donald A. *Interpretive Theories of Religion.* The Hague: Mouton, 1981.

Eliade, Mircea, ed. *The Encyclopedia of Religion,* 16 vols. New York: Macmillan, 1987.

Hackett, Stuart C. *Oriental Philosophy: A Westerner's Guide to Eastern Thought.* Madison: University of Wisconsin Press, 1979.

Hick, John H. *An Interpretation of Religion.* New Haven: Yale University Press, 1988.

Katz, Steven, ed. *Mysticism and Philosophical Analysis.* New York: Oxford University Press, 1978.

Mitchell, Basil. *The Justification of Religious Belief.* New York: Oxford University Press, 1981.

Nakamura, Hajime. *Ways of Thinking of Eastern Peoples.* Revised English translation by Philip P. Wiener. Honolulu: University of Hawaii Press, 1964.

Newman, Jay. *Foundations of Religious Tolerance.* Toronto: University of Toronto Press, 1982.

Noss, David S., and John B. Noss, *A History of the World's Religions.* 8th ed. New York: Macmillan, 1990.

Plantinga, Alvin, and Nicholas Wolterstorff, eds. *Faith and Rationality: Reason and Belief in God.* Notre Dame: University of Notre Dame Press, 1983.

Smart, Ninian. *Doctrine and Argument in Indian Philosophy.* London: George Allen & Unwin, 1964.

———. *The Phenomenon of Religion.* New York: Herder & Herder, 1973.

———. *The Religious Experience of Mankind.* 3rd ed. New York: Charles Scribner's Sons, 1984.

Smith, Wilfred Cantwell. *The Meaning and End of Religion.* New York: Harper & Row, 1962.

Streng, Frederick. *Understanding Religious Life.* 3rd ed. Belmont, Cal.: Wadsworth Publishing Company, 1985.

Trigg, Roger. *Reason and Commitment.* London: Cambridge University Press, 1973.

Wiebe, Donald. *Truth and Religion: Towards an Alternative Paradigm for the Study of Religion.* The Hague: Mouton, 1981.

Christian Faith and Other Faiths

Anderson, Gerald H., and Thomas F. Stransky, eds. *Christ's Lordship and Religious Pluralism.* Maryknoll, N.Y.: Orbis, 1981.

———. *Mission Trends No. 5: Faith Meets Faith.* Grand Rapids: Eerdmans, 1981.

Anderson, Sir Norman. *Christianity and World Religions: The Challenge of Pluralism.* Downers Grove, Ill.: Inter-Varsity Press, 1984.

Cox, Harvey. *Many Mansions: A Christian's Encounter With Other Faiths.* Boston: Beacon Press, 1988.

Cragg, Kenneth. *The Christ and the Faiths.* Philadelphia: Westminster, 1986.

D'Costa, Gavin. *Theology and Religious Pluralism.* Oxford: Basil Blackwell, 1986.

Dewick, E. C. *The Christian Attitude Toward Other Religions.* Cambridge: Cambridge University Press, 1953.

Drummond, Richard Henry. *Toward a New Age in Christian Theology.* Maryknoll, N.Y.: Orbis, 1985.

Fernando, Ajith. *The Christian's Attitude Toward World Religions.* Wheaton, Ill.: Tyndale, 1987.

Hick, John H. *God and the Universe of Faiths.* London: Macmillan, 1973.

———. *God Has Many Names.* Philadelphia: Westminster, 1982.

———. *An Interpretation of Religion.* New Haven: Yale University Press, 1988.

———. *Problems of Religious Pluralism.* New York: St. Martin's Press, 1985.

Hick, John H., ed. *Truth and Dialogue in World Religions.* Philadelphia: Westminster, 1974.

Hick, John H., and Brian Hebblethwaite, eds. *Christianity and Other Religions.* Philadelphia: Fortress, 1980.

Hick, John H., and Paul F. Knitter, eds. *The Myth of Christian Uniqueness.* Maryknoll, N.Y.: Orbis, 1987.

Hocking, William Ernest. *Living Religions and a World Faith.* New York: Macmillan, 1940.

Knitter, Paul F. *No Other Name? A Critical Survey of Christian Attitudes Toward the World Religions.* Maryknoll, N.Y.: Orbis, 1985.

Kraemer, Hendrick. *The Christian Message in a Non-Christian World.* London: Edinburgh House Press, 1938.

Neill, Stephen. *Crises of Belief: The Christian Dialogue with Faith and No Faiths.* London: Hodder & Stoughton, 1984; originally published as *Christian Faith and Other Faiths: The Christian Dialogue With Other Religions.* London: Oxford University Press, 1961.

Panikkar, Raimundo. *The Intrareligious Dialogue*. New York: Paulist Press, 1978.

Reischauer, August Karl. *The Nature and Truth of the Great Religions: Toward a Philosophy of Religion*. Rutland, Vt. and Tokyo: Charles E. Tuttle, 1966.

Robinson, John A. T. *Truth is Two-Eyed*. Philadelphia: Westminster, 1979.

Samartha, Stanley. *Courage for Dialogue*. Maryknoll, N.Y.: Orbis, 1981.

Samartha, Stanley, ed. *Living Faiths and the Ecumenical Movement*. Geneva: World Council of Churches, 1971.

Smith, Wilfred Cantwell. *Religious Diversity: Essays by Wilfred Cantwell Smith*. Edited by Willard G. Oxtoby. New York: Harper & Row, 1976.

————. *Towards a World Theology*. Philadelphia: Westminster, 1981.

Speer, Robert E. *The Finality of Jesus Christ*. New York: Fleming H. Revell, 1933.

Swearer, Donald K. *Dialogue: The Key to Understanding Other Religions*. Philadelphia: Westminster, 1977.

Tillich, Paul. *Christianity and the Encounter of the World Religions*. New York: Columbia University Press, 1963.

Toynbee, Arnold. *Christianity Among the Religions of the World*. New York: Charles Scribner's Sons, 1957.

Index

Allah, 76, 82-84, 86-87
Alston, William, 176
Amida Buddha, 69-72
Anderson, Gerald H., 9, 17
Anderson, Sir Norman, 74, 83, 87,
  247, 270, 272-73
anonymous Christian, 25
Aquinas, Thomas, 139, 218
Ariarajah, Wesley, 293
Aristotle, 145-46

Barrett, David, 8
Barth, Karl, 9, 18, 115
Berger, Peter, 8-9, 30, 31-32, 197,
  291-92
Bhagavad Gita, 44, 196
Bloesch, Donald, 276
Bloom, Allan, 30
bodhisattvas, 66-67, 70-71
Bosch, David, 16, 20
Braaten, Carl, 255-56, 258, 263
Brahman, 45, 47-48, 52-55, 148
Braithwaite, R. B., 121-22, 132

Brunner, Emil, 18, 115-17, 126, 129
Buddha, the Gautama, 28, 57-65,
  71, 153, 229, 261
Buddhism, 8, 37, 56-72, 147-48,
  179, 190-91, 224
  Mahayana Buddhism, 65-72
  Pure Land Buddhism, 69-72
  Theravada Buddhism, 56-66
  Zen Buddhism, 69, 147-48, 179,
    190-91, 224

Carrithers, Michael, 57, 61
Chandler, Russell, 7
Chisholm, Roderick, 180
Christian, William A., Sr., 39-40,
  110-11
Chrysostom, 134
Church's mission
  definition of, 282
  and evangelism, 278-79, 282-83
conflicting truth claims in religion,
  106-11, 112, 124, 200
Conze, Edward, 57-58, 65

319

Cox, Harvey, 9, 234-35, 293
Cragg, Kenneth, 74, 81-82, 85, 87, 89
Crosby, Donald, 156
Cullmann, Oscar, 247
Cupitt, Don, 171

Davis, Stephen, 248
D'Costa, Gavin, 263-64
Deutsch, Eliot, 52-53
dialogue (interreligious), 15, 19,
    234-35, 283-301
    and theology of mission, 19-20,
        285
    and Vatican II, 24-25
    and World Council of Churches,
        19-20
    common presuppositions of,
        290-94
    evangelicals and, 294-301
    formal/informal distinction,
        295-97
    various kinds of, 285-90
Douglas, Robert C., 5-6
dukkha, 60-63

Emmet, Dorothy, 132
enlightenment (Buddhist), 59, 61,
    69-70, 147-48 (see also *satori*)
Erickson, Millard, 270-72
evaluating religious worldviews,
    151-66, 180-95
    functionalist/pragmatic criteria
        for, 157-65
    Hick on, 157-62
    inevitability of, 152-55
    Knitter on, 162-64
    proposed criteria for, 180-95
evangelism, 278-83
    definition of, 280-82
    priority of, 278-79, 282-83, 301
exclusivism, ix-xii, 9-14, 27-35,
    112-13

and tolerance, 32-33, 301-3
definition of, 9-10, 33-34
history of, 10-14
reasons for rejection of, 27-33

Ferguson, John, 11-12, 258
Fernando, Ajith, 266-67
fideism, 178-80
Five Pillars of Islam, 86-88
Four Noble Truths, 60-61
Frege, Gottlob, 214-15

Gandhi, Mohandas K., 28, 310
Geertz, Clifford, 156, 166
Gilkey, Langdon, 9, 27, 174
Greenberg, Blu, 312
Gregory of Nyssa, 134
Guillaume, Alfred, 74-75

Haddad, Yvonne, 5
Heim, Mark, 18, 254-55
Helm, Paul, 126-27
Hengel, Martin, 247
Hesselgrave, David, 299-301
Hick, John H., ix-xii, 9, 27, 128,
    153, 157-62, 189, 198-233, 236,
    240-49, 302-3
    and reinterpretation of religious
        beliefs, 221-33
    on Christology, 240-49
    on conflicting truth claims,
        200-201, 227-33
    on divine *personae/impersonae*,
        204-6, 210-17, 222-25
    on evaluating religions, 157-62
    on religious language, 217-21
    on soteriology, 158-62, 206-8,
        225-27
    on the Real, 204-7, 210-18,
        222-25
    theory of religious pluralism,
        200-233

Hiebert, Paul, 8
Hinduism, 8, 37, 41-56, 148, 190, 224
   Advaita Vedanta Hinduism, 52-54, 148, 190, 224
Hirai, Naofusa, 93-94, 97, 102-3
Hirata, Atsutane, 95, 101
Honen, 70-71
Hopkins, Thomas, 45, 48, 50
Hudson, W. D., 137
human predicament
   in Buddhism, 108 (see also *samsara* and *dukkha*)
   in Hinduism, 108 (see also *samsara*)
   in Islam, 88-89, 108
   in Shinto, 102-4, 108
Hume, David, 29

inclusivism, 9-10, 14-25
   and Vatican II, 21-25
   definition of, 9-10
Islam, 8, 37, 73-93

Jesus Christ
   and the historic creeds, 237-40
   and interreligious dialogue, 234-35
   exclusivism on, 9-11, 34
   Hick on, 240-49
   in the Qur'an, 91-93
   Incarnation, 236, 240-43, 245, 248-49, 260-61, 301
   inclusivism on, 9-10, 14, 22-25
   Knitter on, 249-60
   pluralism on, 10, 26
   uniqueness of, 10-11, 14, 22, 260-62
Justin Martyr, 12

kami, 94-95, 98-103, 194
Kane, J. Herbert, 269

Kant, Immanuel, 29, 167, 203-5
karma, 42-43, 45-46, 52, 55-56, 61-63, 68
Kasulis, Thomas, 69
Kaufman, Gordon, 9, 27, 170
Kitagawa, Joseph, 68, 93-96, 99, 103
Knitter, Paul, xi, 21, 25-27, 142-44, 162-64, 171, 236, 249-60, 288, 291-92, 302
Koestler, Arthur, 191
Kraemer, Hendrik, 9, 18
Kraft, Charles, 39, 168
Krishna, 42, 49-51, 196

Lausanne Covenant, 239, 262-63, 265, 280
Lindsell, Harold, 265

Madhva, 55
Marshall, I. Howard, 247
McGavran, Donald, 268, 282
moksha, 47, 49-51, 53, 56
Motoori, Norinaga, 95, 100
Moule, C. F. D., 246-47, 250
Muhammad, 73-80, 85, 87, 153, 188, 261

Nash, Ronald, 115, 126
Neill, Stephen, 9, 89, 262, 301
Newbigin, Lesslie, 30-31, 178-79
Newman, Jay, 306-7, 309
nirvana, 63-64, 67, 69, 71-72, 184

Ono, Sokyo, 94, 100-103
Otto, Rudolf, 133-34, 197

Packer, J. I., 282
Panikkar, Raimundo, 9, 26-27, 146, 256, 306-7
Parrinder, Geoffrey, 91-92
Pelikan, Jaroslav, 235
Phillips, D. Z., 123-25, 131-32, 173

Pinnock, Clark, 275-76
pluralism (theory of), 10, 25-27
  definition of, 10, 25-26 (see also
    under Hick and Knitter)
principle of noncontradiction,
  141-47, 149, 183-84
propositions, 113-15

Qur'an, 77-80, 83-86

Radhakrishnan, Sarvepalli, 35, 196,
  198, 310
Rahman, Fazlur, 74, 85
Rahner, Karl, 9, 20, 25-26
Rahula, Walpola, 60, 64-65, 191
Ramanuja, 54-55, 72
Reischauer, Edwin O., 97
relativism, 29-30, 166-78
  and religious pluralism, 170-74
  cognitive relativism, 169
  descriptive/normative
    distinction, 167-69
  inadequacy of, 174-78
religion
  defining beliefs of a religion,
    40-41, 181
  dimensions of religious
    phenomena, 38-41
  functionalist/pragmatic views of,
    32, 155-57
  noncognitivist views of, 120-25
  place of belief in, 39, 127-33
religious diversity, 4-8
religious language
  as exclusive, 142-47, 251-53,
    258-60
  as factually informative, 127-33,
    221, 231-32
  as noncognitive, 121-25
  via negativa, 139-40, 218-19
religious skepticism, 28-29, 313-14
religious ultimate

in Buddhism, 106-7 (see also
  nirvana)
in Hinduism, 107 (see also
  Brahman)
in Islam, 106 (see also Allah)
in Shinto, 107 (see also kami)
Robinson, John A. T., 9, 143-44
Rossano, Pietro, 24
Russell, Bertrand, 283

Samartha, Stanley, 19, 166, 288,
  291-93, 303
samsara, 46-48, 52-53, 55-56,
  61-63, 68-69
satori, 69-70, 142, 179, 184
Sanders, J. Oswald, 268
Saunders, Dale, 71
Schuon, Frithjof, 147, 197, 198
Scott, Waldron, 27
Sekioka, Kazushige, 105-6
Sen, Kshiti Mohan, 41, 56, 196-97
Shankara, 35, 52-54, 72, 148
Sharpe, Eric, 285-90, 300
Shinran, 70-71
Shinto, 8, 37-38, 93-111
shirk, 84
Smart, Ninian, 37-40, 127, 165
Smith, Wilfred Cantwell, 9, 27,
  117-20, 127-31, 142, 144, 198,
  286-87, 291, 293, 302
soteriology
  and Jesus Christ, 10-11, 14, 22,
    260-77, 280-83
  Hick on, 158-62, 206-8, 225-27
  in Buddhism, 65, 72, 109 (see
    also satori and nirvana)
  in Hinduism, 49-51, 72, 109 (see
    also moksha)
  in Islam, 88-91, 109-10
  in Shinto, 103-6, 109-10
  universalism, 33, 263, 275
Spae, Joseph, 102, 104

Stott, John R. W., 273-74, 276,
281-82, 296-97, 305
Streng, Frederick, 156
Swearer, Donald, 291, 293
Swidler, Leonard, 285, 287, 290

tolerance/intolerance, 30, 32-33,
151, 301-14
and evangelism, 279-80, 309-13
and exclusivism, 32-33, 301-13
nature of, 304-9
Toynbee, Arnold, 198, 303
Trigg, Roger, 29, 128, 132, 176-77
Troeltsch, Ernst, 172
truth, 40-41, 112-50, 181-84
and principle of noncontradiction, 141-47, 149, 183-84
as ineffable, 133-41
as propositional, 113-33
definition of a true religion,
181-82
priority of question of truth,
160-62, 164-66, 313-14

"two-level" theory of religious
truth, 53, 147-50
W. C. Smith on, 117-20

Ueda, Kenji, 102

Vatican II, 21-25
Vivekananda, Swami, 16

Warren, Max, 8
Watt, W. Montgomery, 74-75, 77
Wentz, Richard, 284
Wiebe, Donald, 131, 133, 156, 165
Winch, Peter, 172-73
Wittgenstein, Ludwig, 29, 122-23,
125, 131-32, 203
World Council of Churches, 19, 20
World's Parliament of Religions,
15-16
worldview, 39-40, 181
Wright, Christopher J. H., 297-98

Yandell, Keith, 183, 185-86, 232